THE AWAKENED LIFE

ASTROLOGY

BY MADELINE GERWICK

ALPHA

Publisher: Mike Sanders
Senior Acquisitions Editor: Janette Lynn
Art Director: William Thomas
Book Producer: Lee Ann Chearneyi/Amaranth@LuminAreStudio.com
Copy Editor: Rick Kughen
Cover Designer: Jessica Lee
Layout/Book Designer: Ayanna Lacey
Indexer: Celia McCoy
Proofreader: Amy Schneider

Published by Penguin Random House LLC
005-317267-JUN/2020
Copyright © 2020 by Amaranth

International Standard Book Number: 978-1-46549-265-4
Library of Congress Catalog Card Number: 2019950632

22   5

Interpretation of the printing code: The rightmost number of the first series of numbers is the year of the book's printing; the rightmost number of the second series of numbers is the number of the book's printing. For example, a printing code of 20-1 shows that the first printing occurred in 2020.

Printed in the United States of America

Reprinted and updated from *The Complete Idiot's Guide to Astrology*

A WORLD OF IDEAS:
SEE ALL THERE IS TO KNOW

www.dk.com
First American Edition, 2019

Contents

Part 3: Heavenly Bodies   109

Chapter 8: Housekeeping with the Planets.................... 111

Appendixes

Foreword

I was on a train going from Grand Central Station in New York City up to New Canaan, Connecticut. I dug into a book I had just bought impulsively—just as you have perhaps bought this one. I found myself immediately fascinated: there were juicy new power words to learn, ways to say things that sounded a little mysterious but, according to the author, were as clear as the Liberty Bell clanging for my personal freedom, my individuality as a birthright gift from the gods! "I'm a Capricorn ♑ because the Sun ☉ was located in that sign when I was born! I mean business. I get things done. (I can be pretty melancholic sometimes, but don't tell anyone.) But I'm in there for the long haul. I age well!"

My brain was racing through the pages to pick up more things about my Capricorn ♑ nature. There was something pointed out about my tremendous attraction to any Pisces ♓ woman who ever lived. I filed that away (and remembered it regularly throughout 27 years with two Pisces ♓ ladies!).

There was a lot about my incompatibility with Aries ♈ people. (And I knew that that explained everything about my relationship with my mother, God take her soul!)

Okay. When I finally settled down, I saw that astrology had *reasons* for these generalities. I saw those reasons were tied to the miracle of creation and to millennia of keen observations by wise people. And I saw that the mysteries of being were easily converted into strategies of becoming—I was hooked!

By the time I had arrived at New Canaan on that hot summer day, I didn't need a cool drink as much as I needed pencil and paper. I was going to follow the guidelines in the book and start to build my birth chart—the portrait of my birth in space and time and the portrait of who I am (the nice stuff, the tough stuff—all of it!).

Books, lines, and thinkers: How hooked was I? I studied, studied, and studied, and gradually, I realized that nothing was more interesting to me in the world than astrology—and it probably was also in a previous life, as I was learning. I saw how I could appreciate myself, my purpose in life, and how I could help others to do the same. Time and space now started to mean something more than three meals a day, a raise now and then, college education for the children, and the IRS.

And that book, with the neat lines and the quotes from all the wise men from Ptolemy to Newton to Einstein to J. P. Morgan, was nowhere as good as this one you're holding right now.

Watch out! Be warned: Madeline Gerwick has the lines that will hook you, too; she's one of those wise thinkers in astrology who really knows what she's talking about.

And Madeline and her book producer at Amaranth, Lee Ann Chearneyi, have style. This book is a breeze. For example (getting back to the Pisces issue, please), their "Fish Facts" talks about Pisces' (delightful) character trait to live largely in the world of the imagination, the realm of dreams, and where objects and events seem to have no connection to outer reality. (I, the

Capricorn ♑ warlord of accomplishment, love it!) But then they tack on the lines that show you the substance within all the fun: "Above all, Fishes [Pisces] are here to give their help, love, and whatever else is needed—not just to those like themselves, but to anyone in need." Isn't that lovely? Isn't that valid? And that's just the beginning. How do all the traits, powers, and interrelationships among the planets within the signs reflect your life, the details of your progress, the outlines of your dreams, and the dynamics of your relationships?

Well, my fateful train ride those many years ago took me to write some 24 technical astrological texts of my own, to lecture throughout the world, and to appreciate this *Astrology: The Awakened Life* guide to the field I love. I can tell you for sure that when I introduce newcomers to this fascinating world of astrology, I will recommend this book. They, and you, will be thrilled with Madeline Gerwick's introduction to seeing stars. It's expert, it's charming, and it's easy.

All aboard!

—Noel Tyl
World-renowned astrologer and co-founder of the Association for Astrological Networking, astrology's global organization

Introduction

You're probably familiar with Sun sign forecasts that appear online in daily horoscope apps. And you probably know your Sun ☉ sign, too. But did you know that Sun signs are just the beginning of astrology? Did you know, for example, that all 12 signs, the Sun ☉, Moon ☽, and planets all appear somewhere in your birth chart?? Have you ever toured the astrological houses?

Based on the date, place, and time of your birth, the planets and signs in the houses of your astrological birth chart create a metaphor for you in the heavens. Your astrological birth chart represents the position of the heavens at the moment of your birth. While there are hundreds of astrology books and apps out there—some general and some intricately technical—this book is unique because it's about *you*. It shows you how your planets in their signs and houses can help you understand more about yourself and your life. It explains what all those symbols for signs and planets mean and how they connect with your everyday life: who you are, who you love (and who you don't!), why you do what you do, why feel like you do, why live where you live, and why you work where you work.

Astrology can explain all that? Yes, it can. Planets are the *what* of astrology, showing the various energies at work in your life. Signs show *how* those energies behave in your birth chart, and houses are *where* the various areas of your life unfold, from relationships to financial concerns and from wishes to hopes and dreams. Curious? Read on to find out more about astrology and you.

How to Use This Book

While some of the more advanced material in this book will make more sense if you have a birth chart in front of you, it's not a requirement. We do strongly recommend, though, that you get your birth chart and study it as you read. When getting your chart, be sure to specify Geocentric view, Tropical Zodiac, Placidus house system, and True Node. Charts appearing in this book are generated with Solar Fire software, published by Astrolabe, Inc. Check out their website at www.alabe.com.

This book is divided into five parts:

Part 1, Astrology Has Its Moment, introduces you to astrology: its history; all about the astrological Sun ☉ signs, including energies, qualities, and Elements, plus the basics of exactly what an astrological birth chart is and what's in it for *you*.

Part 2, Touring the Zodiac: Sun ☉ Signs, Ascendants, and Descendants, takes you through the Sun ☉ signs. This is more than just a cursory look; it's an analysis of each sign in love and health, at work, at home, and with money, as well as each sign's best and worst sides. You'll also look at your ascendant (Rising sign) and your descendant, which shows how you partner.

Part 3, Heavenly Bodies, moves through the planets in each sign so that you become more familiar with the potentials for each one. You'll also learn about the effects of retrograde planets.

Part 4, The Twelve Houses: Where Planets Live explores the signs and planets throughout the 12 astrological houses.

Part 5, Using Astrology: Astro-Nerds Assemble!, discusses more ways to use astrology and moves beyond the basics of a chart to help you understand aspects, transits and progressions. We'll also look at Moon phases and Moon ☽ signs, as well as void of course moons. Also included are two invaluable appendixes. Appendix A details the math and science behind how a computer calculates a birth chart—a must-read for both math/computer geniuses and those of us more technically challenged, too. Appendix B introduces the asteroids and Chiron, which are heavenly bodies that also influence your birth chart and that are important to a serious study of astrology. Appendix C introduces you to relationship astrology, called synastry. You'll learn how compatible you are with another by analyzing a special chart called a synastry grid. By the time you complete *Astrology: The Awakened Life*, you will have the ability to read and interpret an astrological birth chart, unlocking the meaning of the heavens at the moment of your birth and revealing your potential for your best self, and your relationships with others.

About the Author

Madeline Gerwick is an internationally recognized, certified astrologer, specializing in business and economic astrology. With more than 30 years of experience, Madeline consults with individuals and businesses to guide them to higher levels of prosperity by working in harmony with the Universe. She is co-founder of Polaris Business Guides LLC and annually publishes *The Good Timing Guide* and its companion newsletter, which provide good timing and economic trends for all types of businesses and personal activities. Her latest book, *Money Is an Energy Game*, co-authored with Margaret Donahue, is a culmination of more than 20 years of study and teaching prosperity training. Madeline served on two Boards of the Washington State Astrological Association and on the Board of Trustees for The Kepler College of Astrological Arts and Sciences. She is a member of the Society of Astrological Research. Subscribe to Madeline's newsletter at www.polarisbusinessguides.com.

Acknowledgments

Madeline gives many thanks to David and Aria for their support, and to the clients she had to reschedule to meet this book's deadlines. A special thanks also go to Harold J. Langseth, her first business client, and to all her friends, peers, and clients for their continued encouragement. Most of all, she gives thanks to Lee Ann at Amaranth@LuminAreStudio for finding her and for creating a funny, readable book about a complex topic. She dedicates this book to her late brother, James, her family's first author.

A special thanks from Amaranth goes to tarot reader and psychic astrologer Arlene Tognetti at www.mellinetti.com, co-author of *The Complete Idiot's Guide to Tarot, Second edition,* and whose quick astrological insights and birth chart analyses have added depth and insight to the core text of *Awakened Life: Astrology.* Arlene's enthusiasm for astrology and tarot and her joie de vivre inspires her students and empowers her clients. And most of all, thanks to Madeline, a gifted astrologer whose voice and passion for astrology and expert knowledge come through on every page of this book.

We remember the quick wit and bright spirit of Lisa Lenard, whose memory we honor.

Special Thanks to Noel Tyl

We would like to give a very special thanks to world-famous astrologer Noel Tyl, for reviewing and endorsing this book. When we caught up with him, he was preparing for a tour of South Africa, guiding 170 correspondent students, writing a book, and of course, seeing clients! His graciousness in accommodating our special needs was truly tremendous.

Noel Tyl is well known for his more than 30 books on astrology, his frequent talks throughout the world for more than 30 years, and his pioneering work in the connections between psychological need theory and astrology. Mr. Tyl, a graduate of Harvard University, is also an internationally acclaimed opera singer and co-founder of the Association for Astrological Networking (AFAN). True to his Capricorn ♑ nature, Mr. Tyl has distinguished himself in many ways, and we are thrilled to have his endorsement.

Trademarks

All terms mentioned in this book that are known to be or are suspected of being trademarks or service marks have been appropriately capitalized. Alpha Books and Penguin Random House LLC cannot attest to the accuracy of this information. Use of a term in this book should not be regarded as affecting the validity of any trademark or service mark.

ASTROLOGY HAS ITS MOMENT

Astrology is all over the Internet and it is having a cultural moment. Of course, you know your Sun ☉ sign, and even your Rising sign. You read all the daily horoscopes online and subscribe to a daily horoscope app, but you want more. Curious, you've downloaded your birth chart from more than one online source, and you know the sign and house your Moon ☽ is in. But what does all this really mean? How can you read and interpret your own astrological birth chart?

Astrology is so much more than your Sun ☉ sign and your daily horoscope. Astrology is as expansive as the heavens and as unique as you. The chapters in Part 1 help you see the bigger astrological picture and your place in it.

Part

1

ASTROLOGY FOR THE NEW MILLENNIALS

Astrology is about personal agency—*your* agency. It is a system thousands of years old, revealing the divine nature of the Universe in each human being. In astrology, the Universe is a reflection of all humanity. Currently, all you may know about astrology is your zodiac Sun ☉ sign. But astrology is so much more than your daily horoscope … your zodiac Sun ☉ sign. *All* the signs and planets influence *all* of us, no matter what our Sun ☉ signs are! The energies of the signs, planets, and houses "dance" together in many different ways that may make life easier or may create challenges. Your daily horoscope is a very small way to begin to notice that your life has cycles connected to the vastness of the Universe.

In this chapter, we expand from the narrow window of your Sun ☉ sign horoscope to the heavenly vista of your astrological birth chart, so you can begin to see the bigger picture of how astrology works in your life and in the Universe.

Astrology on Trend

Do you read your daily astrological horoscope? Millions of people in the United States read their horoscopes online or subscribe to a daily Sun ☉ sign reading sent to their phones or computers. Millions more are downloading astrology apps, hoping to discover more about their personal relationships and who they are. Interest in astrology is exploding as more and more people turn to this ancient system to make the leap from their daily horoscopes to the complexity of their astrological birth charts. Today, this leap is made possible by the Internet, where calculating your astrological birth chart is simply a click away. An ancient system meets modern computer technology and suddenly, astrology, in all its intricacy, goes mainstream.

The daily horoscopes you receive online still reflect, as they always have, the trends of the day for *everyone* with that particular Sun ☉ sign. However, today's daily horoscopes *do* reveal more than ever before because they are produced by powerful computer algorithms that allow astrologers to factor in the complex movements of heavenly bodies; astrologers are looking at more than just your Sun ☉ sign. They're looking at the planets, their cycles, and the relationships of the planets in their houses to your Sun sign. (We talk about these features, called *aspects* and *transits* by astrologers, in Chapter 17.) All of this added together *can* color a day in a certain way. But a daily horoscope is not particular to *you as an individual;* as ever, you need your astrological birth chart to reveal *your* personal nature and relationships.

To get an astrological birth chart online, all you need to do is enter your birth date, birth time, birthplace, and click. Ancient astrologers calculated birth charts laboriously by hand, tracking and studying the movements of the heavens. These complex calculations and observations today are made by a computer algorithm. (See Appendix A for more on what goes into calculating birth charts.) Easy access to accurate birth charts has fueled current interest in this ancient system. But what exactly *is* a birth chart, and what does a birth chart show about *you?*

An astrological birth chart is a "selfie" of the heavens at the exact place and time of your birth. Easy access to your birth chart means that you have the opportunity to explore and discover your own nature more fully, as well as uncover your infinite possibilities and opportunities to manifest your best self. While you can always get a reading from a professional astrologer—and these readings have great benefits—this book is designed to help you deconstruct your birth chart and gain the tools to do your own readings and reach your own understanding about your life and relationships. We'll say it again: Astrology is about *your personal agency.* What you can discover and learn on your own about your birth chart can only resonate deeper and truer for *you* as you move through this world and this life.

Is It Fate or Freewill?

Astrology connects your outer world to your inner world to reveal your potentials. How you manifest your potentials is where *freewill* comes into play. Sometimes, these manifestations are easy, with supporting energies from the planetary placements in your birth chart. Other times, the placements of planets and other chart factors create energies that make manifesting your potential more challenging.

Sometimes, your behaviors and their consequences clue you in on what lessons you need to learn. For example, you may need to realize when you let others pull your strings and why; then you may need to reclaim that part of yourself. Your conscious self doesn't know about these lessons you need to learn, which is why your birth chart is so important; your birth chart illuminates these lessons, so your conscious self can then go to work on making the changes you need to make. Either way, nothing's going to stop you from learning these lessons. If you ignore your lessons, life's circumstances will continue to present you opportunities for learning until you finally get the message. Later in this chapter, we talk about how your Rising sign (also called your *ascendant*) can reveal the lessons that you need to learn in your life.

For example, based on your present cycles, it's possible to predict that you're going to have major changes to your home life in a certain time period. A change at home made through freewill is one where you have the ability to choose the experiences through which you will learn your life lessons. A change in your home life beyond your control is called *fate*. Fate holds the lessons you need to learn in your lifetime; these lessons are unavoidable. To put it another way, whatever you need to learn, you *are going to learn*, regardless of whether your conscious self wants to learn. This also could be called fate.

Madeline believes that you really don't have a choice in the areas in which you have lessons to learn. The exception to this rule is whether you're going to cooperate and make it easy on yourself or whether you won't cooperate and make it hard on yourself. In other words, you *do* have choices (freewill), but they're not about whether you can avoid learning your lessons; your lessons are fate.

Beyond Your Horoscope: Astrology's Bigger Picture

Put simply, astrology is based on the relationships between the planets, the Sun ☉, and the Moon ☽; 12 *zodiac*, or Sun *signs*; and 12 areas of a person's life, called *houses*. Astrology began as the study of the "wandering" stars (or planets, as we know them today). It's actually the study of planetary cycles and how the energies of these events relate to their concurrent time on Earth. Put another way, astrology uses the harmony of the Universe to observe the possibilities of human behavior and experience. Even after thousands of years, astrology provides a psychological model that offers explanations for phenomena rational science just can't address.

* The **zodiac** is the name of the elliptic pattern Earth follows in its annual revolution around the Sun. This path is always the same and always passes through the same 12 signs.

* **Signs** are the "how" of astrology. The signs of the zodiac are: Aries ♈, Taurus ♉, Gemini ♊, Cancer ♋, Leo ♌, Virgo ♍, Libra ♎, Scorpio ♏, Sagittarius ♐, Capricorn ♑, Aquarius ♒, and Pisces ♓. *All zodiac signs appear in every person's chart.* The needs and styles of the planets are shown by the signs, along with what methods could be used to achieve those needs and styles.

* **Planets** are the "what" of astrology. They represent the various energies of a person, including your mental and emotional nature, desires, vitality, soul, will, consciousness, and subconscious, as well as the people in your life. Throughout this book, we include the Sun ☉, the Moon ☽, and the North ☊ and South ☋ Nodes, even though they aren't actually planets.

* The **houses** are the "where" of astrology. Each of the 12 houses encompasses a specific arena of life and is the stage where the drama of the planets unfolds.

Getting in Touch with Celestial Rhythms

Astrology connects you with the past, present, and future. *Natal astrology* involves the creation of your birth chart based on the position of the planets at the time and place that you were born. It creates a map unique to you and your true self. Using natal astrology, we help you discover your own unique position in the synchronicity of the Universe. We show you how to find out about your Sun ☉ sign, Moon ☽ sign, *ascendant*, and *descendant;* the signs for all your planets; and the houses in which those planets reside.

Your ascendant, or Rising sign, is the sign that was rising over the horizon at the moment of your birth. Your Rising sign represents the "you" that the outside world perceives, as well as your personality traits, needs, and physical characteristics.

Your descendant, located on the cusp of your seventh house, represents how you channel your energies through partnerships and relationships.

It all adds up to a special portrait of you as a unique human being.

Getting in touch with the ancient rhythms of astrology involves being aware of your constantly evolving history—a history that includes both now and then—and understanding your unique position within that history.

Your Chart Shows the Position of the Heavens at Your Birth

A birth chart looks like a wheel. It's a metaphor for *you,* designed for the day and the time and place that you were born. Simply put, your astrological birth chart, also called a *natal chart*, is a map of the heavens for the location, date, and time you were born—it's a unique map of who you are. Its symbols represent the locations of the planets on that map. The odds of anyone else having the same birth chart as you are astronomically small!

Let's take a look at a birth chart. Following is the chart for His Holiness, the Dalai Lama of Tibet. Each of the 12 sections of the chart wheel is called a *house*, and the symbols represent the signs and the planets. In this chapter and throughout this book, we begin to unlock the mysteries of these symbols for you. As we do, we return to the Dalai Lama's chart and unlock the secrets of his heavenly signature for this incarnation on Earth. The Dalai Lama is the fourteenth such leader of the Tibetan people, though today, he travels the world in exile from his homeland. The Tibetan people believe the Dalai Lama to be the incarnation of the Buddha of Compassion. Through reincarnation, Tibetans believe the Buddha of Compassion returns to Earth to serve humanity. So, when we look at the Dalai Lama's birth chart, we may gain insight into the nature of the Buddha of Compassion.

The Dalai Lama's Birth Chart

Now take a look at the Dalai Lama's astrological birth chart. First, notice the information in the top-left corner. It shows his birth date, birth time, and birthplace: July 6, 1935, 4:38 A.M., Takstar, Tibet. The Dalai Lama's chart is calculated for this date, time, and location. Had he been born at another time, place, or date, the chart would be different from the one shown.

The symbols in the birth chart represent the location of the planets and the signs they were in at the time, date, and place of the Dalai Lama's birth. It might help you to think of the center of the chart as the position of the Earth and the placement of the planets as what's in the sky all around it.

The highest point of this chart (the upper, heavy vertical line on the Dalai Lama's chart, marked with an "M.C.") represents the highest point that the Sun ☉ reached on the day of his birth. On the Dalai Lama's chart, this is Pisces ♓. Note, too, the horizon line; this is the heavy horizontal line across the birth chart. Everything above the horizon line was in the visible portion of the sky at the moment of birth, and everything below this line wasn't visible. At its left is the east horizon where the Sun rose at the time of birth, the ascendant or Rising sign is here (Cancer ♋, on the Dalai Lama's chart), and its right is where the Sun sets in the west (Capricorn ♑, on the Dalai Lama's chart). It helps to visualize the directions if you imagine yourself standing on top of the world, facing south, at the moment of your birth: East is on your left.

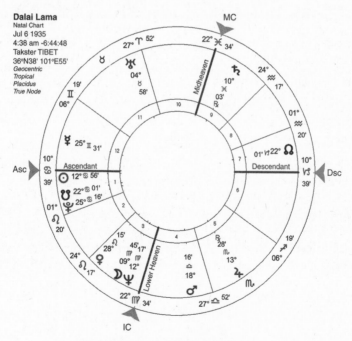

His Holiness the Dalai Lama's birth chart.

Your ascendant (or Rising sign—the mask you wear for the world) is the sign at the easternmost point of the horizon line. With Cancer ♋ as the ascendant, the Dalai Lama's chart reveals insights into how he wants to appear to the world. (You'll find out more about the Dalai Lama's ascendant, and how to figure your own ascendant, in Chapter 3.) Your descendant represents how you relate to others through partnerships and relationships. It's the sign next to the horizon line on the westernmost side of the chart. On the Dalai Lama's chart, his descendant is Capricorn ♑.

The lowest point in the chart, or *lower heaven* (the lower, heavy vertical line marked with an "I.C."), would be the exact opposite side of Earth from the *M.C.*, or the *midheaven*, and is in the sign of Virgo ♍ for the Dalai Lama. Your midheaven represents your ambition and career or your social role and public image. It's the highest point that the Sun reached on the day of your birth and is located on the cusp of the tenth house. Opposite the M.C. is the *imum coeli*, or I.C.—the bottom of the sky. Your I.C. (lower heaven) is the point on your birth chart that represents your life's foundations and psychological roots. It's found on the exact opposite side of Earth from the midheaven, on the cusp of the fourth house.

The Dalai Lama's Pisces ♓ midheaven highlights his life's vocation in a role of compassion, universality, and inclusiveness; his Virgo ♍ lower heaven reveals his foundation in a role of sacred service to others. Of course, this would be true for the incarnation of the Buddha of Compassion. Note, too, that one of the archetypes for Pisces ♓ is Christ! The Dalai Lama received the 1989 Nobel Prize for Peace. When someone asks what inspires him, he often quotes this Buddhist verse:

> For as long as space endures
> And for as long as living beings remain
> Until then may I too abide
> To dispel the misery of the world.

Body Signs

In astrology, connections between the signs and parts of the human body go inward to reveal microcosmic truths, just as astrology holds that the entire cosmos, the Universe, is reflected in each human being. As Shakespeare's *Hamlet* muses on humanity—"What a piece of work is man"—also remember that *all* the zodiac signs (not just the Sun ☉ sign) you are born under are represented in your astrological chart. All the zodiac signs have a bearing on a healthy you. From head to toe, each sign of the zodiac is associated with a particular part of the body. The first sign, Aries ♈, is associated with the head, and the last sign, Pisces ♓, is associated with the feet.

The Signs and Their Associated Parts of the Body

Astrological Sign	Associated Body Parts
Aries ♈	Head and face
Taurus ♉	Neck and throat
Gemini ♊	Head, arms, shoulders, nervous system, and lungs
Cancer ♋	Stomach and breasts
Leo ♌	Back, spine, and heart
Virgo ♍	Intestines, liver, pancreas, gall bladder, and bowels
Libra ♎	Kidneys, lower back, and adrenal glands
Scorpio ♏	Genitals and the urinary and reproductive organs
Sagittarius ♐	Liver, hips, and thighs
Capricorn ♑	Bones, teeth, joints, and knees
Aquarius ♒	Ankles and circulation
Pisces ♓	Feet and the immune and hormonal systems

From ancient to modern times, astrology has been called upon to help identify health problems and assuage pain. The belief that mind, body, and spirit have divine correlations to the Universe, and so to sickness and health, is at the heart of astrology. Today, alternative health practices, such as acupuncture and yoga, also draw upon ancient beliefs in Elemental connections to health—Fire, Earth, Air, and Water. T. S. Eliot's epic early twentieth-century poem *The Waste Land* is filled with astrological references, and four of its sections are named for the astrological Elements: Fire, Earth, Air, and Water. (Learn about the signs and their Elements in the next chapter.)

Astrology: The First Science

For as long as eyes have looked upward to the heavens, humankind has strived to understand its place in the Universe. Astrology, arguably the first science, connects our human souls to the movement of the heavens and celestial rhythms. Long before physics, chemistry, biology, or any of those other subjects you may have tried to avoid in high school or college, there was astrology. As early as 2900 B.C.E., the Sumerians built temples in the form of ziggurats (terraced pyramids) to observe the stars and planets. It's a pretty safe assumption that astrology existed even before this.

From its ancient beginnings, astrology soon developed into an incredibly complex practice. Astrology and astronomy became one science, and *astrologers* were the best-educated people: They had to understand astronomy, math, spiritual symbols and mystic meanings, psychology, and human nature. Early scientists used astrology to explore the relationships between the position of the Earth and the positions of celestial bodies in the heavens.

It shouldn't come as a surprise that astrology was taught in the universities until the 1600s when "rational science" took over. Today, most astrologers are still very well educated and often hold college degrees in various fields as well as certifications in astrology. They frequently have training in psychology or counseling, and in addition to their in-depth knowledge of astrology, they have a great deal of spiritual understanding.

Albrecht Dürer, a contemporary of the mystic Nostradamus, depicted the skies of the Northern and Southern Hemispheres in 1515 C.E., illustrating the blending of science, astronomy, and astrology at this time in human history.

Some brilliant scientists who used astrology:

* **Pythagoras (580?–500? B.C.E.)** Do you remember the Pythagorean theorem? Pythagoras also gave us the musical scale. Pythagoras believed that similar to musical harmonies, the larger harmony of the Universe could be discovered in numbers as well. (It is still believed by many mathematicians that the secret of the Universe can be discovered somewhere in *pi,* the ratio of a circle's circumference to its diameter.)

* **Nostradamus (1503–1566 C.E.)** Nostradamus's famous astrological predictions, written in 1555 C.E., foretold everything that would happen from that date until the end of the world, which he posted at 3797 C.E. (thank goodness!). He predicted a Golden Age— 1,000 years of peace—beginning around the millennium. (Let's hope Nostradamus is right and that world peace is just around the corner!)

* **Isaac Newton (1642–1727 C.E.)** Long before he sat under the proverbial apple tree, Isaac Newton was a practicing astrologer and astronomer. Among Newton's many ponderings were questions about the secret of the Universe, the nature of gravity itself (yes, it *exists*—but *why?*), and a belief in the existence of animal spirits in the human body. It's ironic that scientists after Newton would use own Newton's laws to discount any further examination of astrology as a science.

* **Carl Gustav Jung (1875–1961 C.E.)** The co-founder with Sigmund Freud of psychology, Jung recognized the synchronicity that is the basis of astrology, and he once said, "We are born at a given moment, in a given place, and like vintage years of wine, we have the qualities of the year and of the season of which we are born. Astrology does not lay claim to anything more."

Three Wise Men

Turn-of-the-century financier J. P. Morgan might have summed it up best when he said, "Anyone can be a millionaire, but to be a *billionaire*, you need astrology." But then, money isn't everything, right?

Have you ever wondered why the Three Wise Men were looking for that star over Bethlehem in the first place? The answer is that they were astrologers! It is believed that they learned from their study of the stars that the Christ child would be born at the time of a *conjunction* of planets that signaled the arrival of a new age (the Piscean). A conjunction of planets means that the two planets appear in the same place in the sky at the same time. Conjunctions begin new cycles that reflect the planets involved.

This wasn't quite as easy as it sounds. The two planets involved in the conjunction—Jupiter ♃ and Saturn ♄—were bright, but they were not something an average person would have noticed. So, even though they were trained astrologers, it took the Three Wise Men some time to actually locate Jesus in Bethlehem. But if they hadn't studied the stars, they might not have been looking in the first place.

The Three Wise Men looking for the conjunction of Jupiter and Saturn.
Written in the symbols of astrology, this is: ♃ ☌ ♄.

Astrology Is Fake, But I'm Still So Obsessed by It!

In our new millennium, the twenty-first century, the rational scientific underpinnings of astrology have been undermined, while its intuitive foundation grows stronger. Our scientific knowledge of the human body, the Earth, and the Universe convince us there is something more—an elusive intuitive link that binds all existence. We yearn and search for such a link, and we find access to its promise in astrology.

Astrology is the perfect intuitive science for the modern age. It holds the unique melding of modern technology (which makes birth charts accessible to all) and an understanding of human psychology and the behavioral sciences; astrology also melds discoveries in astronomy and space exploration with our hunger to understand our own actions and relationships and humanity's place on Earth and in the Universe.

Astrology Memes Are So Relatable

Why do we behave the way we do? Will we love, and be loved? Where are we going? Where are we? Who are we?

Astrology remains a tantalizing method for self-discovery. Understanding astrological cycles over time reveals the celestial heartbeat of the Universe coursing through human experience on Earth.

While exploring each nuance of our astrological birth charts, we discover that we are as large as the Universe. We contain multitudes. We crave celestial resonance—a spiritual connection of our lives to the Earth.

Astrology is a symbolic system from which we can learn the interconnection between external reality and internal reality. Your astrological birth chart, a representation of the heavens at the place and time of your birth, expands in all directions and is an infinite record of your potential. When you begin to uncover the meaning of the symbols in your chart, you enhance your embodiment of that potential. How wonderful to have a tool to discover who you are, what you want, *who* you want.

Robert Downey Jr.'s Meme-worthy Chart

You don't have to be famous to have a meme-worthy chart. Just look on social media to see people posting thousands of memes about astrology. Is your Jupiter ♃ rising? Will you survive Mercury retrograde ☿ ℞? Is this the dawning of the Age of Aquarius ♒? You'll find *your* own answers to these questions in a study of your birth chart. What are you waiting for?

We're going to throw a birth chart at you right now, before you've read further in this book and learned all about what the symbols mean and how to read them. Here's the chart for former wild child and gifted actor Robert Downey, Jr.

For a quick and dirty birth chart reading, you need to look at three things: the Sun ☉, the Moon ☽, and the ascendant. Robert Downey Jr.'s Sun ☉ is Aries ♈, his Moon ☽ is Taurus ♉, and his ascendant (Rising sign) is Leo ♌. Aries and Leo give him the power to focus his passion—whatever he is momentarily attracted to. Aries can be sporadic, innovative, and futuristic; Robert has a lot of energy built up, and he must get it out there into the world and use it. The Rising sign is Leo ♌, which is leadership; Robert wants to be independent, self-reliant, and be his own boss. So, Robert's Sun and Rising sign give him charisma, the power to be confident about what he wants to accomplish, even if he does like to take chances. The Moon ☽ is exalted in Taurus ♉, meaning that in astrology, the Moon is favored in Taurus. In his emotional self, no matter what happens in his life, Robert can understand loyalty, integrity, and perseverance; hard work pays off. Robert's heart is attached in the right place in the right direction; he doesn't scatter his energy. Robert knows when he either loves something or he does not. He's a speedball who gets easily bored, Aries/Leo, yet has the power to reflect and reground himself in his Taurus Moon. He goes from one extreme to another.

How did we know so much about Robert from only considering three points in his chart? Read on and find out.

Out of billions of people on Earth, there is only one you. The heavens shone down on you in a particular orientation at the moment of your birth. Astrology will help you explore the heavens to find out exactly who you are, and who you can be.

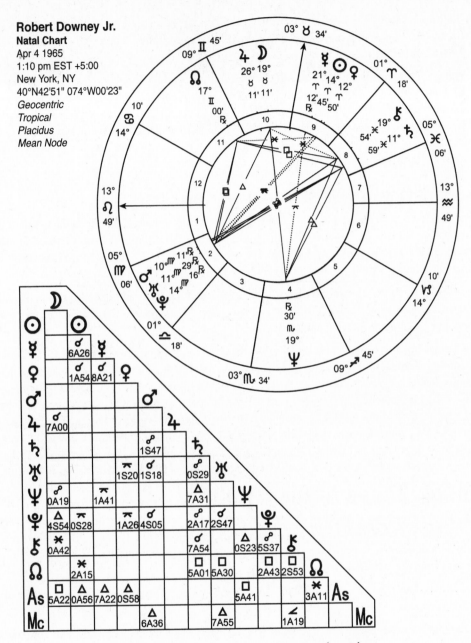

Robert Downey Jr.
Natal Chart
Apr 4 1965
1:10 pm EST +5:00
New York, NY
40°N42'51" 074°W00'23"
Geocentric
Tropical
Placidus
Mean Node

For a fast chart reading, look at the Sun 3, Moon 4, and ascendant.

Chapter 2

SUN ☉ SIGNS: ENERGIES, QUALITIES, AND ELEMENTS

Your Sun ☉ sign gets you to your horoscope. It even gets you to the beginning of your astrological birth chart—and we could say it is the center of your birth chart, just as it's the center of the heavens. However, to move beyond your horoscope to learn about your birth chart, you need to broaden your horizons! There are 12 signs in the zodiac—one of which, of course, is your Sun ☉ sign. In astrology, there are 10 *planets*; astrologers count the Sun and the Moon in that number, too. Each planet represents your different energies and parts of yourself. Each *sign* manifests those energies in different ways and has its own unique combination of character traits—its energy, quality, and element. All these things combine to make you who you are.

Making Sense of the Symbols

Astrology uses a unique language of symbols. When you first look at your birth chart, this language looks hard to decipher. But learning to translate these symbols into their meanings is actually pretty straightforward—and the ability to do it gives you the ability to "read" your birth chart just like astrologers do.

The following tables show the symbols that represent the signs and planets. In addition, we've included the symbols for the *Nodes*, which are points astrologers use to look at Karmic destiny.

The Signs and Their Symbols

Astrological Sign	Symbol
Aries	♈
Taurus	♉
Gemini	♊
Cancer	♋
Leo	U
Virgo	♍
Libra	O
Scorpio	♏
Sagittarius	♐
Capricorn	♑
Aquarius	≈
Pisces	W

The Nodes and Their Symbols

North Node	☊
South Node	☋

The Planets and Their Symbols

Planet	Symbol
Sun	☉
Moon	☽
Mercury	☿
Venus	♀

Planet	Symbol
Mars	♂
Jupiter	♃
Saturn	♄
Uranus	♅
Neptune	♆
Pluto	♇

There's even more to your astrological birth chart than what you've learned here. But for now, all you need to remember is that your chart shows the position of the heavens at *your* birth—just as the Dalai Lama's shows the alignment of the Universe at the time of *his* birth. With this chapter, we start at the beginning, with a look at the zodiac signs and their interpretation in placement as your Sun ☉ sign.

It is nearly impossible for two people to share the same astrological birth chart, but it is mathematically possible. However, the odds of that happening are astronomically small. We've seen those odds calculated as high as 1 in 10^{312}, a number that would take up this whole book if you wrote it down. This number also reveals something of the complexity of astrology and the complexity of people, something no other model about people is able to do, except maybe DNA. No other model can come up with so many different combinations. Translation: You are unique!

The First Spark: You and Your Sun ☉ Sign

You might know what your Sun ☉ sign *is,* but do you know what it *means?* That is, can you understand the significance of your birth sign beyond your horoscope forecasts? Just as the Sun is the strongest light in our solar system, *your* Sun ☉ sign is the strongest representation of who *you* are. It's what you'll notice the most because it's like the fuel you burn.

Symbolically, the Sun represents you, your willpower, and your creativity. And mythologically, the Sun represents the *Source,* the unlimited resources of the Universe or the god of your understanding. Remember that the Sun's symbol ☉ is a perfect circle, an endless whole. Many believe that the Universe, people, and people's creativity are interconnected.

So, who decided just where the Sun signs begin and end, and why they are the way they are?

Remember those ancient astronomers, watching the apparent movement of the sky over Earth? Well, they're back! Part of their sky-mapping determined that the Sun went through certain constellations at certain times of the year, and that people born at that time of year seemed to share certain characteristics.

Now, this isn't really so mysterious. Scientific evidence corroborates that people born at night might be night owls, for example, and that people born in the summer might love warm weather. But if you know anything about astronomy, you also know that the constellations are *not* overhead at the times of year the zodiac indicates. So, what's going on here?

A very long time ago, the constellations of the signs *were* in the area of the sky that was named for them. But because of the Earth's wobble and the fact that the Earth shifts a tiny bit in space over a long period of time, the constellations have shifted out of those positions. So, Western astrology uses the seasons, which don't change over time, as its basis for Sun signs and has kept the names the same.

Finding Your Sun ☉ Sign

So, what's the big deal about knowing your Sun ☉ sign? Knowing it means you can …

  5. Reveal whether the love of your life is a potential perfect match or a stupendous dud.

  4. Always have something to talk about at parties.

  3. Make excuses for your inexcusable behavior.

  2. Have the best pickup line ever.

and …

  1. Have the best tattoo ideas.

You know your birthday, right? Then you have what you need to find your Sun ☉ sign using the following illustration. Doing so is the first step in creating the astrological map—your birth chart—that reveals your uniqueness. Note that if you were born at the beginning or end of a sign, you might need to have your horoscope calculated to determine which Sun sign you have because the Sun doesn't go into a sign on exactly the same day every year.

The Dalai Lama's Sun ☉ Sign

Now, let's look at the Dalai Lama's birth chart to see how you find the Sun ☉ sign in astrological terms. When you look at the legend for the Dalai Lama's chart, you will see that his birth date is July 6, 1935. This means that his Sun ☉ is in Cancer ♋. Can you find the Sun ☉ symbol on the Dalai Lama's chart? We've highlighted it for you in the following illustration.

After you find the circle with a dot in the center that represents the Sun ☉, find the symbol for Cancer ♋ between the numbers to the side of the Sun symbol. This cryptic presentation tells you the Dalai Lama's Sun is in Cancer (and the numbers tell the precise location; more about that in later chapters).

That this fourteenth incarnation of the Dalai Lama has a Cancer Sun ♋︎☉ sign is no surprise to us. Rather than simply *lead* his exiled people, the Dalai Lama has chosen to reach out to the larger world, communicating his ideas through speaking engagements and books that appeal to humanity's need for a more intuitive and holistic approach, sharing a vision that encompasses all of humanity, while never losing his larger vision for the future.

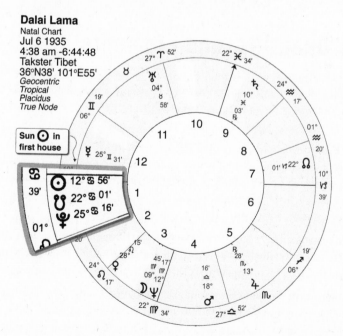

Dalai Lama
Natal Chart
Jul 6 1935
4:38 am -6:44:48
Takster Tibet
36°N38' 101°E55'
Geocentric
Tropical
Placidus
True Node

Sun ☉ in first house

The Signs and Their Energies, Qualities, and Elements

Sign	Energy	Quality	Element
Aries ♈	Yang	Cardinal	Fire
Taurus ♉	Yin	Fixed	Earth
Gemini ♊	Yang	Mutable	Air
Cancer ♋	Yin	Cardinal	Water
Leo ♌	Yang	Fixed	Fire
Virgo ♍	Yin	Mutable	Earth
Libra ♎	Yang	Cardinal	Air
Scorpio ♏	Yin	Fixed	Water
Sagittarius ♐	Yang	Mutable	Fire
Capricorn ♑	Yin	Cardinal	Earth
Aquarius ♒	Yang	Fixed	Air
Pisces ♓	Yin	Mutable	Water

Energies, Qualities, and Elements

Each of the 12 zodiac signs is categorized in a number of ways. First, there are two *energies,* or genders, and each sign is either one or the other. The energies represent whether the energy manifested by a Sun sign is yang (direct and externally oriented) or yin (indirect and internally oriented).

Then there are three quadruplicities, called *qualities,* each of which appears in four signs. Qualities represent different types of activities and are related to where in a season a sign falls. Cardinal signs begin each season, so they represent beginnings; fixed signs, in the middle of each season, are preservers, which keep things as they are; and mutable signs occur as the season is changing and are associated with transitions.

Last, there are four triplicities, each of which appears in three signs; these are called *Elements.* The four Elements describe the basic nature of the signs and of life: Fire, Earth, Air, and Water, and each represents distinct temperamental characteristics. Let's take all that a little more slowly.

People born in signs with the same energy, quality, or Element have certain things in common. For example, people born in signs with a *cardinal* (or first) quality are likely to be leaders; people in signs with an Air Element might always seem to be thinking or communicating.

Now, each combination of energy, quality, and Element appears in only one sign. Aries ♈, for example, has a yang energy, a cardinal quality, and the Element of Fire. This means that when you understand what each of these characteristics represents, you also can begin to understand certain aspects of an Aries personality. See? It's not so hard.

The ancient symbol for the union of yin and yang energies
evokes a heavenly sphere of celestial balance.

Energies: Two for the Show

Every sign is either direct or indirect, male or female. You'll see the energies called "feminine" and "masculine" in some books, but we prefer to call them yang (direct/masculine) and yin (indirect/feminine), which avoids all that gender-based nonsense. All Fire and Air signs are yang, while all Earth and Water signs are yin. Each energy has certain characteristics that, coupled with the qualities and Elements, create a unique picture for each zodiac sign.

The Signs and Their Energies

Yang	Yin
Aries ♈	Taurus ♉
Gemini ♊	Cancer ♋
Leo ♌	Virgo ♍
Libra ♎	Scorpio ♏
Sagittarius ♐	Capricorn ♑
Aquarius ♒	Pisces ♓

The following table will help you differentiate between yang and yin more easily.

Yang	Yin
Specific	Holistic
Positive	Negative
Left brain	Right brain
White	Black
Morning	Evening
Conscious	Unconscious
Heavy	Light
Male	Female
Heaven	Earth

As this table reveals, yang signs tend toward direct action rather than waiting for things to come to them, like the bee that pollinates the flower. Yang represents the outgoing, the positive electrical charge, an external orientation, and the direct, "male" side of things.

Yin represents the indirect forces and actions, those that understand what is needed to attract and create the desired outcome, like the flower that blooms to attract the bee. Yin is also called the receptive, the negative electrical charge, an internal orientation, and the "female" side of things.

People with yin energy signs tend to use a holistic approach, intuiting what needs to be done rather than insisting on specific, ordered steps. It's not surprising to find that the Dalai Lama's Sun ☉ sign is yin Cancer ♋.

Qualities: Three to Get Ready

The qualities represent different types of activity. Think of the way a season progresses, from its forceful beginning, its fixed middle, and its transitional ending. These *qualities* represent each season as it moves through its paces, as well as its three signs.

As there are 3 qualities and 12 signs, there are 4 signs for each quality. Signs that share a quality also share certain characteristics.

The Signs and Their Qualities

Cardinal	Fixed	Mutable
Aries ♈	Taurus ♉	Gemini ♊
Cancer ♋	Leo ♌	Virgo ♍
Libra ♎	Scorpio ♏	Sagittarius ♐
Capricorn ♑	Aquarius ♒	Pisces ♓

Qualities and Their Characteristics

Cardinal	Fixed	Mutable
Independent	Persistent	Adaptable
Impatient	Consistent	Flexible
Go-getting	Reliable	Mercurial

You'll notice in the following figure that the qualities in each of the signs form a square; that's one of the reasons they're called quadruplicities. (The other reason is that there are four signs for each quality.)

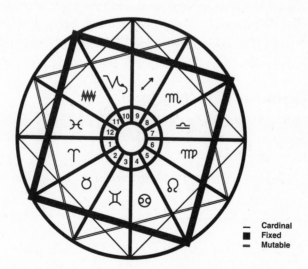

The qualities form a square.

The first quality is called *cardinal*. The first quality is the first sign in each season—Aries ♈ in spring, Cancer ♋ in summer, Libra ♎ in autumn, and Capricorn ♑ in winter. People with cardinal quality signs are independent. They seek to move ahead and start new things, and they can be proactive and enterprising. They also can be impatient if others don't move as quickly as they do, but they're independent, too—the signs of beginnings. Of course, once they get something started and established, cardinal people tend to lose interest in the project. Instead, they're off to start something else. Remember, it's a certain type of person who likes to start things, and if you have heavy cardinal influences in your chart, you're just that kind of person.

In the midst of each season, we have what is called the *fixed* quality. People with fixed quality signs—Taurus ♉ in spring, Leo ♌ in summer, Scorpio ♏ in autumn, and Aquarius ♒ in winter—are consistent, reliable, determined, and persistent. They often have great reserves of power, but they also can become stubborn or set in their ways. These are, after all, characteristics needed to preserve what has already been started. Remember, though, that people with fixed quality signs are the ones who take over once cardinal people have started things.

The end of each season signifies a time of change, so the signs in this placement are called *mutable*. People with mutable quality signs—Gemini ♊ in spring, Virgo ♍ in summer, Sagittarius ♐ in autumn, and Pisces ♓ in winter—adapt easily, are flexible and resourceful, are quick to learn, and can see issues from more than one angle. They also can lack perseverance, but this is precisely because they're adaptable and flexible. That's what's needed to make transitions. After all, they've already seen the beginning and the middle of the process.

Elements: Four to Go

Think of the Elements as tendencies of the temperament: Fire, Earth, Air, Water. Everything that exists is composed of these characteristics, and every astrological sign manifests one of them as well. In addition, all Fire and Air signs are yang, and all Earth and Water signs are yin.

The signs that share an Element share certain characteristics, depending on what that Element is.

The Signs and Their Elements

Fire	Earth	Air	Water
Aries ♈	Taurus ♉	Gemini ♊	Cancer ♋
Leo ♌	Virgo ♍	Libra ♎	Scorpio ♏
Sagittarius ♐	Capricorn ♑	Aquarius ♒	Pisces ♓

The Elements and Their Characteristics

Fire	Earth	Air	Water
Energetic	Practical	Intellectual	Emotional
Courageous	Skillful	Social	Intuitive
Passionate	Down to earth	Thoughtful	Romantic

You'll notice in the following illustration that the Elements in each of the signs form a triangle; that's one of the reasons they're called the triplicities. (The other reason is that there are three signs for each element.)

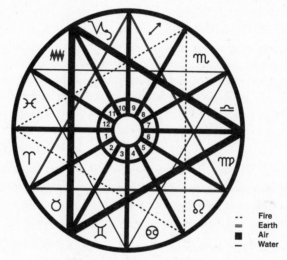

The Elements form a triangle.

The first Element is Fire. Fire signs (Aries ♈, Leo ♌, and Sagittarius ♐) are energetic, idealistic, self-assertive, courageous, and often visionary. If you remember that *Fire is first*, it might help you remember that Fire signs are very active, stimulate creative expression, and are always passionate. People with lots of Fire planets are often known as "fireballs."

The second Element is Earth. Earth signs (Taurus ♉, Virgo ♍, and Capricorn ♑) are practical and skillful, good at managing physical assets, financial matters, or any form of matter. Thinking of Earth signs as *down to earth* will help you remember their characteristics. People with lots of planets in Earth signs are sometimes called "grounded" or "rooted."

The third Element is Air. Air signs (Gemini ♊, Libra ♎, and Aquarius ♒) represent social and intellectual abilities: ideas, communications, thinking, and social interrelationships. People with Air signs operate on a mental plane, through air, so to speak, which might help you remember what Air signs are like. People with lots of Air planets are often known as "airy" or just plain "head in the clouds."

The fourth Element is Water. Water signs (Cancer ♋, Scorpio ♏, and Pisces ♓) are sensitive and emotional; they think with their feelings, intuitively, and are often romantic. Cancer represents the lake, Scorpio represents the river, and Pisces represents the ocean. Thinking of water as emotion will help you remember the characteristics of Water signs. People with lots of Water planets are often known as "water babies" or "in the flow."

Throughout Earth's history, the Elements have evolved as our planet has transformed and evolved through time. In our time, as we experience the Earth's sixth mass extinction event and witness the ravages of climate change, the Elements play a strong role in our changing world. Volcanic eruptions and raging forest fires, including the burning of the Amazon forest (the Earth's lungs) show Fire's fast all-consuming power. As more and more living beings become endangered, more refugees (microbes, fungi, plants, and animals) move and adapt to find the safe places for life on Earth. Droughts and storms manifest as the Air patterns swirl around the Earth, affected by the release of carbon in the atmosphere. This happens as the Air we breathe in is influenced by industry's chemicals, for better or worse. Rising sea levels will change the Earth's shorelines, while the oceans warm up and humankind faces the challenge of removing plastic and toxins from its depths.

In our time, the Elements are carving a new map of the world, and humanity—indeed all that lives—must find its place. An imperative exists. In astrology, this means we feel the influence of the Elements in the signs more strongly, and we must heed their message or ignore it, potentially at our collective peril.

Looking Beyond Your Sun ☉ Sign

Look again to find the Sun ☉ sign placement in the Dalai Lama's chart, and already you can begin to interpret extra meaning. With his Sun ☉ in Cancer ♋, we already know that Cancer has a yin energy, a cardinal quality, and Water as its Element.

Each planet and sign appears in your birth chart. You can find these by locating the appropriate symbols (use the charts at the beginning of this chapter to identify them). For example, let's find the Dalai Lama's Moon ☽. We've highlighted the Moon for you … see it there in the third house? Can you identify its sign? Look up the symbol ♍; it's Virgo. Can you identify the energy, quality, and Element of the Dalai Lama's Moon? The domain of the Moon ☽ is the emotions; these characteristics tell us how the Dalai Lama interacts emotionally. The Dalai Lama's Moon ☽ in Virgo ♍ is yin, mutable, and Earth, which signifies someone who is receptive to new ideas and change, yet grounded and solid in his emotional interactions with the world around him. The third house is the house of Knowledge. (You'll learn all about house energies in the next chapter.) With Virgo's love of sacred patterns and the Moon's soft light shining in the third house of knowledge, which gives way to illuminating what is hidden, the Dalai Lama proves to be a grounding source of faith and inspiration for humanity as we seek to understand our changing, transforming world.

Chapter 3

YOUR BIRTH CHART DECONSTRUCTED

Though your Sun ☉ sign is the basis of your birth chart, it is only the beginning of astrology. Every one of the 12 signs of the zodiac appears somewhere on your birth chart, and every sign is a part of who you are in some way. In this chapter, we look in more detail at ascendants, planets, and houses because there's a whole lot more to you than just your Sun sign.

Your ascendant, or Rising sign, shows the "you" the world sees, and it reveals the lessons you'll learn during this lifetime. Planets hold the energy of the Universe, representing different energies in yourself and in society. Planets reveal why you behave the way you do. Each astrological house on the chart wheel is an area of your life; houses are where the action is.

Your Vital Statistics: Your Birth Chart's Foundation

Before you can explore these astrological features, you need your birth chart. The information you need to create your birth chart is usually easy to obtain. You just need these three simple numbers:

* Your date of birth
* Your time of birth
* Your place of birth

Now, this sounds pretty easy, right? For most of us, it is. Your birthday is your date of birth, of course. And you probably know where you were born. Most of us have heard the stories of our births. ("Oh, I was in labor for 2 days with you, and I thought I'd have to wait forever to meet you.") But it may be a little harder to find out your precise birth time.

Okay, go ask your mother. She'll say, "Let's see, we'd just fallen asleep, and I woke up and said to Daddy, 'Something's funny, honey,' and next thing I knew, we were off to the hospital, and then you were born." "What time, Ma?" you ask. "Oh, it must have been around three or four. Somewhere in the middle of the night. I'm just not really sure."

Or, maybe your mother recalls exactly when and why her C-section was scheduled for your birth on a particular day and maybe even what part of the day, but maybe she doesn't remember the precise recorded birth time. And although you were there, you didn't yet know how to tell time. Well, isn't "around three or four" good enough? The answer is, it's not. And in a moment, we'll tell you why.

The best option is to check your birth certificate. But not all birth certificates include the time of birth—especially if you're, well, shall we say, older, or if you were born in a country other than the United States. And depending on your age and where you live, if you are adopted, you might not know any of your actual birth information.

Let's look more closely at each of the three—your birth date, birth time, and birthplace.

Your Most Important Day

Happy birthday! As you already know, your birthday determines your Sun ☉ sign. But it's also the first number you need to start your astrological birth chart. This is the number that tells you which pages of the reference books to use to find the numbers to calculate your chart or the first number you punch into the computer for your personal chart calculation. (If you were doing manual calculation, see Appendix A.) You need your full birth date, including the month, day, and year. For the Dalai Lama, whose birth chart we're beginning to grow quite familiar with, the birth date is well-known: July 6, 1935.

The Time of Your Life

The exact time you were born can be an elusive piece of information. Lots of people know that they were born "around 10 A.M." But the minute astrologers see a rounded number like that, they begin to think it's an approximate time rather than the exact time. Even a few minutes can mean the difference between a planet appearing in one sign or another or in one house or another. Your ascendant or midheaven could change as well. As we've already discovered, these are *important* differences. You'll want to be aware of the time zone in which you were born, which is also very important for ensuring that the calculations used to create your birth chart are correct.

Your midheaven changes degrees at least every four minutes, and depending on your birth chart, it could be even more often. Because the interpretation of a chart can't be more accurate than the information used to calculate it, it's worth doing some research to get your birth time right, such as sending away for your birth certificate. Otherwise, you might end up with a birth chart that's not entirely accurate.

But the big question remains: If your mother can't remember your exact birth time, and it's not on your birth certificate, how do you determine your birth time? Astrologers, for a fee, will do a *rectification* for your birth time. This is a consultation in which you tell the astrologer about important things that have happened in your life and how you behave in various situations, much as you might tell a therapist. The astrologer will then determine your birth time by using this information. It's kind of like finding your birth time by doing your chart, instead of the other way around. Rectification is still an estimate of birth time, remember, but is the next best thing to having the precise birth information.

Of course, if you don't want to pay for a rectification, you can always ask the astrologer to use a noon chart, which uses noon as the time of your birth. While it is less accurate than a chart with your specific birth time, especially when it comes to your Moon ☽ placement and your ascendant, a noon chart will nonetheless give you an overview of your planetary placements. Your noon chart will help give the astrologer an "eagle eye" view of your natal planets and how they were placed in the sky. The astrologer can view your birth planets' cycles and derive helpful trends in your life. To see an interpretation using a noon birth chart, look at civil rights legend Rosa Parks's chart in Chapter 18.

Just how much does knowing a precise birth time *really* matter? For years, there has been quite a controversy over the precise birth time for Hillary Clinton. Numerous reports give varied times of birth, but most astrologers focus in on whether Clinton was born at 8 P.M. or 8 A.M. on October 26, 1947. Many astrology stans feel Clinton has been purposefully obscure about her birth time to thwart public discussion of her chart. And the difference between Clinton's morning chart and evening chart are stark. Only the morning chart revealed a rise to high office, while the evening chart has many Clinton astro-nerd stalker fans, "stans," depressed. While many astrologers cling to the morning birth time for Clinton despite her defeat in the 2016 U.S. presidential election, her precise birth time is still unknown as of this book's printing. Many astrological sites online use a ranking system to indicate how reliable precise birth time data is for their birth charts of famous people, and they sometimes list a source for the time.

For the Dalai Lama, though the precise birth time is not documented, the time of birth is placed by his mother at sunrise, so astrologers commonly use the time of sunrise, 4:38 A.M., on July 6, 1935. The power of the 4 A.M. birth time continues to resonate in the Dalai Lama's life, as this is the time he rises daily to meditate and pray. Each day presents a new rebirth, perhaps?

Where Did You Come From?

The last number you need to create an astrological birth chart comes from a place: where you were born. Though you know your place of birth by its name on the map (like Victoria, British Columbia, Canada, or Baltimore, Maryland, United States), every place on the planet Earth can be translated into its latitude and longitude. This location information is written in degrees and minutes. Latitude measures the distance north or south of the equator. 00 degrees is the equator.

Places to the north are shown in degrees and minutes as 00N00, and places to the south are shown in degrees and minutes as 00S00.

Longitude is the distance east or west of the Greenwich Meridian. Places east of the Greenwich Meridian are shown as 00E00, and places west are shown as 00W00.

To give you an example, Aspen, Colorado, has a latitude of 39N11 and a longitude of 106W49. This means that Aspen is 39 degrees, 11 minutes north of the equator, and 106 degrees, 49 minutes west of the Greenwich Meridian.

It's pretty unlikely that you'll know the latitude and the longitude for the place that you were born. But never fear! Computer programs calculating your birth chart use GPS data to do all the work for you. For example, when we entered the birth date, birth time, and birthplace of the Dalai Lama (July 6, 1935; 4:38 A.M.; and Takstar, Tibet), the latitude and longitude for the birth chart is correctly calculated as 36N38 and 101E55.

Creating Your Birth Chart

From your vital statistics, an online astrology site or app uses an algorithm to calculate your birth chart and presents it to you in the familiar form of the zodiac wheel. This wheel represents what you might've seen if, as a newborn, you'd looked up at the heavens at the moment of your birth (though, of course, you were far more interested in looking at your mother and everyone else gathered to welcome you into the world). The planets and their signs appear in the 12 segments of the zodiac wheel, called the astrological houses, ready for you to interpret!

Ascendants

Your ascendant, or Rising sign, is the sign that was rising over the horizon at the moment of your birth. This sign is your outward manifestation—the "you" that the outside world perceives. At the same time, your ascendant also is the way you express yourself (which is probably why the outside world perceives you that way). Usually, your Sun ☉ sign and ascendant sign are different, which is why your ascendant usually is perceived as a "mask," hiding your true self—your Sun sign.

Each of the 12 signs rises over the horizon during a 24-hour period, so in rough terms, each ascendant rises over the horizon for 2 hours (more or less, depending on how quickly a particular sign rises) every day. In addition, the sign the Sun is in will be the sign rising at sunrise that day.

For example, in the early spring, Aries ♈ is rising at sunrise, but Leo ♌ is rising at sunrise in the middle of summer. This means that if you were born at sunrise, both your Sun ☉ sign and ascendant would be in the same sign, which means others would see you behaving like your Sun sign. Or to put it another way, rather than wearing a different mask, you'd behave like your Sun sign—just as the Dalai Lama, whose Sun and ascendant are in the same sign.

We'd like to add another dimension to your consideration of your ascendant. Think of it as "training" for the person you are becoming. In other words, your Rising sign indicates the skills and traits you're learning to develop during your lifetime. For example, if you're born with a Scorpio ♏ ascendant, much of what you do might be connected with learning about control, both self-control and a need to control others.

Your ascendant might also be revealed in the clothes you wear, the car you drive, the art or novels you admire, or any of the other ways you "show" yourself to the world. Your ascendant is as much a part of you as your Sun sign, but it's often more obvious to others.

Now, when we look at the Dalai Lama's birth chart, we see that his Sun and ascendant are both in Cancer ♋. This tells us that this spiritual leader truly is "out there" with who he is; he hides nothing in his presentation of himself. See Chapter 4 to find out how to interpret the meaning of your Sun sign and ascendant. When you look at your birth chart, your ascendant is the sign that appears on the cusp of the first house. This is the line that separates the first house from the twelfth house. See it there, the symbol for Cancer ♋, on the Dalai Lama's chart?

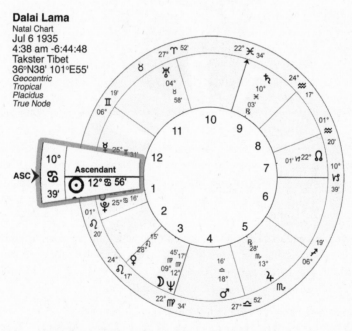

The Dalai Lama's ascendant is in the sign of Cancer ♋.

Planets: Every Heavenly Body Tells a Story

Planets are the "what" of astrology. They represent the various energies of a person, including things like mental and emotional nature, desires, vitality, soul, will, consciousness, and subconscious, as well as the people in a person's life. Every planet, in other words, tells a story.

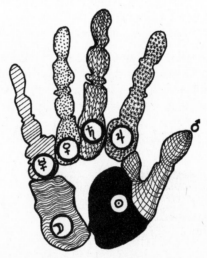

The planets appear in other intuitive arts as well aside from astrology. In palmistry, the fingers and mounts of the hand are named for the planets.

Because each planet's story is connected to the way that planet seems to behave, they are, in turn, stories about *you*. These stories are based on a number of things, such as what sign a planet is in and where it appears in your birth chart, as well as which planets it associates with and how well they get along with each other.

Astrology is complex, just like the planets, and so we'll be telling you some of these stories when we tell you more about each planet. After all, humans are storytellers for good reason. Stories help us understand who we are and why we're here in the Universe. Because astrology has a similar purpose, it's natural the two should hook up in this book.

Planet Power: Where Do You Put Your Energy?

Planets represent different energies within ourselves and our society, and are divided into the luminaries (Sun ☉ and Moon ☽), personal planets (Mercury ☿, Venus ♀, and Mars ♂), social planets (Jupiter ♃ and Saturn ♄), and transpersonal planets (Uranus ♅, Neptune ♆, and Pluto ♇).

Knowing the signs your planets are in can help you see why you behave the way you do. For example, if your Mercury ☿ is in Gemini ♊, this might indicate that you're a person who's quick thinking.

Some people have several planets in a sign other than their Sun ☉ sign. This means they'll exhibit strong characteristics of that different sign. Similarly, some people might have lots of planets in a particular *house* of their chart, so they might spend a lot of energy in that area of their life.

In Part 3, we'll show you just what each planet in each sign reveals in more detail. For now, just remember that the signs *your* planets are in describe how you use their particular energies or functions in your life. For example, a Leo Moon ♌☽ means you will seem sunny and optimistic, but someone with an Aquarian Moon ♒☽ will seem aloof and detached.

The Sun ☉ and the Moon ☽: Luminaries

In astrology, the Sun and Moon are called the *luminaries* because they are responsible for lighting up our world. For simplicity, the Sun ☉ and the Moon ☽ also are called planets because from Earth's vantage point, they move across the sky just as the planets do. Because it stands for yourself, your willpower, and your creativity, your Sun ☉ sign is the strongest representation of who you really are. The chapters in Part 2 talk all about Sun ☉ signs.

Your Moon ☽ represents the emotional and intuitive parts of you and the ways you express your feelings. The Moon also influences how you nurture. You'll learn much more about Moon ☽ signs in Chapter 9.

In Chapter 2, we located the Dalai Lama's Sun ☉ in Cancer ♋ in his first house and Moon ☽ in Virgo ♍ in his third house; you can look back to review the placement of his luminaries.

The Luminaries

Planet	Symbol	Energies
Sun	☉	Self, essence, life spirit, creativity, willpower
Moon	☽	Emotions, instincts, unconscious, past memories

All About You: The Personal Planets

The energies of the *personal planets*, also called the *inner planets*, influence who you are and how you express your inner self. Chapter 9 gives you the full scoop on the personal planets. Here are the Dalai Lama's personal planets: Mercury ☿ in Gemini ♊ in the twelfth house, Venus ♀ in Leo ♌ in the third house, and Mars ♂ in Libra ♎ in the fourth house.

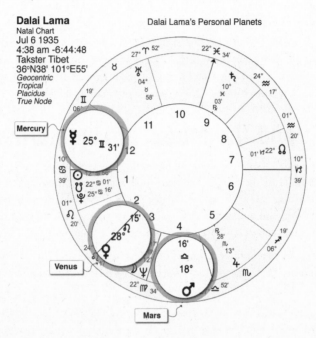

Dalai Lama's Personal Planets

The Personal Planets

Planet	Symbol	Energies
Mercury	☿	Mental activities, communication, intelligence
Venus	♀	Love, art, beauty, social graces, harmony, money, resources, possessions
Mars	♂	Physical energy, boldness, warrior ways, action, desires, anger, courage, ego

Interactions: The Social Planets

The energies of the *social planets* have a broader reach than those of the personal planets, influencing how you interact with and relate to your community, society in general, and the world at large. Because the orbits of the social planets are longer, these planets also stay in each of the zodiac signs. The social planets affect large groups of people in similar ways. Jupiter's 12-year journey around the Sun, for example, means that this social planet visits each sign for a full year. Everyone born during that year has Jupiter in the same sign and experiences a similar influence of Jupiter's energy. Chapter 10 covers the social planets through the signs of the zodiac.

When we look at the Dalai Lama's social planets, we see that he has Jupiter ♃ in Scorpio ♏ in his fifth house and Saturn ♄ in Pisces ♓ in his ninth house.

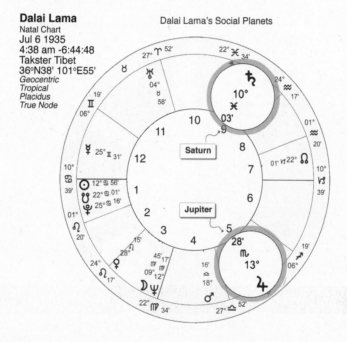

The Social Planets

Planet	Symbol	Energies
Jupiter	♃	Luck, abundance, wisdom, higher education, philosophy or beliefs, exploration, growth
Saturn	♄	Responsibilities, self-discipline, perseverance, limitations, structure

The Bigger Picture: The Generational Planets

The planets farthest from the Sun, the *transpersonal planets*, have the longest orbits and the broadest influences on people. Uranus stays 7 years in each sign, Neptune stays 14 years, and Pluto sometimes hangs around for so long it should be required to have a visa: 11 to 32 years. Astrologers sometimes call these the *generational planets* because their energies influence entire generations of people. Chapter 11 tells you all about the transpersonal planets.

When we look at the Dalai Lama's birth chart, we can see that the placements of his transpersonal planets are Uranus ♅ in Taurus ♉ in the eleventh house, Neptune ♆ in Virgo ♍ in the third house (right with his Moon ☽), and Pluto ♇ in Cancer ♋ in the first house (near his Sun ☉).

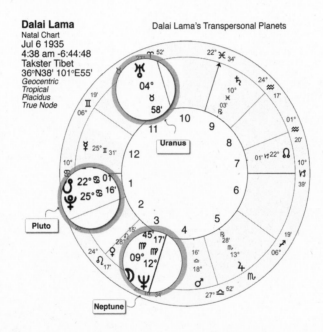

Dalai Lama's Transpersonal Planets

The Transpersonal Planets

Planet	Symbol	Energies
Uranus	♅	Sudden or unexpected change, originality, liberation, radicalness, intuition, authenticity
Neptune	♆	Idealism, subconscious, spirituality, intuition, clairvoyance
Pluto	♇	Power, regeneration, destruction, rebirth, transformation

Accomplishments and Possibilities: The Nodes ☊☋

Although the *Nodes* ☊☋ of the Moon are not heavenly bodies, they nonetheless add some essential information to your birth chart. The Nodes physically represent moving points that relate to the Moon's orbit around Earth. Exactly opposite each other, these points are often called your past and your future. Let's look at them a little more closely.

The *South Node* ☋ represents your heredity or past. Some call the South Node the "point of letting go." This means that you have already learned these lessons and mastered these skills; if you continue along this path, it will be the "easy way out." In other words, because you know how to do these things extremely well, there is no growth, no challenge, and no learning gained from doing them. Your "comfort zone" is your South Node, but being comfortable isn't necessarily your best path.

The *North Node* ☊ is always exactly opposite the South Node in its placement and represents your possibilities, your area of greatest growth, and where your future lies. If you follow the path of your North Node, you can gain new confidence as you learn new ideas. This is the path to developing new skills, abilities, and growth. Of course, it's also the path that is less comfortable for you.

In the Dalai Lama's birth chart, we find his North Node ☊ of challenge and potential in Capricorn ♑ in his seventh house, and his South Node ☋ of comfort and accomplishment in Cancer ♋ in his first house. It is interesting to note that the Dalai Lama's Sun sign, Rising sign, and South Node are all in the sign of Cancer, the nurturer.

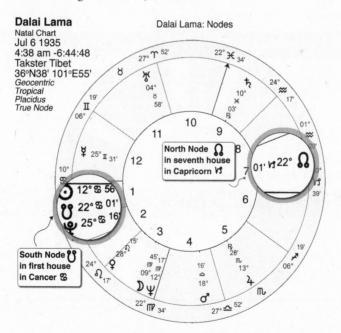

The Nodes ☊ ☋

Node	Symbol	Energies
North Node	☊	Lessons to learn, potential, possibilities, challenges, tension, the future
South Node	☋	Lessons already learned, accomplishments, talents, skills, comfort, the past

Planetary Rulers

It seems that the planets would be busy enough traveling through the signs of the zodiac and the houses of your astrological chart. But they have more responsibilities. Every planet naturally "rules" one or more of the signs, and so, also naturally, certain planets and signs share certain characteristics. Planetary *rulership* means that a planet is "in charge" of a sign; these planets and signs share certain characteristics. For instance, no matter what sign Mars ♂ or the Sun ☉ are in, they are still in charge of Aries ♈ and Leo ♌, respectively. Leo, like the Sun, is bright and optimistic, and Aries, like Mars, is energetic and on the move. We talk a little more about planetary rulers later in this chapter.

This table shows the planets and the signs they rule.

Planetary Rulers

Planet	Sign(s) Ruled
Sun ☉	Leo ♌
Moon ☽	Cancer ♋
Mercury ☿	Gemini ♊, Virgo ♍
Venus ♀	Taurus ♉, Libra ♎
Mars ♂	Aries ♈, co-ruler of Scorpio ♏
Jupiter ♃	Sagittarius ♐, co-ruler of Pisces ♓
Saturn ♄	Capricorn ♑, co-ruler of Aquarius ♒
Uranus ♅	Aquarius ♒
Neptune ♆	Pisces ♓
Pluto ♇	Scorpio ♏, co-ruler of Aries ♈

The Houses of Astrology

Now, looking at the next figure, it's time to discuss what those pie slices on the chart wheel *really* represent: They're the houses, or the places where everything in your life occurs. Each of the 12 houses encompasses a specific arena of life, or the stage where the drama of the planets unfolds.

Everything in your life happens in one of these houses, from where you brush your teeth to where you keep your secrets. When you look at a chart, the first house is always the pie slice just below the eastern horizon, and the other houses follow, counterclockwise, around the chart.

It might help you to think of each house as representing the horizon at the time of your birth: Half the sky was visible, and half of it was not. Below the horizon are the six houses of *personal* development, which are invisible but oh-so-important. This includes areas such as your personality, personal resources, knowledge, home, creativity, health, and responsibilities.

Above the horizon are the six houses of your development in the larger world; in other words, these are the visible houses. These houses include areas such as your relationships, joint or shared resources, social concerns, career, goals, and the subconscious.

Are you starting to wonder how you're going to keep this all straight? It might help if you remember that planets are the "what," signs are the "how," and houses are the "where."

Each House Is an Area of Your Life

Bear in mind that the following chart is just the tip of the iceberg when it comes to what's in each house. We've tried to give you word associations that you'll be able to remember. Planets *in* signs appear *in* houses; in other words, they show *how* you do *what* you do in certain *areas* of your life.

The house and sign a planet is in is where the story of you *really* begins. This is where the particular mathematics of astrology come into play: Planets + Signs + Houses = You. For example, if you have Mars ♂ in Aries ♈ in your first house, you're always going to put yourself first!

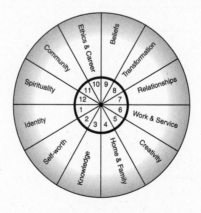

The houses are where the activities of your life unfold.

House	Area of Life
1st	Physical self, personality, early childhood
2nd	Possessions, earning abilities, self-esteem
3rd	Knowledge, siblings, environment
4th	Home and family, foundation of life
5th	Creativity, fun, romance, risk, children
6th	Personal responsibilities, health, service
7th	Primary relationships, partnerships
8th	Joint resources, sex, death, rebirth
9th	Social areas of higher education, philosophy, religion, law, travel
10th	Reputation, career, social responsibilities
11th	Goals, groups, friends
12th	Subconscious, privacy, past karma

There's nothing arbitrary about the house divisions. Astrologers have been studying what's going on in each house for thousands of years, and these correlations are borne out again and again in the way we all behave.

Let's peek into the Dalai Lama's birth chart to see what's in his fourth house of family and foundations. Can you identify the symbol? It's Mars ♂, the planet of action, in Libra ♎, the sign of harmony and balance. Want to do another? Let's look, then, at the Dalai Lama's eleventh house of goals. There, we find Uranus ♅, the transpersonal planet of sudden change, liberation, and authenticity, in the home-happy sign of Taurus ♉.

So, are you ready to learn what's in all these houses? We give you the short tour here; in Chapters 8 through 12, you'll learn more about each house, and you'll *really* get to see behind those doors.

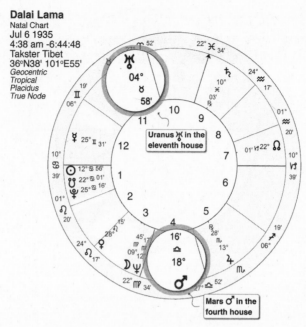

Dalai Lama
Natal Chart
Jul 6 1935
4:38 am -6:44:48
Takster Tibet
36°N38' 101°E55'
Geocentric
Tropical
Placidus
True Node

Uranus ♅ in the eleventh house

Mars ♂ in the fourth house

The planets in the Dalai Lama's 4th and 11th houses, as shown in his birth chart.

House Rulers: Who's in Charge?

The houses of your astrological chart are busy places. They are, of course, where the action is—where the energies of the heavens meet you and your life. Who keeps all this action under control?

In addition to being connected to each other through rulership, signs and planets are associated with certain houses. Just as certain planets naturally rule certain signs, they also rule certain houses. And which planet rules which house is determined by which planet naturally rules the sign on the *cusp* of the house. Cusps are the *beginning* of each house. For example, the ascendant is the beginning of the first house, the house of Self, and the next cusp is the beginning of the second house, and so on. The cusps also separate the houses from each other. The following figure shows which planets and signs are naturally associated with each house.

Now, your houses, as indicated on your birth chart, likely have different signs on the cusps, which indicate that your personal house rulers are not the same as your natural house rulers.

Remember, the planets are in continual motion through the zodiac. Your birth chart represents where they are in the heavens at the moment of your birth. Through this movement, the planet and sign on the cusp of each house changes. The planet and sign that land on the cusp at the time you're born rule that house; these are your *personal* rulers.

Natural planets and natural signs in their houses.

A house's *natural* ruler is important because it establishes the general "flavor" or design of the house. Your personal ruler "decorates" the house, personalizing it for how you will live your life. Astrologers look at both rulers to assess how the rulers' energies influence what happens for you in the house.

The house's energies are further influenced by the planets that may reside in the house. If you have more than one planet in a particular house, this indicates an emphasis on that area of your life. Even if there are no planets in a house, the energies of the natural rulers influence what happens in that house. And when your personal house ruler is the same as the house's natural ruler, sit up and take note! Such a configuration is a twin beam of focus.

Beyond the Sun ☉ Sign

We've looked at pieces of the Dalai Lama's chart to illustrate the many concepts we've introduced in this chapter. Now we're going to put all these concepts together as we look at a different birth chart, that of Scarlett Johansson, who portrays Black Widow in Marvel's *Avengers*. Take a moment to look at Scarlett's chart before we begin your step-by-step tour.

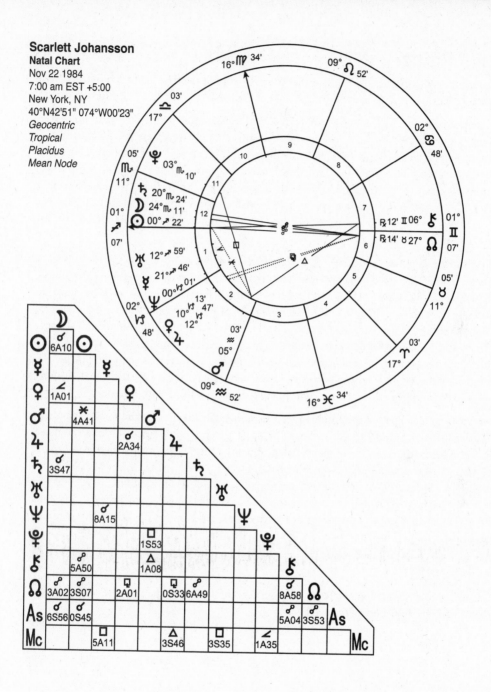

Scarlett Johansson
Natal Chart
Nov 22 1984
7:00 am EST +5:00
New York, NY
40°N42'51" 074°W00'23"
Geocentric
Tropical
Placidus
Mean Node

What's Rising?

The ascendant, or Rising sign, is the sign that is on the cusp of the first house. Scarlett's ascendant is Sagittarius ♐. What does this say about the mask that Scarlett wears for the world?

For a simple beginning, let's use what you learned in Chapter 2 about energies, qualities, and Elements. Sagittarius ♐ has a yang energy, mutable quality, and Fire Element. This means that someone with a Sagittarius ♐ ascendant will appear direct (yang), flexible (mutable), self-assertive, energetic, and courageous (Fire). Scarlett's early degrees of the Sun ☉ in Sagittarius ♐ in the 12th house of spirituality and the early degrees of her Sagittarius ♐ ascendant show an intensity of purpose. In this lifetime, she wants to finish up everything that has been unfinished for her. She wants completion and the resolution of problems and she'll shoot her arrow for the stars to find it.

People with Fire signs have the power of *"they get it,"* the enthusiasm of *"let's go,"* and the enthusiasm for change. Scarlett has the double power of a Sagittarius ♐ sun and ascendant. This Fire in the 12th house means she will be very committed to whatever she is doing, and when she is done, she can also step back and say, *"Good, we did it!"* Her mutable nature means that when she is presented with something she wants to do, she never wavers. However, she is also open-minded to trying new things and stretching for new roles. At the same time, her yang energy knows what resources are needed for the bottom line, and she knows what is most important to accomplish for the greater good of herself, her family, and perhaps even her country. She is very dedicated. Ruled by Jupiter ♃, the Sagittarius ♐ ascendant loves life and does everything with full gusto.

Scarlett's ascendant and all of the 12th house relate to her spiritual nature and mission, so the Sun ☉, the Moon ☽, Saturn ♄, and her South Node ☋ are all integral parts of her sacred quest in this life. The Sagittarius Sun has an optimism about the future, while the Moon in Scorpio, the Water sign Moon, is compassionate about reaching and completing her goals, and she will never give up. Her Scorpio Saturn, the compassionate taskmaster, will make sure of it. The South Node in Scorpio as well emphasizes a desire to come back, almost like a past-life motivation, to finish or complete her work.. This means Scarlett's karmic focus in this lifetime is aimed squarely on the future.

The Planets

The planets are represented by the large symbols in each house. Use the table we've provided to locate the sign for each of Scarlett's planets.

Scarlett Johansson's Planets in Their Signs

Planet	Symbol	Sign	Symbol
Sun	☉	Sagittarius	♐
Moon	☽	Scorpio	♏
Mercury	☿	Sagittarius	♐
Venus	♀	Capricorn	♑
Mars	♂	Aquarius	♒
Jupiter	♃	Capricorn	♑
Saturn	♄	Scorpio	♏
Uranus	♅	Sagittarius	♐
Neptune	♆	Capricorn	♑
Pluto	♇	Scorpio	♏

Next, locate Scarlett's North ☊ and South ☋ Nodes. That's right: Her North Node ☊ is in Taurus ♉ in her 6th house, which means her South Node ☋ is in Scorpio ♏ in her 12th house. If you'd like to find out what this nodal pairing reveals about what's easy and difficult for Scarlett, you can sneak a peak at Chapters 11 and 13. *Hint:* It's about using her roles as an actress to *"try on,"* that is, to explore, new values. Meanwhile she is building a strong core sense of being. She's ready to move on. And what about that exotic-looking symbol in Scarlett's 7th house in Gemini ♊? That's the planetoid/comet Chiron ⚷, the wounded healer. Find more about Chiron in Appendix B.

Who's in Charge?

To illustrate planetary rulership, let's look deeper into the 12th house in Scarlett's chart. This house is ruled by the planet on the cusp of its beginning. In this case, the sign on the cusp is, again, Scorpio ♏, which is co-ruled by Pluto ♇ and Mars ♂. This reinforces Scarlett's determination to fight for transformation in her life and in the world. Are you beginning to see how the signs, planets, and houses come together in your birth chart? The next thing we want to note about Scarlett's chart is that all of her planets, except for the planetoid/comet Chiron ⚷, are clustered on the eastern side of the chart wheel. The eastern side of the wheel emphasizes the ascendant. Scarlett is independent and self-reliant, and she likes being those things. However, she is also here to teach those things to others, especially women and young people. Her Moon ☽ in the 12th house shows that she can be a great inspiration, giving others the confidence to believe in their own callings, to understand there is a purpose to each of our lives, and it is our duty to find that purpose. Johansson's Sun ☉, Moon ☽, and ascendant show an independent, self-reliant human being who is devoted to whatever she believes she should do and believes there is a belief system in her being that is strong. She can adapt and fit into any society, any culture, and any role. She can change according to what's going on, and she observes people well. She reads the crowd and the room. That's her. This is Scarlett's birth chart in an elementary way. She's here to complete whatever she's supposed to do, and she's willing to do it! .

Whew! And we've only just begun to learn how to interpret an astrological birth chart. Daunted? Never fear. We'll take you one step at a time. To begin, in Part 2, we reveal everything you ever wanted to know about the astrological signs.

SUN ☉ SIGNS, ASCENDANTS, AND DESCENDANTS

We'll look at the personal signs—Sun ☉, ascendant (Rising sign), and descendant—that represent you in the world. These signs symbolize your core characteristics (your Sun sign), the "mask" or persona you present to the outside world (your ascendant), and what you seek in partners (your descendant).

The chapters in Part 2 tour the wheel of the zodiac from Aries ♈ to Pisces ♓ to take a closer look at the characteristics of these signs and their placements in your birth chart. "Where's your sign?" is the key question!

Part

2

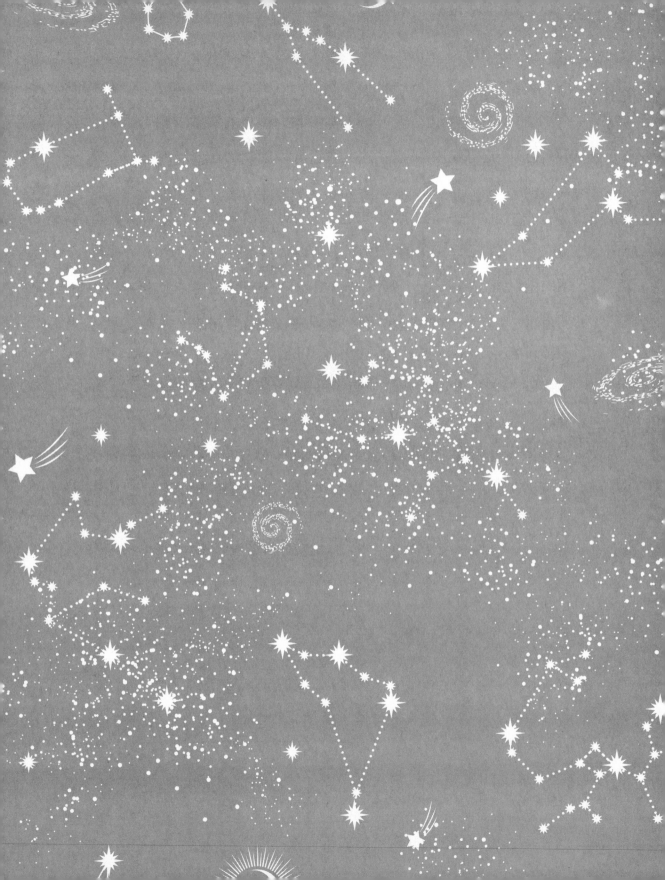

Chapter 4

SPRING SIGNS: ARIES ♈, TAURUS ♉, AND GEMINI ♊

At first glance, these three zodiac signs appear to have little in common: Aries ♈ likes to get things going, Taurus ♉ likes to keep them as they are, and Gemini ♊ talks on and on about it all! But the spring signs share one key characteristic: They create. Spring is all about new growth and new life, and the three signs of spring are all about getting things started. But these signs *do not* need anybody to tell them what to do or how to do it. Aries, Taurus, and Gemini are out and about already, making things happen.

As you're reading about the spring signs, consider the influences of the signs of your ascendant and descendant. As we talked about in Chapter 3, your ascendant, or Rising sign, is the "you" that you show to the outside world, sometimes with more intense energy than your Sun ☉ sign. The sign of your descendant suggests the partners—romantic, business, or even just friends—who attract you. You'll need your birth chart to know your ascendant and descendant signs.

Aries ♈, the Ram

It's no accident Aries is the first sign; if it hadn't been, it would have rearranged the zodiac to get there! Aries is the sign of the pioneer, the innovative early adopter, and the person who just won't say "No." In legend, the Ram often came to the rescue, and, that's how Aries ended up as a constellation. Jupiter rewarded Aries to become a constellation, for trying to save some children from the machinations of their wicked stepmother.

Nothing can stop the Ram (just try!); as the first of the cardinal signs, no one has a stronger will. Rams want to be where the action is and will do anything to make sure they get there first. Don't stand in a Ram's way; you're likely to get run down by this hard-charging leader of the zodiac!

Rams are the only Fire sign with a cardinal quality, which means they like to start things but might not want to finish them. Cardinal signs—Aries ♈, Cancer ♋, Libra ♎, and Capricorn ♑—start each season and are signs of beginnings. Aries see the start of something new as the fun part … but when it comes to finishing, they'd rather delegate the details.

Because Rams are also a Fire sign, they're enthusiastic and impulsively go off to start new ventures without giving much thought beforehand to what may follow. Fools rush in where angels fear to tread, but rushing in does take great courage, and Rams have enough courage to share!

The First Zodiac Sign

Aries, the Ram ♈	March 21 to April 20
Element	Fire
Quality	Cardinal
Energy	Yang
Rulers	Mars ♂ and Pluto ♀
Color	Red
Gem	Diamond
Anatomy	Head and face
Keywords	Early adopter, leader, new beginnings, adventure
Archetypes	Aragorn, *Tomb Raider*'s Lara Croft, Luke Skywalker, Neo from *The Matrix,* the astronaut
Celeb Rams	Lady Gaga, Matthew Broderick, Keira Knightley, Steven Tyler, Reese Witherspoon, Kristen Stewart, Russell Crowe, Sarah Jessica Parker, David Letterman, Jane Goodall, Nancy Pelosi, Akira Kurosawa, Tennessee Williams, Vincent van Gogh
Rams Rising	Rihanna, Beck, Chris Rock, Bette Midler, Ron Howard, Dale Chihuly, Walt Whitman
Tarot Suit	Wands
Tarot Major Arcana	0 The Fool, innocence and openness, going headfirst

The Best and Worst of Ram

Rams are assertive, direct, straightforward, and brimming with enthusiasm, but this also means they can be aggressive, blunt, or impatient. Strong-willed Rams can be remarkably single-minded when they have a goal in sight, but this single-mindedness can render Rams tactless, blind to side issues, obsessive learners but bad listeners, or just plain irritating.

The symbol for Aries ♈ could be interpreted to represent the eyebrows and the nose—the face, in other words—the parts of the body that are under Ram's rulership. Or it could be interpreted as a sign of the emergence of self and of beginnings. It also represents the constellation Aries, which appears in the sky standing erect, its head facing toward Mars.

Rams like challenges and are often wonderful leaders. Their determination can inspire others to follow their lead, and their early confidence gets everybody where they're going. But don't expect the Ram to follow through or stick with the plan. When the novelty wears off and routine sets in, Aries sheds responsibility like the Ram sheds his winter coat!

But anyone who likes a challenge also likes a good fight, and Rams can be argumentative. At their worst, they're steamrollers, running over anything that stands in their way. But at their best, Rams are idea people, innovators, and early adopters who can inspire others to embrace those new ideas.

Rams in Love

Rams in love won't take no for an answer; they'll pursue their beloved to the ends of the world—after all, Rams are explorers. Rams have the happiest love matches with other Fire signs: other Aries ♈, Leos ♌, or Sagittarians ♐; signs who, like Ram, crave excitement and passion.

If those fires don't keep burning, don't expect Rams to stick around. They like relationships that can contain the fire, and they may seek lovers who are dependent on them for love but independent in other ways. It can be tough to love a Ram!

Rams can be jealous; they expect their love to give them the same fiery attention they're giving. But Rams also enjoy sharing everything with a lover they trust. Their ambition for those they love, like their ambition for themselves, knows no bounds.

Rams and all Air signs do well together: Ram's opposite, Libra ♎, for example, can provide some air to keep the fire burning, but Ram may get tired of Libra's standards. The other Air signs, Gemini ♊ and Aquarius ♒, can also feed Ram's fire. But Ram is not a "householder" sign, and that's one reason why it doesn't do well with Cancer ♋ and Capricorn ♑. Love requires compromise and meeting the needs of others, and this is very hard for Rams to do.

From a mythic or archetypal point of view, Aries ♈ is the cowboy of the American West, the rugged individualist, the wild woman, or even the goddess Diana/Artemis. None of these types is high on settling down to build a nest, especially when young. These are adventurers.

One of the most important lessons Rams can learn is cooperation. If they learn that the help of others can only further their own creativity and desires, they can move beyond their Ram-centeredness and make enormous marks on the world.

The Healthy Ram

Aries ♈ rules the head and face, and it also represents the eyes and the brain. With this influence, it's easy to see why Rams are the quick thinkers of the zodiac, but it's also why they're prone to injuries—they sometimes leap before they look. At the same time, because they're quick to anger at both real and imagined slights, Rams may be susceptible to headaches and nervousness. The best health advice Rams could get would be to slow down—but don't expect them to listen.

Mars ♂, Aries's ruler, represents the blood and iron, so Rams need to get enough iron to keep them oxygenated and keep their hemoglobin up. They also need vitamin B_{12}, which is required for the formation of red blood cells and metabolism, and potassium, which is necessary for maintaining their muscles and heart rate.

Rams at Home

There's never a dull moment with a Ram at home. Like adolescents, Rams see all that the world has to offer—and want to experience it all, too. But, also like adolescents, Rams might see the world from a self-centered point of view, and that can make life with a Ram a challenge. One thing's for sure: Don't expect to find Rams snoozing next to the fire. They're the ones fanning the flames, just to see what happens!

Rams at Work

Rams need work that holds their interest; they need to do things that totally involve them and allow them the freedom to express themselves. They don't like to take orders, and they'll always try to climb to the top themselves. Their love of competition means they won't let setbacks stand in their way, and their eagerness for new experiences means they'll jump when they see a new opportunity.

Rams are often found in positions that need "idea incubators"; they're project leaders—as long as there's a team to handle the details and bring projects to fruition. Rams also do well in creative fields, where their fiery independence can find self-expression.

Some Aries like to work outdoors, like the archetypal cowboy of the American West or in construction, and many prefer work that enables them to maintain their independence. This can include areas like sales consulting, or independent contractor work.

Rams and Their Money

Impulsive Rams sometimes spend first and think later—or don't even bother to think later! Money for a Ram is one more way of getting ahead, and getting ahead is Ram's credo. Rams can be—and often are—generous, especially when it comes to pursuing something or someone they want. Aries know that as long as they are working, they always have money—but don't expect them to stash much of it in the bank. Rams are often the ones to see ways to make money, but others might take advantage of Ram's moneymaking ideas.

Ram Rising: Aries ♈ Ascendant

Rising Rams are learning to develop a strong, individuated self, learning how to play, and learning to become independent, spontaneous, and free of restrictions in the process. Rising Rams are also learning qualities of courage, trust (especially in themselves), and even innocence.

Ram ascendants really *are* ascending, always pushing themselves forward and striving for the next peak. Those with an Aries ascendant are often the ones making the decisions, and they've got strong likes and dislikes to back up those decisions.

But Ram ascendants might mistake impulsiveness for a need for action and might not stop long enough to see what they really want. Rising Rams may appear pushy or rude; but remember, an ascendant is a mask, and what appears to be arrogance may be covering up something else entirely.

Ram in Partnership: Aries ♈ Descendant

A descendant Aries seeks independent and reliable partners, be they in marriage or business. Only the self-confident need apply! Do you love to work hard and play harder? Are you cool, calm, and fast to respond to crisis? Do you relish going where others dare not tread? A Ram in partnership is fearless, decisive, and dynamic. Rams love action and adventure, and they want their relationships to be adventures, too.

Taurus ♉: Keeping the Home Fires Simmering

Taurus, the Bull, is consistent, methodical, and dedicated, just the characteristics that projects of all kinds, from gardens to work to family, need to grow and to reach their full potential. Bulls turn over every little rock. They like to know the game plan and stick with it, so no surprises, please.

No one is more down to earth than the passive, fixed, Earth sign Taurus ♉. All the Bull's feet are planted firmly on the ground, and Bull's calm and dependability make a Bull a friend you can count on. Hand in hand with that dependability, Bulls can be conservative and cautious, so they usually like to stay with what works. If it's not broken, don't fix it—that's the Taurean motto!

Bulls' connection with the earth means they're often materially wealthy, but Bulls' wealth can also be found in the cozy homes they create: Bulls like to sit calmly in their favorite chair, reading a favorite ebook, perfectly content. Bulls' exquisite taste makes them terrific social media influencers; people feel comfortable with Bulls' trustworthy posts, pins, and tweets. Before you know it, Bulls are recognized as trendsetters who understand how to make things beautiful.

But this desire for beauty and harmony goes beyond the self: Bulls also seek a harmony with everything on Earth. Taurus loves to see things grow—gardens as well as people, situations, and money. You're likely to find Bulls living in the country, but even if they live in the city, you'll find them surrounded by plants or working in their gardens. Bulls crave silence, too—the silence that comes with inner serenity. Bulls are the most physical of the signs; everything they know, they know through the body. This is because they're ruled by Venus ♀, the ruler of the senses.

The Second Zodiac Sign

Taurus, the Bull ♉	April 20 to May 21
Element	Earth
Quality	Fixed
Energy	Yin
Ruler	Venus ♀
Color	Green
Gem	Emerald
Anatomy	Neck and throat
Keywords	Ownership, dependability, sensuality
Archetypes	Marmee from *Little Women*, Captain America, Aphrodite, Osiris
Celeb Bulls	The Rock, Cate Blanchett, Djimon Hounsou, Donatella Versace, George Clooney, David Beckham, Aidy Bryant, Jerry Seinfeld, George Lucas, Ho Chi Minh, Bertrand Russell, Charlotte Brontë
Bulls Rising	Snoop Dogg, Sigourney Weaver, Josh Brolin, Merce Cunningham, Charles Bukowski, Nikola Tesla
Tarot Suit	Pentacles
Tarot Major Arcana	5 The Hierophant, steadfast conformity

The Best and Worst of Bull

At their best, Bulls create a calm in the midst of storms all around them. They're connected solidly to their bodies and to their homes, and have good jobs, good friends, good marriages, and good children. Bulls are disciplined, orderly, and reliable. They're the people everyone else turns to: They're who you text at 2 A.M. when you need a friend or a ride home, and though they may be reluctant to get out of bed, they'll be the ones you know you can rely on.

But consistency can become complacency. Bulls may be resistant to change and can become dogmatic or even preachy. Bulls can't understand what all the excitement's about, and they may be the first to tell you that all this astrology stuff is unscientific (while insisting on doing a synastry grid on your birth charts to see how you'll be in a relationship). Bulls can become lazy as well—too comfortable to make a move—or they can get so caught up in their earthly possessions that time passes them by.

Bulls in Love

Security and stability … a Bull in love stays in love. Romance and love are one and the same to sensuous, earthbound Bulls, and they're nothing if not patient when it comes to making sure the love they find is the right one. A Bull will always be there for you—and expects the same in return.

The goddess Aphrodite represents Taurus ♉. After all, Taurus is ruled by Venus. She embodies the qualities of deep intimacy, as well as beauty. Aphrodite was beautiful not to attract men but to celebrate her divine womanhood. She was intimate only with those men who met her high standards for honor and love. Consider carefully before you decide to slide into her DMs; you may not be welcomed!

Bulls don't like change, so they might show some jealousy if the stability they create seems threatened in some way. A Taurean partner is one you can always depend on, though, and, although it may seem dull at times, you can rest assured that this person is with you for the long haul.

Bulls are attracted to Water signs, especially Cancer ♋ and Pisces ♓. But many Bulls or Rising Bulls find their mate in a Scorpio ♏, Bull's opposite. Bulls get along well with householder Cancers because Bulls like their comfort. Remember: Earth and water go well together, creating beautiful lakes.

Taureans are often attracted to the livelier signs, like Aries ♈, Gemini ♊, or Sagittarius ♐, but they quickly become annoyed when all these signs want to do is go out and play. They're most comfortable with other Earth signs, whose reliability and need for established routine matches their own. Don't expect many fireworks here, though—just everything in its place, as it should be.

The Healthy Bull

Taurus ♉ rules the neck, throat, and the entire metabolic system. The thyroid gland, in particular, can be a problem for Bulls: They might not properly convert what they eat into energy, which means they can be prone to gaining weight. Their love of inaction feeds this tendency as well. But the throat is also where singing comes from, and many Bulls are well-known singers: Adele, Lizzo, Barbra Streisand, Stevie Wonder, Willie Nelson, and Ella Fitzgerald, to name just a few.

Iodine is necessary for the development and functioning of the thyroid gland, which is ruled by Taurus. Other vitamins and minerals that are important to Taurus are selenium, bioflavonoids, and vitamin E, which work together to maintain beauty and promote normal body growth, fertility, and metabolic action. With Venus being Bulls' ruler, getting enough of these nutrients is even more important than usual.

Bulls at Home

Home is where Bulls thrive: They gather, they arrange, and they organize to make home a place they and those they love can comfortably relax in. Bulls may be collectors, too; with their Venus ruler, they have an appreciation for beauty. Their homes might be filled with music and books, as well as paintings and sculpture. They're also likely to know a great deal about some special area of expertise, such as the cultivation of orchids or the batting averages of White Sox pitchers.

Bulls crave comfort, security, and calm, and their homes reflect that desire. A Bull's home is always a good place to show up at dinnertime. Not only will there be a wonderfully farm-to-table meal cooking, but you're sure to be invited to stay! Chef Alice Waters, after all, is a Bull.

Bulls at Work

No one knows a good opportunity like a Bull, especially an opportunity that promises long-term stability. Tauruses love to take over the lead after the project is under way, and they will see it through—detail by detail—to completion. Connected to Earth, Bulls can do well with real estate or land deals. But Bulls don't want to build the homes and buildings (Aries ♈ do that); they want to *own* the land, home, or building as an investment that will grow in value.

Bulls' connection to Earth makes them practical in nature. They aren't going to set off on an impulsive whim. For example, they might be interested in finance, banking, or the things they can build with money and resources.

Bulls make wonderful employees, too: They're the ones who show up even on snow days and the ones who get the proposal in on time. Because Venus is their ruler, many Bulls are talented folks who sing, write, or perform music; sculpt; or enjoy other creative endeavors. Many Bulls use their voices for voice-overs or are radio announcers or disc jockeys.

Bulls and Their Money

Bulls are wonderful providers and may acquire a great deal of money and a wealth of possessions. But they also need to be careful not to cross the line into materialism, wealth for its own sake, or extravagance. There's a danger of stinginess, and Bulls might hoard cash or hide it away where it will be "safe." But as the ultimate Taurean desire is for earthly harmony, Bulls are far more likely to use their wealth to share their desire for comfort with those they love. Expect a Bull to pick up the tab, share a Netflix password, or send you a plane ticket to come out for a visit.

Bull Rising: The Taurus ♉ Ascendant

Rising Bulls seem placid and easygoing, have charming manners, and never impose their opinions on others. They don't want to upset the apple cart. They like the cart the way it is—full of apples.

Rising Bulls' lesson is to understand the nature of physical experience, intimacy, and aesthetics. As shamanic astrologer Daniel Giamarro says, the enlightened path for one with this training "is the Garden of Eden, to bring spirit into matter all the way, so one can totally enjoy it." This training helps Bulls learn to be fully present in life and increase their life-force energy.

Bull ascendants seek their identities through substance, whether it be possessions, connections, or creation. Rising Bulls always seek to "keep a handle" on things, but their love of food, drink, and yes, sex, can make them momentarily forget that stability is their main goal. Like those with a Taurean ♉ Sun sign, Rising Bulls need to remember to love things for their own sake rather than for what they might represent. For Rising Bulls, possessions are merely a mask.

Bull in Partnership: The Taurus ♉ Descendant

Taurus ♉ descending seeks a loyal, easygoing, peaceable partner. Only those who can truly walk the talk will catch the interest of Bull descending, who needs to know the partnership is solid, secure, and long-term. The Bull in partnership needs emotional, physical, and spiritual enjoyment to feed and fulfill its sensual side. Taurus descendant requires partnerships that share such enjoyment.

Gemini ♊: Quick-Witted, Quicksilver

Twins are like two people who share one body, often appearing to go in two directions at the same time. They may even refer to themselves as "we"! Always thinking and observing, Twins never miss—or forget—a thing and will leave you in their dust if you can't keep up. Cerebral and witty, Twins talk all the time. Pay attention because Twins *always* do what they say.

Gemini ♊, the twins, is a mutable sign, which signifies change; a yang sign, which signifies motion; and an Air sign, which signifies the mind. In their quest for knowledge, Twins are always in motion, always alert, always trying to live not just two, but as many lives as they can, all at one time. Often called a dualistic sign, Twins are really deceptively simple: It's all based on avid curiosity, on finding things out and then quickly moving on to something else.

Twins have been called the Great Communicators, too, and with Mercury as their ruler, it's easy to see why. But sometimes words can mask meaning, and that's another paradox of Twins: Meaning is not really what they're after; they're after the ideas themselves.

The Third Zodiac Sign

Gemini, the Twins ♊	May 21 to June 22
Element	Air
Quality	Mutable
Energy	Yang
Ruler	Mercury ☿
Color	Yellow
Gem	Agate
Anatomy	Hands, arms, shoulders, lungs
Keywords	Mentality, communication, versatility
Archetypes	Fleabag, Hermione of *Harry Potter,* "Natasha Romanoff" the Black Widow, Castor and Pollux, Coyote the Trickster
Celeb Twins	Kendrick Lamar, Natalie Portman, Rafael Nadal, Tom Holland, Prince, Helena Bonham Carter, Joyce Carol Oates, Michael J. Fox, Bob Dylan, Vanessa Bell, Allen Ginsberg, Frances Crick
Twins Rising	Julianne Moore, Kristen Stewart, Lady Gaga, North West, Mick Jagger, Margaret Atwood, Alan Turing
Tarot Suit	Swords
Tarot Major Arcana	6 The Lovers, options and choices

The Best and Worst of Twins

Twins can be amusing, witty, quick, and flexible—and they can be glib, sarcastic, fickle, and devious. Two sides of the same coin, and it's all too easy for a Twin to flip back and forth between them. Geminis can appear devious or deceptive when they shift gears in midconversation and seem to take the opposite side of what they've just said. Often, though, their brains are working so fast that they've carried the dialogue to conclusion before others have the chance to participate!

At their best, Twins are masters of invention, clever, adaptable, and never afraid to try something new. But this same eagerness to try everything can lead them to be scatterbrained or restless—even unreliable or ungrateful.

The symbol for Gemini ♊ may be merely the Roman numeral II, but it also represents the parts of the body ruled by this third sign: the hands, arms, shoulders, and lungs. Taking it still one step further, this symbol suggests the dual sides of human nature: body and soul. On the other hand, maybe it's just a pair of twins!

At their weakest, Twins can run themselves to emotional exhaustion or feel that nothing matters. At their strongest, their wide variety of interests brings them many friends and experiences, and their quick minds enable them to take it all in. You can always count on a Twin to be the publicist who throws the perfect pop-up party!

Twins' flexibility and adaptability arise because this is a mutable sign, and mutability means changeability. Mutable signs, such as Gemini ♊, occur as the season is changing and thus, they are associated with transitions. Other mutable signs are Virgo ♍, Sagittarius ♐, and Pisces ♓.

Geminis are also very resourceful because they've seen so much, and that's part of their mutability, too. After all, the more you're willing to change, the more you're going to see.

Twins in Love

The Twins of the Gemini myth, Castor and Pollux, chose to be united forever in the sky rather than separated for even a moment, so Gemini ♊ is obviously a sign of relationships. Translated to love, though, Twins have so many relationships that they can all seem a little too casual. This is because Gemini is a mutable sign. It's not that a Twin won't give you all the attention you want; it's that a Twin can't. There's too much else going on!

Here's where Twins' fickleness can come into play: Someone who seemed fascinating last week (swipe right!) is a known quantity this week and is no longer interesting (swipe left…). But Twins also can be the ideal match: They're charming, witty, generous, and genuinely interested in you; keeping that interest is the hard part. Meet them on their own ground—wit and imagination—and let them know they can trust you by trusting them.

Other Air signs—other Geminis ♊, Librans ♎, and Aquarians ♒—are always good matches for Twins; Air signs are lighthearted and understand each other's need for mental stimulation. At the same time, two Air signs might never come down from the clouds. If they do, they might find there's no place to land.

Because air feeds fire, Twins can do well with Aries ♈, Leo ♌, and Sagittarius ♐, the Fire signs. Down-to-earth Virgo ♍ is a good match, too: With the same quality (mutable) and ruler (Venus) as Gemini, Twins and Virgos can both challenge and learn a lot from each other.

Healthy Twins

With Geminis Ⅱ, the mind often is thinking one thing, and the body is doing another. No other sign can benefit quite so much from learning to breathe, learning to relax, and taking deep breaths and letting them out. Twins are always on the move, and all this rushing around can mean they don't stop and smell the roses like they should. Gemini rules the hands, arms, shoulders, and lungs, and this grouping reflects yet another of Twins' dualities: the need to flit about and the need to breathe deeply and relax. If Twins don't learn to relax, all that flying around can lead to emotional exhaustion and insomnia. Twins would benefit a lot from yoga, the perfect practice to unite body, mind, and spirit through movement and concentration.

Twins at Home

Twins at home—now, there's a phrase that's hard to interpret: Twins don't often stay put long enough to let them see where home is. But maybe that's exactly it: Twins are at home wherever they happen to be. Twins are seldom content to sit still and watch the world go by; they'd rather be on that world and going by with it!

Don't forget that Twins are great communicators, so if they *are* at home, you're likely to find them on the phone or gathering new information from surfing the Internet or watching TV.

Twins at Work

Multitasking was around long before Microsoft … just ask Geminis what they're thinking! Twins need mental challenges to keep them stimulated on the job, and it can't be the same challenge over and over again. Careers like advertising, writing, broadcasting, and public relations appeal to Twins because they're always presenting new challenges to Twins' inquiring minds. Don't rule out technical fields, though; the right opportunity might offer Twins just the mental somersaults they need.

Twins are often found in media positions or in other jobs where there is a lot of contact with other people. They can be "silver-tongued" with their wit and communication abilities, so they're excellent at persuading or influencing others. Twins are the ultimate social media influencers. With their ability to connect, Twins can dictate trends (and even set them). Twins know how to build and use social media platforms that attract enough likes, clicks, and comments to create online communities with hundreds of thousands of followers.

Twins and Their Money

Twins like to spend their money on information, digital media, computers, smartphones, travel, cars, and things that will feed their need for the newest technology, communication, movement, and action. Twins don't worry much about spending, either, and they are apt to max out their credit cards and then sign up for another. It's not money that concerns Twins; it's information they want, and they will get it any way they can get it, including buying it. Remember that Gemini ♊ is the first of the Air signs. Air is the element of mental activity, so Rising Twins are always thinking about what's next.

Twins Rising: The Gemini ♊ Ascendant

Motion. That's what you're going to see in Rising Twins. Restlessness is the hallmark of this ascendant, and Rising Twins find their identities by making as many contacts as possible. Rising Twins are often the life of the party and are often *giving* the party.

At the same time, Rising Twins are learning to be the eternal youth, change agent, free spirit, entertainer, artist, or comedian. They can also be the troubadour minstrel, court jester, trickster, clown, or the coyote that leaves a surprise. Remember that the court jester was the only one who could tell the king the truth and not be killed for it (another form of messenger). Rising Twins are learning how to speak truth to power without getting penalized for it.

A Gemini ♊ ascendant man will be a patient gentleman, with eloquence and sharp wit. But he can sometimes appear excitable and quick to disconnect. There's an aloofness here: Twins' connections are made on a mental field, which can often leave emotions out in the cold.

Twins in Partnership: The Gemini ♊ Descendant

Twins in partnership want exactly who they are … they want other Twins. Restless to find these others, Twins descending often find partners who look quite like them. Twins in partnership need the other to be witty, sharp, and quick, especially in thought, to keep up with their speed-of-light multitasking. "Thoughts have wings"—this is the quintessential Twins partnership in marriage, family, business, and friends. The challenge with Twins descending is that Twins sometimes simply can't make decisions.

Chapter 5

SUMMER SIGNS: CANCER ♋, LEO ♌, AND VIRGO ♍

Summer is for vacations, fun, and family. The signs of summer revel in the joy of gatherings, fostering emotional connections among people and between people and community. All things grow and flourish during the summer season.

The signs of summer—Cancer ♋, Leo ♌, and Virgo ♍—share a season, but each contributes unique influences. Emotional Cancer ♋ nurtures under the influence of its ruler, the Moon ☽; bright, sunny Leo ♌, personification of the Sun ☉, seeks the spotlight; and meticulous Virgo ♍, under the influence of thoughtful Mercury ☿, improves herself by helping others learn about sacred patterns.

Cancer ♋: Wear Your Heart on Your Sleeve

The first day of summer starts the sign of Cancer ♋, and the Crab joyously leads into graduations, weddings, and reunions—the gatherings of family and friends. The Crab loves traditions and will create them when they don't already exist. Are you a Rising Crab? Don't be surprised to find yourself in charge of this year's family barbecues! The Cardinal Crab loves to be the one who nurtures and guides, urging siblings to get along … at least during the event of celebration that brings them together. Crabs lead with the heart.

But they are touchy, touchy, touchy: No one else feels like a Crab. And no one retreats like a Crab, either. They are quick to hurt, and they're also quick to crawl into their shells. But remember, Crabs' shells are also their houses. Crabs are nurturers, too, and they are the mamas and papas of the zodiac.

Wound Crabs, and they'll never forget it; Crabs will carry grudges for life. Befriend Crabs, and they'll never forget, either; Crabs are famous for keeping in touch with old friends, old loves, and old times. And what a memory! Need to know who was wearing what at that party back in 1985? Ask any Crab; chances are, the Crab will remember the menu as well!

People look to Crabs for warmth and understanding, and Crabs always lend a sympathetic ear, lap, or shoulder. But these Moon-ruled ☽ children won't look to get the same from you. They might be the most sensitive sign of the zodiac, but they're also the least likely to let you know what they're feeling. Crabs hide their emotions behind what they believe is an impenetrable shell.

For Crabs, it's all about security; that's the major point of Cancer. Crabs are learning about emotional and physical security, as well as responsible nurturing. After the primal instincts of Ram, the building of Bull, and the thinking and mental development of Twins, there's the emotional foundation of Crabs, which can take many forms as disparate as a house and an Instagram account—or maybe, a shell.

The Fourth Zodiac Sign

Cancer, the Crab ♋	June 22 to July 23
Element	Water
Quality	Cardinal
Energy	Yin
Ruler	Moon ☽
Color	Silver
Gem	Pearl
Anatomy	Stomach and breasts
Keywords	Feeling, sensitivity, nurturing
Archetypes	Meryl Streep's Clarissa in the film *The Hours,* Forrest Gump, Peeta Mellark in *The Hunger Games,* Aunt Em
Celeb Crabs	Tom Cruise, Mindy Kaling, Harrison Ford, Meryl Streep, Margot Robbie, Tom Hanks, the Dalai Lama, Ernest Hemingway, Rembrandt
Crabs Rising	Hugh Grant, Cher, Lisa Kudrow, Stephen King, Robert Pattinson, Albert Einstein
Tarot Suit	Cups
Tarot Major Arcana	14 Temperance, patience and adaptation; 18 The Moon, imagination and feeling

The Best and Worst of Crabs

At their best, Crabs are dependable, loving, adaptable, and self-sacrificing, which means at their worst, they can be clingy, oversensitive, moody, and smothering. Want a financial adviser? Let a Crab handle it. Need an advance? Better have those numbers ready! Late for dinner? Tell Crab your sob story. Didn't show up at all? Better move to another town!

Crabs are easily distracted; just about anything can set Crabs' imaginations running—in another direction. Crabs are always off on tangents. Picture a crab on the beach, always scrambling sideways rather than moving forward. They *do* get where they're going, often without the rest of us realizing they've done it. Don't ever take the clever Crab for granted, that's for sure. They'll leave you standing in the sand, wondering which way they've gone!

Many of Cancer's myths involve turtles or tortoises. In ancient Egypt, the constellation was called Stars of the Water, and its symbol was two turtles. In Roman mythology, the Crab assisted Jupiter's wife, Juno, in trying to slow down one of the many labors of Heracles (Hercules in Greek mythology). The unfortunate Crab got caught underfoot, though, so all Juno could do to reward it was place it in the heavens.

Crabs in Love

No one sends more confusing messages than a Crab; just when you think they might be interested, off they go into their shells. Crabs are so afraid of being hurt that they may *never* let you know they're interested, but on the other hand, if they decide they've got a chance with you, look out: Crabs can hang on very tightly.

Crabs who didn't feel coddled as children might seem cold and distant as adults. But in their indirect Crab way, they're really craving your attention. Crabs have a natural fear of revealing themselves—those soft insides are very vulnerable—so they're never going to approach you directly. You know those conversations that go "What's the matter?" and then "Nothing"? Chances are, they're with a Crab. If you can't get a Crab to give you a face-to-face conversation, try breaking through by text; the intimacy of talking in person may be too difficult for delicate Crab.

Water signs—other Cancers ♋, Scorpios ♏, or Pisces ♓—understand things the same way Crabs do, and Pisces, in particular, may inspire Crabs to use their intuition. Still, there can be too much emotion and too little thinking with these pairings. Crabs are good with Earth signs—Taurus ♉, Virgo ♍, and even their opposite, Capricorn ♑—keeping them watered and fertile. Gemini ♊ can be fun but might feel smothered, and Leo ♌ might love the attention but not return it.

As a Water sign, Crabs require trust in a relationship and are very cautious about giving their hearts away. The things they need most are love and security. Deep down, Crabs really do believe love makes the world go 'round, and if you love a Crab, you'll love being along for the ride.

According to Greek (and Roman) mythology, Demeter (Ceres), goddess of Earth, was responsible for agriculture and growth. When Demeter found out that Pluto (Hades) had stolen her daughter, Persephone, and taken her to the Underworld, Demeter grieved and forbade anything on Earth to grow. Zeus (Jupiter) had Hermes (Mercury) go to the Underworld to strike a deal with Pluto. Because Persephone had eaten seven pomegranate seeds and had toured the Underworld, however, Pluto insisted that she be returned to him each year for three months (our winter months). Because of her motherly devotion, Demeter is associated with Cancer ♋, the sign of motherhood and responsible nurturing.

The Healthy Crab

Nurturing Crabs rule the stomach and the breasts, sources of food and nourishment. So, naturally, sensitive Crabs are prone to stomach troubles and, with their love of creating comfort through food, can also be prone to being overweight.

No sign is as sensitive to touch, and Crabs are always reaching out and touching. But they're sensitive to hot and cold, too: You'll see Crabs wearing sweaters in July or, if it's very hot, scuttling into the shade or the water to cool off. Remember that Crabs' ruler is the Moon ☽, and the Moon has no light source of its own. Crabs reflect everything around them, and their emotions ebb and flow like the tides.

Vitamin A and beta-carotene are especially helpful for growth and maintenance of all mucous membranes, including the stomach and digestive tract, which is very important to a Crab. They also help build strong bones and teeth (ruled by Capricorn ♑, the opposite sign). Crabs also may have allergies, which are often aggravated by dairy products, so if digestion becomes a problem, it's best for Crabs to monitor what they eat in relation to how they feel.

Crabs at Home

Crabs' homes are their safe havens, even if they do carry their houses on their backs. It might be the pillows tossed about for comfort, or it could be those good smells coming from the kitchen, but you'll always feel like a Crab's home is a place where you can relax and unwind. Crabs may be likely to rent a room or cottage as an Airbnb, and you'll be sure to feel right at home there and perfectly welcome.

Within their cozy home, though, there is a place that is the Crab's alone. It might just be a corner of the living room, but in that corner will be Crab's favorite chair; a tablet filled with beloved books, movies, and music; a love-worn blanket; and maybe a picture or two. Chances are, Crab's dog or cat will snuggle up in that spot, too, regardless of whether Crab's there at the moment. But rest assured, there *will* be a dog or cat, or maybe there will be more than one. Crabs nurture any creature that comes their way.

But beware a Crab who takes things a bit too far and begins hoarding possessions and pushing loved ones away in the process. In our consumer culture, it's easy to take advantage of a sale or stock up on bulk products; it's easy to buy one too many books (never!) or that extra kitchen gadget. Before long, the clutter is everywhere. You'll need patience and love to draw this Crab from its shell and rediscover the joys of home again.

Crabs at Work

Although it might seem Crabs can be too dreamy or unfocused to do well in business, it often happens that the opposite turns out to be true. Intuitive and sensitive to change, Crabs can often sense future trends and be on the cutting edge. Cancer's mothering quality might come out at work by birthing new products, projects, or companies, taking care of others by feeding them or nurturing their emotional selves via teaching.

Crabs are often found in creative areas like writing, too, because writing involves the part of genesis that requires gestation, creating something new and unknown, and then birthing it. In addition, Crabs' empathy for others and their prodigious memories comes into play with the creative arts, helping them generate works that connect with everyone. Crabs will do well with online businesses involving cooking, home arts, and offering advice and services on the web.

Crabs and Their Money

Tenacious Crabs hoard their money just like they do everything; no matter how much they accumulate, they may never feel entirely secure. Crabs don't differentiate between things and security, and because of their nature (hard on the outside, soft on the inside), they hold on to everything with a tenacious grip.

Sometimes this hoarding tendency can move into selfishness. This is not because Crabs don't want to help; Crabs' selfishness comes from their fear of being hurt from the outside and they'll do anything they can to protect themselves, including keeping all their assets to themselves.

You won't often find Crabs broke; they're far too concerned with security. And because Crabs want this security for those they love as well, they'll make sure to create a safe haven.

Crab Rising: The Cancer ♋ Ascendant

Rising Crabs are learning about emotion. They are talkative, especially about feelings, but they're also moody and changeable because their ruler, the Moon ☽, changes signs every few days. At the same time, Rising Crabs are compassionate and receptive. They know what's happening with everyone around them because they're sensitive to others. Family and traditions are important to them. But they can be crabby and irritable at times, too. It can seem deceptively easy to get to know a Rising Crab because they seem so soft and personal. But like those with Crab Sun ♋☉ signs, Rising Crabs wear a hard, tough shell that can sometimes get in the way.

Rising Crabs are learning about the nature of family, home, and roots. They also are learning how to responsibly nurture, love, and support their offspring or creative projects until they reach maturity. Rising Crabs may be indirect in their approach to things and quick to take things personally. Above all, they seem to react to all things emotionally, feeling rather than thinking their way through conflict.

Crab in Partnership: The Cancer ♋ Descendant

Crab descending focuses on attaching to partners, be it in romantic or business relationships, who love to be nurtured and who nurture in return. When the descendant is this Water sign, taking care of business means taking care of family. This means taking care of children and pets, and even feeding the birds and squirrels. Crab descending seeks the intuitive, sensitive type who will devote time and patience to the family unit. In the business setting, Crab descending seeks partners who can work to create projects that are fulfilling.

Leo ♌: King of the Jungle

Fixed Leo, the Lion, is a fire sign, filled with pride for family, friends, and accomplishments. Summer is the season to shine, and Leos bask in the glory of the Sun ☉, Leo's ruler. Talk about self-confidence, Lions invented it. Leos love the spotlight. They're dramatic, they're bold, they're creative, and they're strong; no other sign can grab and hold center stage the way a Lion can. Who's telling the jokes, leading the songs, rallying everyone for a game on the field? Leo, of course!

Lions are great fun to be around, too. Their exuberance is contagious, and when they get to the party, everyone knows it's really time to party. Not only *can* Leos lead, they *will* lead: Lions expect to be at the head of the line and at the head of the pride.

Lions are at one with the creative principle. When Leo is your ascendant, your purpose is to learn how your willpower affects what you create in your life. Self-expression and creativity are everything to Lions. Eventually, they learn to follow more than just their own will, aligning themselves with the higher Self and the creative principles of the Universe. Will a Lion give up? Never.

The Fifth Zodiac Sign

Leo, the Lion ♌	July 23 to August 22
Element	Fire
Quality	Fixed
Energy	Yang
Ruler	Sun ☉

Leo, the Lion ♌	July 23 to August 22
Color	Gold
Gem	Ruby
Anatomy	Back, spine, and heart
Keywords	Willpower, creativity, expressing the heart
Archetypes	King Arthur, The Lion King, Hindu goddess Sarasvati, Celie in *The Color Purple*
Celeb Lions	J.K. Rowling, Jennifer Lawrence, Chris Hemsworth, Lisa Kudrow, Tom Brady, Robert DeNiro, Barack Obama, James Corden, Richard Linklater, James Baldwin, Andy Warhol, Beatrix Potter
Lions Rising	Eddie Murphy, Jennifer Lopez, Robert Downey Jr., Sting, Al Pacino, Frida Kahlo, Pablo Picasso
Tarot Suit	Wands
Tarot Major Arcana	8 Strength, fortitude and compassion; 19 The Sun, self-confidence

The Best and Worst of Lions

Because Leo ♌ is a fixed sign, Lions can be determined, stubborn, or even habit-bound, but confident Lions are born to lead, and they're proud, courageous, and self-assured to a fault. Lions can be generous, commanding, ambitious, and proud, and this means that they can also be intolerant, demanding, self-righteous, and vain. Lions can lead others to tremendous victories, but they can be ruthless with their enemies. Because their memories are short, however, they are quick to forgive.

Because Lions are always leading, they are often surrounded by people who tell them what they want to hear. This, in turn, can lead to gullibility because Lions are easily flattered and can forget that not everyone loves them. And as much fun as they can be, they also can become overbearing or self-centered if things aren't going their way.

Lions are exceptionally loyal and expect loyalty in return as well. They are very up-front about their needs and expectations, and this lack of guile can also be their undoing. Lions might do well to trust a little less, but they expect adulation, and others can't help but give it to them. Why do so many Leos go by one name? Because they can! With the Sun ☉ as their planet, Lions live in and for the spotlight, and with that kind of lighting, they can go by any name they choose. Jackie, Lucy, Mick, Madonna, and Napoleon are just a few Leos we recognize from singular names. Others include Fidel, Tipper, and Lawrence (of Arabia).

It takes creativity to generate excitement, but Lions are among the most creative signs of the zodiac. The Sun ☉, after all, provides illumination, and it is through that light that Lions truly shine.

Lions in Love

Generous Lions expect generosity in return: They love being in love and the drama that being in love provides. Lions are loyal, too, which can actually make it difficult to end a relationship with them. Try ghosting a Lion, and you'll hear them roar!

Lions expect adoration, but they'll give it as well. Like kings, they'll graciously give their loyal subjects all they can. As a Fire sign, they'll usually do best with other Fire signs—other Leos ♌, Sagittarians ♐, or Arians ♈—but Lions also can be caught up in the intensity of Scorpios ♏ or the refinement of Libras ♎.

Airy Geminis ♊ and Aquarians ♒ (Lions' opposite) are also good matches; remember that opposites attract. Lions learn a lot, in particular, from the detached Aquarian, who can provide them with perspective and give them balance.

The Healthy Lion

No one is healthier than Lions; the ailments that touch the rest of us seem to pass them by. This strength is due in no small part to Leo's rulership of the back, spine, and heart: even the words suggest Lions' strength. A lion features prominently in the Strength card of the Tarot. Just as Leo ♌ is a sign of both strength and generosity and childishness and ferocity, this Major Arcana card suggests the fearless and fearful child in us all.

Lions can sometimes be less strong emotionally. When they fail to get the adoration and respect they deserve, they can actually become physically ill. And Lions, like all cats, can be lazy, too; the only evidence of life in them may be the continual twitching of their long tails.

Because Leo rules the spine and heart, these areas also can cause them trouble when things don't go well. They might need a trip to the chiropractor or a cardiologist to get them back on track, but it's also important for them to deal with the underlying emotions that set off such problems to begin with.

Lions need plenty of magnesium and calcium on a 1:1 ratio to protect their hearts (a muscle) and circulatory systems. And Lions need to pay more attention to their potassium and salt balance than other people because that balance is very important for their hearts. Coenzyme Q_{10}, an enzyme that strengthens the heart, might also provide them with additional energy when they get older.

Lions at Home

Lions call their homes their "castles," and they love to show them off almost as much as they love to show off themselves. Lions give great parties and won't hesitate to keep the food and wine coming. Home is another place where Lions' generosity is evidenced: There's always a place for everyone to sleep, and friends are welcome to stay as long as they please.

If they're not entertaining, you might find Lions roaring when they're upset, but you might also hear them purring like kittens when everything is in order and they get the attention they need.

Lions at Work

No one leads like a Leo, and Lions will naturally gravitate toward careers that allow them to shine. They might be generals or presidents, but Lions might be teachers as well, firing up their students' enthusiasm with their own.

Lions can often be found in the performing arts, shining with the brightness of the Sun. Not surprisingly, many rock stars are Leos (among them the inimitable Mick Jagger). In the public eye, a Lion is charismatic and magnetic, but a Lion shines even in less visible fields.

Above all, Lions need an audience (what good is it to be king without subjects?) and often choose jobs in which they can get one. These fields include sales, teaching, consulting, tour guiding and travel, management, and, of course, performing.

Lions and Their Money

Image matters a lot to Lions, so if the checking account balance and Lions' needs are saying different things, the needs are going to win out. Big night out with the gang? Count on Leo, broke or not, to pick up the tab.

Nothing's too good for Lions, so they're not likely to notice what something costs when it's something they want to have. Lions seldom think to bargain; when they see something they want, they get it. Yet they always seem to know the best place to find the highest affordable quality. Living the good life, according to Lions, has nothing to do with what things cost, and this makes them most generous—nearly royal in their magnanimity.

Lion Rising: The Leo ♌ Ascendant

Rising Lions present the world with a bright, sunny, confident exterior, coupled with a flair for the dramatic. How much has this got to do with the inner being beneath the show? That depends on the individual. Beneath all the roar, Lions can be real pussycats.

One of the primary lessons for a Rising Lion is learning to give up needing approval, respect, and admiration from others. An ascendant Lion might help to develop self-confidence because the outer person will be projecting self-confidence as a matter of course. After a while, this can become second nature, helping those who are less confident overcome a lack of faith in themselves. Self-approval is the key to a Rising Lion.

Lion in Partnership: The Leo ♌ Descendant

The Leo descendant seeks leadership in all partnerships, both personal and professional. Lions descending love to show off their partners' intelligence, beauty, and diplomacy because proud descending Leo says, "What you see in my partner is a reflection of me!" When descending Leos share the spotlight, it's with themselves as much as with their partners.

Virgo ♍: Practical Perfection

Purity. Perfection. Practicality. These are the Virgo's Virgin values. But what does this translate to? Virgins, more than any other sign, are identified with analyzing—with examining everything in great detail, so as to improve not just themselves but the world. And improving the world means serving more than one's self; it means serving the greater good. Virgins are very responsible people.

Virgins are about order and connection; they see things very clearly, and they see each part of a whole in a way that few other signs can. A Virgo sees perfection where others see (or leave) messes, and a Virgo does whatever is necessary to bring that perfection out, so everyone can see it in the same way.

Virgins are about finding the patterns, especially sacred patterns. In Native American tribes, the Virgin is represented by the spider, which weaves the sacred patterns in its web. In ancient cultures, Virgins were the sacred priests and priestesses, who often were responsible for reading the natural cycles and patterns correctly so there would be enough food to feed everyone.

Virgo brings in the harvest. By the end of summer, it's time to reap the fruits of their labor, and Virgins are at the ready, waiting until precisely the moment of ripeness. Waste not, want not when Virgo is in charge.

Organized and duty-bound, Virgins are always looking for what *could* go wrong … so they can head it off, or at least correct its course. This grounded Earth sign almost always appears calm, cool, and collected. Virgins keep their restless energy contained and under control until they resolve any negative issues behind the scenes. Virgo is happiest when everything is perfect.

The Sixth Zodiac Sign

Virgo, the Virgin ♍	August 22 to September 22
Element	Earth
Quality	Mutable

Virgo, the Virgin ♍	August 22 to September 22
Energy	Yin
Ruler	Mercury ☿
Color	Blue
Gem	Sapphire
Anatomy	Intestines and colon
Keywords	Service, self-improvement, sacred patterns
Archetypes	Mexico's Virgin of Juquila, Astraea, Sherlock Holmes, Renaissance monks who created illuminated manuscripts
Celeb Virgins	Beyoncé, Salma Hayek, Melissa McCarthy, Keanu Reeves, Zendaya, Idris Elba, Amy Poehler, Jada Pinkett Smith, Colin Firth, Sophia Loren, River Phoenix
Virgins Rising	Renee Zellweger, Keanu Reeves, Madonna, Usher, Marion Cotillard, Ryan Reynolds, Kurt Cobain
Tarot Suit	Pentacles
Tarot Major Arcana	9 The Hermit, truth and inner guidance

The Best and Worst of Virgins

Calm-on-the-outside Virgins will fool you like no other sign. On the inside they're all restless energy, constantly seeking, constantly improving, and constantly *fixing* whatever needs to be fixed. Here is one of the zodiac's liveliest minds, a consummate problem solver, a diligent fixer, a model of methodical efficiency, bent on beauty and perfection.

Because Virgo ♍ is an Earth sign, Virgins are very practical, and because their quality is mutable, they're resourceful as well. That same mutability can translate into flexibility, so Virgins can be chameleon-like, too. They might agree with you when they sense that you're not going to change your mind (practical and flexible), but privately, they won't change their minds either, unless doing so suits their purposes.

Virgins can think too much. They can find fault wherever they look—even where there's none to be found. They can be inflexible, and they can worry too much along with all that thinking. Because Virgins measure their self-esteem by weighing what they accomplish in a given day, they can increase their self-esteem by giving up this narrow view of what they're good for. Then they'll see themselves as whole people, with love, feelings, and other important things to offer others.

No one is more organized than a Virgin. While the rest of the world is collapsing around them, Virgins are calmly making lists of what's left. No one's more committed or more willing to make sure it goes smoothly for everybody. If there's someone in the kitchen cleaning up after dinner while everyone else has gone on to another party, it's most likely a Virgin, who's probably perfectly happy to be there. Virgins *like* to work, and they do it very well.

Virgins have long been known as healers and those who serve, and the mythological archetypes here are no exception. Chiron was the wounded healer who couldn't heal himself but nonetheless healed others, and Astraea was a healer as well. Oaxaca, Mexico's tiny Virgin of Juquila used Earth energy to survive the ravages of fire. Many faithful make the pilgrimage to her shrine each year to ask for special favors.

Virgins in Love

There's no denying that Virgins seek the perfect mate. If you find a Virgin on a dating app, they're sure to have strict criteria and qualifications for partners in love. But they also enjoy the pleasures of intimacy, especially when those pleasures can lead to personal growth. In her constellation in the sky, Virgo appears to be dancing, and one of her greatest joys is the fruit of consummated love.

Because Virgins like to serve, they will do whatever they can to take care of those they care about. Sometimes they can go too far, leaving the beloved with nothing to do, but they often anticipate the needs of others with prescient clarity.

As seekers of order, it's natural that Virgins seek out other Earth signs—Virgos ♍, Taureans ♉, and Capricorns ♑—but it might be the fixed intensity of Scorpio ♏ or the mutable water of Pisces ♓ that really plants the seeds of contentment for this mutable sign. Watery Cancer ♋, too, can make for strong emotional connections. But Virgins shouldn't necessarily settle for complacency just because it's tidy; they may find far more compatibility with the excitement of Gemini ♊ or Sagittarius ♐.

The Healthy Virgin

Virgins are often more concerned with health and its applications than other signs. In an Earth sign like Virgo ♍, the ruler, Mercury ☿, is very practical and interested in practical applications of knowledge. Often, Virgins will know about vitamins or aromatherapy; they'll know which herbs cure which ills and why your antibiotic isn't working on your pesky cold. Virgins' interest in health is largely because they're interested in practical knowledge and in sacred patterns (and what's more sacred than healing?), as well as in keeping themselves healthy.

Virgo rules the intestines and colon, and it is in these areas that problems often arise. Colon cancer is on the rise among younger people. It is important to eat well and exercise; this is age-old advice that rings true. And remember that colonoscopy screenings may be protective against colon cancer. Busy Virgins need to stop what they're doing periodically to eat, and they need to relax while they eat, not rush through—or, worse, work through—their meals. Virgins need to learn to serve themselves as well as they serve everyone else.

Virgins at Home

Here again, Virgins' love of service shows itself clearly. The Virgo home is tidy, efficient, and organized, but that just makes it easier to take care of all those who enter. You won't find Virgins sitting down to eat until everyone else has enough on their plates, and even then, Virgins may hover rather than sit down and join in.

Virgins are great lovers of beauty, and coupled with their understanding of botany, this can mean homes surrounded by lovely gardens and filled with thriving plants and herbs. Virgins are likely to have aloe vera growing somewhere and are even more likely to snap off a leaf to rub on your wound.

Virgins at Work

Count yourself fortunate to have Virgins on your work team. With their love of challenges and constant need for self-improvement, they'll bring a strong dose of clarity.

Virgins can be good planners, good organizers, and good finishers, but the same knack for details can also make them very strong in any field in which they use their hands. Best of all, no matter what they do, Virgins are always reliable, whether they're the boss or an employee. With their desire to serve, they'll see that the job gets done in a fine way. The two largest employment areas for Virgo are in the health field and in any jobs that require analysis, including marketing, systems analysis, and computers. Virgins love details and excel at jobs that require detail-oriented work. Of course, as Madeline can tell you, Virgins' attention to detail makes them fine astrologers, too.

Virgins and Their Money

Detail-oriented, organized Virgins always have their checkbooks balanced and often know exactly how much money they have in their pockets as well. Money is an area in which Virgins, with their eye for every detail, can tend to be highly critical of their own abilities; in reality, however, they are able and clever money managers, always staying within their budgets and never frivolous.

Virgin Rising: The Virgo ♍ Ascendant

Rising Virgins might not say much until they've adequately sized up you and the situation. Because these people are analytical, they'll probably ask you several questions rather than assume anything. Rising Virgins also can be very witty people because they're Mercury-ruled. Rising Virgins are learning to develop a new understanding of how they can contribute to our present culture and the nature of sacred work in today's world. When they understand what their sacred work is, they can learn to co-create with the patterns of the Universe. Rising Virgins may be learning to put things in perspective, or they may have a tendency to let small details take on meanings far beyond their actual importance. Work matters a great deal to Rising Virgos.

Virgin in Partnership: The Virgo ♍ Descendant

The Virgo descendant represents the quest for a perfect match—in love, work, and life in general. A Virgin descending needs partnerships with perfect communication, partners who pay attention to the details, and partners who can serve the greater good. The ideal (perfect!) Virgin partner is someone who takes health and well-being seriously. Descending Virgins aren't looking for lots of partners. They want only the few good men and women who can fulfill the job of partnering with total equal commitment.

Chapter 6

FALL SIGNS: LIBRA ♎, SCORPIO ♏, AND SAGITTARIUS ♐

With the start of fall, we move from the signs of personal development into the signs of external development: Libra ♎, the seeker of harmony; Scorpio ♏, the transformer; and Sagittarius ♐, the explorer. These are the signs that begin to integrate self and family with community. In the fall, the desire to connect to others rises; this is the season of cooperation.

Fall, like spring, is a season of transition. Nature begins its retreat in preparation for winter. Leaves turn colors and fall from the branches, the remnants of the harvest enter the soil to reinfuse it with nutrients, and the external environment appears poised to turn inward. So it is, as well, with the energies of the fall signs.

Libra ♎: A Fine Balance

Harmony. Balance. No one wants to even things out like a Libra ♎. Libra, the Scales, begins at the autumnal equinox, a time when the length of the day equals the length of the night, and Scales strive for such balance in all they do. Libras know that although there's a time and place for doing things on your own, you can't do everything alone. Scales realize the need to cooperate with others to maintain equilibrium and stability and to connect heart and mind to achieve unity and peace.

Libras are charming, and their charm is primarily because of the rulership of Venus ♀. Scales see *everything* from both sides and have a great appreciation for art and beauty. As a yang, cardinal sign, they generate a great deal of activity as well, especially in starting things, from diplomatic talks to friendships.

But Libra is an Air sign as well and, like all Air signs, has an active mind. In Scales' case, this takes the form of looking at one side and then the other, weighing everything over and over again. Like other cardinal signs, Libra seems constantly in motion, moving around and enjoying life.

The Seventh Zodiac Sign

Libra, the Scales ♎	September 22 to October 23
Element	Air
Quality	Cardinal
Energy	Yang
Ruler	Venus ♀
Color	Blue
Gem	Opal
Anatomy	Kidneys, lower back, adrenal glands
Keywords	Balance, harmony, justice
Archetypes	King Solomon, Lady Justice, Joni Mitchell song *Both Sides Now*, parents who encourage kids to share
Celeb Scales	Donald Glover, Kate Winslet, Hugh Jackman, Neil deGrasse Tyson, Cardi B, Brie Larson, Gwyneth Paltrow, Kamala Harris, Serena Williams, Bruce Springsteen, Eleanor Roosevelt, Mahatma Gandhi
Scales Rising	Benedict Cumberbatch, Jennifer Aniston, Beyoncé, Leonardo DiCaprio, Yoko Ono, Jimmy Carter
Tarot Suit	Swords
Tarot Major Arcana	11 Justice, fairness and honor

The Best and Worst of Scales

Scales are social creatures, ready to share their experience with others and quick to form partnerships. Friendly, popular, and attractive, they often are idealistic as well, and they are eager to talk about their high principles and lofty ideas with any who will listen.

But Scales can seem affected or insincere, too eager to compromise, or worse, indecisive. Scales are often so busy weighing each side of an issue that they can never come to a conclusion or decision. Also, in their need to please others, they might forget to please themselves. Scales need to be aware of their own needs and meet them, too, not just those of other people. The prime purpose of Scales is to create relationships with others. Libra ♎ is the opposite of Aries ♈, who are concerned with themselves. Here, we see the concern for others and the incorporation of both perspectives: "mine" and "theirs."

At their best, Scales understand that their strength lies in creating and maintaining relationships. Scales seek to find their perfect complement—their other half—to complete the balance. They also want to find balance in other things, not just relationships.

Libra is the sign of justice and is represented by a blindfolded Venus ♀, who holds the scales of Libra ♎ in one hand and the sword of Mars ♂/Aries ♈ (its opposite) in the other. The goal for Libra is the attainment of inner harmony and a reconciliation of opposites. This is not an easy task, but if anyone can do it, Libra can.

Scales in Love

Scales love to be loved and admired, and they give much in return. Constantly testing their powers of attraction, they may seem flirtatious and flighty, but Scales are seeking their other half. Scales are romantics, too, and they love to "set the mood" for romance by creating an atmosphere of beauty to match their feelings.

Air signs—Geminis ♊, Aquarians ♒, and other Librans ♎—with their easy talk and quick minds—are an obvious match for Scales, but there are interesting possibilities with Scales' opposite, Aries ♈, though each sign might believe the other too selfish. Scales can thrive with Leo's ♌ generosity, or they might find the balance they seek through an adventure with Sagittarius ♐.

Scales are at their strongest with other people, yet their focus in a relationship is on themselves. Scales' self-concept is a reflective one, seen through others' eyes rather than their own. At the same time, Scales might hide their feelings to give an appearance of balance. Scales would do well to remember that making a decision is not always a tipping of the scales!

Signs ruled by Venus ♀ are the most romantic of the zodiac, and Libra is no exception. But this same romanticism can translate to a search for an ideal mate as well, and Librans should beware of the disappointment that can occur when such high expectations are brought down to Earth. Another danger is that Scales may refuse to acknowledge the beloved's true self and instead keep their notion of their ideal partner up on a pedestal.

Healthy Scales

Graceful Scales should pay attention to inner fitness as well as outer fitness; their tendency toward lower-back or kidney problems is a direct result of keeping things inside to avoid creating discord. For Scales, extra potassium might be needed to balance the water level in the body and stimulate the kidneys to eliminate wastes. Vitamin E, selenium, and bioflavonoids are very helpful for preserving the beauty of Libra.

As in love, healthy Scales need to bring their ideals down to an earthly scale. Scales also can benefit from holistic aids like aromatherapy, and the lovely scents and properties of rose oil or jasmine can help create the inner harmony Scales seek. After all, as a sign ruled by Venus, Scales are very sensitive to smells all around them.

Scales are strong social media influencers because they bring all facets to the forefront for consideration, balancing pros and cons to find the best path forward. Scales actress and influencer Gywneth Paltrow combined her performance, research, and holistic skills to create the ultimate holistic and lifestyle online company, Goop. Through various broadcast, Internet, and print media platforms, Goop covers it all to bring Gywneth's message of harmony and healing to the public.

Scales at Home

Scales' homes are lovely places filled with *objets d'art*, reflections of the beauty of Librans themselves. True to their need for others, Scales are among the great hosts of the zodiac, filling their homes with other people as well as those people's conversations and, ideas, and often, their music.

Scales also enjoy the comforts of life and will not hesitate to make certain that their home reflects them. Because Scales seek harmony and balance above all, this is what you will find in their homes.

Still, all that waffling we've mentioned can make life with Scales rough going at times. Their constant weighing of things can make decision time difficult, and their ideals can mean that they seek a harmony impossible to find here on Earth. "Let me think about it," Scales say. Still, this results in a personal space that is singularly lovely, as befits the home of a Venus-ruled sign!

Scales at Work

Social Libras shine at work. They are often leaders who show others the way; however, with their need for balance and harmony, they are often partners, too, using their knack for balance and harmony with others to achieve great things.

Scales' charm comes into play at work, too, and they may have a knack for public relations or sales. Or Scales' love of beauty might translate into a career in the arts, fashion, or interior design. Scales could be found starting an online couture clothing rental site. Another good Scales profession could be font designer, with all its requirements for balance and harmony of form and function. You might expect Scales to be judges and lawyers, but though they often are found in these fields, their tendency to vacillate rather than come to a final decision can sometimes hamper them.

On the other hand (a favorite Libra phrase), these same qualities can make Scales fine counselors, where their ability to hear two sides of an issue rather than take sides is a decided asset. And for the same reason, they can be remarkable teachers, translating a broad array of ideas into a range of possibilities.

Scales and Their Money

Money for Scales is a means to an end, and that end is beauty and harmony. Scales need to be aware, however, that things and their appearance cannot give or replace inner security and harmony. Also, they might find that hanging on to a little "mad money" could bring them much closer to such balance than they would have thought possible.

Scales are more likely to invest in things and people than in long-term securities because they like to see an immediate return on their investment—in the form of beauty and harmony. The inward reflects the outward here as in no other sign. To Scales, appearances really *do* matter.

Scales Rising: The Libra ♎ Ascendant

Rising Scales are learning about consciousness, equal relationships, and partnerships. This is not about defining who you are by whom you're with. Instead, it's about actually learning—through constant interaction—about relationships as a spiritual path.

Rising Scales' need for companionship or partnership is balanced by their desire for fair play, peace, balance, and harmony. After their need for love is satisfied, their desire for social justice kicks in. They might have a well-developed sense of diplomacy and refined social graces, and often they are very personable and charming as well.

Scales in Partnership: The Libra ♎ Descendant

Descending Scales seek partners who are equal to themselves. They need and want partners who are fair, honorable, harmonious, and adaptable. After all, this is how Libra descendants treat their partners. Descending Scales also look for balance in partnership, countering their need to get down to business with companionship. Work or pleasure, partnerships for Libra ♎ descendant are always about collaboration and fairness.

Scorpio ♏: Intense Power

Scorpios, the Scorpions, are intense. After all, they're dealing with life and death, and by extension, with birth and sex. Scorpions are all about mystery and about how that poison stinger can so quickly change life into death. Scorpios can be both penetrating and incisive. Scorpio ♏ is one of the signs that has two rulers, Pluto ♀ and Mars ♂. That's why this sign can be quite a warrior and very powerful. Combined with their fixed nature, these people never give up.

Like all Water signs, Scorpios are more concerned with feelings than appearances, and as a fixed sign, they're often resistant to change. Scorpios' ability to see through others' facades can serve them well, and they can wait forever for the right moment to get even or make their move. But give up? Never! Scorpios persevere until they attain an outcome that is their truth.

Scorpios are constantly probing beneath the obvious face of things, seeking what lies beneath. One of their rulers is Pluto ♀, the invisible planet that rules beginnings and ends, both of which—like Pluto itself— occur out of natural sight. Scorpios tend to keep ideas and thoughts close to the vest, taking time to observe and to formulate a powerful plan of action when it is needed. According to Navajo myth, Scorpio Grandmother Spider is the Grandmother of all the people (the Diné, as the Navajo call themselves). When the people seem lost or confused, it is Grandmother Spider who speaks to them from her ever-evolving web, to remind them that they already know the way—and that they must simply look inside themselves!

Scorpions' intensity and probing might make them sound humorless and frightening, but these same characteristics create both passion and excitement as well. You might feel as if a Scorpion is looking right through you, but the feeling might be an invigorating one.

The Eighth Zodiac Sign

Scorpio, the Scorpion ♏	October 23 to November 22
Element	Water
Quality	Fixed
Energy	Yin
Rulers	Pluto ♀ and Mars ♂
Colors	Burgundy, black
Gem	Topaz
Anatomy	Genitals, urinary and reproductive systems
Keywords	Desire, transformation, power
Archetypes	James Alexander Malcolm MacKenzie Fraser of *Outlander,* The Phoenix, The Scorpion King, Grandmother Spider
Celeb Scorpios	Björk, Ethan Hawke, Bill Gates, Roy Lichtenstein, Terry Gilliam, Julia Roberts, Prince Charles, Sylvia Plath, Aaron Copland, Georgia O'Keeffe, Marie Curie, John Keats
Scorpios Rising	Tom Cruise, Diane Keaton, Natalie Portman, Chris Pratt, Gwen Stefani, Tracey Ullman, Chelsea Clinton, Samuel Beckett, Camille Claudel, Sigmund Freud
Tarot Suit	Cups
Tarot Major Arcana	13 Death, transformation and regeneration

The Best and Worst of Scorpions

Scorpios use what many astrologers call Scorpionic power to achieve their ends. But maybe we should just look at that power itself because Scorpio ♏ is the zodiac's most powerful sign.

Scorpio ♏ appears in the zodiac at a time when Earth seems to be retreating: Leaves fall from the trees, hibernating animals seek haven in their caves, and even humans go inside their houses and get cozy. But this retreat is, in reality, more like cocooning—a regeneration of self, a rebirth, and this is the true source of Scorpio's power. In Scorpio's case, still waters really *do* run deep!

In pop astrology, you'll often find this power called sex, and yes, Scorpios *do* have a strongly developed sexuality. Sometimes, though, they might disguise this even from themselves, in which case they may constantly be seeking something they can't quite name. The quest for intimacy—sensually, both spiritual and physical—may take them (or push others) to the edge. Scorpio's symbol ♏ is a pictorial representation of a scorpion's stinger connected to the human reproduction organs. In ancient times, it also represented the mythical phoenix, a bird that continually regenerated from its own ashes. Scorpio was believed to represent the serpent in the story of Adam and Eve and an eagle.

One thing's clear: no other sign of the zodiac is so concerned with the cycles of life. Sometimes, Scorpios sublimate this passionate life energy into other projects, and they might be very aware of doing it. Björk's avant-garde music and Pablo Picasso's genius drawings and paintings reflect the passions of their lives as transformed into their art. At Scorpios' worst, they may choose to use personal magnetism to coerce others in fanatical ways, like Scorpio Charles Manson.

Scorpio is also associated with death, but in its astrological sense, death refers to transformation, rebirth, and creation through the life cycle rather than oblivion. The Death card of the Tarot represents the potential for transformation and personal growth through a fresh start, which is the essence of Scorpionic power as well. Just as the garden dies back from the fullness of summer, Scorpio energy draws passion inward; here, Scorpios can see their emotions and goals, analyze them, and know how they feel about planting the seeds of passion for a transformed future.

At their best, Scorpios are magnetic leaders, like Robert F. Kennedy—shrewd, faith inspiring, compassionate, and brave. At their worst, they're manipulative, vengeful, or even cruel. Like the nuclear energy that shares Pluto's ♀ rule, Scorpios can use their power for good or evil, and Scorpios would do well to use their tremendous energy and power in positive ways, such as healing and learning control.

Scorpios in Love

Although Scorpios might know everyone else's heart of hearts, they'll seldom reveal their own. When they do, though, they share a depth of passion no other sign can. Like their relatives the spiders, Scorpios will weave a web of romance, attracting partners with their intricacy and magnetism. But they're also quick to retreat if they feel threatened, and after Scorpios have hidden, it might be hard to get them to reveal themselves again. You'd also do well not to injure a Scorpio in love; their vengeance has a long memory and a fierce sting. An archetype for Scorpios in love is surely Katniss Everdeen, a young woman forced to learn about love and betrayal while growing up in the arena of *The Hunger Games*.

Don't forget that Scorpio ♏ is a Water sign, sometimes emotional, sometimes moody, always slow to commit, but very loyal when they do. Other Water signs might be the most comfortable match for Scorpio romance: Scorpios may see other signs' approaches to love with too much clarity for romance. Earth signs, like Taurus ♉, Virgo ♍, and Capricorn ♑—fed by Water—can do very well with Scorpios. And Taurus ♉ is Scorpio's opposite, also very sensuous and pleasure loving, an interesting match for Scorpio's intensity.

The Healthy Scorpio

So reluctant are they to let anything out in the open, retentive Scorpios may be prone to urinary tract infections or constipation. But they also have the potential to be great healers, not just of themselves but also of others because of their strong regenerative and transforming powers.

Healthy Scorpios pay attention to their dreams, for both their informative and their imaginative power, and they should pay attention to what they eat and drink as well. A Scorpio's intake can truly make a big difference in how they feel. Any relaxation techniques that help Scorpios get rid of old resentments and anger could also help them feel their best. But a Scorpio's most important health lesson is to let go of repressed jealousy, anger, and resentments.

Scorpios need to get adequate amounts of zinc or zinc supplements in their diets. This is essential for the growth, development, and functioning of the reproductive organs and prostate gland, as well as the general healing process, both of which are important for Scorpios.

Scorpios at Home

Because Scorpios require power and control, life at home can be full of struggles—power struggles! Or it can be a place where Scorpios keep "everyone in line" until they leave home to start lives of their own. But no matter what the kids or spouse do, Scorpios are ready to defend them with their lives and stingers, if necessary. Loyalty is very important to them.

When Scorpios are unhappy, though, they head off to be alone—and heaven help you if you disturb them! Scorpios usually need and want regular time alone to process their intense feelings. Without time alone, it can become very hard for Scorpios to maintain their sense of control. For this reason, Scorpios need their own hiding place at home, where no one else will bother them. This isn't just a corner in a room, either; it's an entire room they can call their own. When Scorpios *can* control themselves instead of others, they are very loving and loyal, and they can give a great deal of themselves to their families and mates.

Don't be surprised if Scorpios need to sign off social media from time to time. While you can expect Scorpios to be tenacious supporters of causes they believe in, too much oversharing of strong opinions can lead to tension and the conflict. Don't take it personally when Scorpios withdraw; they'll soon regroup and be right back in the good fight, making comments and posts.

Scorpios at Work

Scorpios thrive on change, and a career that requires any renovation or strategy works very well for them. They might find creative outlets for those transforming energies, or they might be in the healing arts as doctors or counselors. Scorpios also can do very well in fields like research or science—anything requiring that penetrating, probing eye will benefit from a Scorpio touch. Scorpios also are often involved in reviving the environment or cleaning up waste in some way. Scorpios are involved in eliminating toxins and regeneration, and that's why they excel at these jobs. Look at Nobel scientist Marie Curie, whose passion for science led to the discovery of polonium and radium and the theory of radioactivity. Her contact with these toxic elements led to her death from radiation poisoning.

As the most powerful zodiac sign, Scorpios also do well in any position from which they can wield that power, be it management, finance, or directing. But that power also means that any field Scorpios choose will benefit from their influence. Even the seemingly meaningless is transformed when a Scorpio is in charge.

Scorpios and Their Money

Here again, Scorpios' retentive ways come to the forefront, and Scorpios and their money are not soon parted. Scorpios understand the dynamics of power and money, and their conservative approach pays off here as well.

Scorpios will amass cash quietly in the background and then use it to achieve their ends. Outward appearances mean little to Scorpios; to them, it's all about control and transformation, and they'll apply their money only where they feel it's necessary.

Scorpio Rising: The Scorpio ♏ Ascendant

There's nothing halfway about a Rising Scorpio; they put the whole force of their intense personality behind everything they do. Rising Scorpios are often very magnetic and attract others easily. Watery Rising Scorpios aren't really interested in surface chitchat, and their intensity might initially intimidate others. Rising Scorpio author Emily Brontë used her talent to reimagine the Victorian novel, penning the ultimate romantic conflict in *Wuthering Heights*. Her heroine Catherine Earnshaw must choose between Edgar Linton, who is stable, kind, and cultured, and her own soul, Heathcliff, with his wild, headstrong nature that could be dangerous and even cruel. Scorpio Rising is a strong indicator of people born with a need to control because that's when things feel safest to them. Major difficulties in the early environment and home life may have encouraged them to take control, so they would feel safe. After all, people don't worry about feeling safe unless they feel very vulnerable. Rising Scorpios' greatest challenge is to learn how to control themselves and stop controlling others.

Rising Scorpios are learning about the life force as a path to the Universe, or the Source of the All. Rising Scorpios are magnetic iconoclasts, like filmmaker Stanley Kubrick. They are bold thinkers, rugged individualists with strong visions, and they are shrewd, innovative, and brave. Kubrick's epic sci-fi classic *2001: A Space Odyssey* still inspires and challenges young screenwriters and directors to imagine the Earth's future and humanity's future on it. The mask of Scorpio is secrecy; Scorpio Rising can act as a double disguise. Rising Scorpios might use manipulation or deception to rise to power, and they might move quietly in the wings until their rise has been completed.

Scorpios in Partnership: The Scorpio ♏ Descendant

Scorpio ♏ descendant seeks partners who are passionate about life and serious about productivity. Scorpios descending demand loyalty, monogamy, and integrity from their business, as well as their romantic partners. Can you play archetypal Spider-Man to the Scorpio descending's Iron Man? Scorpio ♏ descendant desires shared devotion to common causes. Scorpios descending persist until they find the right partner who can grow with them to become a very powerful duo.

Sagittarius ♐: Aim for the Stars

The Sagittarius Archer's arrow searches for meaning, and Sagittarius ♐ can be thought of as the gypsy, the student, and the philosopher, all rolled into one. No other sign is so focused on finding life's basic truth. Archers burn with this need to understand, and, as a mutable sign, they thrive on the changes this search can provide.

Because it's a yang sign, Archers are always moving toward more experience. It's also a party sign, and the party starts with the Fire sign's enthusiasm, high spirits, plus a whole lot of fun. Archers' optimism is contagious, and their honesty and directness (when they apply it) can be a breath of fresh air or a shock to the system.

The Ninth Zodiac Sign

Sagittarius, the Archer ♐	November 22 to December 22
Element	Fire
Quality	Mutable

Sagittarius, the Archer ♐	November 22 to December 22
Energy	Yang
Ruler	Jupiter ♃
Color	Purple
Gem	Turquoise
Anatomy	Liver, hips, and thighs
Keywords	Understanding, enthusiasm, exploration
Archetypes	Guardians of the Galaxy, Indiana Jones, Diana the Huntress, the Centaur
Celeb Archers	Billie Eilish, Brad Pitt, Emmanuel Macron, Nicki Minaj, Jon Stewart, Taylor Swift, Woody Allen, Kim Basinger, Jim Morrison, Jimi Hendrix, Jane Austen
Archers Rising	Pink, Angela Merkel, Goldie Hawn, Sean Penn, Bob Dylan, Patti Smith, Émile Zola, Charles Darwin
Tarot Suit	Wands
Tarot Major Arcana	7 The Chariot, winged victory

The Best and Worst of Archers

Archers thrive on independence and freedom, and they never tire of a change of scenery. Sure, they might forget your date or miss that important deadline, but you can also count on them to find where the fun is. Archers are ruled by Jupiter ♃, the king of the Roman gods, and the planet of good fortune, optimism, expansion, and abundance. (The word *jovial* is a derivative of the Latin form of *Jupiter*.) Jupiter is a fortunate ruler, and Archers tend to be freedom loving and energetic people.

Archers' enthusiasm is bound to be contagious, but their lack of commitment can annoy other more responsible signs. Their generosity might spill into excessiveness, their optimism might make them blind to details, and their honesty can make their remarks sound blunt or inconsiderate. But the carefree adventurousness of Sagittarius can be a welcome release.

Most dangerous to Archers can be their tendency toward dogma. Because they're seeking a universal truth rather than an individual one, they might mistake a trend for that truth and then become rather preachy about its powers. But Archers truly do wish to unite all people under one idea, and if they believe they've found it, they're eager to share it with all. Archers speak their truth regardless of whether you ask for it. They're candid and outspoken, yet intensely introspective and philosophical.

In the long run, for Archers, it's the getting there that's more than half the fun. Archers love travel, new places, and seeking. Go along for the ride, if you dare. Of course, if you're an Archer yourself, you won't think twice.

Archers in Love

Commitment? Sure. Just don't expect it to go on too long. Mutable Archers are always on the move, and if they do find their true love, they might have left a bevy of admirers behind, trying in vain to find their tracks.

Love is fun! Romance is a gas! Passion is excitement! See how Sagittarius breeds exclamation points? Those who require loyalty and longevity in love might do well to look elsewhere, but if you're looking for a good time, text ARCHER. Fun-loving influencer Archers make pop-up events exciting; they excel at organizing parties and gatherings that bring people together to spark connections. Who knows who you'll meet, and where it may lead?

Archers aren't just looking for a good time, although that's part of it: They want a trail-mate to travel along on their journey. Archers are here to seek, and householder types like Cancer ♋ aren't particularly interested in living a life on the trail. It takes a special person to want to adventure off with an Archer; the future is so open to possibilities, but it's also so unsettled. This isn't the person you want if you're after a mate to "settle down" with. But for another adventuring heart, an Archer is a great journeyer.

Archers aren't concerned with details, which means they can drive more detail-oriented signs like Virgo ♍ to distraction. And Archers expect that everyone will want to have as much fun as they do, which tends to leave Scorpio ♏ and Taurus ♉ back in the dust, too. Archers will do best with other Fire signs, with which the romance can be both fiery and adventurous. Just don't forget that air feeds fire, too: Gemini ♊, Libra ♎, and Aquarius ♒ might have just the kind of surprises that Archers love. With a water sign, such as Pisces ♓, love can be steamy as long as Pisces can share dreams and visions on a journey of discovery.

The Healthy Archer

Energetic Archers sometimes forget to slow down. And while galloping along, they might be gathering so many new projects that it's nearly impossible to finish all they've started. Constant motion can make Archers prone to nervous exhaustion or just plain confusion. Sometimes it's necessary for racing-ahead Archers to S-T-O-P.

Sagittarius ♐ rules the hips, thighs, and liver, all of which can be severely harmed by overindulgence. Archers would do well to work on exercises that help them stay centered physically, and this, in turn, will help them not to lose sight of the big picture they envision.

Archers need to be aware of the problems of excess sugar, fat, or even alcohol; all can harm the liver. Too much overindulgence in food can really slow Archers down and make them sick.

Archers need adequate amounts of vitamin K, inositol, manganese, and molybdenum to maintain normal liver function and metabolize fats. Detoxifying the liver around midlife also can prevent major health problems later.

Archers at Home

Archers are great entertainers, and everyone loves a party at an Archer's house. Yes, they might forget to serve—or even to make—a main course, but everyone will be having too much fun to care.

You won't often find children at an Archer's house, though. This adventurous sign doesn't want to be tied down and Archers are slow to come to parenthood, if at all. Archers like to feel free to set out for the next adventure, and home can just as easily be a tent in the Serengeti or on Denali, a studio in Manhattan or Vancouver, or just a backpack and a sleeping bag. But wherever Archer's tent is pitched, you can be sure that's where you'll find the action.

Archers at Work

Because Archers tend to lose interest before a project is completed, it's best to have them on your idea team. Archers do well, though, in all areas of communications or anywhere a sense of humor and excitement are needed; also, they may be meme makers, clowns, tricksters, or even court jesters. They'll also do well as *National Geographic* photographers—or any kind of photographer or web videographer.

One of the best-known Archers at work was Gene Roddenberry, the creator of *Star Trek*. Deep in the heart of the 1960s, Roddenberry created a crew that included an African American woman, a Russian, an Asian, and an alien! Old *Star Trek* shows may look dated now, but back then, Roddenberry's vision was truly revolutionary—and very Archer-like.

Archers also can be found in positions that require risk, from the stock market to test piloting. They may be gamblers: Archers believe in their luck, and that optimism really does make them lucky.

Archers are often found in education, medicine, the legal system, foreign relations, the travel industry or travel for business (such as importers/exporters), or sales. Archers tend to be highly educated and very well read; Sagittarius often produces philosophers, preachers, or anyone associated with inspiring others.

Archers and Their Money

Overconfident Archers tend to overextend themselves (and, by extension, their resources) for the sake of a good time. But here again, their luck comes into play. Archers will put their last $100 on that 50-to-1 shot, and with their luck it has a good chance of coming in. You can bet that, if they can hang in the game long enough, Archers will go for the high stakes whether or not they have a safety net. Look for Archers to start crowdsourcing funds for start-up projects, launch humorous videos on social media that generate ad revenue, or take donations to support their sites online.

Because they're more interested in the big picture than the little details, Archers may forget that they borrowed $20 from you as soon as the money is in their hands. Their irresponsibility with cash may irk their more dependable friends to no end. But those same dependable friends will always come through for Archers, and because Archers know it, they don't sweat it. As a mutable sign, Archers can be very resourceful, so they're able to scrape something together, even if they're broke.

Archer Rising: The Sagittarius ♐ Ascendant

The world of Rising Archers is filled with possibilities, and these people are unusually optimistic. Rising Archers are explorers. They need to see new territory, so goals and challenges are very important to them. Rising Archers tend to hide their problems and troubles behind humor, and they don't want others to be worried about them. Part of this is because Rising Archers can't stand to worry about themselves, so they don't want others to do so, either.

With Jupiter ♃ as the ruler of the Sagittarius ascendant, Rising Archers are often jovial, happy-go-lucky, enthusiastic, and optimistic, always seeking to find the truth, and they will approach the world as if it's their own oyster, filled with possibilities. They are learning about the meaning of life and expanding their inner selves to the farthest horizons possible. Adventure and spiritual growth go hand in hand with Archer Rising.

Archer in Partnership: The Sagittarius ♐ Descendant

The Archer descending needs a partner who has a strong sense of humor, with a healthy dose of intelligence for good measure. Sagittarius ♐ descendant tells it like it is and appreciates others who can do the same. Archer descending looks for communicators who can connect with suits and sweats, hiking boots and high couture, with equal ease. But more than anything, Archer descending needs partnership in which the pair will surely discover something new about each other.

Chapter 7

WINTER SIGNS: CAPRICORN ♑, AQUARIUS ♒, AND PISCES ♓

Perhaps no three signs are more different than the signs of winter: Capricorn ♑, Aquarius ♒, and Pisces ♓. Capricorn is the organized, goal-setting achiever; Aquarius is the inventive, humanitarian revolutionary; and Pisces is the compassionate, all-understanding healer.

It's no accident that these signs appear during the dark and heavy winter months. These signs understand the hardships of the world and can readily walk a mile in someone else's shoes. What grows in the winter? Some might say nothing—as it appears—but the signs of winter know this is the time to look under the surface to formulate ideas, goals, and a plan of action.

Capricorn ♑: Climbing Everest

No sign's public persona is closer to its values than a Capricorn Goat's, and no sign is more directed toward its goals. Intense and practical, Goats will bide their time, waiting for the right moment to climb that peak, because after they do, they intend to stay at the top.

Self-control, of both will and emotion, helps Goats achieve their aims. As the cardinal Earth sign, the Goat is decidedly down-to-earth in its efforts and with its yin energy; a Goat uses the mind rather than physical force to reach its goals.

But Capricorn ♑ isn't just any goat; it's a sea-goat, and as a creature that's half fish, it also can use water's deeper powers to its advantage. (Even the highest mountain is covered with snow.) Ultimately, though, Goats' goals are always down-to-earth, so no matter their means, their ends are always practical and constructive.

Capricorn is society's "elder." Goats are here to accept responsibility for helping others and building a society that meets the needs of the people. They also want to build something stable and enduring; after all, this sign is ruled by Saturn ♄, also known as Father Time.

Goats are meant to create a balance between conscientious nurturing and meeting the responsibilities of being the elders. People don't become elders when they're young, though, so Goats understand the patience required to learn what's important.

The Tenth Zodiac Sign

Capricorn, the Goat ♑	December 22 to January 21
Element	Earth
Quality	Cardinal
Energy	Yin
Ruler	Saturn ♄
Color	Brown
Gem	Garnet
Anatomy	Bones, joints, and knees
Keywords	Achievement, structure, organization
Archetypes	Father Time, Cronus, Nepali sherpas, Joan of Arc, Doctor Who
Celeb Goats	Greta Thunberg, Michelle Obama, Timothée Chalamet, Lin-Manuel Miranda, Zooey Deschanel, Emily Watson, Jude Law, David Bowie, Muhammad Ali, Martin Luther King Jr., Stephen Hawking
Goats Rising	Ariana Grande, Daniel Day-Lewis, Meg Ryan, Lorde, Dave Grohl, Roberto Benigni, Billie Jean King, F. Scott Fitzgerald, J. M. W. Turner
Tarot Suit	Pentacles
Tarot Major Arcana	15 The Devil, materialism, obsession; 21 The World, attainment, experience

The Best and Worst of Goats

It can be lonely at the top, but if Goats want to be there, they'll learn to live with solitude. At their best, Goats are ambitious, organized, efficient, and responsible, but they also can be cool, calculating, suspicious, and rigid. Though Goats can get a little heavy with the rest of the zodiac while thinking that all the other signs are not disciplined or structured enough, they are often hardest on themselves.

In the effort to achieve security, Goats might step on anything or anyone that stands in their way. But they can be surprisingly kind, too, especially to those who have done them favors or kindnesses. Goats are motivated by pride; they don't like to be beholden, and they'll repay favors generously.

Goats' practicality can be a welcome asset in the cold of winter: the logs will be stacked and ready next to the door, and the cupboard will be filled with all that's needed to get through the cold months. And Goats will surprise you, too, with their quiet, dry wit helping to pass the deep, dark winter nights.

Goats in Love

Goats seek their approval from the world at large, which might make personal relationships seem secondary to them, but after you discover Goats' dry sense of humor, you'll find a way to their hearts as well.

When you penetrate a Goat's icy reserve, you'll find the possibilities for deep love and strong loyalty. With their deepest feelings buried beneath the surface, Goats protect those they care for, and they'll stick around when the going gets tough.

Stability matters more to Goats than to any other sign, so when it comes to romance, they'll seek comfort over pleasure and longevity over romance. Goats do well with other Earth signs, but it is with Water signs that the best connections may occur. A nurturing Cancer ♋, passionate Scorpio ♏, or sympathetic Pisces ♓ might help a Goat grow in new ways.

It's cold at the start of winter, and Capricorn's a cold sign—cold and calculating. Unlike another climber, the Ram, the Goat's steps are slow and sure: Goats want to make sure they get where they're going, so they're careful to take their time. With their energy turned inward, toward self-control, Goats quietly and steadily work toward their goals. Because they are ruled by practical Saturn ♄, they're bound to get there, too.

The Healthy Goat

Goats can be pessimistic, and they need to beware of the melancholy that pessimism can bring. Goats need time to rest and retreat into quiet time. But cautious Goats often live long, long lives: Helena Rubinstein, Albert Schweitzer, and Carl Sandburg lived well into their 90s, for example. What seems to shorten Goats' lives most often is their potential power. After all, both Joan of Arc and Martin Luther King Jr. were Goats.

Many Goat afflictions are due to too much rigidity in their thinking or behavior. The difficulty of representing tradition is getting too rigid about representing tradition. Eventually, this can translate into arthritis or rheumatism.

As for vitamins, goats need calcium (what else?). They need calcium to build those bones and teeth, as well as to keep their nerves under control. Goats also need plenty of vitamin C, which is necessary for healthy skin, ligaments, bones, teeth, and gums. And they need to get enough vitamin D and magnesium for utilizing the calcium to build their bones.

Capricorn rules the skeleton, bones, and teeth—all the structural aspects of the body that Goats are associated with. For this reason, alternative therapies that deal with the structure of the body, such as chiropractic therapy or Feldenkrais (a form of structural and physical therapy), are very appropriate for Goats.

Goats at Home

Our favorite Goats seem to understand the importance of a place of their own—a quiet, private retreat from all the trappings that can come with power. Here, they'll have their favorite music playing, their favorite pictures on the walls, and their favorite books stacked up next to their favorite chair.

Like all Earth signs, Goats appreciate the comforts of home, but they're more likely to use it as a getaway than a base of operations. Goats know the importance of strong foundations, and their home will be warm and secure, a haven from those cold winter storms.

Have you heard the one about Cronus (another name for Saturn ♄, Capricorn's ♑ ruler), who ate his children because he was certain one of them was going to overthrow him? Talk about being rigid and sticking to tradition! Fortunately, his wife substituted a rock for one of the kids, who just happened to be Zeus, also known as Jupiter. Jupiter later went on to lead his brothers and sisters, who were freed (alive) from their father's stomach, in what seems to be a justified revolt against their father.

Goats at Work

Goats like to be in charge, and if they don't start there, it's usually where they'll end up. Rags-to-riches Goats abound in history, such as Howard Hughes and Aristotle Onassis, as well as powerful Goats, such as Mao Tse-tung and Joseph Stalin. As today's social media influencers, Goats are most likely to be the gatekeepers to valuable content. Goats know that information is currency in the twentieth century, just as knowledge has always been power. Depend on Goats to show the way to the highest guarded treasure of all in contemporary culture—access.

The older Goats get, the more rewarding their lives are likely to become. After they've achieved the power they've sought, they can relax with the wisdom they've gained and the lessons they can share with others. Many Goats live long lives as writers or artists, including J. R. R. Tolkien, Alfred Stieglitz, and Anton Chekhov. And Goats are found in business, where there are a lot of mountains to climb. As Goats are very achievement-oriented, you'll find them at the tops of many fields—and mountains.

More presidents of the United States have been born with their Sun ☉ or Moon ☽ in Capricorn ♑ than any other sign. Why? Because Goats' ambitions, shrewdness, and slow, steady movement toward their goals are just what are required for executive positions. Goats aspire to the top spot, and they get there, too!

Goats and Their Money

Goats understand the power that can come with money, and, as a cardinal sign, they're likely to do things with investments to turn them into even more value: buying, selling, and making deals. Goats use their money to attain and maintain power. Money means control to a Goat, and control and power are Goats' driving forces. They also are generous with their money when they have it, but the generosity is tied to their power and prestige. Goats truly understand the phrase "Money talks." Goats are good at creating value, which can mean many things, from starting a company and building it into a global powerhouse to investing in alternative currencies, such as Bitcoin.

Goat Rising: The Capricorn ♑ Ascendant

Rising Goats are learning about what it means to be responsible for not just themselves but others, too. Part of this is learning the rules, and part is being available to help others. The tough side is that Rising Goats might begin to believe they are responsible for *all* the problems around them (rather like a scapegoat!) and that they must carry the burden for others.

Rising Goats can be worriers. They'll worry about what's going wrong in their youth, what can go wrong in their middle age, and death in their old age. And they can tend to be quiet and reserved, though this often masks an active mind and tremendous willpower. It's often hard for Rising Goats to show their feelings; their mask of reserve might be doubly thick because Capricorn ♑ is a naturally quiet sign. What you'll find on the surface with a Rising Goat is a need for order, a constant checking of the details to make sure everything is going smoothly. You'll also find that they also have a sometimes obsessive certainty that things are not going smoothly.

Rising Goats may remind other less practical signs that they need to attend to what matters, so Goats sometimes seem to be "wet blankets." But underneath all this careful planning, you may find someone who's a whole lot of fun.

Goat in Partnership: The Capricorn ♑ Descendant

Descending Goats take a cautious, serious, and practical approach to picking partners. The descending Goat observes his or her prospective partner to decide whether he or she can remain loyal to the relationship and prosper from the partnership. Partnership, personal or professional, is serious business for a Capricorn ♑ descendant. If you are the one who wants to be that partner, you might think, you should send in your résumé!

Aquarius ♒: The Quiet Revolutionaries

Aquarius ♒, the Water Bearer, is where you'll find the zodiac's eccentric individualists and crazy inventors. Anything out of the ordinary interests this independent sign, and Water Bearers are often trend-spotters and trendsetters (or, in modern parlance, disrupters). Count on Aquarius to throw the world up in the air because the impossible simply doesn't exist for Aquarius! You never know what new invention a Water Bearer will bring to us. Aquarius is the futurist of the zodiac, the eccentric inventor always thinking up new possibilities.

Water Bearers' fixed Air represents persistent development of the intellect through communication, and their planetary influence, Uranus ♅, means they'll be committed to innovation and change. Aquarians will often be progressive and open-minded, but that fixed quality means they'll often be fixed in their opinions as well.

Most Water Bearers find Earth to be a very dense place. Most of them are 50 years or more ahead of their time, and talking to the rest of us can seem like a difficult and laborious process. Aquarians often feel like they're visiting from another planet because their ideas are so advanced. Trouble is, sometimes they forget their missions after they get here and find out how dense this place really is.

So, why is it that Aquarius, the Water Bearer, is an Air sign, not a Water sign? Good question. But look at this sign's symbol, ♒, to find your answer. This water is in the form of waves, caused by wind: the motion of air on water. These wavy lines also represent the serpents of knowledge, which are the parts of the body ruled by Aquarius (ankles and circulatory system) and lightning that cleans air and leaves that "ozone buzz." You can be sure that Aquarians are in tune with the mysterious "global Hum" phenomenon. Remember that the "Water Bearer" name doesn't refer to the water itself, but to its carrier: Aquarius is the "water bearer," the most human of the signs.

Water Bearers will do anything to avoid boredom, and they care little for what others think, especially after they've determined their own particular cause. Water Bearers firmly believe that change is good, and innovation can lead to enduring transformation.

Water Bearers bear the standard as the embodiment of innovation to address climate change. The Water Bearer's ambition is for understanding humankind's place in the Universe as well as humanity's duty of care here on Earth. You'll find that some of the great progressive thinkers are Water Bearers, including Galileo, Charles Darwin, Abraham Lincoln, Thomas Edison, and Franklin Delano Roosevelt. Aquarius has a genuine belief (and goal) that everyone can have their needs met, including Mother Earth.

The Eleventh Zodiac Sign

Aquarius, the Water Bearer ≈	January 21 to February 19
Element	Air
Quality	Fixed
Energy	Yang
Rulers	Uranus ♅ and Saturn ♄
Color	Violet
Gem	Amethyst
Anatomy	Ankles and circulation
Keywords	Humanitarian, unique, revolutionary
Archetypes	Gaia, Earth Mother, *Star Trek*'s Spock, Glinda from *The Wizard of Oz*
Celeb Water Bearers	Jennifer Aniston, Ed Sheeran, Oprah Winfrey, Ellen DeGeneres, Chris Rock, Yoko Ono, Jackson Pollock, Virginia Woolf, Chuck Yeager, Charles Dickens
Water Bearers Rising	J.K. Rowling, Michael J. Fox, Whoopi Goldberg, Bob Fosse, William Butler Yeats, Auguste Renoir
Tarot Suit	Swords
Tarot Major Arcana	17 The Star, hope and faith, inspiration, the water bearer

The Best and Worst of Water Bearers

Idealistic, inventive, and original, Water Bearers can all too easily seem aloof, detached, or just plain cranky. Water Bearers' tendency to go against the grain can separate them from other people, even the more abstract "humanity" they are trying to help.

More than any other sign, Water Bearers have a human connection, and they seek to bring all humans together without regard for any of the imaginary divisions humans themselves have created. This same disregard for human difference, though, might leave Water Bearers without any close relationships. Have you ever heard the line, "I love humankind. It's people I can't stand"? It's likely this meme was first expressed by an Aquarian.

Water Bearers' strongest trait is their intellectual independence, their refusal to be pigeonholed. Water Bearers really do hear a "different drummer," and it may even be they who are playing those drums. They can be radicals, renegades, or bohemians, too, but depending on other factors in their birth charts, this might not be obvious. Water Bearers can look perfectly normal yet have very different ideas. So, even though they might pass for one of us, they don't *feel* like us.

It's almost as though Water Bearers are aliens from another star system, living in human bodies. They often experiment with or observe friends, mates, or partners, just to see what they will do under a particular set of circumstances, and they can be very detached about this process—although the results might be enough to keep them interested in a person!

There's a lot of disagreement about just when the Age of Aquarius will or did begin. But we are agreed on what the Age of Aquarius means, and you'll see a lot of those same traits in an Aquarian person: tolerance, independence, progressiveness, and altruism. The Aquarian Age heralds important leaps in science and technology, logical progressions, and greater global connections. Does this sound familiar? It should because many believe the Age of Aquarius has already begun.

Water Bearers in Love

Independent Water Bearers need partners who understand their independence and who won't feel threatened by it, and in return they'll offer their partners the same kind of freedom. With the right partner, Water Bearers will be constant and true. Remember, Aquarius is a fixed sign, meaning Water Bearers are reluctant to change after establishing what they consider to be the right path.

Some Water Bearers may sacrifice personal relationships to pursue a greater good, and some may seem aloof even in the best of relationships. Sometimes Water Bearers' relationships themselves will become laboratories for their creativity, as they did in the cases of James Joyce, Federico Fellini, Gertrude Stein, and W. Somerset Maugham. Water Bearers are always seeking what's best for humankind, and they can sometimes lose sight of individual humans in the process.

Air signs—Gemini ♊, Libra ♎, other Aquarians ♒—will naturally combine well with Aquarius, but pay attention to the fire-feeding capabilities of air, too. The innovation of a Water Bearer might be just what Aries ♈, Leo ♌, or Sagittarius ♐ needs for some mutual excitement.

The Healthy Water Bearer

The ankles and the circulatory system are ruled by Aquarius ♒. The ankles support our ability to stand, and circulation is the movement of our very lifeblood through our bodies. Water Bearers are the very essence of human existence, and it's important they don't allow their tendency to think and see globally to make them lose sight of these areas closer to home.

Vitamins and, of course, eating right can keep Water Bearers at their fittest. Water Bearers need magnesium—and plenty of it—in their diets to keep their circulation and heart (Leo is their opposite) in good shape. Magnesium also is needed for the electrical charges that move nutrients in and out of cells, as well as for absorbing and using vitamins and minerals.

Water Bearers might heal well with acupuncture or chiropractic care because Saturn ♄ is their co-ruler and these healing techniques deal with the nervous system and their energy. Exercise also plays an important role; with their heads in the clouds, Water Bearers might forget that they have bodies to take care of as well!

Water Bearers hold the mind and spirit in high esteem, but they also need to pay attention to what connects them to the rest of humanity and to keep their lifeblood circulating freely.

Water Bearers at Home

A Water Bearer's home is the world, and they populate that world with a variety of people, especially the unusual, the eccentric, and those who are just plain different. "Live and let live" is a Water Bearer motto, and they'll open their doors to anyone who needs their shelter. Water Bearers believe they can change people's lives just by being a part of them, and if their homes sometimes resemble Noah's Arks of humanity, it's no coincidence.

Even though they may seem aloof, Water Bearers' individual goals are always based on a greater good. This holds true at home, too. Altruistic and giving, Water Bearers share their homes with all. Water Bearers realize an essential human truth, which is that each human being holds the birthright to Mother Earth. A curiosity about the Earth and humankind's home on it leads Water Bearers to pursue life-nurturing goals. Water Bearers understand that human life depends on Mother Earth. As humanity evolves through technological and genetic discoveries, the human body will become an evolving life form. Expect Water Bearers to be at the forefront of research into what it means to be human, both in body and mind.

Water Bearers at Work

Clever, original Water Bearers can excel in any profession in which creativity is a plus. This isn't limited just to the arts, either; this can extend to scientific innovation and invention, to public service or civil rights reform, and even to owning their own businesses or marketing someone else's unique ideas. Water Bearers may rent out a room in their home as an Airbnb, walk dogs, design websites, deliver groceries, or drive Ubers. They'll thrive in the gig economy and will use their positions to nurture compassion by helping others. Many also work in broadcast media.

Water Bearers understand that the future is where innovation lies, and their careers often lead others toward that future. Charles Lindbergh was a Water Bearer, for example, as was Ronald Reagan. Also, Water Bearers may be geniuses within their chosen fields, like golfer Jack Nicklaus or dancer Mikhail Baryshnikov.

Water Bearers can be revolutionaries, sometimes associated with actual government revolutions, like Boris Yeltsin and Angela Davis. They're often associated with ideas, causes, or inventions that eventually revolutionize the world.

But no matter where they work, you can count on Water Bearers to be the ones at the cutting edge, the ones with ideas, and the ones with creative solutions to problems, such as the extreme weather patterns of climate change, which many believe insoluble.

Water Bearers and Their Money

Water Bearers are givers rather than keepers, and with their vision focused on the future, they're not likely to concern themselves with the here and now. This can translate into a disregard for money, including a tendency to go beyond their budgets or overextend themselves in other ways.

With their vision for the future, though, Water Bearers can potentially do well in speculative ventures, especially in areas that will use new technology. Well-selected investments in these areas now can protect Water Bearers who are moving into their more uncertain futures. Water Bearers of all nationalities and socioeconomic statuses often benefit from innovative sources of funding, such as crowdsourcing, microlending, and alternative currencies.

Water Bearer Rising: The Aquarius ≈ Ascendant

Rising Water Bearers appear to be forward thinking and progressive, friendly, and open to new ideas, but they also may be intolerant of others' shortcomings and quite sarcastic. Rising Water Bearers are full of contradictions: they love to travel, and they love to stay at home; they're friendly and outgoing, and they're moody and aloof. Mindwise, they can be both scientific and artistic, and they might be involved in two very separate areas of work. No matter what the challenge, Water Bearer Rising always goes forth with a spirit of adventure. They might forsake human connections for ideas, but they are always on the forefront.

Rising Water Bearers are magnetic—this sign is associated with electricity—so people with this Rising sign appear unusual in some way and attract many people to them. This is often the ascendant of celebrities or people who work in broadcasting. David Bowie, for example, has Aquarius Rising, as do Michael J. Fox and Alice Munro. They're on Earth to learn how to detach from the physical and emotional planes so they can focus on spirit and the higher planes.

Water Bearer in Partnership: The Aquarius ≈ Descendant

The Water Bearer descending takes an easygoing, friendship-first approach to all forms of partnership. For the Water Bearer descending, friendship is the foundation for marriage as well as business relationships. But don't try to tie down Water Bearer descending—that's the surest way to send them looking in other directions. Aquarius ≈ descendant seeks the unusual, the nontraditional, and the creative when it comes to partnerships of any kind, from embracing blended families to seeking unlikely (and so perfect) business alliances. Water Bearer descending will be a champion of human rights, dignity, and basic equality among all human beings.

Pisces ♓: How Deep Is the Ocean?

Water is mutable, meaning it can exist as solid ice, as liquid, or as a gas (vapor). This is the character of Pisces ♓, the Fishes, who changes according to outside conditions. Pisces has the ability to match its nature to what the surrounding conditions demand—becoming the rigid molecular lattice structure of ice, the flow of water that will find its way, or the wisp of water vapor that humidifies the room. Metaphorically speaking, of course. And yet Fishes retreat to live largely in the world of their imagination, the realm of dreams, where objects and events seem to have no connection to outer reality. What's going on here?

This last sign of the zodiac is truly Universal. Pisces nature creates the possibility to move beyond self into transcendence—what others understand as the world of dreams and faith. Pisces can follow its karma to evolve as a bodhisattva, bound for enlightenment. But this also can evolve as a world of sheer escapism, a false enlightenment where dreaming is done for its own sake, and addictions can take hold. Fishes, we could say, can either sink or swim.

Put another way, Fishes know which way the river is running and might swim with it or against it. Swimming against it can mean that they might find a way to another stream ("hooked" Fishes can channel their addictions, for example), while swimming with it might mean, quite literally, "going with the flow" and living intuitively.

Fishes are highly intuitive, and Pisces is the sign that merges with others so easily that these people don't always know what's theirs and what belongs to someone else. As the last sign of the zodiac, Pisces carries the knowledge of the preceding 11 signs, knowing and understanding the light, dark, and shadowy in-betweens of human nature. Fishes are frequently so sensitive to the vibrations of others that they can walk into a room and instantly feel how others are doing. Unfortunately, they also might unconsciously take responsibility for how others are doing or wonder why others feel so bad—especially when Fishes woke up feeling so good!

For this reason, Fishes can have a hard time maintaining boundaries and knowing what *they're* feeling, as opposed to what others are feeling. The reason for this boundary stuff goes back to the main point of Pisces, which is to merge with others and, eventually, the Source or God. Fishes are in a highly spiritual sign, living in a very nonspiritual world. For this reason, it's easy for Fishes to swim off-course by merging with the wrong people and abandon their true spiritual focus.

Above all, Fishes are here to give their help, love, and whatever else is needed—not just to those like themselves, but to anyone in need. Pisces want to heal and will sacrifice for the greater good of their families, communities, countries, and humanity.

True to the Piscean paradox, here's a symbol ♓ with multiple meanings:

* Two fishes tied together

* A picture of the human feet, which Pisces rules

* Two crescent moons connected by a straight line—emotion and higher consciousness tied down to the material world

No wonder Fishes so often feel misunderstood and yet have so many possibilities. Even their symbol is all-encompassing! Pisces is associated with baptism, spiritual cleansing, and renewal. Venus ♀ is "exalted" here, which means that the love and beauty she rules are of a Universal rather than a personal nature. Fishes are a symbol of divine purity; the birth of Christ is associated with the beginning of the Age of Pisces.

The Twelfth Zodiac Sign

Pisces, the Fishes ♓	February 19 to March 21
Element	Water
Quality	Mutable
Energy	Yin
Rulers	Neptune ♆ and Jupiter ♃
Color	Sea-green
Gem	Aquamarine
Anatomy	Feet, immune system, hormonal system
Keywords	Compassion, universality, inclusiveness
Archetypes	Empath Mantis from *Guardians of the Galaxy*, Buddhist goddess Kwan Yin, fairy godmothers (and godfathers, too)
Celeb Fishes	Rihanna, Chelsea Clinton, Rachel Weisz, William Hurt, Frank Gehry, Mikhail Gorbachev, Steve Jobs, Albert Einstein, Galileo
Fishes Rising	Gwyneth Paltrow, George Clooney, Laura Dern, Ryan Gosling, Robert Redford, Richard Pryor, Yogi Berra
Tarot Suit	Cups
Tarot Major Arcana	18 The Moon, unconscious knowledge, deep emotions

The Best and Worst of Fishes

Compassionate Fishes can see deep into the human psyche, probe the depths of emotions, lend a sympathetic ear, or play an intuitive gambit. But they can also be oh-so-sad, shy, timid, or just plain impractical. Fishes can seem both lazy and overtalkative, seeming to muse on and on about any number of possible scenarios.

But Fishes can be changeable, too, and change can be good because it means adaptability. Pisces Fishes can seem to be swimming both with and against the current at the same time, and they do possess this remarkable ability. Because of their extraordinary sensitivity, Fishes are often creative artistically, and their understanding of people sometimes seems limitless (though the understanding doesn't always extend to themselves).

Pisces ♓ is the sign that represents spirituality (not religion, like Sagittarius ♐), a true need to have a relationship with the divine. When these spiritual needs aren't fulfilled, Fishes can become involved in the negative side of this energy, which is escapism. That's where the drug, alcohol, or sugar addictions come in, as well as the wrong people.

Fishes need to learn to live by faith and intuition: When they do this, they're on the right course. Physicist and mathematician Galileo was a Pisces, and his theories were "inconvenient" but correct. After recanting to the Spanish Inquisition his assertion that the Earth revolves around the Sun, Galileo famously added *"E pur si muove"…and yet it moves*. Does the Universe need dreamers who can transcend the boundaries of reality as it is currently understood in its time? And does that make those people impractical? Or are they just different from the rest of us?

Fishes in Love

Kind, perceptive, sensitive Fishes look at the inner soul of others and at the essence rather than the surface. Fishes are truly seeking their soul mates, the most profound love possible, and so they might be disappointed when real people fail to live up to their idealistic expectations.

Fishes in love can create an enchanting place where love happens, a space separate from the rest of the world for Fishes and their loved ones alone. You'll always know when you're the object of Fishes' empathetic affection.

Water, water, water. Of course, Fishes will do well with Cancers ♋, Scorpios ♏, and other Pisces ♓. But here's a sign in which empathy can go far—if Fishes are careful. More flighty signs like Gemini ♊, Libra ♎, and Aquarius ♎ may leave Fishes swimming in their wake—or raise them to new heights of awareness.

Spiritual Fishes can be drawn to Virgo's love of sacred patterns, and even appreciate Virgo's detail-driven worldview. (Pisces love a good plan!) Fishes can do especially well with nurturing Earth signs, and Earth signs' practicality can also keep Fishes' tendency toward flights of fancy a little more rooted. As in all areas, though, Fishes need to beware of those who would take advantage of them. They're quick to trust, and all too easily hurt. Impressionable Fishes can fall for just about any hard-luck story; dreamers themselves, they can easily get caught up in the dreams of others as well. Fishes can tend toward addiction, too. Sometimes, their lives can seem filled with trouble.

Healthy Fishes

Fishes can tend to overindulge and need to be careful to limit their intake of everything from bread to wine. Fishes may be overweight or have a tendency to retain water. Pisces rules the feet, and Fishes should take particular care to avoid sprains or even breaks to that sensitive area.

Fishes don't always take care of themselves as well as they do others, but one way to start is through a holistic fitness regimen that takes into account both body and soul. One vitamin that can help Fishes feel their best is pantothenic acid, which helps stimulate their adrenal glands and strengthen their immune systems. Because Pisces appears to rule the immune system, all aids to this system—such as astragalus or echinacea herbs—are helpful for Fishes.

Pisces also seems to be in charge of hormones, so keeping them in balance is very important. Fishes are very sensitive to foods and poisons in their environment, and they might need to be detoxified more frequently than any other sign. Alcohol and drugs are very difficult for them to process. Even prescription drugs can wreak havoc on their systems, so it's very important for Fishes to watch their intake and notice the changes in their bodies.

Fishes at Home

Fishes use their homes as places for spiritual renewal—or spiritual abuse. Just as they might swim with or against the current, they might use their homes as refuges or dens of iniquity, and the choices they make will spill over into other areas of their life.

If Fishes find true love, they're more likely to create a home as a refuge, and Fishes would do well to create their own hidden cave, a place to renew themselves, to meditate, and to be introspective. Retreat can bring healthy renewal.

Fishes are often keen readers of novels and poems, curled up in a favorite reading chair in their home library. Fishes' intuition and passion lead them to seek out the imaginative worlds created by great books. Books can represent both refuge and escape to Pisces readers. Pisces will tend to think in metaphors and take existential worldviews. Pisces can make passionate arguments for reading in both print and electronic media, swimming in both directions, as usual.

Fishes at Work

Because Fishes love to combine their real life with their imaginary one, they can often be found in the world of theater or film, or in any of the arts. But they also can do quite well in business or even politics, where their sensitivity can give them powerful insights that less-intuitive signs might miss.

Fishes like to work behind the scenes or alone. Fame and recognition aren't what drive them. Because of this, Fishes can be great manipulators or builders, or they may be photographers, beautifully capturing others' spirits on film.

Fishes often channel their imagination and creativity into the arts. The great Italian Renaissance artist Michelangelo Buonarroti was a Pisces, and so were French Impressionist painter Auguste Renoir and Polish Romantic composer Frederic Chopin. Fishes do best when they believe in themselves and their dreams the same way they believe in others' dreams—but this isn't always an easy task.

Fishes are often found, too, in areas where their capabilities for the spiritual can be used. They may be astrologers or monks, poets, religious leaders, or healers. Fishes are known for their ability to sacrifice themselves for others.

Pisces also deals with images, so these people are gifted at leading others through visualization experiences and meditations and bringing people to a higher level of awareness and consciousness. Above all, Fishes are here to help the rest of us transcend our normal ruts, beliefs, and boundaries, and they can help us see the illusions we live under.

Fishes and Their Money

Here again, Fishes need to be wary of others' stories. They're all too easily convinced to hand over their life savings to help a friend (or anyone) they think is in need. Money can swim in and out of Fishes' lives as mysteriously as everything and everyone else does, and impractical Fishes don't always understand why.

Because they're not really prone to moneymaking enterprises themselves, Fishes' money might come from outside sources, and it might go back outside, too. Many Fishes work in the service sector, so they may not get the kind of money that business enterprises pay. But what Fishes *are* good at are the dreams where all good ideas—including potential moneymaking ones—begin. Here's a sign whose intuitive hunches are always worth pursuing.

Fishes Rising: The Pisces ♓ Ascendant

Rising Fishes want the world to appear ideal, and if it doesn't, they'll ignore anything that doesn't color the picture the way they want. They'll show endless goodwill toward others, often to their own detriment. Also, they often get caught up in pipe dreams and get-rich-quick schemes, both their own and others'. Rising Fishes need to learn about giving in a healthy way, including giving unconditional love to everyone—not just family, clan, tribe, or race.

Rising Fishes also are learning how to be in the flow of life instead of trying to control things. Quick to be sentimental, Rising Fishes will cry over anyone's spilled milk. Their bodies are basically one big antenna, catching all the pain and pleasure the world has to offer, and their moods will change as often as the tides—or even more often.

Fishes in Partnership: The Pisces ♓ Descendant

Fishes descending want partnerships based on devotion to shared beliefs about life, love, happiness, and commitment. The ideal partner for Fishes descending is a soul mate, someone who can complete the perfect union. When they find such partners, Pisces ♓ descendants are generous and forgiving, sometimes—to the eyes of others—to a fault. Fishes descending give a partner not one chance, but two (or three or four …) to recover from falls and shortcomings.

HEAVENLY BODIES

Planets rule! No, really, they do. Each sign has a planetary ruler—the energy behind the scenes. As the planets move through the zodiac, they visit other signs, too. Your birth chart captures what signs the planets are in at the moment of your birth.

The movements of the planets also affect you—and the world at large— throughout your life. Some influences are deeply personal, and others shape entire generations. Most of the time, the planets cruise through the zodiac in a forward direction. Now and again, though, a planet looks like it's moving backward instead. This is a retrograde ℞, and it has special meaning.

Part
3

Chapter 8

HOUSEKEEPING WITH THE PLANETS

Houses are the stages where the drama of your planets in their signs unfolds—the places where *who you are* is made visible by *what you do*. Think of the houses as the various places where you live your external life, just as your home, your office, your place of worship, and your car are some of the locations for your life. Some may be places you'd rather avoid, and some may be places you'd love to never leave, but each of them is very much a part of you.

The planets that appear in a house reflect tendencies toward unconscious choices. These tendencies offer opportunities for learning and growth. The planets that appear in your sixth house, for example, influence how you relate to your work environment and the kinds of jobs that best suit you. In addition, the planets in the sixth house influence how you approach your physical health and your daily responsibilities.

Lessons in Housekeeping

You will recall that each of the 12 houses encompasses a specific arena of life. Among the 12 houses are all the areas of experience any human will encounter, so *everything* in your life shows up in one of your houses—everything from early childhood to sex, death, and taxes! The first house is the pie slice just below your eastern horizon, and the other houses follow, counterclockwise, around your astrological birth chart. The dividing lines between the houses are called cusps. Each cusp begins a new house; think of them as doors into the houses.

The houses of your chart also represent the space above and below the horizon of your birth chart: half the sky is visible, and half of it isn't. Below the horizon are the six houses of *personal* development that aren't generally visible to others. The houses below the horizon represent your basic needs as an individual and how you deal with yourself and your core family. These include areas such as your personality, knowledge, possessions, earned income, home and roots, children and creativity, responsibilities to work and the way you serve others, and health.

Above the horizon are the six houses of your development in the larger world that others can more readily see. The houses above the horizon represent your development toward cooperating with others and with the extended family of your community. These include areas such as your relationships and partnerships, shared resources and money matters, social concerns and community contributions, career, goals, and your unconscious.

A House Is More Than a Home

Houses reveal *where* in our lives we have lessons to learn. For example, if you seem to have a pattern of picking the wrong type of friend or lover, you probably have a lesson related to your seventh house that you haven't quite mastered yet. Or if every time it seems you've finally settled down "for good," you find yourself suddenly up and moving again—or you find yourself couch-surfing—maybe you haven't quite resolved a home issue that would make your fourth house feel comfortable or stable.

Your first house is also called your ascendant house, so it is where we find the *you* that the world sees: your personality and your physical self.

Each house, just like each sign, also has a quality. The first house, for example, is also one of four *angular* houses (which correlate to the cardinal signs and are houses with the potential for dynamic action). The angular houses represent your strongest personal influences. The first house is your "identity project"; the fourth house is your "foundation or home project"; the seventh house is your "relationship project"; and the tenth house is your "social role or career project." The angular houses correlate to leadership. They correspond to the natural cardinal signs, which are Aries ♈, Cancer ♋, Libra ♎, and Capricorn ♑.

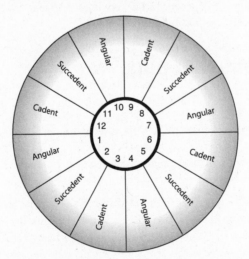

The cardinal houses represent personal influences, the succedent houses represent areas of personal stability, and the cadent houses represent social areas and higher purposes.

The Cardinal, or Angular, Houses

The First House	Physical self and personality, public persona
The Fourth House	Home and the foundation of your life, family ties
The Seventh House	Primary relationships, personal and business partners
The Tenth House	Reputation and career, community contributions and leadership

The second set of houses, called the *succedent* houses, corresponds to the natural fixed signs and represents the areas of your life concerned with resources: what you own, how you earn money, your creative capabilities, your shared resources, and the friends and groups that help you achieve your goals. The succedent houses correlate to individualism. The succedent houses are houses that give us stability and purpose. They're the second, fifth, eighth, and eleventh houses. They correspond to the natural fixed signs: Taurus ♉, Leo ♌, Scorpio ♏, and Aquarius ♒.

The Succedent Houses

The Second House	Possessions, self-esteem, earning abilities
The Fifth House	Creativity, children, risk-taking, romance
The Eighth House	Shared resources, taxes, insurance, intimate relationships, transformation
The Eleventh House	Groups you work with to achieve your goals and desires

The last set of houses corresponds to the mutable signs. These *cadent* houses are concerned with your human relationships and transitions; notice how each of these houses encompasses a much *wider* scope of activities than do the angular and succedent houses. The cadent houses correlate to flexibility and are the most adaptable. The third, sixth, ninth, and twelfth houses are cadent. They correspond to the natural mutable signs: Gemini ♊, Virgo ♍, Sagittarius ♐, and Pisces ♓.

The Cadent Houses

The Third House	Knowledge, short trips, siblings, local environment, neighbors
The Sixth House	Daily responsibilities, health, service to others, coworkers
The Ninth House	Social areas: higher education, philosophy, religion, law, travel, foreign concerns
The Twelfth House	Subconscious, the unknown

What's Behind Those Doors?

In addition to being divided by quality, houses are divided by Element. The following chart shows these divisions and their meanings.

Houses by Element

Fire: Houses of Personal Life	
First House	Body
Fifth House	Soul
Ninth House	Spirit, mind
Earth: Houses of Substance	
Second House	Possessions and earning abilities
Sixth House	Occupation and daily work
Tenth House	Reputation and social role
Air: Houses of Relationships	
Third House	Relationships we don't choose (siblings, neighbors)
Seventh House	Relationships we do choose (lovers, partners, friends)
Eleventh House	Relationships of shared interests
Water: Houses of Endings	
Fourth House	The end of the physical body
Eighth House	Liberation of the soul, death
Twelfth House	The results of the life we choose

Remembering these divisions also will help you to learn which area each house represents. Yes, we know: there's a *lot* to learn. Think of it as home schooling!

Star Gazing: Heavenly Bodies in Your Astrological Chart

Knowing which planets appear in which signs and in which houses begins to reveal your personal story. The following keywords will help you remember what's what among the heavenly bodies.

Heavenly Keywords

Signs	The way you do things	How
Planets	Energies; what you like to do	What
Houses	Areas of your life	Where

Here's an example: If you have Venus ♓ in Libra ♎ in your second house, what you own will be very attractive. You'll also count your ability to create harmonious relationships as one of your important talents.

Where Are the Heavenly Bodies?

Here, we've provided that terror-ific writer Stephen King's birth chart. In Chapter 3, we looked at Scarlett Johansson's birth chart to see what signs the planets appeared in. Now, with Stephen King, we're going to add the planets' houses as well. Here are King's planets in their signs and houses.

Stephen King's Planets in Their Signs and Houses

Planet	Symbol	Sign	Symbol	House
Sun	☉	Virgo	♍	Third
Moon	☽	Sagittarius	♐	Fifth
Mercury	☿	Libra	♎	Fourth
Venus	♀	Libra	♎	Third
Mars	♂	Cancer	♋	Twelfth
Jupiter	♃	Scorpio	♏	Fifth
Saturn	♄	Leo	♌	First
Uranus	♅	Gemini	♊	Eleventh
Neptune	♆	Libra	♎	Third
Pluto	♇	Leo	♌	First
South Node	☋	Scorpio	♏	Fifth
North Node	☊	Taurus	♉	Eleventh

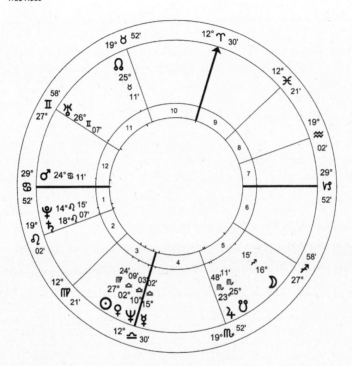

Stephen King
Natal Chart
Sep 21 1947
1:30 am EDT +4:00
Portland, ME
43°N39'41" 070°W15'21"
Geocentric
Tropical
Placidus
True Node

The Planets as Landlords

When a planet is the ruler of a particular sign, we think of it as the "landlord" who owns the house. It might help to actually think of these planets as the ones that are collecting the rent, making sure the plumbing works and the garden gets tended. We can then think of other planets that are within the house as the house's renters, or occupants.

Because landlord planets "own" the houses they're in charge of, they have the final say about what's happening in that area of your life. In other words, no matter which planets are "renting," or located in a house, the landlord is the one calling the shots.

Here's where we need to review the rulership of signs to determine the ruler of each house in your chart. We'll use Stephen King's chart to show you what we mean. And we've also provided you with a list of planetary rulers.

Natural Planetary Rulers

Planet	Sign(s) Ruled
Sun ☉	Leo ♌
Moon ☽	Cancer ♋
Mercury ☿	Gemini ♊, Virgo ♍
Venus ♀	Taurus ♉, Libra ♎
Mars ♂	Aries ♈, co-ruler of Scorpio ♏
Jupiter ♃	Sagittarius ♐, co-ruler of Pisces ♓
Saturn ♄	Capricorn ♑, co-ruler of Aquarius ♒
Uranus ♅	Aquarius ♒
Neptune ♆	Pisces ♓
Pluto ♇	Scorpio ♏, co-ruler of Aries ♈

King's Landlords

House	Sign on Cusp	Landlord(s) or Ruler(s)
First	Cancer ♋	Moon ☽
Second	Leo ♌	Sun ☉
Third	Virgo ♍	Mercury ☿
Fourth	Libra ♎	Venus ♀
Fifth	Scorpio ♏	Pluto ♇, Mars ♂
Sixth	Sagittarius ♐	Jupiter ♃
Seventh	Capricorn ♑	Saturn ♄
Eighth	Aquarius ♒	Uranus ♅, Saturn ♄
Ninth	Pisces ♓	Neptune ♆, Jupiter ♃
Tenth	Aries ♈	Mars ♂
Eleventh	Taurus ♉	Venus ♀
Twelfth	Gemini ♊	Mercury ☿

Remember, even if a house appears "empty" on a birth chart, it nonetheless has a landlord. The planets in any house are sort of "renting" the area, but the landlord has the final say about what goes on in that area of life. The exception to this is when a landlord actually occupies the house it rules; in that case, the landlord is not a renter. Instead, the landlord is an in-residence landlord. This means that it's going to be keeping a particularly close eye on what goes on in that house.

No matter where the landlord "lives," though, if the landlord is not in the house it rules, whatever is happening to the landlord affects the house it *owns* as well. We could say that the house is "owned" by an absentee landlord.

Let's use King's Capricorn ♑ on the seventh-house cusp as an example. Saturn ♄ would be the landlord here. Now, whatever sign the landlord is actually in will change the way it acts; in other words, the sign affects its style.

On King's chart, his Saturn ♄ is in Leo ♌ in the first house, indicating that although he's supremely self-assured, he also has a need for recognition that he can fulfill through self-discipline, organization, and persistence. Additionally, Saturn ♄ is next to his Pluto ♀, which is also in Leo ♌, providing plenty of independence to fulfill his special destiny.

This brief example begins to show you the interconnectivity of all areas of your life. Although you might have already intuitively "known" these things about yourself on some level, astrology charts them out for you in a way that's easy to locate. That's why we call your chart the heavenly map of you.

When Planets Seem Backward: Retrogrades ℞

When planets are *retrograde*, they appear from our vantage here on Earth to be moving backward; however, this is not actually so; planets can move in only one direction along their orbits. Think of it as that moment when you pass a car going in the same direction you are traveling, and the other car appears to be going backward. When this same thing happens to our earthly view of other planets—because each planet travels its orbit around the Sun at a different speed—we call it retrograde motion. The symbol to denote a retrograde planet on an astrological birth chart is ℞.

When you have retrograde planets in your birth chart, you need to pay special attention to those planets' energies. Chapter 12 is devoted to this concept.

Why Neptune ♆ and Pluto ♀ Are Special

Poky Neptune ♆ and Pluto ♀ are such "slow" planets from our earthly vantage point that they're called "generational" planets. A whole generation usually has these planets in the same sign, and they apply to the collective.

Right now, Pluto is on the "fast" part of its cycle: It's taking "only" about 11 years to get through a sign! At its slowest, Pluto takes about *30* years (speed is relative, after all), which might help explain why time seems sped up these days. Neptune also takes a while to go through one sign—about 14 years—so it's called a generational planet, too.

Both Neptune and Pluto are "late" discoveries. Three planets were discovered relatively recently: Uranus ♅ was first noted in 1781, Neptune ♆ in 1846, and Pluto ♇ in 1930. Naturally, modern astrologers have had to study these new discoveries to find how they fit into the larger scheme of the Universe.

With new technologies such as long-range telescopes and camera-equipped space probes, astronomers have recently made many discoveries about our solar system. One result: in 2006, after decades of debate, astronomers crafted a new definition of *planet* that saw Pluto ♇ reclassified as a dwarf planet. However, the designation has proved controversial, and many researchers continue to believe Pluto should be considered a planet once more. In 2019, the NASA Administrator declared in a speech to much applause that Pluto should be upgraded to planet status based on its buried oceans, moons, and multilayered atmosphere. As our understanding of the nature of heavenly bodies evolves, so too does our understanding of their energies. The meaning of Pluto's astrological characteristics has only deepened with discoveries of its properties and nature. Astrologers continue to classify Pluto as a planet.

The discovery of a new planet reflects a major change in consciousness on Earth. Discovering a new planet is like discovering something new about ourselves and our society. In studying these most recently discovered planets, astrologers have learned that Uranus is associated with scientific invention and innovative ideas, as well as revolutions; Neptune is connected to film, psychic abilities, and psychology; Pluto is aligned with both atomic energy and the collective emerging unconscious.

Discovering New Energies

There's a correlation between a planet's first discovery and concurrent scientific discoveries connected with that planet's energies. For example, there was no psychology at all until Neptune was discovered in 1846—and then Freud unlocked the subconscious. And we had to wait for Pluto's "discovery" in 1930 to unlock the secrets of nuclear power. Because Neptune and Pluto move so slowly, we only look at each of them in the signs for people who are (or soon will be) alive now, approximately a 100-year span, more or less.

As humanity's reach through science becomes greater and we see further into the Universe, astrologers may need to expand their understanding and add new classifications to its method for casting and interpreting birth charts. For example, in Appendix B, you'll learn about the influence of asteroids and comets. What other heavenly bodies might be important for understanding astrology's map of the heavens that is your birth chart? It may take future generations to redefine the influence of astrology's signs, planets, and houses and to designate new influences affecting humankind's understanding of itself and its place in the Universe. As the Universe expands, why shouldn't our collective understanding?

Chapter 9

WHO YOU ARE: SUN ☉, MOON ☽, MERCURY ☿, VENUS ♀, AND MARS ♂

Do you have your birth chart? You'll want to have it in hand as you read these next chapters so that you know the locations of the planets in your chart. If you don't have a birth chart (also called a natal chart) yet, remember you can generate one online, or consider getting a chart from a professional astrologer at a nearby metaphysical bookstore or an online astrology site (and maybe a professional chart reading, too?).

In this chapter, we look at the *luminaries* and the *personal* planets, which reveal the behavior and characteristics that make you unique. The luminaries, the Sun ☉ and the Moon ☽, are so named because they are the planets that provide light to us here on Earth. The personal planets and the luminaries are focal points of the energy that is *you*. They reflect and reveal your personal tendencies—who you are and how you relate to the world around you. The personal planets are Mercury ☿, Venus ♀, and Mars ♂.

Lighting Your Way: The Luminaries

The luminaries are the heavenly bodies of light, the Sun ☉ and the Moon ☽. The Sun represents your ego, your soul, the outer you. The Moon represents your emotions, your feelings, and the inner you. The luminaries are stronger and more influential than any other planet or point in your natal chart.

The Sun ☉: Here Comes the Sun King

As the central, life-giving force of our solar system, the Sun naturally plays an important role in what you are like, describing the nature of your individual approach to life itself. When you ask people what their sign is, the answer will be the Sun ☉ sign.

Whether you are male or female, the Sun represents masculine, or yang, energy. The Sun is your will and your ego. It characterizes your sense of purpose, creativity, and willpower, and it characterizes how you develop consciousness. It also begins to answer the question, "Who am I?" But there's a whole lot more to you than your senses of self and purpose, right? As you can see by now, your Sun sign is only the beginning.

For more information about the specific possibilities of the Sun in each zodiac sign, you should refer to the detailed Sun sign profiles in Chapters 4 through 7. But for information on other dimensions of yourself and that "whole lot more," keep reading.

Grandmother Moon ☽

The Moon is the third part of what could be called the most important triangle of astrology: the combination of Sun ☉ sign, ascendant, and Moon ☽ sign. We explored these in the birth chart of Scarlett Johansson in Chapter 3, "Your Birth Chart Deconstructed." Grandmother Moon, the body closest to Mother Earth in the sky, represents what could be called your feminine side— and the Moon has four primary phases, each one representing a different aspect of the feminine nature. The Moon's phases consist of the New Moon, Waxing Moon (First Quarter), Full Moon, and Waning Moon (Third Quarter). But there are also Dark Moons and Blue Moons to consider! Native Americans revered Grandmother Moon and her cycles as the leader of feminine life, the beating heart of Mother Earth, and the Source of intuitive knowledge.

The phases of the Moon ☽. In Greek tradition, the Moon, who was called Selene, fell so in love with a beautiful young man named Endymion that she chose him to lie beside her for eternity. The legend goes that Endymion sleeps forever unconscious, the stuff of dreams and the natural territory of the Moon.

* The early crescent, or New Moon, is the young maiden—also represented by Taurus ♉—and its corresponding myth is Diana the Hunter with her bow. This Moon enjoys all the possibilities before her. She is about initiation and incubation, the planting of ideas, thoughts, and feelings.

* The Waxing, First Quarter Moon represents a young woman just ready to flower, including the mythical Persephone, who's spirited away by Hades at the height of her beauty because he can't resist her. This Moon is associated with Aries ♈, the first sign of the zodiac. She manifests those ideas and thoughts, and she applies action to move them toward fruition. Then there's the Full Moon, the mother who is pregnant and full with her baby and who then gives birth. This Moon is associated with Cancer ♋ and the fertility goddesses. Many believe that all sorts of odd human behaviors are due to the Full Moon, and many legends have grown from that belief. This Moon heightens emotions and intensifies intuition. (Think of howling at the Moon as one example.)

* What's a Blue Moon? And why do things happen only "once in a Blue Moon"? Well, there are usually 13 Full Moons each year, and, although the lunar cycle is about 29½ days, months are anywhere from 28 to 31 days. Once in a Blue Moon, there are two Full Moons during one month, and that second Full Moon is called the Blue Moon.

* Next, there's the Waning or Third Quarter Moon, associated with Virgo ♍, the Earth Goddess, who is responsible for the harvest. This Moon represents the mature woman who must release her children (like Demeter and her daughter, Persephone, or the Virgin Mary and Christ) so they can fulfill their destinies.

* The Dark Moon is associated with the old crone, the wise woman. This is also Scorpio ♏, or Hecate, who has knowledge of healing and other ancient wisdom and who mourns for the loss of her child. This Moon is about wisdom and acceptance and the completion of karmic lessons. The old ends here.

The Moon is the main model for all the feminine energies and roles, whether you are male or female. The Moon is the planet of giving nourishment. She is the bonding planet between family members, mother and child, and lovers or partners.

In the past, people knew their Moon ☽ sign instead of their Sun ☉ sign because the Moon was considered more important. Because our Western society prefers to emphasize the more "masculine" characteristics of individuality, achievement, and goals, the Sun sign is now considered more important. Although women tend to express their Moons more directly, men often project their Moons through the women in their lives: mothers, lovers, or wives, for example. The Moon also represents the nurturing person who raised you.

Your Moon ☽ is your emotional self, your feelings, and your intuition. On your birth chart, the sign where your Moon ☽ is placed reveals your emotional nature, memories, habits, and patterns, especially your unconscious patterns. The Moon reveals the intuitive side of your nature and your ability to connect to your "gut feelings" about any issue at hand. The Moon is also associated with dreams and premonitions.

The Moon's light is not its own, but is reflected from the Sun, and the emotions the Moon rules can change as quickly as that moonlight. Your Moon, in other words, illuminates how you feel.

The Moon ☽ in Each Zodiac Sign

The Moon ☽ moves very fast (about 12 degrees per day), so on the days when the Moon changes signs, your Moon could either be in the sign the Moon was in the previous day, or it could be in the new sign. Your birth chart should show the correct Moon ☽ placement, but if the birth time you used for the chart calculations is off even a little, your Moon ☽ might be incorrect. For this reason, if the description of the Moon sign that appears here doesn't seem quite right to you, read the descriptions before and after it to see if your Moon may actually be in a different sign.

Moon in Aries ☽♈

An Aries Moon indicates directness and spontaneity, an emotional nature that is energetic and sometimes excitable, and a person who is both daring and independent. People with an Aries Moon won't be long on patience as a rule, but they will have a knack for getting others to do what they want. Self-confident in love, they'll have little use for shrinking violets or those who seem to hesitate. Life for a person with an Aries Moon might hide a sense of insecurity, but it's also a life that is always moving forward. More than any other sign, Aries feels with its *head*.

Moon in Aries ☽♈ Notables: Zandaya, Daniel Radcliffe, Jane Campion, Daniel Day-Lewis, and Jacqueline Kennedy Onassis

Moon in Taurus ☽♉

In the stable sign of Taurus, the Moon is at its best: its emotional nature is trustworthy, warm, and affectionate. It may take a Taurus Moon a while to make up its mind, but once it does, nothing will make it change. People with a Taurus Moon marry for life. Taurus's Venus ♀ ruler is manifested here as a love of beauty, and people with a Taurus Moon are artistic and romantic, and they have a great love of creature comforts. The downside is that a Taurus Moon can be rigid or obstinate (remember, Taurus is a bull) because, above all, it needs to feel stable, safe, and secure. But Taurus feels with its *senses*, making this a steady and reliable Moon sign overall.

Moon in Taurus ☽♉ Notables: Sergey Brin, Saoirse Ronan, Oona Chaplin, Christian Bale, and Marcel Proust

Moon in Gemini ☽♊

Mutable Gemini makes for a restless and erratic Moon, but this Moon sign also is marked by a lively, inquisitive, and emotional nature that is quick to laugh and make others laugh, though it is just as quick to flip-flop to a darker mood. A Gemini Moon is curious, too, needing constant stimulation; also, talkative Gemini makes this Moon quick to let others know its feelings. Gemini Moons also spend a lot of time trying to analyze their feelings themselves because Gemini is a thinking sign. A Moon in Gemini feels with its *mind*, a most unusual combination.

Moon in Gemini ☽Ⅱ Notables: Shiloh Jolie-Pitt, Julie Delpy, John Barth, Catherine Aubier, and Louis Pasteur

Moon in Cancer ☽♋

The Moon is at home in Cancer, the sign that it naturally rules. Cancer Moons have an emotional nature that is both receptive and retentive; it stores away impressions, reactions, information, and, yes, feelings, until they need them. This often makes them writers or actors (or both). With a Moon in Cancer, a person is likely to be both imaginative and creative, while underneath feeling vulnerable, touchy, moody, and easily hurt. All this, though, is hidden under Cancer's hard shell. But because a Moon in Cancer feels with its *feelings*, it is also a warmhearted and romantic combination.

Moon in Cancer ☽♋ Notables: Taylor Swift, Dean Koontz, Zelda Fitzgerald, Christian Dior, and Antoine Lumière

Moon in Leo ☽♌

Exuberant Moon in Leo has strong emotions and refuses to be limited by what it feels are narrow-minded or limiting ideas; it likes its heart to be in whatever it's doing. Leo Moons have an emotional nature that is usually both affectionate and outgoing, and it's often charismatic as well. However, they can easily be hurt if they feel they're not being appreciated, which can happen any time the spotlight's not shining on them. A natural performer and a hearty lover, Moon in Leo feels with its *heart*—strongly, openly, and joyfully.

Moon in Leo ☽♌ Notables: Sacha Baron Cohen, Jane Fonda, Paul McCartney, Queen Elizabeth II, and James Joyce

Moon in Virgo ☽♍

Virgo Moons like to see things—and figure them out—for themselves. Intelligent and practical, they spend whatever time is needed to get to the bottom of what they're feeling; they want to take their feelings apart and put them together again so that they make perfect sense, which is a prospect that delights Virgo to no end. Step by step, Moons in Virgo approach everything they do with logic and efficiency, so they can be frustrated by less methodical minds. Conversely, their precision can sometimes seem too rigid to others, but a Moon in Virgo feels with its *logic*, using its discriminating emotional nature to create a well-ordered emotional life for itself.

Moon in Virgo ☽♍ Notables: Serena Williams, Channing Tatum, Charles Bukowski, Vladimir Nabokov, and Alexander Graham Bell

Moon in Libra ☽♎

Moons in Libra are partnership Moons. They love the way things and people fit together to create harmony, and they seek to create an atmosphere in which everything seems to fall naturally into place. The most social of Moons, Moon in Libra can seem superficial or shallow, but in reality, its emotional nature cannot help but express its feelings through the way things look and feel. Naturally gracious and the most hospitable of hosts, Moon in Libra feels good when everyone else feels good. To Moon in Libra, the outward appearance reflects the inward; Moon in Libra feels through *others*.

Moon in Libra ☽ ♎ Notables: Anne Hathaway, Jay-Z, Ferdinand Porsche, Louis Vuitton, and Nikola Tesla

Moon in Scorpio ☽ ♏

A Moon in Scorpio is so intense that it spends a great deal of energy protecting itself from its own emotions. Well aware of how powerful emotions can be (and never satisfied with superficial answers), Scorpio Moons can be suspicious of others, be quick to judge, and hold grudges for a very, very long time. At the same time, they have a desire to understand deep mysteries and get to the bottom of things, which makes Scorpio Moon's emotional nature intuitive, potent, and capable of stronger feelings than any other Moon sign. Scorpio Moons often seek their soul mates. Above all, Scorpio Moons feel with their *intense emotions*.

Moon in Scorpio ☽ ♏ Notables: Lady Gaga, Roger Federer, Julie Andrews, Hank Aaron, and Isadora Duncan

Moon in Sagittarius ☽ ♐

Adaptable Moon in Sagittarius is always out there with an emotional nature that is made for making friends and experiencing the new and unexpected. Sagittarius Moons love adventure, excitement, discovery, and a plain old good time. You won't find shrinking violets here, nor will you find moody brooders. You might not find anyone here: Sagittarius Moons love to be free, and they may be off on yet another trekking adventure. Moon in Sagittarius is eager for the truth, and in seeking that truth, they will feel through its *experiences*.

Moon in Sagittarius ☽ ♐ Notables: Adele, Amal Clooney, Magic Johnson, Ludwig van Beethoven, and Vincent van Gogh

Moon in Capricorn ☽ ♑

Cool and cautious Moon in Capricorn might seem reserved and remote, but what it's really doing is planning its own success. Capricorn Moons thrive on challenges and the successes that completing challenges can bring them, and they're not very big on what they view as excessive emotion. With a self-controlled and cautious emotional nature, those with a Capricorn Moon's discipline and determination can achieve tremendous successes in their lives, but there also can be an emotional cost. Capricorn Moons often become world leaders, but this might be because they mistake control (external approval) for love (internal approval). Capricorn Moons need to be needed, but because they feel through *control*, they may not allow others to get too close.

Moon in Capricorn ☽ ♑ Notables: The Rock (Dwayne Johnson), Amy Winehouse, Federico Fellini, Abraham Lincoln, and George Eliot

Moon in Aquarius ☽♒

You might find it hard to get close to an independent Moon in Aquarius. Being different is as necessary to this Moon as breathing, and anything that furthers Aquarian Moons' uniqueness holds their attention. Intuitively strong, Moons in Aquarius often make new discoveries, but they also might discover that new territories are lonely places. Others adore Moons in Aquarius, but they'll find that what really attracts these independent Moons is unattainability. Progressive Aquarian Moons feel through their *individuality,* with an emotional nature.

Moon in Aquarius ☽♒ Notables: Eminem, Sophia Loren, Princess Diana, John Lennon, and Carl Linnaeus

Moon in Pisces ☽♓

Dreamy Moons in Pisces always believe the best about everyone and everything, so they're constantly setting themselves up for disappointment. With their sensitive and compassionate emotional nature, Pisces Moons forgive just about anything, too, but they're easily hurt and may sometimes feel sorry for themselves. Moons in Pisces can confuse dreams with reality, which makes this a most creative Moon. However, when they find that they really live in reality—not in a dream—it can be a jarring jolt. Idealistic and romantic Pisces Moons feel through their *imaginations.*

Moon in Pisces ☽♓ Notables: Rita Ora, Kanye West, Usain Bolt, Martin Luther King Jr., and Marie Curie

Mercury ☿: Instant Messaging in Real-Time

Mercury ☿ is in charge of thinking and communications—what we know and how we know it. As the planet closest to the Sun, Mercury is fast, it's hot, and it's small—small but mighty, that is. Mercury stays in a sign from 15 to 60 days, and always stays within 2 signs from the Sun. Here is where you'll find all the faculties of the mind: logic, reason, intelligence, and education. Mercury's tool is language (whether English, mathematics, Braille, sign, Mandarin, French, Egyptian hieroglyphs…), and its method is transmittal.

How You Think: Mercury ☿ in Each Zodiac Sign

Are you the one that strangers on airplanes tell their stories to, or are you reading a book by the fire or posting one of your newly written stories online? Reading and writing, commenting and listening, watching and thinking: this is your brain on Mercury. Any questions? The sign your Mercury is in describes your mental nature, how you think and communicate. In Greek mythology, Mercury was called Hermes and was the messenger for the gods. Naturally, modern Mercury loves instant messaging, as well as smartphones, overnight delivery, video streaming, and ebooks. It's no coincidence that Mercury's corresponding sign is Gemini ♊. The two are probably sliding into each other's DMs right this moment!

Mercury in Aries ☿♈

Quick, imaginative, and always trying to be first in everything: that's Mercury in Aries. Of course, this can also indicate an impetuous, premature, and headstrong nature, but no matter which way Mercury goes, in Aries, it's always spontaneous and immediate. Running ahead before it gets all the facts, Mercury in Aries might jump to conclusions, but it is always an *active* mind.

Mercury in Aries ☿♈ Notables: Mark Zuckerberg, Sofia Coppola, Mariah Carey, Iggy Pop, and Samuel Beckett

Mercury in Taurus ☿♉

If Mercury is in Taurus, it's always prepared. And it's always sure, too, that its ideas, opinions, and beliefs are the right ones. This can mean that Taurus Mercury won't always listen. But why should they when they already know the answer? Mercury in Taurus isn't one to jump to conclusions, though; this is Mercury in its easy chair, a *comfortable* mind.

Mercury in Taurus ☿♉ Notables: Dev Patel, Kirsten Dunst, Liberace, Isak Dinesen, and Robert Browning

Mercury in Gemini ☿♊

Mercury in Gemini is full of unprocessed data and ideas, and it has the words to let others know what it means. Mercury is at home in Gemini, a quick, agile mind that's witty and charming. Although sometimes this can slip over the line into gossip, Mercury in Gemini wants to get the message across, you know? Mercury in Gemini is a *communicating* mind and an inquiring mind that wants to know.

Mercury in Gemini ☿♊ Notables: Prince William, Peter Dinklage, Miuccia Prada, Bob Hope, and Frank Lloyd Wright

Mercury in Cancer ☿♋

Mercury in Cancer might be picking up everyone else's signals; Mercury is as much a receiver as a transmitter in this sign. If there's such a thing as an earthly empath, Mercury in Cancer might be it. These people always seem to intuit what others are thinking without a word being said, and Mercury in Cancer is an *intuitive* mind. There's also a good chance that with their good memory and strong metaphoric powers, they'll write it all down, paint, compose, or photograph it!

Mercury in Cancer ☿♋ Notables: Tom Hanks, Lana Wachowski, Alan Turing, Carl Gustav Jung, and Paul Gauguin

Mercury in Leo ☿♌

Here's Mercury with heart! Leo Mercury thinks with its heart. Outspoken and optimistic, Leo Mercury is also strong in purpose, dramatic, and idealistic, and it isn't likely to sweat the little stuff. This is Mercury with the charisma to lead and to convince others to follow its lead. Mercury in Leo is a *creative* mind, one that others will willingly be drawn to and follow.

Mercury in Leo ☿♌ **Notables:** Benedict Cumberbatch, Robin Williams, Ray Bradbury, Edgar Degas, and Mata Hari

Mercury in Virgo ☿♍

Impartial Mercury in Virgo sorts all those details into their proper files, where its logic and precision can find the heart of the matter. That's where Mercury in Virgo works its magic using its fine intelligence to systematically clarify and refine the information, while understanding the patterns and symbols. Mercury in Virgo is a *logical* mind; it is analytical, practical, and a quick learner, and it might excel in mathematics.

Mercury in Virgo ☿♍ **Notables:** Brie Larson, Alejandro González Iñárritu, Renzo Piano, Karl Lagerfeld, and Leo Tolstoy

Mercury in Libra ☿♎

Rational Mercury in the sign of balance will endlessly weigh both sides of any issue and make comparisons, seeking to find the perfect choice. Of course, there is no perfect choice, but that doesn't mean Mercury in Libra won't keep looking. Diplomatic and charming, this Mercury might do best if someone else can make the final decisions, but they will be sure to provide information that covers every angle. Mercury in Libra is a *balancing* mind.

Mercury in Libra ☿♎ **Notables:** Sean Lennon, Bill Gates, T. S. Eliot, Eleanor Roosevelt, and Niels Bohr

Mercury in Scorpio ☿♏

Mercury in Scorpio sees right through semantic disguises to the real meaning behind the words. Mercury here can be critical and quick to judge, and it's not going to waste time with frivolity, either. Intense and secretive, these people make good detectives and will search with great passion for the answers to their questions. This Mercury placement is fascinated with deciphering ancient languages, scientific inquiry, or the study of genealogy. Mercury in Scorpio is a *probing* mind, one that gets to the heart of the matter.

Mercury in Scorpio ☿♏ **Notables:** Katy Perry, Marina Abramovic, Luciano Pavarotti, Sylvia Plath, and Mark Twain

Mercury in Sagittarius ☿♐

Frank and open-minded, Mercury in Sagittarius may speak before it thinks. Sagittarian Mercury loves to learn and is quick to explore new ideas, but it also might not stick to any one idea for very long. For this reason, lengthy projects are not always Mercury in Sagittarius's forte. But Mercury in Sagittarius is a *seeking* mind, and it is almost childlike in its discovery of whatever it finds.

Mercury in Sagittarius ☿♐ **Notables:** Mary J. Blige, Frank Sinatra, Jimi Hendrix, Claude Monet, and Isaac Newton

Mercury in Capricorn ☿♑

In Capricorn, Mercury is a hard worker, storing up those facts and figures for future practical use. Cautious and methodical, Mercury in Capricorn knows what it wants and how it plans to get it. These people are careful deliberators who are grounded and meticulous researchers. Because what matters here is how the mind is used and what it is used for, Mercury in Capricorn is an *organized* mind.

Mercury in Capricorn ☿♑ Notables: Greta Thunberg, Amal Clooney, Dolly Parton, Susan Sontag, and Emily Carr

Mercury in Aquarius ☿♒

Mercury in Aquarius seldom misses a thing and has a knack for grasping abstract ideas. As an observer of people and their motivations, Mercury in Aquarius loves to predict human reactions, too. With its open mind and scientific approach, Mercury in Aquarius might be on the forefront of new discoveries. Unconventional and often seeming aloof, these people espouse wildly original ideas that can champion the underdog and may prove game changing. They are fascinated by the concept of building artificial intelligence (AI). Always original and unorthodox, Mercury in Aquarius is an *inventive* mind.

Mercury in Aquarius ☿♒ Notables: Harry Styles, Chris Rock, Steve Jobs, John Steinbeck, and Gertrude Stein

Mercury in Pisces ☿♓

Mercury in Pisces moves to the intuitive side of the mind, which means that its conclusions might not be based on solely upon logic. Steeped in metaphor, Mercury in Pisces has the mind of the poet. Imagination is the most finely tuned trait, and Mercury in Pisces is often sensitive and receptive. Well-tuned, Mercury in Pisces may seem psychic, though at its worst, it can seem pessimistic and confused. No matter which, though, Mercury in Pisces is a *reflective* mind.

Mercury in Pisces ☿♓ Notables: Barron Trump, Carrie Underwood, Grumpy Cat, Alexander McQueen, and Charles Darwin

Venus ♀: 53 Miles West of Venus

Whether your mind hums along to the B-52s' song about space travel to the second-brightest heavenly body in the sky (after the Moon), or sees the Italian Renaissance classic depiction, the Birth of Venus, painted by Botticelli, the conjuring of Venus always brings with it an association with feminine beauty. This connection to the goddess of beauty is so deeply entrenched it can make us forget the other areas that the planet closest to us rules. Venus is the planet of balance and harmony, and it is in charge of how we feel about our relationships, our social connections, and what we possess. Many believe that if you are male, your Venus sign will represent the type of woman to whom you will be attracted, and if you are female, your Venus sign is your ideal feminine self. But Venus also is strongly associated with your creativity and self-esteem, and those are certainly not divided along gender lines! Venus ♀ stays in a sign about 30 days, and like Mercury ☿, it is never more than 2 signs from the Sun ☉.

Venus's Earth nature is represented in her rulership of Taurus ♉, where she manifests herself as a connection to resources and inherent gifts. In Taurus, Venus is sensuous and devoted to comfort and pleasure. Your possessions and your self-esteem are closely connected; without good self-esteem, you might not be able to attract the resources you need. And both of these are tied through Venus.

Venus's Air nature can be found in her rulership of Libra ♎, which concerns itself with the social graces and marriage. This is where you'll find the Venus of romance and partnerships.

How You Love: Venus ♀ in Each Zodiac Sign

A prominent Venus ♀ in your birth chart means that how you love and connect to your surroundings is very important to you. Venus in the signs describes your love nature, your ability to attract money and worldly goods, and how you deal with relationships in general. So, let's walk Venus through each of the signs and see what they indicate.

Venus in Aries ♀♈

In impulsive Aries, Venus can fall head over heels in love and then might later realize that she was falling in love with someone other than the person she thought! Physical appearance will be what grabs Aries Venus first, and they don't much go for slobs or messes. Demonstrative and enthusiastic, Venus in Aries loves to give gifts but also can be demanding and selfish. But these people are also quick thinkers, creative, and artistic. Most of all, Venus in Aries is an *enthusiastic* love.

Venus in Aries ♀♈ Notables: Rihanna, Cate Blanchett, George Clooney, William Wordsworth, and Nicolaus Copernicus

Venus in Taurus ♀♉

Venus in Taurus is never impulsive. They take their time in love, as they do in everything. And because love can be everything to Taurus Venus, they can become very possessive about those they do love. Venus is in its Earth rulership sign here, so in addition to its stability, it has a strong aesthetic sense, which often manifests itself in beautiful surroundings. Charming, sensual, and artistic, you could call Venus in Taurus a *steadfast* love.

Venus in Taurus ♀♉ Notables: Common, James Taylor, Carly Simon, Henry Kissinger, and Nikolai Vasilievich Gogol

Venus in Gemini ♀♊

Venus in Gemini is both lighthearted and emotionally objective. Venus here likes intellectual stimulation as much as romance. There's a tendency toward lack of commitment: They're far too lighthearted to stay in one place for long and can be quite the flirts. With Venus here, you may find literary talent or, at the very least, a love of language. Sociability is very important as well. Not surprisingly, Venus in Gemini is a *communicating* love.

Venus in Gemini ♀Ⅱ Notables: Sofia Vergara, David Beckham, Tupac Shakur, Frida Kahlo, and William Shakespeare

Venus in Cancer ♀♋

In watery Cancer, Venus is both romantic and sensitive. Venus here can become a little too attached to people and possessions. But security is important to people with Venus in Cancer, too, so they're not likely to rush into anything. When they do feel secure, though, they are sensitive and loyal and make everyone feel at home. If they don't have a home to take care of, they'll care for the world. For these reasons and more, Venus in Cancer is a *nurturing* love.

Venus in Cancer ♀♋ Notables: Mary-Kate and Ashley Olsen, Rafael Nadal, Ernest Hemingway, Grand Duchess Anastasia, and Geronimo

Venus in Leo ♀♌

Venus in Leo can translate into a love of self-expression and a flair for the dramatic, but this also is a generous and selfless association. Leo Venus seems to attract the love of others without even trying because they're just plain likable. They also love fine things, and when they're in love, they love to share those things, too. Ardent and romantic, above all, Venus in Leo is a *passionate* love.

Venus in Leo ♀♌ Notables: Sufjan Stevens, Edward Snowden, the Dalai Lama, George Orwell, and Louis XIV of France

Venus in Virgo ♀♍

Precisely tuned to social, emotional, and artistic values, Venus in Virgo knows what it likes—and what it doesn't. Venus here can be more sincerely affectionate than in any other sign, and it also can manifest itself as someone with a strong business sense or who loves to serve others in some way. Sometimes shy or soft-spoken, more than anything, Venus in Virgo is a *discerning* love.

Venus in Virgo ♀♍ Notables: Demi Lovato, Angela Merkel, John McCain, Ginger Rogers, and Ray Kroc

Venus in Libra ♀♎

"Falling in Love with Love" could be a Venus in Libra's theme song. Romantic ideals seem to have been invented here. Because Venus is in its natural Air sign in Libra, its ideals might be manifested in strong partnerships or an ability to create harmony and beauty in one's environment. Venus in Libra can care so much about the social graces that it might sometimes be seen as superficial or snobbish, but that's not really what's going on. Gracious and appreciative, Venus in Libra is a *romantic* love.

Venus in Libra ♀ ♎ **Notables:** Beyoncé Knowles, Emma Stone, Rose McGowan, Matthew McConaughey, and Warren Buffett

Venus in Scorpio ♀ ♏

In Scorpio, Venus can be an all-consuming passion. After all, this sign is both sensuous and intense. Love has power in Venus in Scorpio and consequently, there's a deep need to find true love and all the passion that true love can bring. Venus in Scorpio also cares about security, which can translate into partnerships that lead to that security—or a deep-seated resentment, if hurt. Passionate and intense, Venus in Scorpio is a *powerful* love.

Venus in Scorpio ♀ ♏ **Notables:** Amanda Seyfried, Ang Lee, Jane Birkin, Grace Slick, and Marie Antoinette

Venus in Sagittarius ♀ ♐

Lighthearted and idealistic, Venus in Sagittarius is all about the adventure and excitement love can bring, so it's not always a love that lasts. Friendships do last here, though, and a Venus in Sagittarius always has lots of friends. Venus's aesthetic sense usually manifests itself in a creative lifestyle in Sagittarius because Venus loves its freedom here. Outgoing and perhaps even flirtatious, Venus in Sagittarius is an *expansive* love.

Venus in Sagittarius ♀ ♐ **Notables:** Margaret Atwood, Margaret Thatcher, Jackson Pollock, Charles Addams, and Hayao Miyazaki

Venus in Capricorn ♀ ♑ Notables

Careful, cautious Venus in Capricorn makes for a steadfast and loyal companion, one who will stand the test of time. Venus here takes personal attachments very seriously and is often attached to its possessions as much as to people. After love has been proven to Venus in Capricorn, you'll find commitment, honesty, and a lover who is constant and resourceful. Responsible and loyal, Venus in Capricorn is a *dedicated* love.

Venus in Capricorn ♀ ♑: Elijah Wood, Lisa Marie Presley, Elvis Presley, Henri de Toulouse-Lautrec, and Benjamin Franklin

Venus in Aquarius ♀ ♒

Venus in Aquarius can seem emotionally detached, but there also can be a great originality to the way Venus approaches love here. Helpful, charitable, and giving, Venus in Aquarius has not only many friends but also often a variety of friends. Of course, we know that Venus in Aquarius can't stand what it perceives as emotional drama and will just walk away. Because Venus in Aquarius cares a great deal about freedom and openness, it's not likely to be possessive and might even be curious about sharing its love with others. Cool, calm, and collected, Venus in Aquarius is a *detached and magnetic* love.

Venus in Aquarius ♀♒ **Notables:** Catherine, Duchess of Cambridge; Olivia Wilde; Nicolas Cage; Elton John; and Akira Kurosawa

Venus in Pisces ♀♓

Compassionate and sympathetic, Venus in Pisces can actually love too much, although we're not sure there really is such a thing. Venus in Pisces is intuitive about love, and with its true empathy for others, Venus in Pisces relates to art, poetry, nature, and animals. Venus in Pisces is often highly imaginative and creative as well, putting feelings into writing, acting, or music. Generous Venus in Pisces is often attracted to the underdog and is, above all, an *unconditional* love.

Venus in Pisces ♀♓ **Notables:** Emma Watson, Matt Groening, Akio Morita, Edgar Allan Poe, and Charles Lewis Tiffany

Mars ♂: War and Peace

There's a long-lived tendency to equate Mars ♂ with aggression and war, and that's no accident. After all, this is the planet of action and warrior ways. Fiery Mars is the war god, but that's not all there is to him. The Hebrew word for Mars is *M'Adam*, which should look vaguely familiar because it's Adam, the first man, according to Judeo-Christian dogma. Just as Venus ♀ is the archetypal woman, Mars ♂ can be thought of as the archetypal man: goal-oriented, physical in his approach, and a protector of those who need protecting. Don't think of him as just a warrior, though; think of him as the one in the lead—like Adam.

In Mars, we find how we manifest everything from physical energy and desires to our egos and how we deal with (or don't deal with!) our anger. Mars also represents courage and so is bold and courageous in certain signs—but not all of them. You could think of your Mars as your "assertiveness training." Your Mars can show you how you're going to fight your battles—and how you might have seemingly pointless conflicts.

How You're Driven: Mars ♂ in Each Zodiac Sign

Because this is how your independence can be found, your Mars ♂ sign can indicate how you're going to begin to separate your battles from the battles of others and in the process, find your path to personal achievement and success. Mars in the signs describes how you express your energies, assert yourself, and go about meeting your needs and desires. Mars ♂ moves from one sign into another approximately every 2 months—that is, unless is goes retrograde ℞ (see Chapter 12), when it can stay in a sign up to 7 months!

Mars in Aries ♂♈

Independent Mars in Aries is energetic, self-assured, and a courageous change agent who doesn't often let anything stand in its way. Because there's lots of enthusiasm here, you'll often find Mars in Aries leading, and that's fine with them because they love to get their way. A Mars in Aries can be aggressive and even pushy, but Aries is Mars's natural home, which makes it a *courageous and honest* energy.

Mars in Aries ♂♈ **Notables:** Alicia Vikander, Zachary Quinto, Kristin Scott Thomas, Eddie Van Halen, and Walt Whitman

Mars in Taurus ♂♉

Dogged and persistent, Mars in Taurus is not easily deterred from its steady course toward success. Mars in Taurus is a skilled artisan, often very successful in business, and passionate and sensuous as well. Sometimes Mars in Taurus's patient movement toward its goals can seem more like plodding, and its sensuous nature can become jealous and possessive. But Mars in Taurus is a *determined* energy that is methodical and practical.

Mars in Taurus ♂♉ **Notables:** Janet Jackson, Michael Jackson, John Irving, Diane Arbus, and André Citroën

Mars in Gemini ♂♊

Versatile Mars in Gemini is a real innovator who is quick to think, quick to act, and quick to move on. Mars here often has great dexterity and is incisive, decisive, and resourceful. At the same time, Gemini Mars can appear to jump to conclusions, manifest nervous energy, or appear restless or even flighty. But Gemini Mars can be magical in its ability to communicate; this is a *lively* energy.

Mars in Gemini ♂♊ **Notables:** Emma Roberts, Victoria Beckham, Courtney Love, Terrence Malick, and Joseph Heller

Mars in Cancer ♂♋

Mars in Cancer might keep things inside, but this can translate into enormous power of will. Mars goes subtle in Cancer, getting what it wants, often in indirect ways. However, because Mars is also intuitive and instinctive here, it might know exactly how to get what it wants. Mars in Cancer's protective custody can make it defensive, or even argumentative, but it also knows what it wants and will stay the course to get it. Mars in Cancer is a *protective* energy.

Mars in Cancer ♂♋ **Notables:** Miley Cyrus, Nick Jonas, Liza Minnelli, Ian Fleming, and Lord Byron

Mars in Leo ♂♌

Mars's Fire element gets accentuated in Leo, and it has no problem putting its big ideas into action. Mars is generous here, too, and its enthusiasm and drama lead others to follow its often-magnetic drive. There's also a tendency toward vanity and self-righteousness in Leo Mars, but those can be part of what makes this sign such a self-confident placement. In Leo, Mars is a *passionate* energy.

Mars in Leo ♂ ♌ **Notables:** Jennifer Hudson, Andrew Garfield, Anne Frank, Bob Fosse, and Dante Alighieri

Mars in Virgo ♂ ♍

Cool, logical, and precise, Mars in Virgo works very hard to achieve its ambitions and may even be a workaholic. Mars in Virgo is good at separating its emotions from what needs to be done, bringing both discipline and industry to everything it wants to do. Mars in Virgo is highly skilled with fine motor skills or handwork; surgeons and craftspeople often have this placement. Mars here can be strongly passionate, especially for what it sees as the right cause. Mars in Virgo is a *systematic* energy that is clever and shrewd.

Mars in Virgo ♂ ♍ **Notables:** Hilary Swank, Judi Dench, Graham Greene, George Everest, and Paul Cezanne

Mars in Libra ♂ ♎

Charming, generous Mars in Libra has a strong sense of justice but cannot always take a side. The primary need here is for active, equal relationships. Social Libra translates into someone who may be making the introductions and connections to further projects, but it also can mean an aversion to standing alone. Principled, cooperative, and idealistic, Mars in Libra is a *balanced* energy.

Mars in Libra ♂ ♎ **Notables:** Seth Rogen, Oliver Stone, Freddie Mercury, Louis Armstrong, and Martha Gellhorn

Mars in Scorpio ♂ ♏

In Scorpio, Mars manifests itself in self-reliance, self-discipline, and determination. With its powerful desires (which it prefers to keep to itself because this is a very secretive energy), an intense Mars in Scorpio means to get what it wants, often at great emotional cost. (Scorpio is one of Mars's planetary rulers, along with Aries.) Mars here can be courageous or set in its ways, so it can also be charismatic or stubborn—or both. Forceful and thorough, Mars in Scorpio is a *highly focused* energy.

Mars in Scorpio ♂ ♏ **Notables:** Michelle Williams, LeAnn Rimes, Philip Seymour Hoffman, Jean Paul Sartre, and Auguste Renoir

Mars in Sagittarius ♂ ♐

Far-sighted Mars in Sagittarius is often at the forefront of adventure—and might be just as quickly off on yet another adventure. Mars here is daring and bold, and it is also open and honest, but its energies can be scattered, and its openness is a little too frank for some. Because Mars in Sagittarius has strong philosophical or religious convictions, it can manifest itself in a cause or patriotism. Above all, Mars in Sagittarius is an *exploring* energy.

Mars in Sagittarius ♂ ♐ **Notables:** Gael Garcia Bernal, Harry, Duke of Sussex, Christopher Reeve, Agatha Christie, and Oscar Wilde

Mars in Capricorn ♂ ♑

In Capricorn, Mars has everything under control. It's persistent, ordered, disciplined, and authoritative. A Mars in Capricorn wants success, and it's willing to work hard to get there. There's no impulsiveness here; a Mars in Capricorn always makes plans and then follows through on them methodically. Depending on what Mars in Capricorn wants, it can seem disinterested in areas that don't matter to it. Mostly, Mars in Capricorn is a *controlled* energy.

Mars in Capricorn ♂ ♑ Notables: Jake Gyllenhaal, Jeff Bezos, Larry Page, Lily Tomlin, and Anne Brontë

Mars in Aquarius ♂ ♒

Mars in Aquarius can be the intellectual eccentric's success story. This placement can be unpredictable in its choices, but it is determined in following them through, so you should expect the unexpected. Mars in Aquarius isn't afraid to experiment, and it has high principles and technical expertise to go along with its originality. Mars in Aquarius can be impatient with those who don't share its ideals, and it can seem decidedly detached from the mainstream, but Mars here is a *progressive* energy, looking toward the future as if it were already here.

Mars in Aquarius ♂ ♒ Notables: Lilly Wachowski, Julian Assange, Ridley Scott, Serge Gainsbourg, and Joan of Arc

Mars in Pisces ♂ ♓

Mars in Pisces has the gifts of imagination, sensitivity, and intuition, which are often manifested in the creative fields. Mars here seeks involvement, whether with a partner, an idea, or a passion; often, it will shoulder others' responsibilities without complaint. Mars can be self-sacrificing here, or it can inspire others in some way. Also, Pisces Mars can be unfocused, pulled in two directions, or even restless. Above all, Mars in Pisces is a *subtle* energy.

Mars in Pisces ♂ ♓ Notables: Heidi Klum, Jessica Chastain, Michael Fassbender, Yuri Gagarin, and Simone de Beauvoir

Chapter 10

YOU AND YOUR WORLD: JUPITER ♃ AND SATURN ♄

The *social* planets, Jupiter ♃ and Saturn ♄, manifest their energies in your interactions with the world around you. Their longer orbits mean they have broader influences than do the shorter orbits of the luminaries and personal planets—the Sun ☉, the Moon ☽, Mercury ☿, Venus ♀, and Mars ♂. (You read about these in Chapter 9.) These longer orbits also mean that people of a certain age share these planets in the same sign and, correspondingly, have common social values. Jupiter, for example, takes 12 years to complete its cycle around the Sun, so it takes 1 year to pass through each sign of the zodiac. That means every 12 years, your Jupiter ♃ returns to the sign in which you were born, and every 12-year cycle represents new possibilities for Jupiter's influence in your life.

Jupiter and Saturn are planets associated with the social aspects of life. Jupiter ♃ represents philosophy or beliefs, higher education, growth, and abundance; Saturn ♄ represents responsibilities, structures, communities, and organizations. They balance and complement each other. Saturn brings discipline and order and is a cosmic taskmaster to help you get your life's work done. Lighthearted Jupiter brings fun, exploration, and good fortune.

Jupiter ♃: Try Your Luck

Benevolent and magnanimous, Jupiter represents your confidence and vitality and symbolizes growth, optimism, success, and generosity. In mythology, Jupiter, the father of all gods and men, was the god of the sky, bringing the energy of light, well-being, and protection. Jupiter's appearance in the sky was a good omen. Because it's always expansive, generous, and cheerful, it should come as no surprise that the Jupiter archetype perhaps most familiar to Western cultures is Santa Claus. That's right, jolly old St. Nick!

Astrologers look at Jupiter in your birth chart to find your opportunities for expansion and success, as well as to see how you might use your higher mind and education, faith, religion, or philosophy to achieve those goals.

On the other hand, Jupiter can be excessive, as it is also the planet of overindulgence and overextension. Jupiter can represent getting too much of a good thing—like winning the lottery—with the result of excesses that can cause you a little trouble. It's easy to go overboard with an unexpected windfall or to take on more projects and commitments than you could comfortably do. But your expansive and optimistic Jupiter will always reveal how you grow and change, how you can expand to fit your needs, and the lessons you can learn.

How You Grow: Jupiter ♃ in Each Zodiac Sign

Jupiter ♃ in the signs describes how you expand yourself by working with others in society. It also reveals your belief system, your interest in higher education, and how you do things on a large scale. Jupiter in the signs also shows how you might benefit materially, as well as how you might be confident—or overconfident.

Jupiter in Aries ♃♈

In Aries, Jupiter has a child's enthusiasm, an independent spirit, and a need to strike out on its own. This also is a very courageous Jupiter, but because of this exceptional courage, it can also be the "fool who rushes in where angels fear to tread." A Jupiter in Aries has a natural talent for leadership and is often an innovative disrupter of the status quo as well. Although it can sometimes be rash or naïve, Jupiter in Aries grows *enthusiastically*.

Jupiter in Aries ♃♈ Notables: Michelle Obama, Tiger Woods, 50 Cent, Salvador Dali, and Frederic Chopin

Jupiter in Taurus ♃♉

Jupiter in Taurus understands the value of life, money, and resources, and it likes the things that money buys. Taurus is the money sign, and Jupiter brings abundance, so it's a good match. Not only does Jupiter in Taurus have an eye for art, but it often is artistic itself and might conduct its career at home. All this stability can make it a tad smug, but Jupiter in Taurus grows *steadily*.

Jupiter in Taurus ♃♉ Notables: Robert Downey Jr., Vladimir Putin, Andy Warhol, John F. Kennedy, and Pablo Picasso

Jupiter in Gemini ♃♊

Adventurous Jupiter in Gemini has a knack for getting into advantageous situations and usually does best in intellectual areas. Jupiter in Gemini is sociable, popular, and knowledgeable about a wide variety of interests and can actually become an intellectual snob. Jupiter here may travel a great deal, too. Jupiter in Gemini grows *mentally*.

Jupiter in Gemini ♃♊ **Notables:** Björk, Barbra Streisand, J. K. Rowling, Stephen Hawking, and Jane Austen

Jupiter in Cancer ♃♋

Generous Jupiter in Cancer is sympathetic toward others, with a good nature, a good sense of humor, and an optimistic disposition. Jupiter in Cancer is good with money, too, and everything that Jupiter in Cancer cares for prospers. These people can become overindulgent, both with themselves and with others, but Jupiter in Cancer grows *emotionally*.

Jupiter in Cancer ♃♋ **Notables:** Jennifer Lawrence, Adam Sandler, William Shatner, Leonard Nimoy, and Leonard Bernstein

Jupiter in Leo ♃♌

Noble Jupiter in Leo is big-hearted and self-confident and radiates warmth and generosity. Jupiter in Leo thinks big, and as a change agent, it can inspire others to think big as well. Jupiter in Leo creates leaders that groups eagerly follow. With its flair for drama and its charismatic charm, Jupiter in Leo can sometimes get big-headed, but overall, Jupiter in Leo grows *magnanimously*.

Jupiter in Leo ♃♌ **Notables:** Bill Gates, Usher, Mick Jagger, Debbie Reynolds, and Toshiro Mifune

Jupiter in Virgo ♃♍

Practical Jupiter in Virgo values work and service to others and can succeed through its smarts and perseverance. Even though many point to a conflict between Jupiter's expansiveness and Virgo's need for precision, these qualities don't need to cancel each other out; Jupiter in Virgo can actually use its methodical approach to growth to reach great ends. Jupiter in Virgo grows *pragmatically*.

Jupiter in Virgo ♃♍ **Notables:** Julia Roberts, Molly Ringwald, Roman Polanski, Yoko Ono, and Carrie Fisher

Jupiter in Libra ♃♎

Artistic Jupiter in Libra is cooperative and charming and often finds its greatest area of growth through partnership. Morally conventional, Jupiter in Libra has a strong sense of justice and is always honorable in its dealings with others. Because this isn't a sign for the sole practitioner, Jupiter in Libra grows *socially*.

Jupiter in Libra ♃♎ **Notables:** Tim Burton, Diane Keaton, Cher, Judy Garland, and Marcel Duchamp

Jupiter in Scorpio ♃♏

Shrewd Jupiter in Scorpio has great faith in itself and takes itself very seriously. Jupiter in Scorpio indicates a strong need to probe for the truth behind religious doctrine or belief systems. These people are often involved in large-scale joint or corporate finances, and they can have a strong desire to gain wealth or control currency over others. Jupiter in Scorpio grows *powerfully*.

Jupiter in Scorpio ♃♏ **Notables:** Ethan Hawke, Stephen King, Roy Lichtenstein, David Bowie, and Alfred Hitchcock

Jupiter in Sagittarius ♃♐

Farsighted Jupiter in Sagittarius can see its opportunities and act on them; with Jupiter in its rulership, the planet's expansiveness and generosity enjoy the spotlight. Optimistic and enthusiastic, Jupiter's enthusiasm pays off here. Jupiter in Sagittarius is heavily interested in philosophy, belief systems, foreign cultures, travel, and higher education. It has a strong tendency to choose a particular set of beliefs and then often tries to convert others to it. Jupiter in Sagittarius grows *zealously*.

Jupiter in Sagittarius ♃♐ **Notables:** Mila Kunis, Prince Charles, Robert Redford, Julia Child, and William Butler Yeats

Jupiter in Capricorn ♃♑

Ambitious Jupiter in Capricorn seeks financial and material wealth and is patient and dedicated enough to achieve its goals. Hard work and willpower pay off here, as does fiscal conservatism. Jupiter in Capricorn has high integrity, especially in business ethics and its responsibilities. Although Jupiter in Capricorn is often charitable, it can become miserly. Jupiter in Capricorn grows *expediently*.

Jupiter in Capricorn ♃♑ **Notables:** Scarlett Johansson, Bruce Springsteen, George Foreman, Adolf Hitler, and Boris Pasternak

Jupiter in Aquarius ♃♒

Open-minded Jupiter in Aquarius might find its fortune through the people it meets because it's always open to new ideas and is both intuitive and impartial. Jupiter in Aquarius wants a world without class, race, or religious distinctions, and works for a world that's impartial, democratic, and universal. With their tolerance for different values and lifestyles, people with Jupiter in Aquarius are idealistic and humanitarian. Sometimes rebellious and easily bored, Jupiter in Aquarius nonetheless grows *innovatively*.

Jupiter in Aquarius ♃♒ **Notables:** Mos Def, George Clooney, Michael J. Fox, Keira Knightley, and Dwight Eisenhower

Jupiter in Pisces ♃♓

In one of its home signs, Pisces, Jupiter's strength is its emotional depth. Others find people with Jupiter in Pisces friendly and unassuming. Having Jupiter in Pisces can mean that you achieve your secret ideal. You're imaginative and creative, often finding great success in the arts.

Altruistic and compassionate, Jupiter in Pisces also can be mysterious and reclusive. Jupiter in Pisces grows *imaginatively*.

Jupiter in Pisces ♃♓ **Notables:** Alanis Morissette, Will.i.am, Joaquin Phoenix, Sidney Poitier, and Louisa May Alcott

Saturn ♄: Let's Get to Work!

Celestial taskmaster Saturn ♄ is all about responsibility, rules, and regulations. Your Saturn is concerned with self-discipline and self-respect, and it is concerned with your lessons, duties, and limitations. Saturn also represents the authority figures in your life. Later in life, Saturn represents your own authority. Saturn reminds us that to live as social creatures, we must abide by certain laws that are both terrestrial and universal. In Blackfoot myth, Saturn is called "The Old Man." In one story, he says to the people whom he has created: "What is made law must be law. We will undo nothing that we have done." Saturn is not a fun guy to have at parties!

Although Saturn is not going to be telling a whole lot of jokes, it *is* responsible for whatever lasting achievements you earn, especially your triumphs over obstacles. Saturn is your ambitious side and thus, it is well aware of your strengths and weaknesses. Saturn also is about security and safety, and it is the teacher of the zodiac, with many lessons to impart—if we pay attention. In other words, there won't be any reward until you get your homework for your life lessons done!

Because Saturn represents the tasks in your life—your life's work, if you will—wherever Saturn falls in your chart is where you take a serious approach to the work at hand. Saturn brings focus and concentration to your energies and efforts. Your Saturn is reflected in your perseverance, too. However, an overactive Saturn can produce rigid, inflexible structures with too much bureaucracy and not enough freedom.

Knowing Your Limits: Saturn ♄ in Each Zodiac Sign

Saturn in the signs describes the kinds of responsibilities that will challenge you, as well as the lessons you must learn. It also gives clues about the type of career you will have and how you relate to authority figures.

Saturn in Aries ♄♈

Saturn placed here forces impetuous Aries to slow down … breathe, Aries, breathe! Aries loves to move quickly to complete a task—let's get it done and over. But Saturn in Aries wants to study the situation and then respond with a steady, gradual approach. Saturn in Aries is learning independence, self-reliance, patience, and initiative, and it can become singularly self-reliant—or headstrong, defiant, and defensive. Saturn in Aries needs to *learn to cooperate* with others to be successful.

Saturn in Aries ♄♈ Notables: Lorde, Lisa Marie Presley, Tina Turner, Albert Einstein, and George Washington

Saturn in Taurus ♄♉

Saturn's great strength, combined with its strong purpose, is mirrored in Taurus, and this placement can be determined and responsible. Saturn in Taurus sticks to its guns, never wavering from the task at hand. When Saturn is in Taurus, we can guarantee that the task will be complete, no matter how long it takes! Saturn in Taurus can seem downright selfish, but that's because the lesson here is to *learn perseverance and continual progress toward completing the task.*

Saturn in Taurus ♄♉ Notables: Christopher Nolan, Bob Dylan, Placido Domingo, Richard Pryor, and Mother Teresa

Saturn in Gemini ♄♊

Saturn in Gemini can translate into a great capacity for problem solving, and this placement indicates lifelong learning. Saturn grounds flighty Gemini, giving Gemini's natural intelligence the patience it needs to succeed. Saturn in Gemini enjoys debate and delights in arguing points of detail about the task. Saturn supports the decisions Gemini reaches through this process of weighing the pros and cons. Saturn in Gemini is a master of disambiguation, removing ambiguity and clarifying meaning. The lesson for Saturn in Gemini is to *learn to communicate as well as listen.*

Saturn in Gemini ♄♊ Notables: Snoop Dogg, Lance Armstrong, Michael Palin, Coco Chanel, and John Keats

Saturn in Cancer ♄♋

Saturn in Cancer is an interesting combination of nurture and discipline. Remember your favorite elementary school teacher who nudged you through lessons you didn't understand—even if that meant keeping you in at recess to finish your assignment? This is Saturn in Cancer personified. Saturn in Cancer seeks approval and security from others, though it does not always receive or accept it. The lesson for Saturn in Cancer is to *learn to self-nurture rather than depend on others.*

Saturn in Cancer ♄♋ Notables: Fergie, Chloe Sevigny, Eric Clapton, Robert McNamara, and Henrik Ibsen

Saturn in Leo ♄♌

Saturn is tremendously self-assured in Leo and can be downright bombastic if there's nothing to stop it. People with this placement desire positions of leadership and power to fulfill their need for recognition and importance. Leo loves the limelight, and Saturn lets Leo shine in public through leadership. Saturn in Leo loves to teach and to see young people grow into their potential. In relationships, Saturn in Leo creates longevity and endurance. Saturn's lesson in Leo is to *learn values for managing others and for dealing with creativity, children, love, and romance.*

Saturn in Leo ♄♌ Notables: Patti Smith, Steven Spielberg, Albert Brooks, Lawrence Ferlinghetti, and Charlie Chaplin

Saturn in Virgo ♄♍

Responsible Saturn in practical Virgo is efficient and effective. Somewhat conservative, Saturn helps Virgo achieve its goals to perfection with a "waste not, want not" attitude and approach. At the same time, Saturn in Virgo can be driven, letting nothing stand in its way, especially pleasure. This can make for a serious nature in this placement, and the lesson for Saturn in Virgo is to *learn to work first but then enjoy life and living.*

Saturn in Virgo ♄♍ Notables: Pink, Meryl Streep, Venus Williams, Chelsea Clinton, and Johannes Brahms

Saturn in Libra ♄♎

Saturn in Libra is responsible and fair, and it works very well with others. Saturn adds decisiveness to Libra's good judgment and often heralds great success in public life. Saturn the taskmaster brings out the best in Libra's desire to understand partnerships and cooperate with others. Saturn in Libra understands the need to continually develop long-lasting relationships. The lesson for Saturn in Libra is to *learn cooperation with others … no need to go it alone!*

Saturn in Libra ♄♎ Notables: Ryan Gosling, Ivanka Trump, Tony Blair, Stan Lee, and Camille Claudel

Saturn in Scorpio ♄♏

Saturn in Scorpio understands what makes people tick and studies people to further its awareness. Serious, capable, resourceful, and insightful, Saturn in Scorpio is likely to probe beneath the surface. Saturn in Scorpio knows still waters run deep. Close observation helps penetrate mystery and emotion to acquire power. Saturn in Scorpio may want to put people in boxes, so its lesson is to *learn that each person is unique and to use its power wisely and appropriately.*

Saturn in Scorpio ♄♏ Notables: Whoopi Goldberg, Joel Coen, Debra Winger, Marilyn Monroe, and Buster Keaton

Saturn in Sagittarius ♄♐

Saturn in Sagittarius can bring ideas into reality through its capacity for intellectual discipline. The celestial taskmaster in Sagittarius can apply a philosophical, spiritual approach to work, partners, and the world. Saturn in Sagittarius is the armchair philosopher, sitting back to observe, think, and introspect. This placement learns wisdom as it goes but maintains a never-ending wonder for what remains unseen around the corner. The lesson for Saturn in Sagittarius is to *take to heart patience and perseverance.*

Saturn in Sagittarius ♄♐ Notables: Madonna, Jamie Lee Curtis, Prince, Carrie Fisher, and Fred Astaire

Saturn in Capricorn ♄♑

Saturn in Capricorn is happily ambitious, industrious, and persistent; it means to succeed, and it probably will because Saturn rules Capricorn. Saturn here is unswerving in its goals, it is disciplined, and it is hardworking. The more there is to do, the happier Saturn in Capricorn is because there's nothing this placement likes more than completion. Though Capricorn in Saturn runs the risk of being a bit ruthless in its pursuit of the goal at hand, it really just loves the work. (What ... you don't?) The lesson for Saturn in Capricorn is that *there is more to life than one's position.*

Saturn in Capricorn ♄♑ Notables: Rihanna, Kristen Stewart, Emma Thompson, Neil Armstrong, and Walt Disney

Saturn in Aquarius ♄♒

Saturn in the freedom-loving sign of Aquarius wants to run the whole show. It wants both freedom and order. And for this placement, it's all in the same package—Saturn in Aquarius teaches that discipline *is* freedom! Discipline opens the flow to the goal, and everything falls into place. Saturn can actually manifest quite well in individualistic Aquarius, especially when it is "allowed" to keep its stance of detached observation. Saturn in Aquarius needs to *learn to set itself free.*

Saturn in Aquarius ♄♒ Notables: Selena Gomez, Brad Pitt, Carl Sagan, Winston Churchill, and William Blake

Saturn in Pisces ♄♓

Saturn in Pisces can be very resourceful because it refuses to be pigeonholed. This placement can be the master of disguises, adapting and shapeshifting to meet the circumstance. Saturn in Pisces knows that to walk in someone else's shoes is to better relate with others. Its imagination can lead to creative success, but its sensitivity can mean that great disappointments occur with this placement, too. But those rose-colored glasses can help Saturn in Pisces become more realistic when they show that what is disappointing in life may actually be the path that develops life's wisdom. The lesson for Saturn in Pisces is to *learn to trust in the journey itself rather than focusing on the journey's outcome.*

Saturn in Pisces ♄♓ Notables: Justin Bieber, Sarah Jessica Parker, Kurt Cobain, Luciano Pavarotti, and Emily Brontë

When Will Saturn ♄ Return?

Saturn ♄, the planet of structure and responsibility, visits each sign/house every 28 to 30 years. That means it takes Saturn 29½ years to complete its orbit and return to its placement at your birth. And when it comes for a visit, it settles in for about 2½ years. With a visit this long, you're not likely to overlook its effect on you. This return point, called your Saturn return, can be thought of as a major life progress report.

If you look at a Saturn return chart (astrologers will prepare an event chart, as discussed in Chapter 19), it can show you what will happen for you when Saturn comes to call. As the teacher of the planets, Saturn will have some lessons for you in terms of responsibility, self-discipline, and perseverance. During a Saturn return, you'll feel challenged to evaluate your present career, your family, and/or your relationships and partnerships. Saturn's return enables us to look back on the areas of our lives where we have not yet accomplished our goals. We review our lives and become aware of our successes or failures up to that time. Of course, success and failure is all a matter of perception!

Because Saturn returns occur every 28 to 30 years, most of us will see at least 2 in our lifetimes—maybe 3! That means you'll have a few chances to work on this one, and you should be prepared to learn new lessons from Saturn during each return. The first Saturn return generally happens near age 28 to 30; the second between ages 58 and 60; and the third from age 88 to 91. How old are you now? When will Saturn come calling for *you?*

Chapter 11

YOUR PLACE IN THE UNIVERSE: URANUS ♅, NEPTUNE ♆, PLUTO ♀, AND THE NODES ☊ ☋

Uranus ♅, Neptune ♆, and Pluto ♀ are the *generational* or *transpersonal* planets, which are concerned with energies beyond the self and universal connections. These are the planets of the bigger picture. They represent events that help us reflect on our lives. Uranus ♅, the planet of the unexpected, rules revolution and invention; it is the planet of surprises. Neptune ♆ is the planet of dreams, hunches, and the realms of the unconscious; it symbolizes idealism and spiritual focus. Pluto ♀ is the planet (albeit formally still classified a dwarf planet by astronomers!) of societal or cultural change and transformation; it symbolizes the death of old conditions and their replacement with new approaches and beliefs.

Always paired in opposite signs, the Nodes of the Moon ☊ ☋ represent the tensions of your life and the comfort of your past versus the uncertainty of your future. Through your Nodes, you can discover which lessons you've mastered and those you've yet to learn—otherwise known as your karma.

Remember that planets with longer orbits, the slower planets around the Sun, have a more profound effect than faster planets that prove more changeable. The sign in which you find Uranus, Neptune, and Pluto creates generational influences. Because these planets stay a long time in each sign, the sign placements do not have strong, distinct individual meanings, though they do have personal meanings when considering house placements and aspects. Instead, the sign placements speak to a generational influence. We've listed the dates under which generations are born during Uranus, Neptune, and Pluto cycles. These planets sometimes go retrograde and direct for a short period of time before settling in for the long haul, so do your research on the start and end of cycles to be sure where your exact placement lies.

Uranus ♅: Born to Be Wild

Uranus is the Ice Man: invention, originality, sudden or unexpected change, and revolution, as well as breakthroughs and radical ideas. The first of the three "late discoveries," Uranus was first found in 1781, so its connection with revolution should not come as a surprise. Uranus both questions and challenges authority, and it transcends business-as-usual social and cultural ideas to arrive at new solutions. Uranus insists on our freedom, but it also understands that humans need to learn about freedom one step at a time.

Uranus is the planet of intuition and the sixth sense, the ruler of astrologers and inventors, and is also closely associated with electricity, technology, and electronics.

It takes Uranus 84 years to complete its orbit around the Sun and 7 years to move from one sign into another. An individual would have to live a long life to meet people in each of Uranus's sign placements,, but as the human life span continues to extend, that occurrence is increasingly likely to happen. Expect exciting and surprising changes. Uranus is the planet of the future, science, and innovation, and its domain is all that is unusual, different, or unorthodox.

Your Liberator: Uranus ♅ in Each Zodiac Sign

The sign Uranus ♅ is in reveals how your age group is unusual and shows how it manifests its desire for freedom, authenticity, and individuality. You'll see dates here that correspond to the lives of your grandparents, your peers, and your (future?) children and even grandchildren. The house your personal Uranus is in describes your own uniqueness and where you need to "break the rules." It also heralds the kinds of historical changes that occur during its seven-year cycles. A planet's aspect relationship to Uranus shows the nature of Uranus's profound influence on the planet it aspects to. (See Chapter 17 for more on planets and their aspects.)

Uranus in Aries ♅♈ (b. 1927–1935, 2010–2019)

Uranus in Aries is a pioneer, quick to make a break from the conventional and take off in new, unexplored directions for both social reform and new breakthroughs in science. The twentieth century's Uranus in Aries generation has a strong desire to do what it wants to do. Bound and determined to stick to their guns, much of their lives were blown up by them, too. This generation's lives were heavily torn apart by World War II and the Korean War. As this generation ages, it tends to tell younger ones that they have no respect for "the good old days," which, during this last transit, included the heyday of everything from labor unions to bootleggers. The twenty-first-century Uranus in Aries generation, Gen Z, is, even in childhood, advocating for climate change and embracing the disruption of traditional customs and organizations. More than previous generations, this one believes radical change is the world's hope. Uranus in Aries liberates *impetuously*.

Uranus in Taurus ♅♉ (b. 1935–1942, 2019–2025)

Uranus in Taurus is very strong and signals both willpower and determination. Generationally, Uranus in Taurus's reform instincts regard attitudes toward money and freedom. This was the time of the worst of the Great Depression and the onset of World War II. Uranus in Taurus can be too materialistic, but that can be because early needs can fuel desire. The generation of Uranus in Taurus now being born eschews too much regulation and will feel the need to reform the financial system with urgency. "Wherever you lay your hat, that's your home" is the motto of a generation who will champion unconventional experiences of home. Uranus in Taurus liberates *improvisationally*.

Uranus in Gemini ♅♊ (b. 1942–1949, 2025–2033)

In Gemini, Uranus is both inventive and original, taking creative approaches to everything from literature to electronics, both of which concern communication. Communication of any sort is highlighted here. These were the years of great twentieth-century leaps forward in science, physics, technology, metaphysics, and universal education. The upcoming Uranus in Gemini generation will develop models for artificial intelligence (AI), revolutionizing communication and reimagining the Internet. Is the storyteller human or an algorithm? These twin forms of communication will shape our world and reveal the nature of sentience. Uranus in Gemini liberates *mentally*.

Uranus in Cancer ♅♋ (b. 1949–1956, 2033–2039)

Uranus in Cancer is very sensitive to others, with well-developed intuitive powers and a flair for the eccentric and unpredictable. This generation rebelled against its parents during the Summer of Love (1967) and Woodstock (1969). Uranus in Cancer people have nontraditional ideas about home and family, preferring to be friends with their parents instead of relating to them only as traditional authoritarian figures, and they desire emotional freedom and excitement. The next generation will have to face the shock of the mass displacement of populations because of climate change, politics, and other factors. They'll experience intense emotions surrounding the metaphysics of family, home, and country. Self-development will foster emotional maturity. Uranus in Cancer liberates *emotionally*.

Uranus in Leo ♅♌ (b. 1956–1962, 2039–2046)

Uranus in Leo has boundless determination and is perfectly willing to overthrow anything that doesn't go along with what it feels works best. New tools and new techniques for using those tools are found here, especially in areas of creative expression. Born during the era of the Beat generation and John F. Kennedy's "New Frontier," this generation reveled in creating new pleasures and wavered between being "cool" and an enthusiasm to impress. The coming generation will find new ways to enjoy life, manifesting a vibrant counterculture in an era of disruption, for better and for worse. Uranus in Leo liberates *creatively*.

Uranus in Virgo ⛢♍ (b. 1961–1968, 2046–2053)

Uranus in Virgo is concerned with reforming work methods and attitudes toward health. Note that this period was when computers were first being used in the workplace, though not at home. Technical advances are Uranus in Virgo's forte, as the renewed interest in ecology, natural foods, and environmental concerns began during this time. In the twenty-first century, people will benefit from advances in genetics and biology that will revolutionize the practice of medicine. Along with that, this generation will continue to use alternative health modalities such as meditation and acupuncture to effect healing. Technology, including 3D imaging and printing, quantum computers, and advancements we can only imagine now, improve the quality of life for millions. Uranus in Virgo liberates *discriminately*.

Uranus in Libra ⛢♎ (b. 1968–1975, 2053–2059)

Uranus in Libra has a strong social conscience and is interested in bringing about new ways of looking at old social traditions like marriage, partnership, and other social areas. One of the results of this was the late twentieth-century notion of "political correctness," a well-meaning idea gone somewhat amok, but Uranus here often finds unusual solutions—and friends and lovers. Those born in the next cycle will be diplomatic and harmonious about alternate lifestyles and relationships. They'll be eccentric but steadfast in personal relationships and will fight to welcome refugees into the new, expansive social order. Uranus in Libra liberates *socially*.

Uranus in Scorpio ⛢♏ (b. 1975–1981, 2059–2066)

Uranus in Scorpio is a powerful pairing, and during this time, both the Three Mile Island nuclear power plant and the volcano Mount St. Helens had unexpected explosions. Those born with Uranus in Scorpio are just now beginning to discover their power for change and also are discovering what can happen when power and sexuality are misunderstood, as in the case of gender identity. The future generation will awaken to self-discovery though making profound, transforming changes that involve coming to terms with strong emotions. They will ponder the larger intellectual questions of how emotion shapes identity and destiny. This pairing has the potential to awaken others to what is really happening and liberates *powerfully*.

Uranus in Sagittarius ⛢♐ (b. 1981–1988, 2066–2072)

Uranus in Sagittarius is optimistic and seeks the future, with a liberal and progressive outlook. This generation's intention is religious, legal, cultural, and academic reform, and all these institutions underwent a period of public distrust during this era of the 1980s. Individuals born during this time have a strong belief in universal laws and the freedom to follow their own convictions. The future generation will examine dogma and innovate belief systems. They'll travel the world and likely beyond to discover new cultures to create ways to expand tolerance and gather knowledge. Uranus in Sagittarius liberates *progressively*.

Uranus in Capricorn ♅♑ (b. 1905–1911, 1988–1996)

Uranus in Capricorn works at breaking down old, worn-out structures and organizations to create a better future. At the start of the twentieth century, the Second Industrial Revolution ushered in electric, petroleum, and steel technology. The first Model T Ford rolled off the line October 1, 1908. Its most recent transit saw the toppling of the Berlin Wall and dissolution of the Soviet Union. The marriages and divorces of Prince Charles and Princess Diana, and Prince Andrew and Fergie, occurred while Uranus was in Capricorn, wreaking havoc with British royal tradition and beginning a new era of adaptation to the times for the British royal family. The next cycle will occur during the lives of the last cycle's children and grandchildren. Capricious Uranus is channeled into constructive directions in Capricorn and it liberates *constructively*.

Uranus in Aquarius ♅♒ (b. 1912–1919, 1996–2003)

In its own sign, Uranus is radical, inventive, scientific, and universal with a deep desire to change *everything* for the better. At the start of the twentieth century, this planet/sign pairing coincided with the start of World War I and the sinking of the *Titanic*. In the most recent period, scientists cloned a sheep, the use of e-mail exploded worldwide, and the global stock market saw a dramatic rise and fall. During Uranus in Aquarius everyone from heretics to eccentrics has their day. This pairing likes things to work democratically, impartially, and universally, so anything that's not working according to those principles is subject to change. The next cycle will occur during the lives of the last cycle's children and grandchildren. Uranus in Aquarius liberates *inventively* and *democratically*.

Uranus in Pisces ♅♓ (b. 1919–1927, 2003–2011)

Uranus in Pisces has an abiding sense of mystery—and of the mysterious. Uranus in Pisces saw everything from the Russian Revolution to the "anything goes" Roaring Twenties, as well as the great rise of the motion picture as mass entertainment. During our most recent Uranus in Pisces transit, we experienced the global Great Recession, sought creative solutions to previously insoluble problems such as climate change, and observed the ongoing refugee crisis. The need for a universal sensibility arose and grew strong, though peoples and governments grapple with what that means. The next cycle of Uranus in Pisces will occur during the lives of the last cycle's children and grandchildren, and we hope by then, lasting solutions can be initiated. Uranus in Pisces people are often actors or might be known for other creative and versatile abilities. Uranus in Pisces liberates *universally*.

Neptune ♆: Sweet Dreams

A billion miles beyond Uranus, invisible to the naked eye, orbits Neptune, the planet that governs the idealisms of society. Neptune makes us collectively more aware of all belief systems and reflects the collective quest for a higher spiritual plan. Neptune was discovered in 1846, shortly before Sigmund Freud was born. And the glimmer of Neptune may have been felt as early as

1612, when Galileo sketched the planet in his notebooks. After all, the areas a planet represents don't find their earthly manifestations until we on Earth "discover" that planet.

In Greek mythology, the Universe was divided into three realms at creation: the heavens, ruled by Zeus (Jupiter); the underworld, ruled by Hades (Pluto); and the oceans, ruled by Poseidon (Neptune). So, Neptune, the sea god, is the ruler of the waters, the ruler of dreams; in other words, Neptune is the ruler of the unknown. Neptune naturally represents all matters related to water and liquids, music and movies, glamour, dreams, and illusion. It also rules spirituality, ideals, hunches, and things we intuitively know. Neptune is the planet of the mystical, of fog and flattery and fragrance, of allusion and addiction, and of hypnosis and hypochondria.

It takes Neptune 165 years to orbit the Sun and approximately 14 years to pass through each sign. Like all the generational planets, Neptune's influence is felt during its times, as well as by its *natives,* and its personal importance is ascertained through its house position and aspect relationships as well. Planetary natives have an astrological commonality, such as a planet in the same sign or house. The generational planets stay in one sign for many years, establishing a connection among all people born within it. As the human life span has not yet reached beyond 120 years, an individual will not be able to encounter people who have their Neptune placement in each of the 12 signs—at least, not in one lifetime! Neptune's movement is so slow, its energy may be felt to be as outside of normal time as the dream world.

How You're Inspired: Neptune Ψ in Each Zodiac Sign

Neptune Ψ, through the signs, represents both your generation's spiritual urge and its urge to escape; in other words, Neptune represents your generation's dreams and illusions. The house your personal Neptune lies in describes your own dreams, illusions, and spiritual needs. Most of all, Neptune's sign placement reveals how each generation is inspired.

Neptune moves very slowly and retrogrades about half of each year, so it often takes two years to transition to a new sign. You'll see dates here for Neptune placements that correspond to the lives of your great-grandparents, your grandparents, your peers, and your (future?) children and even grandchildren and great-grandchildren. Neptune Ψ is currently in Pisces ♓ until 2026, after which it rounds the zodiac wheel again by returning to Aries ♈ until 2039.

Neptune in Aries Ψ♈ (b. 1862–1875, 2025–2039)

Emerging from the chrysalis of spiritual transformation in Neptune in Pisces, Neptune in Aries becomes the time to translate dreams for the future into action for the present. During the last period, Americans grappled with Reconstruction after the Civil War and the start of the Gilded Age—both examples of profound progress and also great corruption. In the coming period, people will implement solutions to global climate change; develop exciting new medical technologies leading to treatments and cures for intractable illness; continue to explore the possibilities of artificial intelligence and quantum computing; and explore the nature of boundaries between nations and cultures. Neptune in Aries possesses high energy to achieve what may seem impossible to many. Brash and headstrong Aries natives will need to remember to listen while they harness the urgency of the moment to make dreams into realities. Neptune in Aries is *urgently* inspired.

Neptune in Taurus $\Psi \, \Diamond$ (b. 1875–1888, 2039–2052)

Your children and grandchildren will live through Neptune in Taurus, just as did your parents (if you are elderly now) and, more likely, your parents or even great-grandparents. You can begin to see how long planetary cycles spread their energy like the circular ripples of a stone tossed into a pond. Here, the energy is focused on dreams of possessions, home, fashion, artworks, and especially food. The last period saw the emergence of the Impressionist painters and a new way of seeing our home environment with its depictions of still life, landscape, and routine home life. Neptune in Taurus focuses on creating new interpretations of home. Natives are methodical and fixed on manifesting their dream visions of comfortable domestic environments, and they enjoy exploring cuisines and savoring new flavors to make the tastes their own. Neptune in Taurus is *domestically* inspired.

Neptune in Gemini $\Psi \, \mathbb{I}$ (b. 1888–1902, 2052–2065)

The last period of Neptune in Gemini saw the spread of the newfangled telephone in homes and businesses, operational electric power stations in some American cities, and the birth of flight. Transmission of energy, quickness of thought and its expression—these are hallmarks of Neptune in Gemini. Natives are versatile, well educated, and passionate about enhancing any method of communication to reach more people, more efficiently. With all the innovation occurring today in the field of communication, there's no doubt that our children and grandchildren and great-grandchildren will enjoy a revolution in communication as profound as the one our ancestors lived through. Neptune in Gemini is *fleetly* inspired.

Neptune in Cancer $\Psi \, \mathfrak{S}$ (b. 1902–1915, 2065–2078)

Neptune in Cancer has a deep sentiment for nature and anything having to do with roots or family, and is often psychic, spiritual, and idealistic. This placement indicates an abiding faith in "the good old days," and Neptune's last transit was a period when the world headed toward wars about patriotic nationalism and ethnic issues. Also, during that time, President Teddy Roosevelt led a campaign against big business (opposite Capricorn, in other words) to protect the rights of the common people. Freud's work with the subconscious mind became recognized during this time as well. Those born during this placement are the Greatest Generation, the first children of the twentieth century. Neptune in Cancer natives are emotionally sensitive and intuitive and are *sentimentally* inspired.

Neptune in Leo $\Psi \, \Omega$ (b. 1915–1928, 2078–2092)

Neptune in Leo is romantic, idealistic, and artistic. Just think about the art styles like Cubism and Dadaism that appeared and how the big jazz bands broke through the restrictions on self-expression during this period. The Neptune in Leo generation had a flair for the dramatic and a sometimes unrealistic sense of what love and romance are all about. But Leo also rules speculation. During this period, there was a lot of unwise investment and market speculations, which led, as you might recall, to the big stock market crash and the beginning of the Great Depression that occurred when Neptune moved into Virgo. Either way, though, Neptune in Leo is *creatively* inspired.

Neptune in Virgo ♆♍ (b. 1928–1942, 2092–2105)

Neptune in Virgo is the Silent Generation, the first generation to feel the pull between reason (rational science) and emotion (psychiatry), and it is the generation of both the Great Depression and World War II. Virgo rules employment, and there was a great lack of employment during this period. Remember, Neptune dissolves, and it certainly dissolved the high times of the Roaring '20s. During this period, the greed and pleasure of Leo were replaced with a concern for working people and service to society. Neptune in Virgo natives have a careful approach to life, which is a result of their tough early years; they are concerned with using ideals to achieve practical ends, although they might learn to rely more on their intuition. Martin Luther King Jr. is born in this placement. Neptune in Virgo is *practically* inspired.

Neptune in Libra ♆♎ (b. 1942–1956)

Neptune in harmonious Libra emphasizes both idealism and love, and this generation—the start of the Baby Boomers—is interested in new ways of looking at relationships and laws. This is the generation that confronted sexual equality, marched for peace, experimented with LSD, and cares deeply about injustice throughout the world. Sometimes, this Neptune's intentions can have unfortunate results. The Neptune in Libra period saw the end of World War II and then the beginning of the Cold War. Neptune in Libra was also when marriages were subject to uncertainty (wartime made this difficult) and disillusionment. This period is when the divorce rate began increasing, too. Still, Neptune in Libra is *idealistically* inspired.

Neptune in Scorpio ♆♏ (b. 1956–1970)

Neptune in Scorpio can be self-destructive—and potently powerful. The purpose of Neptune in Scorpio is to encourage spiritual regeneration, the exploration of inner and outer worlds. This generation—the second half of the baby boomers—was born during the rise of the counterculture, the civil rights movement, protests for peace, second-wave feminism and the birth control pill, and the historic Moon landing; this generation internalized the idealism of Neptune in Libra and nurtured the dream of achieving oneness in the Universe. This generation took the lyrics of John Lennon's "Imagine" to heart. They feel deeply and still rely on direct face-to-face communication as the most emotionally valid experience; these people put away their smartphones during meals and prioritize personal conversation without the interruption of texts and web searches. Neptune in Scorpio natives have an enormous capacity for renewal, especially spiritually, and there also can be an extraordinary capacity for psychic awareness or an interest in alternative belief systems, including the intuitive arts. This period saw the beginnings of tremendous change in every facet of life; after all, Neptune in Scorpio is *intensely* inspired.

Neptune in Sagittarius ♆♐ (b. 1970–1984)

Neptune in Sagittarius corresponds to Gen X and is open, honest, and idealistic. Astrologers put great store in the generations born in Sagittarius, the sign of higher learning, philosophy, and freedom. During its last transit here, we saw Watergate brought out in the open, and Jimmy Carter, an idealistic Washington outsider, elected president. Neptune's Sagittarius transit also was a period of universal travel, as millions of people began to see the world. New and mystical religions sprang up all over, and music and art were often spiritually oriented. Personal fitness and outdoor sports also became popular. Neptune in Sagittarius natives often feel a need for greater religious and philosophical values and might revise existing laws or ways of thinking to reflect that need; they are more realistic in their world view than the Baby Boomers and focus their dreams on human dignity. Neptune in Sagittarius is *prophetically* inspired.

Neptune in Capricorn ♆♑ (b. 1984–1998)

This period was a time that was recognized for its dissolving of worn-out governments and economic structures. The USSR dissolved, the Berlin Wall fell, and all around the world, new countries were formed or reformed after years of being swallowed up by others. Communism collapsed, and here in the United States, we began facing the need for socialized medicine and other necessary reforms. Economic and political structures—society's organizations—are associated with Capricorn. Neptune in Capricorn natives encompass the Millennials, sometimes called the "echo Boomers" because their parents are Baby Boomers. These Neptune in Capricorn natives have a deep sense of responsibility, self-discipline, great courage, and purpose to achieve their goals. This is the first generation to grow up with the Internet. They are disruptors of industries—taking new ideas and making them practical for mass consumption. Mark Zuckerberg is born during this placement. Communication is a practical tool, best experienced through the shorthand of text or social media and without face-to-face interaction. Neptune in Capricorn is *constructively* inspired.

Neptune in Aquarius ♆♒ (b. 1998–2012)

When Neptune was in Aquarius from 1834 to 1847, it was a time of the transcendental literature movement, the first use of anesthetics, and the discovery of uranium. This was a period when many people pursued idealistic causes, campaigned for reforms such as the end of slavery, and strove for humanitarian and utopian ideals. Neptune in Aquarius natives have a knack for the abstract, resulting in new approaches to everything from the arts to the sciences. The period of Neptune in Aquarius in our lifetimes coincided with the period of the Great Recession; the rise of the gig economy; the flood of refugees from political and environmental strife around the globe; the return of nationalistic fervor not seen since World War II; the discovery of the gene-editing tool CRISPR; and an awareness that the Earth—and humankind with it—is experiencing the effects of the sixth mass extinction even as physicists probe deeper into the mysteries of space and the Universe. Natives comprise Gen Z, and they are ready for unconventional solutions to problems. They don't like to drive, they are Internet natives, and they take seriously their role in facing humanity's many challenges. Neptune in Aquarius is *inventively* inspired.

Neptune in Pisces ♆♓ (b. 2012–2026)

Pisces rules Neptune, enhancing the effects felt during this powerful time. Not experienced since the American Civil War, Neptune in Pisces is a time of spiritual transformation. A time of great upheaval prompts a renewed emphasis on intuitive and psychic insight as a pathway to understanding and beneficial change. Restored harmony is possible through deep thinking in service to the dream of a greater good for self, family, community, and country. Neptune in Pisces natives feel deeply the ravages the Earth experiences and feel oneness with all that lives, including plant and animal life suffering from the extremes of climate change. There is a danger of depression and despair, as in a waking nightmare, so vigilance must be practiced to keep dreams of a better world alive. Neptune in Pisces is *compassionately* inspired.

Pluto ♀: Soul Journey

Pluto ♀ is so far from Earth that it wasn't even discovered until 1930. And it was only after its discovery that scientists learned how to split the atom and about the atomic power that comes with it. As we noted in Chapter 8, astronomers reclassified Pluto as a dwarf planet in 2006, but astrologers still consider it to have the same transformative influences.

It takes Pluto approximately 248 years to orbit the Sun, and it spends anywhere from 11 to 32 years in each sign, making it the most generational of the transpersonal planets. Learning what your Pluto is about takes time, as its energies are abstract but also very deep and far-reaching.

As the ruler of the underworld, Pluto is naturally associated with death, but death also is about renewal and transformation, as in the Tarot's Major Arcana Death card. Sometimes it takes an enormous setback or challenge to force us onto a new course—and remember, too, that the same force can be either creative or destructive, like atomic energy. It all depends on how that energy gets used.

Pluto's position in your birth chart can show how you're changing and represents both your transformative and destructive urges. Your Pluto truly is both your end and your beginning.

How You're Changing: Pluto ♀ in Each Zodiac Sign

On an individual basis, Pluto represents the soul's journey, its evolutionary intent or purpose, and what the soul has chosen to learn throughout the entire life. Although astrology leaves the question about belief in past lives up to each person, there is generally an understanding that each person or soul is evolving during his or her lifetime.

Certain branches of astrology also believe that each person is evolving over many lifetimes until he or she is ready to return to and merge with the Source or the God of their understanding.

Because it is the most generational planet, Pluto is personally revealed by its house position rather than its sign's position. So, to find your soul's evolutionary purpose, see your Pluto's house placement in one of the four chapters devoted to the houses (see Chapters 13 through 16), and study how Pluto is aspected in your birth chart (see Chapter 17).

Generationally, Pluto through the signs always indicates permanent changes for the world, both regenerative and destructive; these changes occur in the areas associated with the sign it's in and describe the major global and collective changes occurring at the time. Because Pluto moves so slowly, we look into the past or imagine the future for generations. In an average lifetime, a human being may live through as many as five or six periods of Pluto in the signs. The number of people they'll be able to meet with Pluto sign placements other than their own will vary according to when they were born.

Pluto in Aries ♀♈ (b. 2068–2098)

The last placement in Aries was 1822 to 1853, coinciding with the rise of slavery in the United States and the growing controversy surrounding it. Harriet Beecher Stowe published her novel *Uncle Tom's Cabin* telling the plight of plantation slaves in 1852, selling 300,000 copies in the first year. By the end of this period, tension would begin to explode, presaging the Civil War. Pluto in Aries natives reject old identities to search out new ones. There is a profound and urgent need to understand the nature of being, both personally and in society. There's no looking back because Pluto in Aries doesn't *want* to look back; it's a new persona for a new time. Like Tarot's Ten of Swords, the slain man awaits the dawn of rising to a new life and a new world. Pluto in Aries seeks ways to achieve *the creative destruction and rebirth of self.*

Pluto in Taurus ♀♉ (b. 1853–1884, 2098–2129)

The last placement in Taurus coincided with the Civil War in America and its aftermath, as well as the birth of the modern city with its skyscrapers. Eastman's introduction of the Kodak camera and Edison's famous first telephone call placed on March 10, 1876, proved revolutionary. Pluto in Taurus natives have a profound interest in what makes a good home. Resources tangible and intangible are directed toward creating a home that meets the needs of the time and facilitates better understanding between the people that live and work in both public and private spaces. Pluto in Taurus seeks new ways to achieve *harmonious, modern spaces for living.*

Pluto in Gemini ♀♊ (b. 1882–1914, 2132–2159)

The last Pluto transit in Gemini opened up the avenues of exploring the human mind through psychoanalysis, a manifestation of the way Pluto's personal power interacts with the Gemini mind. Einstein published his paper on the theory of relativity, and events erupted toward the Russian Revolution. Pluto in Gemini natives are exploring the nature of politics, the physics of being, and the manifesting power of the human mind (and in the future, of artificial intelligence to enhance it), and then watching the world change through their new ideas and discoveries. Pluto in Gemini seeks new ways to *communicate and transform their intellects.*

Pluto in Cancer ♀︎♋ (b. 1914–1939)

Pluto in Cancer means a major upheaval in family life, last witnessed during both World War I and the Great Depression, when millions of families were forced from their homes. Pluto in Cancer also is connected to a patriotic love of country and so is associated with the rise of nationalism during the 1930s in Germany, Italy, and Japan, as well as in the countries of the Allied Powers. Pluto in Cancer natives seek new ways to *achieve emotional security and maturity and often love to break with tradition.*

Pluto in Leo ♀︎♌ (b. 1937–1958)

Pluto in Leo is all about power: witness World War II, the Cold War, the Korean War, and McCarthyism. This period saw the first atomic bomb, dictatorships all over the world, and the creation of the state of Israel and the United Nations. Power can be used for either good or evil, and the Pluto in Leo generation, with its natural self-confidence and sense of authority, seeks new ways to *utilize power*—sometimes for good and sometimes for not-so-good.

Pluto in Virgo ♀︎♍ (b. 1956–1972)

Tremendous changes in labor and industry resulted during the most recent Pluto in Virgo period. Computers arrived in the workplace, new medical discoveries made enormous strides in both preventing and combating disease, and humans set foot on the Moon, a technological feat unparalleled before or since. Humankind's first venture from the Earth to the Moon will resonate through time as our journey beyond our home planet to explore the Universe begins. Pluto in Virgo natives are analytical and often perfectionists, and they seek new ways to *solve profound problems and explore sacred patterns of the Universe.*

Pluto in Libra ♀︎♎ (b. 1971–1984)

The most recent Pluto in Libra period brought changes in the arts and international relations. Robert Mapplethorpe's powerful black-and-white photographic images challenged and shocked the public. Libra's egalitarianism was manifested here in everything from the end of the war in Vietnam, to Nixon's trip to China, to the healing of the nation after the storm of Watergate, and to the election of Ronald Reagan to the U.S. presidency. Pluto in Libra natives seek *harmony and cooperation*, and as this generation reaches adulthood, we can already see the results of their Plutonian energies in their music, art, and writing.

Pluto in Scorpio ♀︎♏ (b. 1983–1995)

Pluto's most recent time in Scorpio saw a resurgence in interest in natural healing and the rediscovery of New Age ideas. The most recent Pluto in Scorpio transit was the beginning of AIDS and the period when all the "taboos"—rape, incest, sexual abuse, and scandals—came out in the open. The basic theme of this period is reform and transform. Pluto in Scorpio natives (remember, Pluto is Scorpio's ruler) are sensitive to their environment, are emotionally intense, are intrigued by the mysterious, and seek *spiritual regeneration,* sweeping away anything that stands in the way of their quest.

Pluto in Sagittarius ♀♐ (b. 1995–2008)

Pluto in Sagittarius signals the transformation of all the major social systems: education, health care, law, and religion. The latter includes a resurgence in fundamentalism and dogmatism as well as growth in spirituality. During that time, the world witnessed the death of Pope John Paul II, the Polish-born pope revered for his political and humanitarian acumen. Questions about Catholic faith in the modern world gained new attention, as did the role of organized religion in modern society. This certainly has proven to be an era of new values tested out in everything from philosophy and religion to politics and foreign affairs. The Pluto in Sagittarius generation seeks *personal freedom,* but it also has a great faith in human nature (thank goodness for that) and is both philosophical and humane.

Pluto in Capricorn ♀♑ (b. 2008–2024)

The last placement in Capricorn was from 1762 to 1778, coinciding with the time of the American Revolutionary War. The Declaration of Independence penned by Thomas Jefferson on July 4, 1776, echoes through the centuries to the present day when questions of constitutional abuse and authority confront the great American democracy. Corporations grow more powerful over the lives of everyday citizens, and vast inequities in wealth fuel division and unrest. Pluto in Capricorn natives believe in shrewd and prudent resistance to authority, and inner motivation prompts them to act with reserved, common-sense surety to manifest changes in power structures. The measured and consistent tenacity of protesters adds to the power and scope of their achievement when they do succeed in breaking down the traditional structure of authority. Natives will oppose the rise of nationalism and authoritarian government to champion democracy and freedom for the world's peoples. Pluto in Capricorn seeks *independence from authority and the removal of inequalities in relationships, governments, and culture.*

Pluto in Aquarius ♀♒ (b. 2024–2044)

The last placement in Aquarius was from 1778 to 1798, and it coincided in America with the birth of the United States and the early years of its government. America's "new world colonies" became its states and territories, as citizens grappled with forging the life of a new nation, along with western expansion. Drastic change can undermine traditions and old conventions, threatening outdated ways of being. Witness the settlement of the West, leading to the establishment of property rights and to the development of new towns and cities, which facilitated the rise of business in the states, all to the detriment of the indigenous culture it replaced. Pluto in Aquarius natives are change agents forced to use ingenuity and intelligence to transform social, political, and personal relationships. The changes wrought are active and tend to be permanent. We will soon enter a new experience of Pluto in Aquarius, seeking the potential for sweeping humanitarianism. Pluto in Aquarius seeks *enduring transformation of human relationships through intellectual means leading to unconventional, disrupting societal change.*

Pluto in Pisces ♀♓ (b. 2044–2068)

The last placement in Pisces was from 1797 to 1823, coinciding with the movement toward literary realism as seen in Jane Austen's novels, studies of manners, and poet William Wordsworth's *Lyrical Ballads.* Realistic portrayals of society and nature quietly asserted the beauty of everyday experience, soon giving rise to the Romantic poets John Keats and John Shelley. Women's rights icon Mary Wollstonecraft gave birth to Mary Shelley (wife of poet John), who published the classic novel *Frankenstein,* considered by some as the birth of science fiction. Pluto in Pisces natives desire an intuitive union with social structures and the natural world, leading to deeply felt and inspiring portrayals of the world, including visionary imaginings of its future. These portrayals inspire both hope and fear for what lies ahead. Pluto in Pisces seeks an intuitive love for humanity and the Universe that prompts visions of potential achievements and challenges.

The Nodes ☊☋: Back to the Future

You could think of the Moon's Nodes as the particular tensions in your life: the pull and comfort of the past versus the fear and uncertainty of the future. Always exactly opposite each other on your birth chart, your Nodes are the push-me/pull-you energies in your life.

Your South Node ☋ indicates lessons and talents that you have already mastered, what could be perceived as the "easy way out." Your South Node is your past, your history, and who you've been, and it is generally believed to represent a composite of your past lives. Because you've already mastered your South Node skills, talents, and lessons, there's no growth, learning, or challenge when you continue to use them. This is the Universe's way of encouraging you to follow the growth path of your North Node.

Your North Node ☊ indicates lessons you are here to learn, what could be perceived as "the hard way"—but worth the effort. Your North Node is your future and your greatest opportunities for growth—in short, your development path. This is where you will find fulfillment, increased confidence, and rewards for your efforts. Here are represented the areas where you'll gain new knowledge, new ideas, and all types of growth, which, in turn, will lead to fruition.

Coming and Going: The Nodal Pairs ☊☋ in Each Zodiac Sign

Because the Nodes are always exactly opposite each other in your chart, their interpretations are likewise presented in pairs. Simply look for your North Node ☊ sign description, and your South Node ☋ will be included there, too.

North Node in Aries ☊♈/South Node in Libra ☋♎

A North Node in Aries/South Node in Libra is someone who has already learned cooperation and how to work with others but might be dependent on others, too. These people now need to develop independence, initiative, and self-confidence, and they need to learn how to stand on their own. It is an excellent placement for developing leadership abilities and using the relationship skills of the past to create a basis of support.

North Node in Taurus ☊♉/South Node in Scorpio ☋♏

A North Node in Taurus/South Node in Scorpio is someone who has already learned about power, the occult, and transformation, but might have had the rug pulled out from under them in the past. These people now need to learn a new set of values to live by, as well as how to stabilize their energies through the wise use of material resources. After they realize that the Universe provides all that they need, they can create beauty, harmony, and trust.

North Node in Gemini ☊♊/South Node in Sagittarius ☋♐

A North Node in Gemini/South Node in Sagittarius is someone who has already become accustomed to freedom and seeking their truth but might still be on a quest. Now the growth of these people comes from communicating with others and looking at both sides of all issues. This is an excellent opportunity to share past philosophies and truth with others through the development of new communication skills.

North Node in Cancer ☊♋/South Node in Capricorn ☋♑

A North Node in Cancer/South Node in Capricorn is someone who has already learned about responsibilities, accomplishments, and ambition. Now these people need to learn about being sensitive, sharing their emotions, and responsibly nurturing others. They're here to give of themselves and achieve their best by doing so.

North Node in Leo ☊♌/South Node in Aquarius ☋♒

A North Node in Leo/South Node in Aquarius is someone who has already learned about being the detached, ingenious inventor or an eccentric humanitarian. Now these people need to learn how to share their love and hearts with others through generous and noble leadership. This is an excellent opportunity to share their innovations for humanity through leadership and love.

North Node in Virgo ☊♍/South Node in Pisces ☋♓

A North Node in Virgo/South Node in Pisces is someone who has already developed compassion, intuition, and strong sensitivity to others. Now these people need to develop discernment and learn how to serve others in practical ways. They will often find opportunities to share their compassion from their past while developing their abilities in medicine, healing, or nutrition.

North Node in Libra ☊ ♎/South Node in Aries ☋ ♈

A North Node in Libra/South Node in Aries is someone who has already developed independence, self-confidence, and initiative and knows how to stand on his or her own. Now these people need to learn about cooperation and harmony and how to work with others. This is an opportunity to grow from loving others, learning objectivity and diplomacy, and balancing one's needs with those of others.

North Node in Scorpio ☊ ♏/South Node in Taurus ☋ ♉

A North Node in Scorpio/South Node in Taurus is someone who has already developed a sensuous nature and stability through the accumulation and use of resources. Now these people need to learn about the deeper aspects of life and might go through a rebirth process to do so. This is an opportunity to learn about true power, transformation, and command of their feelings.

North Node in Sagittarius ☊ ♐/South Node in Gemini ☋ ♊

A North Node in Sagittarius/South Node in Gemini is someone who has already learned how to communicate with others, gather endless data, and see all sides of issues. Now these people are here in search of higher knowledge and truth and to realize that although there are two sides to every issue, it is still the same coin. With effort, they can turn their knowledge into divine understanding.

North Node in Capricorn ☊ ♑/South Node in Cancer ☋ ♑

A North Node in Capricorn/South Node in Cancer is someone who has already developed sensitivity, emotions, and nurturing ways. Now these people need to learn about responsibilities, achievement, and maturity. They now have an opportunity to bring their caring nature from the past into responsible "elder" positions, where they can serve many other people.

North Node in Aquarius ☊ ♒/South Node in Leo ☋ ♌

A North Node in Aquarius/South Node in Leo is someone who has already developed a highly creative and loving nature but has generally been focused on his or her personal life. Now these people need to learn how to develop an impersonal, humanitarian approach to life that serves humankind. This is a chance to use past leadership skills to create universal opportunities for all.

North Node in Pisces ☊ ♓/South Node in Virgo ☋ ♍

A North Node in Pisces/South Node in Virgo is someone who has already learned how to analyze, be practical, and serve others. Now these people need to develop compassion, intuition, and a desire not to judge others. They now have an opportunity to use past abilities to serve others in new ways by developing universal consciousness, empathy, and understanding.

Chapter 12

RETROGRADES ℞: ONE STEP FORWARD, TWO STEPS BACK

Let's remember one thing before we begin: Planets don't really move backward! It just looks that way from here on Earth, which is, after all, our astrological vantage point for all heavenly motion.

In this chapter, you'll learn just what it means when we say a planet is direct and when it is retrograde ℞. We also explain the difference between a personal retrograde and a transiting one. Then we take you on a tour of the planets—in reverse.

A Brief History of Planetary Motion

When planets are in direct motion, they appear from our vantage point on Earth to be moving forward along their orbits. Astrologically, during these times when planets are direct, their energies move smoothly and are clearly expressed. But when planets are retrograde ℞ astrologically, their energies seem to be obscured or obstructed. During astrological retrogrades, planets *seem* to the human eye to be moving backward in their orbits. Now, as we've stated at the very start of this chapter, planets don't *really* move backward in their orbits—it is an optical illusion of human perception from Earth's vantage point.

So, thinking of planets astrologically as energies being expressed: you can view direct planets' energies as being extroverted, while retrograde planets' energies are introspective. Although this is not actually occurring (planets can move in only one direction along their orbits), this is the way it appears to look from Earth's vantage. Astrologically, then, this means planets' energies will be reversed, reconsidered, or turned inward when retrograde.

Mercury retrograde ☿ ℞, for example, rethinks things over and over to get communications or mental processes right, unlike direct Mercury's quicksilver approach. In such situations, there is potential for mental burnout, so to speak. Similarly, Mars retrograde ♂ ℞ must learn not to act on aggressive instincts without thinking first. Retrograde Mars must use less impulsive ways to achieve its desires and learn to reconsider actions before taking them.

Understanding Retrograde ℞ Planets

Retrograde planets aren't "bad." Just as we humans need to retreat periodically to renew our energies, so do planets. And, if you're born with a *personal retrograde,* you will be reconsidering the functions associated with that particular planet. A personal retrograde means that a planet was retrograde at the time of your birth, and its energy affects only you. This isn't "bad" at all. Once you understand what you need to do about that particular retrograde's function in your chart, you usually master it and could become known for this quality.

Transiting retrogrades are related to what's happening overhead at a given moment, and so they affect everybody. They occur as the movements of the planets change, during our daily lives. They affect everyone because while the retrograde planet is off on its retreat, the energy from it will feel "different," though it's not always something we can pinpoint. During transiting Mercury retrograde, for example, there might be communication breakdowns, or your car might stop running. It seems that massive Internet service disruptions or cell phone glitches have become a hallmark of Mercury retrogrades, so much so that it seems everyone experiences trouble logging on and dropped calls during these times.

Note that the Sun ☉ and the Moon ☽ are never retrograde. The Sun, unlike the planets, does not follow an orbit; instead, it is the point around which all the other orbits revolve. And the Moon, of course, revolves around Earth and does not follow an orbit like our own.

When a planet is retrograde ℞, it is closer to Earth than usual, and therefore, its energies are more intense. For this reason, the strengths of the energies from these planets require more effort to be integrated, and until that happens, there can be difficulties with them. Once the planet back in direct motion, its' energies move more smoothly and are straightforwardly expressed.

Personal Retrogrades ℞: Self-Expression

Planets that are retrograde at the time of your birth represent the karmic lessons you need to learn during your lifetime. That they are karmic means you will receive opportunity after opportunity to learn them; these lessons are not going to simply go away! The lessons involve matters in the houses where the retrograde planets occur. For example, if you have two retrograde planets in the seventh house, then you know that you'll be working through some issues with partnerships. The good news is that once you master the lesson, you acquire expertise in that area. You'll learn all about astrological houses in Part 4.

To show you how personal retrogrades work, we've provided the birth chart of boxing great Muhammad Ali. We picked Ali because not one, not two, not three, not even four, but *six* planets (and his Nodes!) were retrograde at the moment of his birth. People who have planets retrograde in their birth charts will have a higher level of awareness about the particular functions associated with those planets. In Ali's case, it's likely that he had much more awareness about many areas of his life than people without these retrograde planets.

Because Ali has so many planets retrograde, we'll take them one at a time. Let's start with his retrograde Venus ♀℞, which indicates someone who will reconsider social norms. Remember that Ali was born Cassius Clay and was among the first African American public figures to convert to the Nation of Islam, and you'll see how this retrograde has manifested.

Next, we have Jupiter retrograde ♃℞ in Ali's chart. This suggests that he might find that society's religions, beliefs, philosophies, and cultural values differ from his own. When someone with personal Jupiter retrograde finds his own belief system, however, his faith will be very strong. Need we say more?

Retrograde Uranus ♅℞ indicates a social reformer, someone who will champion what he believes is right no matter what the personal cost. Ali's championing of African American rights is recognized today as a trailblazing influence during the civil rights movement.

Ali's Neptune retrograde ♆℞ suggests a need to question and develop objectivity about matters of faith. Understanding one's spiritual path is of paramount importance to someone with Neptune retrograde. This placement reinforces Ali's retrograde Venus and Jupiter, making his conversion to the Nation of Islam all the more understandable.

Finally, with Pluto ♀ and Saturn ♄ retrograde and forming a supportive conjunction ☌, Ali is rethinking power, authority, societal conditions, and limitations. (See Chapter 17 for more on conjunctions and other astrological aspects.) This combination actually makes him more powerful because when he decides to do something, he is very clear about what he's doing and what the outcomes are likely to be. After all, he's probably reconsidered them more than once.

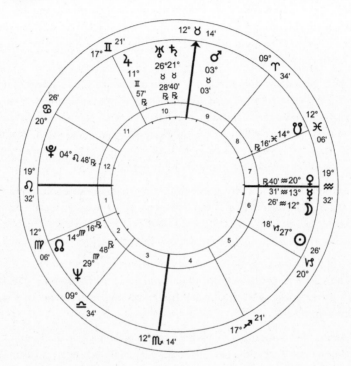

Muhammad Ali
Natal Chart
Jan 17 1942
6:35 pm CST +6:00
Louisville, KY
38°N15'15" 085°W45'34"
Geocentric
Tropical
Placidus
True Node

Transiting Retrogrades ℞: Change Is a Fact of Life

The heavens are constantly in motion. Transiting retrogrades occur because of the movements of the planets during our daily lives, and so affect everybody, every day. During transiting Mercury retrograde ☿ ℞, for example, we all will notice trouble with communications, misunderstandings, missed or rescheduled appointments, and transportation breakdowns. We'll also discover mistakes we made earlier, resulting in schedule delays.

Transiting retrogrades tend to encourage us to reflect on and evaluate decisions we've made. Some astrologers would say that transiting retrogrades cause us to reconsider previous decisions, asking ourselves, "Do you really want to move forward with that decision?" Delays, indecision, and second looks at choices we've made are all part of the energy of retrograde planets.

But hold on—this is not a bad thing! Sometimes the energy of a transiting retrograde brings new information that lets you see a situation in a way you couldn't before. The resulting reconsideration could save you costly mistakes. Transiting retrogrades can be thought of as global wake-up calls to rethink a particular planet's energies. Sometimes the energy is reversed, and sometimes it's intensified; but no matter what, it's just not quite the same as usual.

Many people feel and do better during transiting retrogrades of planets that also are personal retrogrades in their birth charts. Astrologers believe this is because they more keenly resonate with the transiting energy—they are able to march to the beat of their own drum during this time. Muhammad Ali's six retrograde planets, plus the retrograde nodes in his birth chart, reveal his unique karmic duty to challenge the status quo of his time and champion activism. Ali's fight outside the ring, throughout his long life, for equality and personal integrity resonates to the challenges of our own time.

Astrologers chart when planetary transiting retrogrades will occur years in advance, so they can avoid costly errors and misdirected efforts. For example, many won't travel by air during Mercury retrograde ☿ ℞ or sign a contractual agreement. Most wouldn't think of starting a new venture during a Mars retrograde ♂ ℞ when we should be rethinking action rather than beginning it.

Mercury Retrograde ☿ ℞: Crossed Wires

The purpose of Mercury retrograde ☿ ℞ is to encourage us to back up and catch up and to redo things that didn't get done the first time—or were done incorrectly—instead of constantly pushing forward. But it also can mean that expression becomes difficult and that we have trouble communicating through words or, worse, through other methods of communication, like e-mail or text.

During Mercury retrograde, Mercury is at its closest to the Earth. This is its most intense position; because this energy is "in our face," we're forced to deal with things we've glossed over, forgotten, or done wrong. Retrograde Mercury is not "bad" or "good"; it's a change in Mercury's energy. Being aware of it can help you avoid costly mistakes or unnecessary misunderstandings.

Personal Mercury Retrograde ☿ ℞

A personal retrograde occurs when a planet is retrograde at the time of your birth. Because a retrograde planet is out of step with its function in the present culture, personal Mercury retrograde indicates people who are learning to think for themselves, especially because their thoughts and ideas will be different from those of society. This can, of course, lead to some very interesting ideas and perspectives that society needs but hasn't thought of yet. And it's Mercury retrograde people who bring these ideas back to the fold.

People with personal Mercury retrograde are likely to have communication problems with others, either jumping ahead or lagging behind. This can translate to travel as well, where a person can seem perpetually out of step with everyone else. These tendencies often occur when the person is caught up in processing new information and determining direction. Personal Mercury retrograde may find a new way up the mountain (literally or figuratively) or develop a new method of communication that harnesses ideas outside the mainstream.

People born with Mercury retrograde are sorting through ideas, thoughts, and their own communications with greater intensity than people with Mercury direct. It takes time for them to get used to this and start understanding how to deal with it, but in the meantime, people with Mercury retrograde are sometimes likely to think too much, reprocessing the same thing over and over and then hitting mental burnout. However, people born with Mercury retrograde also often have uncanny intelligence and awareness. During transiting Mercury retrogrades, they may experience an extra boost of enthusiasm, acquire greater insight, and accomplish more than people born with Mercury direct.

Transiting Mercury Retrograde ☿ ℞

Because it's the ruler of transportation, when Mercury is retrograde, there are more car breakdowns, traffic mess-ups, and airline delays, and travel often has some unexpected and unpleasant surprises. (Don't you hate when GPS coordinates send you winding roundabout to a dead end?) Rental cars might not be ready or available, or hotel reservations might not have been made or kept. Your baggage might not even show up.

Transiting Mercury retrograde occurs three times every year for about three weeks each time, affecting everyone. This can signal everything from software and computer problems to packages not arriving. In projects requiring communication, signals can seem "crossed" or misunderstandings can occur, and there can be missed appointments, misunderstood texts, and schedule delays as well.

In business of any kind, Mercury retrograde is a difficult time to sign contracts. One or both parties might misinterpret the agreement or wish they hadn't signed on, and contracts often include mistakes. Contract discussions announced or initiated during this cycle are fraught with schedule problems and often fall apart. If you must sign a contract now, be thorough and painstaking, consider enlisting the guidance of a qualified professional, and meditate on opening your eyes and mind to what you may be overlooking in negotiations.

And look on the bright side! Transiting Mercury retrograde gives us three weeks, three times a year, to go back to projects and situations, so we can finish or redo them. Retrogrades always indicate the need to complete or return to something to improve upon the original work. These times are great opportunities to change or correct things you missed. And because you know transiting Mercury retrograde affects communication and transportation, take the extra effort to confirm appointments, project details, and travel plans. During Mercury retrograde periods, if we don't volunteer to redo what needs to be redone, circumstances will prevent us from making any progress until we do. It can be a great time to brush off that to-do list languishing in your computer and consider restarting stalled projects, reorganizing your priorities, and generally making time to catch up. Imagine that when you move in sync … Mercury retrogrades *make time!*

Venus Retrograde ♀℞: What's Love Got to Do with It?

Venus's energies are focused on all things bright and beautiful, and that includes everything from your social life to your love life. This means that during retrograde Venus ♀℞, you will reconsider and reevaluate everything from who and what you love to who loves you.

Personal Venus Retrograde ♀℞

People with a personal Venus retrograde will reconsider relationships and values, especially in terms of societal norms. By comparing their lives and values to others, they realize they can seem a bit eccentric and don't fit easily into the mainstream. They may choose to have relationships that are different from the norm. They might, for example, follow an alternative lifestyle or even enjoy spending most time alone.

Because their values are outside the cultural mainstream, these people also must learn to please and approve of themselves instead of seeking approval from others that may never come. Once they learn this, the social pressure to conform lessens. Personal Venus retrograde people may find themselves activists for great love and understanding and other social causes that improve and expand relationships.

If you have Venus in a personal retrograde, it can lead to feelings of awkwardness, missed connections, and doubts about one's worth as a lover or partner. At the same time, though, this retrograde can free you to pursue new or different social values because Venus's energies are turned inward. You will learn there are many ways to consume and to give love aside from those modeled by mainstream media and target-marketed to our smartphones.

Transiting Venus Retrograde ♀℞

During a transiting Venus retrograde, old lovers and friends may resurface, relationship issues come to the forefront, and all types of contracts and partnerships get reconsidered, especially if they are difficult.

This is also when values get reconsidered to see whether they still make sense or need adjusting. The purpose of transiting Venus retrograde is to reconsider relationship and acquisition needs because these evolve over time for everyone. So, it's important to get in touch with your present values, wants, and needs and become clear about what you want to attract.

Transiting Venus retrograde can pull to the surface talents and abilities you've set aside or didn't know you had. This is most pronounced with talents to develop contentment or prosperity in your life. Transiting Venus retrograde also can support you in attaining former wishes or desires. It is a time to evaluate value and consider what adds or does not add to your experience. In business, transiting Venus retrograde tracks the bottom line. It may be difficult to start a new venture now, access to credit may not be sufficient, or important relationships with vendors and suppliers may not be adequate. During Venus retrograde, rethink finances, relationships, and all questions of value to be sure your ventures—personal and professional—are on track.

Venus is retrograde the least amount of time of all the planets: Out of its 584-day cycle, its retrograde is not quite 6 weeks long.

Mars Retrograde ♂ ℞: Inward Action

Mars is the action planet, so it should come as no surprise that when it's retrograde, inward action is the name of the game. The purpose of Mars retrograde ♂ ℞ is to evaluate what motivates you and determine whether you're on the correct path and doing what you should be doing.

Personal Mars Retrograde ♂ ℞

A personal retrograde Mars means your desires, drive, ambition, and energy are turned inward, and this can result in enormous reserves of power being used to stay the course. With a personal Mars retrograde, you're here to rethink actions, desires, and aims.

With a personal Mars retrograde, you will learn to operate in a different manner, take a different path, and seek to fulfill your desires in new ways. But until you learn to do this, you might overreact or be too forceful in asserting yourself. People with Mars retrograde also tend to compete with themselves instead of with others.

Transiting Mars Retrograde ♂ ℞

During a transiting Mars retrograde ♂ ℞, it's time to adjust your actions and aggressive instincts to ensure that they accomplish your intent, which can include going back over previous actions and redoing them. Old resentments that haven't been resolved in the past will resurface during these periods because this is the time to develop new strategies and approaches for dealing with issues, anger, and learning assertiveness.

Transiting Mars retrograde is not the time to make new starts because this period is for directing your energies inward, determining where you should be headed, and determining how you should get there. So, when you try to push forward with new beginnings under this cycle, you often run into one obstacle after another, or you find you are demolishing everything in your path.

New ventures tend to be launched with too much enthusiasm and too little introspection. Mission statements take aim but miss their targets, and what is intended is not often what is perceived or received. Stock prices can fall or personal portfolios devalue. Transiting Mars retrograde may seem inflexible, wanting everything its own way, and it could benefit from a more equitable exchange of ideas and a longer period of brainstorming with a more team-oriented approach.

Mars is retrograde for a biennial period of about 9 to 10 weeks out of its 26-month cycle. So, every two years, the Universe asks us not to start anything new and to reconsider our directions and goals. "What an inconvenience," you say? Yes, but it is far worse for your venture to fail. Mars retrograde takes stock of our direction on the "right" path and redirects us if needed; it fine-tunes the algorithm. Now we have time to reassess our goals, discover our true motives, and be clear about how we're using energies. When we do so, we're ready to set course for the next two years … with the full force of Mars ♂ now direct to power us along!

Jupiter Retrograde ♃ ℞: Stepping Back

Because Jupiter is the planet of societal growth and expansion, when it's retrograde, you can expect that energy to turn inward. This means a personal Jupiter retrograde ♃ ℞ is someone who will be rethinking society's direction, and during a transiting Jupiter retrograde ♃ ℞, we'll all be evaluating the direction we've been going.

Personal Jupiter Retrograde ♃ ℞

People with a personal Jupiter retrograde find that society's religions, beliefs, philosophies, and cultural values aren't compatible with their own. They have to step back from these belief systems to develop their own "operating systems."

This process often results in very strong and intense faith, and examples of people with personal Jupiter retrograde include Muhammad Ali, the Dalai Lama, Mark Twain, and Karl Marx. People with personal Jupiter retrograde are very intuitive, seeking answers within themselves, and they often find unusual ways to expand their lives.

People with retrograde Jupiter must grow from within before they seek growth in the outer world. What the world has to offer might not be what they need, so they must first look within themselves.

Transiting Jupiter Retrograde ♃ ℞

Immediately preceding a transiting or cycling Jupiter retrograde, society, organizations, and individuals will have "gone too far" in their urges to expand and grow. Their actions in this regard will have exceeded positive limits, and Jupiter retrograde means it's time to step back.

A transiting Jupiter retrograde is the time to grow internally and prepare for opportunities that will be available after Jupiter goes direct. During these periods, it is particularly important to develop more understanding and awareness to determine whether what's being offered to you is what you really want.

Transiting Jupiter retrograde also brings into focus the need to balance extremes in your life. Remember, Jupiter is also the planet of generosity. When it goes retrograde, its energy may support you in completing an activity like going back to college to finish your degree that will bring you prosperity in the future. This is especially likely when you have personal Jupiter retrograde as well.

However, transiting Jupiter retrograde may represent systems that have begun to unravel because of excess or abuse. In such periods, debt can accumulate, such as student loan debt, credit card debt, or the national debt of a country. In such cases, a hard adjustment might be coming, and individuals will do well to take heed to minimize any personal damage from the fallout. These times, though, can hold enormous potential for positive change and the redirection of resources for the greater good.

Jupiter goes retrograde for a period of 4 months every 13 months. For a third of each year, the heavens prompt us to take a look at the balance of energies and resources in our lives and our communities and act upon them. In the words of anti-clutter guru Marie Kondo, it's a time to examine the things that "spark joy."

Saturn Retrograde ♄ ℞: Restructuring

Saturn is the planet of systems and organizations, and when it's retrograde, it's time to reexamine these things and find ways to improve them. If you were born with a Saturn retrograde ♄ ℞, you already know there are systems that need fixing, and you may well be devoting your life to doing just that. Saturn's critical-thinking skills are applied here to analyze systems, as disparate as government or education, which need refurbishing or streamlining.

Personal Saturn Retrograde ♄ ℞

People born with a personal Saturn retrograde ♄ ℞ were born when systems were being reorganized and restructured to work better. Because they're aware of the deficiencies in most systems or organizations, they want to find ways to make them work. Need an example of someone with personal Saturn retrograde? Steven Spielberg's retrograde Saturn ♄ ℞ is found in

Leo ♌ in his second house of material things. (See Appendix A for Spielberg's birth chart.) No wonder the legendary filmmaker questions everything, from the ethics of slavery in *The Color Purple, Amistad,* and *Lincoln* to the Holocaust in *Schindler's List.*

Because Saturn represents limits, people with retrograde Saturn might not have clear or well-defined boundaries with others. This, in turn, can lead to them accepting too many responsibilities for others—or not enough for themselves. In addition, these people will be challenged to find their own definitions of success and their own social roles because they won't relate to society's standards, or their role models might not have given them the needed guidance.

People who have personal Saturn retrograde are always trying to find good role models for authority, but this is actually the lesson of Saturn in retrograde—these people will become their own role models. If you were born with Saturn in retrograde, Saturn the taskmaster is telling you that you are your own boss. Empower yourself! When you meet the challenges Saturn retrograde reveals in your birth chart, your rewards can be great.

Transiting Saturn Retrograde ♄ ℞

During a transiting or cyclical Saturn retrograde ♄ ℞, it's time for all of us to restructure systems, programs, organizations, and rules to make them function better. Processes and policies all benefit from reexamination during this period.

On a personal level, transiting Saturn retrograde is the time to become more aware of your own authority and power, and whether it fits within society's rules. It's also a time to reconsider where *you* fit within society (or any structured organization) and whether you're allowing its rules to limit you. The challenge is to objectively analyze society's patterns and expectations.

Transiting Saturn retrograde is hard work but good work. This energy supports you in developing self-empowerment and responsibility. Through self-discipline, you will eventually acquire strong character, strong will, and focused effort.

Saturn retrogrades every 12½ months for a period of 4½ months. It is a cycle of build and rebuild, create and revise. Saturn's taskmaster makes sure we have a lengthy period each year in which to shore up our prevailing structures, or to tear them down, as needed. Care should be taken with contracts of any nature.

Uranus Retrograde ♅ ℞: For the Times They Are A-Changin'

Uranus is the planet of the unconscious, and even when it's retrograde, this is the area where its energies are concentrated. The difference during a retrograde is that the energy is even more pronounced, so people born with Uranus retrograde ♅ ℞ are often in the forefront when it comes to change.

Personal Uranus Retrograde ♅ ℞

Because Uranus is the Awakener or Liberator, it acts primarily on a person's unconscious. When Uranus is retrograde ♅ ℞ in a person's chart, the desire to reform or rebel is even stronger than when Uranus is direct. For this reason, it's very important for these people to understand the internal workings of structures and systems before they create reforms. When a person has Uranus retrograde, it's important to become as detached and objective as possible when determining what to change.

Both John F. Kennedy and Adolf Hitler had Uranus retrograde in their charts. Although both men were major social reformers, President Kennedy chose to use this energy to champion equal rights and humanitarian changes, while Hitler demonstrated its negative aspects by letting his ego override the welfare of others (among other things).

Transiting Uranus Retrograde ♅ ℞

In cyclical or transiting Uranus retrogrades ♅ ℞, it's time to ask yourself what changes are occurring in the world and how you're contributing to or working against them. It's important to see the connections between your own personal changes and those that are occurring around the world.

Like other transiting retrogrades, Uranus instigates processes of review and reevaluation. While the energy of Uranus in direct motion acts to disrupt the status quo and free us to break out of the box, retrograde Uranus provides an opportunity to explore how we fit as individuals into the scheme of things and teaches us patience in the process of change. Use the energy of transiting Uranus retrograde to plan for the major changes you want to make in your life.

Uranus retrogrades for five months every year. It provides prolonged annual opportunities for disrupting systems to make the world a better place—by championing women's rights or working for climate change policies that benefit the planet, not destroy it. If the world is too daunting a canvas for change, look for ways you can volunteer in your community or make personal changes that are fulfilling, shaking up the status quo to improve both your life and the lives of others.

Neptune Retrograde ♆ ℞: Not Just Blind Faith

Faith and dreams: These are the areas of Neptune's energy, and when this planet is retrograde, nothing is accepted as blind faith. Whether it's the personal spiritual quest of a person with retrograde Neptune ♆ ℞ or the collective quest of society during a transiting Neptune retrograde, this planet's retrograde energy means a reexamination of hopes and beliefs.

Personal Neptune Retrograde ♆ ℞

When Neptune is retrograde ♆ ℞ in a person's chart, there's an even stronger indication that the person needs to question and test all aspects of faith. Instead of blindly accepting faith, they're here to question it and develop objectivity regarding all the intangibles of life, such as truth, fear, hope, and inspiration. Because Neptune is closest to Earth when retrograde, its functions are intensified. For this reason, it's also commonly found in artists, musicians, poets, and those who lead spiritual lives.

Understanding their spiritual path either will be an important part of the lives of retrograde Neptune people, or they may be confused, disillusioned, or full of illusions. For these people, dreams can be an important method of accessing messages from their unconscious.

If a spiritual quest isn't pursued, retrograde Neptune people may fall into drugs, alcohol, or other addicting or escapist behaviors. Because this need to understand spirituality is so emphasized in them, they can't ignore it and must deal with it one way or another. Ideally, they question the ideas society accepts about faith, fears, truth, and understanding, and bring this information not only to themselves but to the rest of the world as well.

Transiting Neptune Retrograde ♆ ℞

When Neptune is retrograde ♆ ℞, cyclically or by transit, it's time for everyone to tune in to the collective unconscious and notice how their fears, illusions, confusion, or spiritual journeys are connected to what's happening with humanity. You should determine whether you're using your own energies in positive ways to develop faith and spirituality, or you're pursuing a path of escapism and disappointment.

Transiting Neptune retrograde acts to dissolve boundaries. It brings awareness—though often frustrated awareness—to our surroundings and to other people. The resulting vulnerability can generate sensitivity and spirituality … or confusion and paranoia. Even though retrogrades are all about completion, transiting Neptune retrograde tends to leave us wanting more. Is the grass really greener in the next valley? With Neptune retrograde, you are willing to climb the mountain to find out.

Neptune retrogrades about five to six months every year. Neptune direct and Neptune retrograde form a kind of yin/yang balance each year, affording opportunities to create a spiritual path and to maintain it.

Pluto Retrograde ♀ ℞: Transformation Time

When Pluto is retrograde ♀ ℞, the one thing you can expect is the unexpected. As the planet of transformation, Pluto's energies equal change, so retrograde Pluto means a reexamination of the changes you (and society) have been making.

Personal Pluto Retrograde ♀ ℞

When Pluto is retrograde ♀ ℞ in a chart, this indicates that people will be much more intensely focused on personal transformation and rebirth to help transform the world. First, these people must be reborn to new ways, so they can begin to affect the world positively. It's also important for them to connect their own actions, behaviors, and changes to those of humanity and see what role they're playing in it. With today's environmental concerns, these people are aware of how they affect Earth with their actions and attitudes.

Transiting Pluto Retrograde ♀ ℞

As a cyclical or transiting period, Pluto retrograde ♀ ℞ is our signal that it's time to step back and review how each of us is either contributing to the future and evolution of humankind and Earth or working to destroy it. These are the periods when it's important to become more conscious of how we impact Earth and others.

Already slow in its actions, Pluto in retrograde becomes even slo-o-o-wer—so slow that we feel stuck even to the point of hopelessness. This is because transiting Pluto retrograde wants us to go deep into ourselves and our experiences to make transformational, not superficial, changes. But then Pluto suddenly throws open the door and completion erupts, the bud blooms, and the chrysalis bursts. Transiting Pluto retrograde is about letting go of those deep pains and issues that hold us back from personal growth. Whatever you let go will be replaced by new opportunity, new consciousness, and new hope.

Pluto is retrograde every year for at least five months. This means that the rumblings of transformative growth and change are there underpinning our experience and prompting us not to hold back but to give in to change.

One Step Forward, Two Steps Back

The dance of planetary retrogrades, forward and back, in ourselves and in our world, is simply the nature of existence and the nature of relationships. Retrograde energies balance direct energies and vice versa, as yin balances yang. The more consciously you consider retrograde energies, the more positively you can understand yourself and the world and the better dancer you become. Remember, all energies can be used for the good, and retrograde energies are no exception.

THE TWELVE HOUSES: WHERE PLANETS LIVE

What we call the zodiac wheel, the planets call home. Each of the wheel's 12 segments is an astrological house, and each house has a planetary ruler—the house's landlord, so to speak. The houses are the areas of your life experiences, where the action is. Houses are the "where" of astrology.

The planets, as you know, are always on the celestial road. So, they stay in different houses as they travel through space and time. Some planets come perilously close to overstaying their welcome, and others move on before you know it.

You'll want your birth chart as you read the chapters in Part 4, so you can discover for yourself the meanings of the houses and your planetary placements. The more you learn, the more comfortable you will be with chart interpretation.

Part

4

Chapter 13

LET'S GET PERSONAL: FIRST, SECOND, AND THIRD HOUSES

From the very beginnings of astrology, astrologers divided areas of life into different categories. The Babylonian astrologers named these areas the houses to represent the arenas where the drama of your life unfolds. Whereas signs are psychological processes, houses are experiential, or as astrologer Steven Forrest puts it, "We *are* our signs, and we *do* our houses."

Because there are 12 signs and 12 houses, learning the symbolism of the signs is a big step toward learning the symbolism of the houses. Still, they aren't at all the same things, so let's make sure you understand the difference.

Houses Are Where the Action Is

There are specific meanings to which *houses* your planets are in—adding more dimensions to unlocking the mystery of you. The houses are the "where" of astrology. Each of the 12 houses encompasses a specific area of your life. Any house in your birth chart with more than one planet in it shows an area of your life that is emphasized and strengthened. At the same time, houses without any planets, "empty" houses, are active as well. It all depends on the house's ruler and the *aspects* it has to it. A house without planets in it could be just as strong as—or stronger than—one with planets visible. When two planets are in aspect to each other, they're related by one of a set of geometric angles between them, some of which are beneficial or well-aspected, while others are challenging. For example, two planets that are 180 degrees apart (±7 degrees) are said to be opposite. There are five major aspects: Conjunctions ☌ 0 degrees, Sextiles ✳ 60 degrees, Squares ☐ 90 degrees, trines △ 120 degrees, and oppositions ☍ 180 degrees. Conjunctions, sextiles, and trines are considered beneficial. Squares and oppositions are more difficult to resolve. Learn more about astrological aspects in Chapter 17.

All houses, whether empty or full, have house rulers, which describe what's happening in that area of your life. An absence of planets in a house doesn't mean there's nothing going on in that house. Remember, all houses have rulers or landlords, which are ultimately in charge of the house. On the other hand, if one of the planets "living" in a house is also its ruler, then that house has, in effect, a resident landlord. Just like a real landlord, that planet's going to have a lot of control over what happens in that particular area of life. Let's look in the Dalai Lama's second house, which has no planets "at home." To know more, we look at the "empty" house's cusp sign. The Dalai Lama's second house of self-worth and personal resources, for example, has Leo ♌ on the cusp.

The second house's *natural* ruling sign is Taurus ♉, which in the Dalai Lama's chart is on the cusp of the twelfth house of spirituality, whose natural ruling sign is Pisces ♓. In other words, the Dalai Lama's second house areas are tied with both his tenth house of ethics' midheaven and his third house areas as well (where his Neptune ♆ resides).

As you read in earlier chapters, the houses in your chart appear as 12 pie slices, 6 below the *horizon* and 6 above. Your horizon divides your chart into north and south, and it runs from your *ascendant* to your *descendant*. On an astrological chart, south is the upper half, or houses 7 through 12; north is the lower half, or the first six houses. It also connects your ascendant, which is the sign on the beginning of the first house, and your descendant, which is the sign on the beginning of the seventh house. The meridian line divides the circle of your chart into eastern and western halves. The line of your meridian connects your lower heaven and your midheaven.

Like Four Points of the Compass

We introduced the concepts of your astrological ascendant, descendant, midheaven (M.C.), and lower heaven (I.C.) in Part 1. Here, we return to the birth chart of the Dalai Lama to look at each of these points in more depth. We'll show you where to find them on His Holiness's chart so that you, in turn, can find them on your own.

As you recall, your ascendant, or your Rising sign, is the same as the sign on the cusp of your first house and represents your self-image and personality. The Dalai Lama's ascendant is Cancer ♋. This tells us he has a compassionate approach to family and humankind.

Your descendant is the sign on the cusp of your seventh house and represents how you channel your energies through partnerships and relationships. The Dalai Lama's descendant is Capricorn ♑. This attracts partners of deep thought and commitment to devoted union.

In addition to the horizon line, your chart is divided by a meridian line, which separates your birth chart into east on the left and west on the right. The lowest point of the meridian is the lower heaven or I.C., and is the same as the cusp, or beginning, of the fourth house. This symbolizes your life's foundation, including your home and psychological roots. The Dalai Lama's lower heaven is Virgo ♍. Virgo is very work- and service-oriented. Its appearance on the I.C. signals a strong commitment to perfect your home and roots.

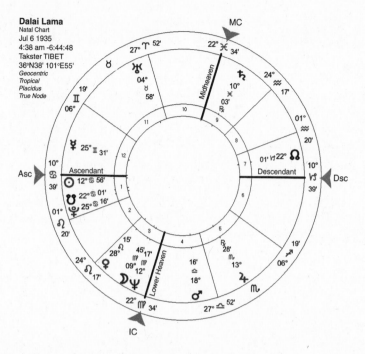

Dalai Lama
Natal Chart
Jul 6 1935
4:38 am -6:44:48
Takster TIBET
36°N38' 101°E55'
Geocentric
Tropical
Placidus
True Node

The highest point of the meridian is the midheaven or M.C., and is the same as the cusp, or beginning, of the tenth house. This represents your ambition, career or social role, and public image. The Dalai Lama's midheaven is Pisces ♓. To the view of the outside world, the Dalai Lama brings spiritual awareness through sacrifice in his personal life.

So, are you ready to grab your birth chart and tour today's open houses? We promise, no pushy real estate agents! We start by taking you through the three houses in the first quadrant, which are all about you. You can look back to Chapter 3 to review the natural associations of signs and houses, and Chapter 2 for a refresher on astrological qualities.

House	Natural Ruler	Natural Planet(s)	Quality
First, Ascendant	Aries ♈	Mars ♂ Pluto ♀	Cardinal, personal influence
Second	Taurus ♉	Venus ♀	Succedent, personal stability
Third	Gemini ♊	Mercury ☿	Cadent, higher purpose

The First House: Taking Care of Number One

This is the house of self, the place where your ascendant—your personality and self-image—resides. Here is where you will find your personal style, from your mannerisms to your temperament, including your disposition, your likes and dislikes, and a key to why you look the way you do. This house also includes your physical body and your early childhood, and it is closely tied to your health. The first house is sometimes called the "house of self-interest" because it shows what you want as well as how you're going to get it. Self-interest sometimes gets a bad rap, but there's nothing wrong with getting what you want from life!

The first house is the house where your ascendant "lives," the place where you will find the mask that best serves your needs. Successfully navigated, the first house shows a sense of control and direction; if it is less successfully navigated, there will be a lack of self-assurance, which might manifest in a number of ways.

Because the planet that rules the natural first house is Mars ♂ and its corresponding sign is Aries ♈, it's clear that the focus of this house is going to be your identity or the "I am" principle. The first house represents the beginnings of your life. With Pluto ♀ as co-ruler of the first house, the soul's journey is represented here as well as what the soul has chosen to learn in this lifetime.

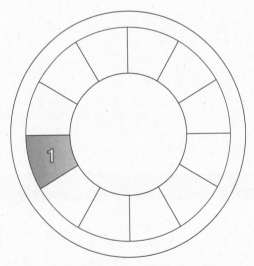

The first house: your physical self, personality, and early childhood.

Heavenly Bodies and Me, Me, Me

Your first house sign describes your self-image and how you express your identity; its ruler describes where and how your identity and self-image are developed. The Aries ♈ house (the corresponding natural sign) shows another area of life that your identity is tied to, providing you with greater self-awareness.

The Sun ☉ in the First House

If the planet of individuality appears here in the house of self, there's a strong sense of self and powerful leadership abilities, as well as a need for lots of attention. A first house Sun indicates a "sunny" disposition and an optimistic nature. A first house Sun *could* mean the ascendant and Sun sign are the same, but it will *always* mean that there's a strong will, tons of energy, a noble manner, and intense self-awareness. The Sun represents *why* you are here; its appearance in your first house tells you that part of your life lesson is learning about yourself.

First house Sun ☉ Notables: Jude Law, Steve Martin, Neil Young, Ingmar Bergman, and Mark Twain

The Moon ☽ in the First House

A first house Moon indicates imaginative self-expression and a desire to be admired and appreciated. To first house Moons, everything can depend on how they feel. Their expression is changeable and moody, and they're highly impressionable, which might also indicate psychic abilities. The Moon is your emotional self. When the Moon is in your first house, you see the world through the lens of your emotions and your feelings. This viewpoint is intuitive and can be impressionable. When you have the Moon in your first house, you may easily become moody because you're always thinking about what other people might be thinking about you! Your feelings and emotions are the basis for your relationships in the external world.

First house Moon ☽ Notables: Kate Winslet, Leonardo diCaprio, Billy Crystal, Charlie Chaplin, and Stanley Kubrick

Mercury ☿ in the First House

Mercury in the first house indicates mental alertness and a person who thrives on intellectual challenges, likes to travel, and enjoys meeting others. Such a person is quite the communicator and can be very eloquent, witty, and funny. Expect to see first house Mercury with a strong social media presence; this is someone who enjoys telling others about their travels and experiences for the sake of sharing resources and information learned (that is, not necessarily for the attention…). Mental initiative and keen intelligence go hand in hand with this placement.

First house Mercury ☿ Notables: Elijah Wood, Scarlett Johansson, Nicolas Cage, Ronald Reagan, and Mahatma Gandhi

Venus ♀ in the First House

First house Venus indicates beauty, harmony, grace, kindness, friendliness, and charm—all those wonderful Venus characteristics. A Venus in the first house cares a great deal about its appearance, and this placement also shows physical beauty and possible artistic talents. People who have Venus in the first house often have a hopeful, positive, optimistic outlook on life. And remember, there are all kinds of physical beauty and Venus espouses them all!

First house Venus ♀ Notables: George Clooney, Queen Elizabeth II, Judy Garland, Buster Keaton, and Andy Warhol

Mars ♂ in the First House

Someone with Mars in the first house isn't going to take the advice of others; this placement indicates both independence and impulsiveness. A first house Mars has plenty of energy and confidence, especially when tackling new projects, but may be impatient with others who don't move as quickly; a first house Mars might even be a bit abrasive. This placement also indicates physical robustness and strength and people who love sports or other forms of physical exercise.

First house Mars ♂ Notables: Brad Pitt, Sandra Bullock, Roman Polanski, Truman Capote, and Lyndon B. Johnson

Jupiter ♃ in the First House

Generous Jupiter in the first house is honest, enthusiastic, and benevolent. Jupiter in the first house brings a great enthusiasm for helping others to see their own potential. If you have Jupiter in your first house, nothing makes you happier than seeing others succeed, which makes sense because Jupiter is the expansion planet. When you have this placement, you may be a social, educational, or religious leader, or you might work in some type of leadership position. People who have Jupiter in the first house often have strong religious beliefs or moral ethics.

First house Jupiter ♃ Notables: Kristen Stewart, Eminem, Ben Stiller, Ringo Starr, and Martin Luther King Jr.

Saturn ♄ in the First House

Self-disciplined, organized, and persistent, someone who has Saturn in the first house can be quite successful. People who have this placement are likely to be very serious and hardworking, too, and they might have had limitations placed on them as children. First-house Saturn is sensible and orderly, and with other good factors, first house Saturn might be very successful in real estate. These people either readily accept major responsibilities or may feel like they are burdened with them. Also, they might have several obstacles to overcome to become independent and free.

First house Saturn ♄ Notables: Laura Dern, Cher, Debra Winger, Fred Astaire, and Andrei Tarkovsky

Uranus ♅ in the First House

Uranus in the first house indicates both eccentricity and inventiveness, a person whose life seems filled with the unexpected, and someone who usually takes it all in stride. Uranus here can indicate people who are ahead of their time, who may be geniuses, or who have very keen awareness. They observe and study everything. Spontaneous and quick to respond, they are exceptionally good in emergencies and crises. Intuition is usually strong, and they often have scientific or advanced talents. Physically, these people might appear striking in some way and have magnetic personalities.

First house Uranus ♅ Notables: Natalie Portman, Johnny Depp, Bruce Springsteen, Audrey Hepburn, and Ray Bradbury

Neptune ♆ in the First House

Neptune is the planet of seeking a higher plane. So people who have Neptune in their first house have great sensitivity to the needs of the spiritual community. They can be very intuitive and might be mystical or clairvoyant, too. They are so sensitive that they feel everything around them, even things at a subliminal level. Also, they are often very artistic and might have musical talents. This is a very creative placement, and people who have it are often attracted to careers in the fine arts, film, theater, and other creative endeavors. Their increased sensitivity, however, may leave first-house Neptune vulnerable to addictions, and they may need to be careful about this. Physically, these people might appear to have a dreamy or otherworldly look to them.

First house Neptune ♆ Notables: Björk, Denzel Washington, Tom Cruise, Marcel Proust, and Benjamin Franklin

Pluto ♀ in the First House

If Pluto is in your first house, your soul has a special evolutionary destiny to fulfill. To pursue this, you need plenty of independence and freedom, so you can find out on your own who you are and become yourself. On the other hand, you may be afraid or timid about evolving beyond what is familiar to you, so you may go through periodic identity crises that force you to become involved with others. Then you can find out who you are and learn your special destiny. Your soul's intent here is to learn to develop equal relationships with others and to balance your need for freedom and independence with the needs of others. First-house Pluto are often self-involved because Pluto is the rebirthing planet, and this is part of their evolutionary development. They're strong-willed, intense individuals.

First house Pluto ♀ Notables: Beyoncé Knowles, Eddie Murphy, Sting, Yasser Arafat, and Abraham Lincoln

North Node ☊ in the First House/South Node ☋ in the Seventh House

If your North Node is in the first house and your South Node in the seventh, you are here to learn how to establish self-identity and become a leader. (Remember, your Nodes are always in complementary houses.) Until now, you've submerged your identity in the affairs of others and have allowed others' opinions to influence your sense of who you are. Now it's time to *become yourself* and learn to balance your needs with those of others.

First house North Node ☊ Notables: Helen Mirren, Martin Scorsese, Jerry Lewis, Johnny Cash, and F. Scott Fitzgerald

The Second House: Are You What You Own?

Your second house reveals how you feel about your assets and also will show the best ways for you to make the most of your earning capacity. The second house is also where you'll find your money and what you own that can be easily moved , as well as what you *will* own and value, including your income and those things you'll come to treasure. (This excludes a home and real estate, which are part of the fourth house.) The second house also reveals how you feel about your possessions.

The second house also represents your self-esteem, earning abilities, and personal resources, which are interconnected, making this the house of productivity and self-worth.

The natural second house cusp is ruled by Taurus ♉, the sign of self-assuredness and possessions. And the natural planet in charge is Venus ♀, whose associations are beauty, charm, values, harmony, and the things you own.

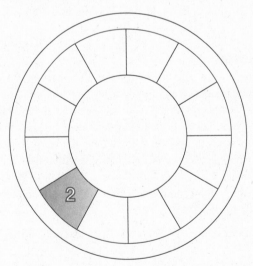

The second house: your possessions, earning abilities, and self-esteem.

What Do I Have in the House?

Your second house is where you develop your values, resources, and self-esteem, so the sign on your second house cusp describes their characteristics. Your second house ruler describes where and how you develop them. The house with the corresponding natural sign of Taurus shows the area to which your values, resources, and self-esteem are tied and where you use them to achieve the results you want. The planets in the second house give clues to your values, resources, and self-esteem.

Poor self-esteem might lead you to try to substitute material things for a feeling of self-worth. If there are challenging factors related to the second house, you may believe that material possessions can be substituted for inner self-worth. Or you may not feel worthy of having sufficient or plenty of money, so you manage to prevent that from happening. For that reason, it's important to truly *value yourself.*

The Sun ☉ in the Second House

A second house Sun indicates the ability and power to become financially self-sufficient. You readily attract resources, get jobs, and earn good income. Many people who have the Sun in the second house are entrepreneurial; they start their own businesses and manage their own money. The lesson of a second house Sun is to learn the correct use of material resources in ways that are beneficial to others as well as to oneself. There is a strong desire to become financially independent—or at least earn a lot of money—because stability and security are very important. These people might earn money from creative talents.

Second house Sun ☉ Notables: Usher, Diane Keaton, Frank Sinatra, Edith Piaf, and Catherine the Great

The Moon ☽ in the Second House

The most important thing for a second-house Moon is its strong need for emotional security, which is often tied to possessions. Also, establishing a strong set of values is important. This placement indicates an ability to earn money from businesses associated with food, homes, and real estate, although finances may go through phases, like the Moon. The Moon in the second house is an easy-come, easy-go placement because there are often fluctuations in earning capacity. People who have the Moon in the second house have an emotional attachment to the job and its income. This placement attracts business contacts and support systems through the feminine side of a person's nature.

Second house Moon ☽ Notables: Beyoncé Knowles, Michael J. Fox, Sophia Loren, Theodore Roosevelt, and Lord Byron

Mercury ☿ in the Second House

Mercury in the second house means the mind and/or communication will be at work for your earning capacity, and a second house Mercury might spend that money on travel, education, information, and time-saving gadgets. People with Mercury in the second house like to translate ideas into financial gain, and with their quick minds, they might be economists, hedge fund managers, corporate planners, salespeople, writers, teachers, broadcasters, journalists, or publishers.

Second house Mercury ☿ Notables: William Shatner, Philip Seymour Hoffman, Bob Marley, Agatha Christie, and Georg Ohm

Venus ♀ in the Second House

People with Venus in the second house are honest and fair in their financial dealings and are generous with financial advice. They believe in the win-win approach; Venus is all about prosperity, including the sharing of it. Venus loves nothing more than to share and see others become prosperous as well. People with a Venus second house placement might pursue careers in areas that promote beauty in some way, such as the arts, fashion, or interior design. Because this is one of Venus's natural residences, people here are often very generous; they also might seek wealth as a means of attaining social status.

Second house Venus ♀ Notables: Brad Pitt, Avril Lavigne, Francis Ford Coppola, Claude Levi-Strauss, and Mao Zedong

Mars ♂ in the Second House

Mars in the second house gains through its own effort and competitive spirit. Money matters, and a second-house Mars will go after it. When it comes to spending, though, people with this placement are often impulsive, lose sight of the budget, or forget there even *is* a budget! But people who have Mars in the second house are hard workers and are always earning money; they have a strong work ethic and need to be productive. This placement is a good one for engineers, mechanics, career military, government workers, those with strong initiative in business, and people who prefer to work for themselves.

Second house Mars ♂ Notables: Will Smith, Jennifer Aniston, Scarlett Johansson, Stephen Hawking, and Tsar Nicholas II

Jupiter ♃ in the Second House

Lucky Jupiter has no trouble with making money in this house and often has good fortune in attracting money. But while people with Jupiter in the second house can make a great deal of money, they also might overspend it freely. This placement indicates someone with a great deal of business acumen and expansiveness, so others also often benefit from this placement's generosity. People with this placement might be found in the travel business or in banking, stocks, import/export, or insurance. Other fields for a second house Jupiter include real estate, food, education, the legal system, fund-raising, and publishing.

Second house Jupiter ♃ Notables: Julia Roberts, Madonna, Jay-Z, Neil Armstrong, and Emily Brontë

Saturn ♄ in the Second House

Saturn's ambition pays out in the second house, where its long-range financial planning can lead to material comfort and success. People with Saturn here want to work hard to achieve financial security, so they can approach their earning capacity. They are cautious spenders, and they are not about to give away the money they've worked so hard to accumulate! Shrewd and conservative, the gain will be slow but steady. Also, second house Saturn might worry about money, even if it doesn't need to, but it can do quite well with real-estate investments, government and business contracts, management, and construction. In short, they are made for the long haul.

Second house Saturn ♄ Notables: Liv Tyler, Drew Barrymore, Steven Spielberg, Sidney Poitier, and Jules Verne

Uranus ♅ in the Second House

Second house Uranus might make its money in unusual ways, with opportunities that seem to literally pop up out of nowhere. There might be wild fluctuations in net worth here, which Uranus might be able to ride out. This can be anything from boom to bust. When it comes to saving money, Uranus in the second house can be erratic, unless there is something in particular it is saving to purchase. In this case, this placement can save scrupulously. This placement indicates people who may do better with their own businesses and who may not "buy into" the value systems accepted by others.

Second house Uranus ♅ Notables: Venus Williams, Robert Downey Jr., Bette Midler, Pablo Picasso, and Lewis Carroll

Neptune ♆ in the Second House

Second house Neptune approaches making money with both intuition and imagination, and it might be surrounded with objects valued more for their aesthetic values rather than their material values. Second house Neptune can be quite resourceful, or they might experience financial difficulties as their finances dissolve. They have an idealistic sense about money and how to use their resources, but there may be unforeseen expenses or circumstances that make holding on to money difficult. They may need to develop faith and a sense of flow where their resources are concerned.

Second house Neptune ♆ Notables: James Franco, Judi Dench, Judy Garland, Carl Gustav Jung, and William Butler Yeats

Pluto ♀ in the Second House

With a second house Pluto, you have a strong survival instinct and need to develop self-reliance and self-sufficiency. Your primary identity might be focused on either your sense of values, including power and possessions, or your abilities, talents, and resources for earning an income. In all cases, your soul's evolutionary intent is to grow beyond the limitations of the way you've identified your self-sustenance by merging your resources, talents, or possessions with others. For example, if you've been equating material gain with self-worth or self-sustainment, you'll need to reassess this and learn about the deeper aspects of life. If, on the other hand, you're focused on your talents, earning abilities, or spiritual values, then you'll need to learn how to tie them to a social need to support yourself. With Pluto in the second house, you possess stability and inner strength, which you can use to promote self-reliance in others.

Second house Pluto ♀ Notables: Emma Watson, Robert Downey Jr., Robert De Niro, Cher, and Louis Armstrong

North Node ☊ in the Second House/South Node ☋ in the Eighth House

A second house North Node/eighth house South Node indicates that you've already learned how to take on the values of others to share in their possessions and resources. You know all about secrets, and you may be so busy keeping them that you neglect your present lessons about where your values really are. You need to discover and establish that which is truly meaningful to you and understand that you can't keep what you haven't acquired honestly. You can develop a completely new and meaningful life for yourself by establishing your own values—and living by them.

Second house North Node ☊ Notables: Winona Ryder, Derek Jacobi, Madonna, Walt Disney, and Fyodor Dostoevsky

The Third House: The Street Where You Live

The third house is often called the house of communication, but this term can disguise the many areas of your life that actually reside there. Because this house contains your capacities for information gathering and sharing, its areas include your knowledge, short journeys, your siblings, and your immediate environment.

You could think of your third house as where you think because it covers logic, memory, and manual skills. It's also about your early education: how and from whom you learned what you know.

The natural third house is ruled by Mercury ☿, of course, and its associated sign is Gemini ♊. Communication, remember, is not just about talking; it's also about listening, our perceptions, and the many other ways we communicate.

Part of your local environment includes the people you haven't "chosen." In other words, this is everyone from your siblings to your neighbors. The third house is the place where all these connections reside, so understanding what's in your third house can help you see why you seem to be stuck with people who drive you crazy—or why you're blessed with people you adore.

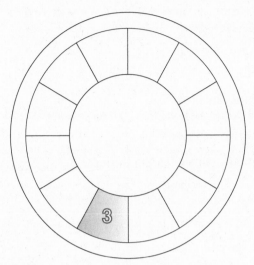

The third house: your knowledge, siblings, and environment.

Heavenly Bodies in Your 'Hood

Because your third house accommodates the nature of your communications, perceptions, knowledge, education, and local environment, the sign on the third house describes the traits of these areas. The landlord planet, Mercury ☿, or ruler of your third-house sign—describes where and how you develop your ideas, how you communicate those ideas to others, and how knowledge from your local environment is used. The house with Gemini ♊ on its cusp shows where you seek new knowledge and information and where you make mental connections with others.

The Sun ☉ in the Third House

An active, creative Sun in the third house wants to communicate ideas and might be a leader in its field. There might be a desire to explore oneself in intellectual ways, or there might even be a driving need for intellectual distinction and a knack for being in the right place at the right time. A third-house Sun is a good communicator and desires to participate in community activities and local affairs.

Third house Sun ☉ Notables: Ivana Trump, Stephen King, Mick Jagger, Jean-Luc Godard, and Paul Cezanne

The Moon ☽ in the Third House

A third house Moon cares a great deal about family and also is involved in education and travel. There's curiosity and a strong imagination here, with a primary tendency to think emotionally. This placement can be restless because it doesn't much care for routine, but it's also a good listener with a remarkable memory for what it hears. Moon in the third house is very attached to siblings and to early home life.

Third house Moon ☽ Notables: Patti Smith, Dana Carvey, Yoko Ono, Elvis Presley, and George Eliot

Mercury ☿ in the Third House

Because this is where Mercury naturally lives, this placement makes for a lively, inquisitive mind and a versatility in handling both people and projects. Mercury in the third house has a quick wit and a good sense of humor, and it is always eager to learn more; those who have this placement can be pretty sharp folks. But third house Mercury also can mean a restless mind that worries a lot, so a profession that keeps this placement on the move can work very well. These people might also be writers, speakers, reporters/journalists, or editors.

Third house Mercury ☿ Notables: Adele, Jared Leto, Ivana Trump, Edgar Allan Poe, and Anton Chekhov

Venus ♀ in the Third House

Venus in the third house is a negotiator, mediator, and facilitator, always seeking harmony through communication. Venus in the third house is always looking for win-win collaborations. Charming and gentle, this placement makes communication seem effortless, and there is both charm and tact in third house Venus people. This placement also can indicate artistic creativity, a love of literature or poetry, and travel for pleasure.

Third house Venus ♀ Notables: Jay-Z, Julia Roberts, Stephen King, Annie Lennox, and Garry Kasparov

Mars ♂ in the Third House

Third house Mars will usually speak its mind, and with its determination, it often gets what it wants through its persuasive or aggressive ways with words. These people are also quick thinkers—especially in emergencies—so they have to be careful about jumping to conclusions. They're quick to react, quick to speak their minds, and quick to get out there and act. Often people who deal with transportation or communication equipment will have this placement, and it also is seen in reporters, journalists, and people in the political arena.

Third house Mars ♂ Notables: Jennifer Lawrence, Hugh Grant, Robert McNamara, Charles Lindbergh, and Martin Luther

Jupiter ♃ in the Third House

Third house Jupiter often has a variety of intellectual interests and might achieve success through education, writing, or communication. This placement signals an enthusiastic, expansive mind with a strong philosophical foundation. Witty and optimistic, this placement is well liked by others. Jupiter in the third house also can indicate a great deal of travel. Because these people are usually very interested in social trends and causes, many writers with this placement pursue topics of this nature, often creating travel logs online to share their experiences and knowledge with the public.

Third house Jupiter ♃ Notables: Sean Astin, Jimmy Carter, Ernest Hemingway, Washington Irving, and Charles Darwin

Saturn ♄ in the Third House

Saturn in the third house wants to learn things to put them to good use. This is a practical placement and can indicate a good student, as well as a strong scientific or mathematical ability. These people might work in printing, publishing, or the communications industry, and they're also good accountants, teachers, researchers, or librarians. With Saturn in the third house, the life task is to get people to understand the basic concepts no matter what the project. There's a possibility that people with this placement might have had relationship difficulties with neighbors or siblings, or they might have had education problems in their early years, but they also have excellent powers of concentration and are conscientious, pensive thinkers.

Third house Saturn ♄ Notables: Tom Hanks, David Beckham, James Joyce, Erich Fromm, and Bertrand Russell

Uranus ♅ in the Third House

Third house Uranus is independent and inventive and, with its unusual and intuitive mind, follows its own drum, however it beats. This placement might indicate a keen and alert mind coupled with a love of new ideas. This placement is futuristic, with people who have it being steps—and sometimes leaps and bounds—ahead of their generation. People with Uranus in the third house might work in communications or broadcasting. There might be unpredictable behavior with this placement or unexpected separation from brothers and sisters.

Third house Uranus ♅ Notables: Heidi Klum, Lisa Kudrow, Tim Burton, Bing Crosby, and Charles Dickens

Neptune ♆ in the Third House

Third house Neptune is a daydreamer and might need to learn how to concentrate but often has strong psychic abilities and a deep need to learn about the unexplained. This placement describes highly developed visualization abilities and a strong interest in learning or writing about mystical or occult subjects. People who have Neptune in the third house are often visual learners or may communicate with music. They're very good with harmonics as well as linguistics. When challenged, this placement may indicate learning difficulties, as well as confusion in communications, contracts, and traveling.

Third house Neptune ♆ Notables: Beyoncé Knowles, Jay-Z, Benedict Cumberbatch, Meryl Streep, and Julia Child

Pluto ♀ in the Third House

If Pluto's in your third house, you have strong intellectual curiosity, and your emotional security is attached to your need to understand the world within a larger framework. However, your desire to constantly take in more information leads to a quest for a deeper meaning that unifies all this data. Your soul's evolutionary intent is to develop your intuition and understand the metaphysical significance behind the information. Someone with Pluto in the third house wants universal communication so everyone can understand; they don't want to stick with one conditioned way of doing things but are constantly forming and reforming with the intent to inspire and motivate to transform the mental patterns of others with their communication skills. Someone with this placement is intelligent and curious and has a deep, penetrating mind.

Third house Pluto ♀ Notables: Katie Holmes, Fergie, Mick Jagger, Carl Sagan, and Neil Armstrong

North Node ☊ in the Third House/South Node ☋ in the Ninth House

If your North Node is in the third house, your South Node is in the ninth house, and you've already worked heavily to gain wisdom and understanding; now, you now need to pay attention to communicating and disseminating information to others and to your relationships. With this placement, you must work to develop clear communications and better relationships with others and resist the urge to sever ties whenever the going gets rough (often leaving loose ends). You're here to translate what you've already learned so that society can learn it, too.

Third house North Node ☊ Notables: Julian Assange, Vladimir Putin, Tina Turner, Mao Zedong, and Nicolaus Copernicus

Chapter 14

WHERE YOU LIVE, WORK, AND CREATE: FOURTH, FIFTH, AND SIXTH HOUSES

The second-quadrant houses are the areas where you connect with your immediate surroundings. Your fourth house is where you'll find your home and family; your fifth house is where you find your pleasure and creativity; and your sixth house is where you find your work and responsibilities. These are the houses where you'll be establishing yourself in all arenas of your world—where you live, work, and create. You can look back to Chapter 3 to review the natural associations of signs and houses, and Chapter 2 for a refresher on astrological qualities.

Fourth, Fifth, and Sixth Houses

House	Natural Ruler	Natural Planet	Quality
Fourth lower heaven	Cancer ♋	Moon ☽	Angular
Fifth	Leo ♌	Sun ☉	Succedent
Sixth	Virgo ♍	Mercury ☿	Cadent

The Fourth House: It's a Family Affair

The fourth house is your home—the place where a house is a home, or a home is a house. But what is a home? In addition to being where your domestic life happens, it's the place where you feel you can be yourself, with all your unconscious habits or patterns and your emotional underpinnings.

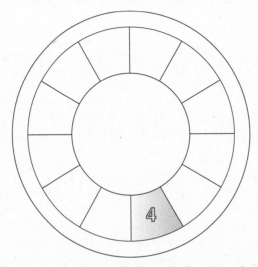

The fourth house: your home and family and the foundation of your life.

Your home is related to your insecurities or your need for emotional security, so when there are lots of disruptions, renovations, or major modifications there, these needs are undergoing major changes as well.

The fourth house ruler is Cancer ♋, so there is a natural association with the Moon ☽. The fourth house holds both your seclusion and your self-protection, is the place you can retreat to and depend on, and is the foundation of your life. Your home is also where you came from (your roots and family), where you are now (your domicile and those you live with), and where you're going (the security of your old age). With the lower heaven (I.C.) as its cusp, your fourth house also indicates the point of your beginnings and psychological roots.

Who's Nesting in This House?

The sign on your fourth house describes the characteristics of your roots, inner foundations, security, and home, and its ruler shows where and how you seek to develop these things. The house where Cancer ♋, the fourth house's natural sign, appears on your chart describes where you search for security and disclose your emotions externally.

The Sun ☉ in the Fourth House

A fourth house Sun indicates pride in your home environment, pride in your family of origin, and a strong need to establish and maintain roots. Family history is very important, and these people may be interested in pursuing their family genealogies and genetic heritages. The Sun in the fourth house means that the creative self will be expressed through the home, which translates to a strong attachment to family and, generally, a happy home life.

Fourth house Sun ☉ Notables: Common, Bill Maher, Bobby Short, May Sarton, and Stephen Crane

The Moon ☽ in the Fourth House

With the Moon in the fourth house, there is a strong emotional attachment to your physical residence, your family, and your children—the foundations of home. This placement indicates a strong desire to be responsible for anybody or anything (including pets and plants) that lives within your home environment. Moon in the fourth house wants to protect; your home is truly your castle. This placement also can indicate a strong parental attachment and a person who identifies emotionally with both family and home, especially with the mother.

Fourth house Moon ☽ Notables: Eddie Van Halen, Keith Haring, Marguerite Yourcenar, Walter Cronkite, and Paul Klee

Mercury ☿ in the Fourth House

Fourth house Mercury has a strong curiosity about family history and will be the keeper of family stories and photographs. This placement needs to have an open flow of communication among those who live within the home. Everybody must have the freedom to speak, and the home is often noisy. Guests are always welcome. When you have Mercury in the fourth house, your home is the neighborhood gathering point for parties, barbecues, and just talking. Many people who telecommute have Mercury in the fourth house.

Fourth house Mercury ☿ Notables: Sonia Rykiel, Gloria Steinem, Gloria Vanderbilt, Evelyn Waugh, and Stonewall Jackson

Venus ♀ in the Fourth House

Venus in the fourth house translates to a beautiful place to live. There also will be happy memories of childhood and a strong attachment to the parents. Venus here is financially secure as well as optimistic and warm. People who have Venus in the fourth house will always have warm, inviting homes, no matter where they live. They are comfortable and harmonious people who love land, flowers, and gardening, and they decorate their homes as beautifully as possible.

Fourth house Venus ♀ Notables: A. J. Foyt, Abbie Hoffman, Gene Rayburn, Mary Pickford, and Le Courbusier

Mars ♂ in the Fourth House

Fourth house Mars indicates a desire for independence within the home life. Mars in the fourth house often develops its own sense of home and environment very differently from those of the family of origin. This placement creates its own traditions and lifestyle patterns, and it takes pride in creating its own roots. People who have this placement may settle far from their original homes. This placement also shows strong efforts to improve the home conditions, and many of these people are "do-it-yourselfers" who fix up their homes.

Fourth house Mars ♂ Notables: Julian Assange, Betty White, Renzo Piano, M. F. K. Fisher, and Henrik Ibsen

Jupiter ♃ in the Fourth House

Fourth house Jupiter is generally happy and comfortable at home and takes pride in its family. There's usually a happy childhood with this placement, and there should be material comfort in later life as well. Fourth house Jupiter loves wide-open spaces and a large home, so they can share their expansive homes with others. This is a warm and compassionate placement, which indicates people who might have many social and educational opportunities. Jupiter in the fourth house often attracts a large extended family, establishing friends within the family circle as well. This support system provides a sense of security. Usually, people who have Jupiter in the fourth house come from a large family circle that is financially secure, and they generally have had a strong religious or ethical upbringing as well. People with this placement might have a second home in another location or country.

Fourth house Jupiter ♃ Notables: J. K. Rowling, Anjelica Huston, Ava Gardner, Margaret Mitchell, and Giuseppe Verdi

Saturn ♄ in the Fourth House

Saturn in the fourth house is strongly devoted to family and might have had to assume responsibilities at an early age. This placement plans carefully to develop security for the future through accumulating and maintaining resources—home, land, money—for the family to enjoy through inheritance. People who have Saturn in the fourth house feel very strongly about both their families and carrying on family traditions generation after generation. This placement also indicates a responsible nature toward elderly members of the family and of the community.

Fourth house Saturn ♄ Notables: Minnie Driver, Bette Midler, Harry Crews, Erik Satie, and Jean Cocteau

Uranus ♅ in the Fourth House

When you walk into the home of a person who has Uranus in the fourth house, you'll encounter a very eclectic environment! Fourth house Uranus is independent and unusual, and may have had a nontraditional home or childhood. This person's life might take a sudden turn in an unexpected direction in later years. There might be sudden and drastic changes in the home arena throughout life, though usually, these are changes for a higher good. This placement also indicates a person who may have spiritual or political values that are very independent of or different from the family of origin.

Fourth house Uranus ♅ Notables: Garth Brooks, Ed Sullivan, John F. Kennedy, Marcel Proust, and Antonin Dvorak

Neptune ♆ in the Fourth House

Fourth house Neptune people might have an idealized picture of what a home life should be like. They want everything in harmony and for the home to be a spiritual oasis in the middle of life's chaos. The home is more temple than castle with this placement—a retreat from the stressful outside world. Accordingly, this home feels peaceful and warm. Its environment supports meditation and spiritual practices, which are important to the person who has Neptune in the fourth house. But if they are challenged by astrological aspects (see Chapter 17), the conditions of their homes might be unsettled, uncertain, confused, or chaotic. This placement also could indicate skeletons or mysteries in the family closet. This placement shows karmic or unconscious emotional ties to the family and home life, and often imaginative parenting.

Fourth house Neptune ♆ Notables: Emma Watson, Robert Downey, Jr., Steven Spielberg, Bill Gates, Sigmund Freud

Pluto ♀ in the Fourth House

With a fourth house Pluto, your soul is learning how to create internal emotional security without the need for others. You might have had emotional shocks early in your family life that forced you to learn the value of internal security, or you might have had many experiences in which your emotional needs were not met. Your evolutionary intent is to learn to become responsible for your well-being, develop your authority or individuality, find the right career or work, and become emotionally mature. This is transformative energy to facilitate the rebirth that your soul needs to liberate itself from old, restrictive traditions. Fourth house Pluto people can be emotionally manipulative and even vindictive if they feel they've been wounded, but they also can be sympathetic and nurturing, as well as intensely loyal to those they care about.

Fourth house Pluto ♀ Notables: Cate Blanchett, Pedro Almodovar, James Dean, Norman Mailer, and Nikolai Vasilievich Gogol

North Node ☊ in the Fourth House/South Node ☋ in the Tenth House

With a fourth house North Node/tenth house South Node, you might have unconscious memories of having an authoritative position and now want to achieve it again. But this time, you're here to learn that it is very important to build the foundation of your domestic life. The South Node in your tenth house of career tells you that you already know how to do this for your career, so now you need to turn your attention to putting down the roots of home. Until you do so, there might be constant conflicts between your home and career. In addition, you will learn to seek achievement for the deeds you accomplish and not for having an automatic audience as an authority figure.

Fourth house North Node ☊ **Notables:** Harry, Duke of Sussex, Kanye West, Tobey Maguire, Tom Waits, and John Belushi

The Fifth House: Do What You Wanna Do

Traditionally, the fifth house is the house of creativity, so it is only natural that this house would also encompass children, risk-taking, and romance—all creative (and risky!) endeavors. It's also the house of investments, which is another risky area. The fifth house is where you find your pleasure, fun, parties, vacations, self-indulgences, and self-expression. It includes everything from gambling to holidays, fun to romance, and creativity to pranks. You also could think of it as the house of joy and the heart.

The natural house ruler here, of course, is Leo ♌, and the associated planet is the Sun ☉. People who wonder whether they'll ever find the right creative outlet would do well to study their fifth house. It's possible the answer is right through Door Number 5.

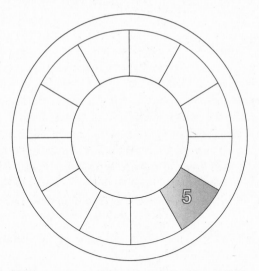

The fifth house: your creativity, fun, romance, risk, and children.

Getting Creative

Your fifth house sign describes the nature of your creativity and self-expression, and its ruler indicates how and where you develop your abilities to express yourself. This is the house where

Leo ♌, its corresponding natural sign, lives; it shows where your creativity and purpose are released and what area of your life will provide your creative potential.

The Sun ☉ in the Fifth House

Fifth house Sun is energetic, powerfully creative, and social, and it enjoys living the good life. There's an interest in the arts and a desire to be with people. This placement loves a good time, and it loves children and others, too. Self-expression can be found through acting, teaching, art, sports, or other creative and artistic pursuits. People with the Sun in the fifth house are also loyal, ardent lovers. They often project themselves with drama or a sense of style.

Fifth house Sun ☉ Notables: Mark Zuckerberg, Yoko Ono, Charles Bukowski, Franklin D. Roosevelt, and Wolfgang Amadeus Mozart

The Moon ☽ in the Fifth House

Fifth house Moon wants to nurture. The Moon's connections are emotional; this placement seeks out pleasure and is both romantic and imaginatively creative. Associations with others are often intimate in some way, and there is a great desire for children. Creative, self-expressive, and romantic urges are heavily influenced by emotional needs. People with this placement might develop emotional attachments to romantic partners, or their feelings for lovers might be very fluid and changeable.

Fifth house Moon ☽ Notables: James McAvoy, Kristen Stewart, Laurence Olivier, Jane Birkin, and Leonard Bernstein

Mercury ☿ in the Fifth House

Fifth house Mercury loves change and new people, and it must be intellectually stimulated to keep the good times rolling. There's a need here to give everything a personal spin, and this placement is capable of dramatic self-expression, especially in speech and writing. This placement can indicate a teacher (especially of the primary grades), a writer, a playwright, or an art critic, as well as a stock market analyst or active investor. Playful cleverness and delight in pulling pranks are also found with this placement. In addition, people with fifth house Mercury are often attracted to intellectual or mentally stimulating romantic partners.

Fifth house Mercury ☿ Notables: James Franco, Jake Gyllenhaal, Geraldine Chaplin, Charlie Chaplin, and Samuel Beckett

Venus ♀ in the Fifth House

Fifth house Venus loves the social spotlight and seems to attract others—romantic partners, children, and even pets—who love life. These people take enormous pleasure in creative work and have a flair for acting, writing, and all types of artistic pursuits. This placement is affectionate and sociable, and it loves to find pleasure and passion. If beneficially aspected (see Chapter 17), there can be gain through investments and speculation as well. People who have Venus in the fifth house also get others to see their own talents and to feel good about themselves.

Fifth house Venus ♀ Notables: Chelsea Clinton, Justin Timberlake, Ewan McGregor, Shia LeBoeuf, and Herbert Hoover

Mars ♂ in the Fifth House

Impulsive fifth house Mars can be impatient in love but has a personal magnetism that draws others. People who have this placement are very passionate, enthusiastic, and impetuous. This Mars placement can be very competitive in sports because these people have natural athletic skill. They also can become very impatient and jealous in romantic matters, or their strong sexual drive might lead to an urgent need for a romantic partner! When well-aspected astrologically (see Chapter 17), Mars here can work very well with children, especially as coaches or physical-education teachers, and these people know the right way to discipline, too. This placement is often found in athletes and in artists who work with tools, such as sculptors.

Fifth house Mars ♂ Notables: Serena Williams, George Clooney, Sarah Jessica Parker, Vladimir Nabokov, and Karl Marx

Jupiter ♃ in the Fifth House

Jupiter in the fifth house loves any kind of recreation, whether it's a sporting event, the theater, or another great party, and it loves adventure, too. This placement indicates a tendency to take risks—and those risks often pay off. Fifth house Jupiter does just about everything in a big way and is often found in teaching, publishing, sales, the arts, the entertainment business, and businesses related to the stock market or investments. This placement is very creative in the arts, sports, education, or anything related to children. Jupiter in the fifth house often inspires teachers, counselors, or advisers, especially when working with young people.

Fifth house Jupiter ♃ Notables: Josh Brolin, Stevie Wonder, Noam Chomsky, Cary Grant, and George Orwell

Saturn ♄ in the Fifth House

Disciplined fifth house Saturn needs to learn how to relax and have a good time, and for this serious, responsible planet, that's not always easy. Because of its seriousness, Saturn's fifth house creativity is often channeled into scientific discovery. This is the placement of Marie Curie, for example. But this is not the only way it manifests. People with Saturn in the fifth house also show structure and organization in art and music, and they show an ability to be creative in politics and business management. They might work in careers associated with education, young people, places of entertainment, or the arts. This placement also can manifest as ambition for leadership or power in artistic areas. Usually, there are serious responsibilities concerning one's own children or the children within society (for example, a teacher taking care of a classroom).

People who have Saturn in the fifth house are often romantically attracted to those who are older or more mature.

Fifth house Saturn ♄ Notables: Shakira, Heath Ledger, Andy Warhol, Winston Churchill, and Zelda Fitzgerald

Uranus ♅ in the Fifth House

Fifth house Uranus takes an inventive approach to creative expression and might make sudden changes in its direction. There's a need for self-expression and romance, but Uranus here also can be reckless or fickle. Unusual circumstances might arise with one's children here, who might be very gifted and talented. It's a wild ride for speculations, investments, and gambling; it's also a wild ride for sudden or unusual romantic attractions, which might break off as suddenly as they started. These people are often attracted to others who are eclectic, different, nomadic, or geniuses, and they like to work for themselves due to their strong independence and need for freedom.

Fifth house Uranus ♅ Notables: Richard Nixon, John Steinbeck, Virginia Woolf, Percy Bysshe Shelley, and Billy the Kid

Neptune ♆ in the Fifth House

Fifth house Neptune loves pleasure and luxury, and it is drawn to anything that involves an element of fantasy. This placement enjoys looking at romance through rose-colored glasses. People who have Neptune in the fifth house have a kind, benevolent attitude toward children and animals who need nurturing. This placement can indicate a childlike or naïve approach to love or risks; in turn, this can mean people might take advantage of them. This placement also indicates idealistic and visionary potentials, and these people might create intuitively or spiritually inspired art or music. They need to be appreciated for their creative talents. Many people who have careers in movies and the film industry have Neptune in the fifth house.

Fifth house Neptune ♆ Notables: Drake, Kate Moss, Eleanor Roosevelt, Frank Lloyd Wright, and Anton Chekhov

Pluto ♀ in the Fifth House

With a fifth house Pluto, you feel as though you have a special destiny to fulfill, and you'll be able to project your special abilities and creativity in any manner in which you want to focus them. However, your soul's evolutionary purpose is to learn how to link your abilities and special destiny with the needs of others or society as a whole; until you do, your creativity might be blocked in some way. It's not enough to just focus on yourself and your talents. You have enormous strength of will, tremendous creativity, and a major need for attention, and you also can be loving, giving, and magnetic.

Fifth house Pluto ♀ Notables: Ashton Kutcher, Donatella Versace, Richard Pryor, Harvey Milk, and Sylvia Plath

North Node ☊ in the Fifth House/South Node ☋ in the Eleventh House

With a fifth house North Node/eleventh house South Node, you're learning about creativity, and you're often a dreamer, apart from the crowd, watching everyone else. With this placement, you need to learn the importance of hopes or wishes and then use them to create your own destiny. Your need for friendships might dissipate your creative energies, so you must learn the self-discipline necessary to avoid this. Instead, constructively apply your hopes to creating reality.

Fifth house North Node ☊ Notables: Emma Watson, Jared Leto, Bill Gates, Whitney Houston, and Paul Cezanne

The Sixth House: 9 to 5

Often called the house of service, the sixth house is concerned with both service and health. This is the area of your daily responsibilities and is the house of your relationships to coworkers, too. You could think of your sixth house as the work you've got to do.

The sixth house is naturally ruled by Virgo ♍, and its corresponding planet is Mercury ☿. This translates into gaining fulfillment through skills that are of value to others. When we develop our own special competence at doing something meaningful to us that also helps others, we find satisfaction in our jobs and careers. When we don't, we tend to end up working at meaningless jobs. Not entirely comfortable in your job? You may be good at it, but if you're not finding the meaningful responsibility of your sixth house, it's never going to fit quite right!

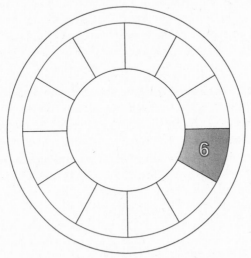

The sixth house: your personal responsibilities, health, and service to others.

But your sixth house is also about your responsibilities, how you help others, and how you are of service to the world. The planets that reside in your sixth house can indicate whether you're an optimist or a pessimist in your daily work and the health problems you might be prone to. When people aren't fulfilled by their work, they have a strong tendency to feel out of sorts or get sick.

Heavenly Bodies at Work

Your sixth house is where you find your desire to be competent. You can be good at many things, but it's in your sixth house that you'll find meaningful responsibility—how the things that you're good at matter to other people and especially to you. Your sixth house sign describes your daily responsibilities and how you prefer to be of service to others. The ruler of your sixth house shows where and how you will meet your regular obligations. The house with Virgo ♍ on its cusp, the sixth house's natural sign, describes where you apply discrimination and analysis to your duties to get the results you desire.

The Sun ☉ in the Sixth House

Sixth house Sun takes pride in its work and is a good organizer, with a need for appreciation. If it doesn't get the appreciation it desires, it'll often leave for a different job! This placement also requires a lot of attention to diet and personal routines to maintain good health. People with sixth house Suns are good problem solvers. This placement may indicate a strong interest in health or healing careers, or an intense desire to establish oneself through service to others.

Sixth house Sun ☉ Notables: Snoop Dogg, Julianne Moore, Billy Idol, Steve Jobs, and John Lennon

The Moon ☽ in the Sixth House

The Moon in the sixth house can indicate a frequent desire to change jobs or positions. This placement needs to have emotional attachment to work and service, and it needs an emotional attachment to believe in the work being done. Moon in the sixth house has great consideration for others, including coworkers. This placement also indicates that these people's health and productivity at work tend to fluctuate with their emotions. Emotional nurturing is very important to them, and they might work in restaurants, nutrition, food preparation, or other businesses associated with food. These people like to serve others by working closely with the public. Moon in the sixth house may indicate fluctuations in health when there is stress in the workplace.

Sixth house Moon ☽ Notables: Beck, Paul McCartney, Michael Jordan, Diana Ross, and Nikola Tesla

Mercury ☿ in the Sixth House

Mercury in the sixth house can be a perfectionist, but that's because this placement understands the importance of details. This natural placement of Mercury has a strong interest in matters of health and well-being as well. There can be a tendency toward unnecessary worry, but that goes with the detail-oriented territory. This placement can also indicate people who acquire specialized skills and knowledge for their work. Normally very systematic and efficient, they also have a strong desire to keep up with the latest research or new techniques. This is a very favorable placement for people working in healing, medicine, science, or engineering, and they'll need lots of vitamin B complex to combat their nervousness.

Sixth house Mercury ☿ Notables: Serena Williams, Barack Obama, Kurt Cobain, Leonard Nimoy, and Sinclair Lewis

Venus ♀ in the Sixth House

Venus in the sixth house wants harmony and good relationships on the job front. This is a good placement for counselors, arbitrators, and health-care workers, or these people might prefer to work in jobs associated with artistic pursuits or in areas that are very social. It's also found in people who work with or for women. Sixth house Venus might have made social connections or found a marriage partner by meeting people through work. This placement indicates good health in general, but there can be a tendency to overindulge.

Sixth house Venus ♀ Notables: Beck, Jennifer Aniston, Prince, Isaac Asimov, and Claude Monet

Mars ♂ in the Sixth House

Sixth house Mars wants to accomplish things, and because it is driven hard, it expects everyone else to do the same. This placement can indicate mechanical ability, but someone with a sixth-house Mars also can find it difficult to get along with coworkers. People with this placement need to beware of accident-prone conditions at work. They commonly use tools (especially sharp ones) and/or machinery in their work and are often mechanics, machinists, mechanical engineers, steelworkers, surgeons, or equipment operators. Their work is normally very skilled or precise, and their identities are usually tied to their work and how well they do it.

Sixth house Mars ♂ Notables: Julia Roberts, Paul McCartney, John Lennon, Robert F. Kennedy, and Duke Ellington

Jupiter ♃ in the Sixth House

Jupiter in the sixth house does well at work and gets along with coworkers, too. People with this placement can be very successful because of their optimism and creativity, but they need to be careful not to overindulge because they have a tendency toward weight and liver problems. These people have a strong interest in and understanding of how the mind and emotions are connected to healing. They might pursue natural healing work, which connects with their interest in serving others in a practical way.

Sixth house Jupiter ♃ Notables: Jennifer Lawrence, Taylor Swift, Leonardo DiCaprio, Eddie Murphy, and George Washington

Saturn ♄ in the Sixth House

Sixth house Saturn is a conscientious and reliable worker, good at taking on responsibility and getting the job done, which often requires specialized skills and knowledge. Sometimes this placement can push itself too hard, resulting in chronic illness. When challenged by aspects, this placement tends to do all the work without asking for any reward, which can lead to internal problems. These people tend to work in medicine, science, engineering, food processing, nutrition, or other areas that require specialized capabilities. Worry and anxiety tend to cause health problems here.

Sixth house Saturn ♄ Notables: Lady Gaga, Pharrell Williams, Robert Pattinson, Nicole Kidman, and Julie Andrews

Uranus ♅ in the Sixth House

Those with Uranus in the sixth house bring new ideas to work but also can be erratic or impatient; they're often people who work well alone. Because sixth house Uranus doesn't much go for routine, these people might find that their health difficulties are not run-of-the-mill, either. This placement also indicates that unusual or advanced methods might be employed at work, and there might be strong interest in spiritual or alternative healing practices or diets. These people might have ingenious scientific or mathematical ideas that lead to important inventions or new understandings, especially ones that have practical applications. Employment might be terminated suddenly or without notice, and illness is normally due to nervousness or irritability. Uranus in the sixth house can be the signature of the entrepreneur.

Sixth house Uranus ♅ Notables: Snoop Dogg, Mariah Carey, Jimmy Carter, Ho Chi Minh, and Indira Gandhi

Neptune ♆ in the Sixth House

With a sixth house Neptune, people tend to be idealistic about their work and sensitive to both their surroundings and their coworkers. This placement can be highly resourceful and very devoted to the work environment, but these people often prefer to work alone or behind the scenes. Health problems can be difficult to pin down. These people are usually learning to view work as a means of serving others in a spiritual way, and there can be many sacrifices asked of them. They also might have an intuitive understanding regarding the most effective work methods and processes, and they might be interested in spiritual healing or other natural forms of healing. When ill, these people could benefit from natural foods or remedies or from a holistic approach.

Sixth house Neptune ♆ **Notables:** Ringo Starr, Donatella Versace, John Lennon, Norman Mailer, and Bob Fosse

Pluto ♀ in the Sixth House

With Pluto in the sixth house, you're learning lessons about service to others, self-improvement, and humility. There's a powerful mind at work here, leading to cycles of introspection and self-analysis and transformations in any aspect of yourself that's not appropriate for your evolutionary intent. Your soul's evolutionary purpose is to learn appropriate relationships between yourself and others, to develop faith, and to find a sense of connection to a higher power or force. In doing so, lessons in discrimination, tolerance, and respect for human imperfections and mistakes will be learned. Sixth house Pluto people are self-effacing, with keen, critical minds. They also might be critical or forgiving, depending on circumstances, and they are sometimes crisis-prone.

Sixth house Pluto ♀ **Notables:** Serena Williams, Miley Cyrus, Demi Moore, Queen Elizabeth II, and Charles Dickens

North Node ☊ in the Sixth House/South Node ☋ in the Twelfth House

With a sixth house North Node/twelfth house South Node, you're someone who spends a lot of time deep in thought. Your tendency to live your life based on fears grounded in the past can undermine your confidence, and those close to you might think you avoid what's real. You are here to live a life of devotion and service to others, so what you really need to do is learn about responsibility and trust, and then develop faith in the Universe. After you do this, you will serve others with compassion and take great pleasure in helping them.

Sixth house North Node ☊ **Notables:** Scarlett Johansson, John Travolta, Barbra Streisand, Paul McCartney, and John Lennon

Chapter 15

THE WIDE WORLD OVER: SEVENTH, EIGHTH, AND NINTH HOUSES

In the third-quadrant houses, you move from your personal world into the larger one. The seventh house is concerned with your relationships and connections with others; the eighth house deals with your ways of coping with everything from money to death; and the ninth house is the area of your social and moral belief systems. These houses, in other words, are the areas where your tools for navigating your world come into play. You can look back to Chapter 3 to review the natural associations of signs and houses, and Chapter 2 for a refresher on astrological qualities.

Seventh, Eighth, and Ninth Houses

House	Natural Ruler	Natural Planet	Quality
Seventh	Libra ♎	Venus ♀	Cardinal
Eighth	Scorpio ♏	Pluto ♀	Succedent
		Mars ♂	
Ninth	Sagittarius ♐	Jupiter ♃	Cadent

The Seventh House: Forever Yours

The seventh house is traditionally the house of partnership and marriage. The natural ruler of the seventh house is Libra ♎, and its associated planet is Venus ♀. When you look at your personal birth chart, the sign that appears on the cusp of your seventh house is your descendant, which reveals what you seek in partnerships and relationships.

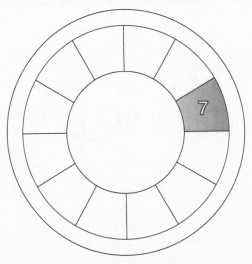

The seventh house: your primary relationships and partnerships.

Your seventh house is the place where you learn to put your own interests aside for the sake of your primary relationships. It can indicate what kind of mate and marriage you'll have, but it also indicates other kinds of partnerships, too: important friends and associates, your business partnerships, and your legal affairs and agreements. Your seventh house can also house your adversaries—the people or things that stand between you, your shared goals, and your open enemies. Enemies in the seventh house are people you know are your enemies, but that doesn't make it any easier to deal with them!

Successful navigation of your seventh house means that you understand shared goals and commitment. This is the house of your primary relationships, and that can include everything from your soul mate to the way your relationships change. Most of all, your seventh house is the place *where you cooperate and share with others.*

Heavenly Connections

Your seventh house sign describes your relationships and partnerships and how you connect with others. This is the house of sharing; it tells how you cooperate with a significant partner through agreements or contracts in all kinds of unions—from romantic (including marriage) to business. This is the house of commitment, cooperation, and connection.

And don't forget: if there are no planets in a house, the ruler and its association with other planets show what's happening in that area of your life. Libra ♎, the seventh house's landlord, is all about relating to others and shared values.

The Sun ☉ in the Seventh House

Seventh house Sun expresses its creative power through relationships, for better or worse. These people's self-expression and willpower are most often shown through their major relationships. If challenged by aspect, they need to learn to respect the rights of others and cooperate. Sun in the seventh house indicates a desire to cooperate and collaborate. When you have this placement, you need to find yourself through partnership. The seventh house is "me *and*" with this placement, that is, you in connection with another. Sun in the seventh house indicates people who work best with others, but at the same time, they must learn to value their partner's needs and goals as much as their own. A seventh house Sun is all about the use of social ties for self-expression.

Seventh house Sun ☉ Notables: Josh Groban, Sam Shepard, Princess Diana, Sharon Tate, and Nathaniel Hawthorne

The Moon ☽ in the Seventh House

Seventh house Moon is concerned with emotional and domestic security in all forms of committed relationships. With the Moon in the seventh house, people usually connect very well with the public because they are very sensitive and responsive to the needs of others. They might marry early in life, and their marriage or business partners might be moody, sensitive, or emotionally changeable. There is an emotional urge to bond with partners, groups, or extended family. Relationships are very important for emotional foundations. Someone with a Moon in the seventh house is not an isolated person; instead, a seventh house Moon is a person who wants and needs to be with others because such connections provide completion. Like the Moon, this person's relationships might go through phases of fullness and barrenness, waxing and waning.

Seventh house Moon ☽ Notables: J. K. Rowling, David Bowie, Steve McQueen, Oliver Hardy, and Henry Wadsworth Longfellow

Mercury ☿ in the Seventh House

A seventh house Mercury seeks intellectual compatibility in all forms of partnerships and loves a lot of verbal give and take. In particular, this placement benefits law, literary, or communications partnerships, as well as salespeople and public relations experts, counselors, arbitrators, or mediators. A seventh house Mercury can have relationship challenges because of misunderstandings or unfulfilled agreements. These people tend to attract like-mindedness, which often manifests in other highly intellectual and well-educated people with a thirst for even more knowledge through partnership.

Seventh house Mercury ☿ Notables: Justin Timberlake, Angela Merkel, Pope Francis I, John McCain, and Edgar Degas

Venus ♀ in the Seventh House

A seventh house Venus seeks harmony and fulfillment in its primary relationships and is able to create a harmonious environment to achieve these goals. This placement can be very successful in legal matters, and with its refined social graces, it gets along well with everyone. Seventh house Venus *needs* to be socially active. This placement also shows a good ability for dealing with the public and works well in sales, psychology, any of the performing arts, or public relations.

Seventh house Venus ♀ Notables: Ryan Gosling, Eric Clapton, Lawrence Ferlinghetti, Umberto Eco, and Henry Moore

Mars ♂ in the Seventh House

Seventh house Mars remains highly independent, even in its relationships, and it is usually the one to impulsively—and aggressively—begin those relationships. This placement, when challenged, might indicate more than one marriage or more than one business partnership. Seventh house Mars can be quarrelsome and restless, and wants everything to happen *now*. No, no, make that *right now!* The need of Mars in the seventh house is to learn patience with partners. Mars in the seventh house can bring a great deal of cooperative spirit and energy to major relationships. This placement infuses partnerships with drive and enthusiasm.

Seventh house Mars ♂ Notables: Chris Pratt, Michael J. Fox, Alfred Hitchcock, Nina Simone, and Bobby Fischer

Jupiter ♃ in the Seventh House

Jupiter in the seventh house supports success and accommodation between partners in a win-win way. The relationship will be fortuitous for both partners because Jupiter brings the desire to cooperate. This placement attracts good counsel, fair and balanced opinions, and equitable and honest contracts that benefit the partnership. This placement can mean that your enemies will later become your associates, or at the very least, that you will have a fortuitous partnership of some sort. Jupiter in the seventh house indicates a very affectionate and optimistic spouse, too. This placement shows someone who is honest and fair in dealings with others and who expects the same in return. If challenged by aspect, though, Jupiter in the seventh house might expect too much from others.

Seventh house Jupiter ♃ Notables: Courtney Love, Tiger Woods, Jim Morrison, Coco Chanel, and Robert Browning

Saturn ♄ in the Seventh House

Someone with Saturn in the seventh house is cautious about all its relationships but also shows a strong sense of responsibility and fairness in dealings with others. Saturn is very businesslike, which works especially well in business partnerships. This is a good placement for working in the legal system or business management. People who have Saturn in the seventh house tend to keep their agreements and improve their lives by working with others, and sometimes, they will delay a personal involvement until they're absolutely certain of the other's commitment. Seventh house Saturn takes relationships very seriously; in return, they want the same commitment they're giving to the relationship. This placement can create difficulties when relating to others, but this is largely because of caution.

Seventh house Saturn ♄ Notables: Alicia Silverstone, Hilary Swank, Diana Ross, Carole King, and James Brown

Uranus ♅ in the Seventh House

Seventh house Uranus can be impetuous and spontaneous. With this placement, a person might find sudden marriage or partnership and is often drawn to people who don't look like they'd be a good match. Seventh house Uranus and their partner might draw others' attention because they are both so unusual, or the connection is unexpected. Relationships are likely to be nontraditional. On the other hand, there might be lots of breakups or sudden divorce and remarriage; there can be a certain lack of permanence in relationships here. The main characteristic of this placement is that these people need a lot of independence and freedom of expression in their relationships.

Seventh house Uranus ♅ Notables: Barack Obama, Daniel Day-Lewis, Debbie Reynolds, Akira Kurosawa, and George Washington

Neptune ♆ in the Seventh House

Seventh house Neptune seeks others with common goals, dreams, and/or visions, and it needs a sensitive, intuitive, and responsive partner. This placement also can attract partners of different philosophies and backgrounds. Neptune in the seventh house indicates a love of global travel and partnerships on a global level. This placement can be genuinely giving, although it also can create an idealistic sense of the partner. Neptune in the seventh house may seek a soul mate or ideal partner, even when choosing a short-term partner. This placement might have karmic ties to major relationships, and seventh house Neptune might have to make a lot of sacrifices for relationships. Ideally, they're seeking their spiritual mates. If challenged by aspect, they could be misled by or deceive others.

Seventh house Neptune ♆ Notables: Lady Gaga, Darren Aronofsky, Janis Joplin, William Styron, and D. H. Lawrence

Pluto ♀ in the Seventh House

If you have a seventh house Pluto, you're learning how to participate in relationships. Your soul is now ready to relate with others on an equal basis so that neither person in the relationship *needs* or *controls* the other. The evolutionary intent for your soul is to learn how to launch your own life changes and make your own decisions, with regard for how those decisions affect others. At the same time, you need to minimize your dependence on others, learn how to trust yourself, and likewise respect the decisions and paths of others.

Seventh house Pluto ♀ Notables: Condoleezza Rice, Laura Dern, Jane Fonda, Sandra Day O'Connor, and Carrie Fisher

North Node ☊ in the Seventh House/South Node ☋ in the First House

With a seventh house North Node/first house South Node, you're learning about cooperation with others because you've already developed yourself as a strong individual. Now, you will learn to give and sacrifice for the sake of relationships, develop consideration for others, and ultimately detach from yourself and the ego-centered ideas that governed you in the past. This lifetime is an opportunity to share your strength with others by helping them see their own self-worth.

Seventh house North Node ☊ Notables: Elijah Wood, Anne Hathaway, Ringo Starr, Hillary Clinton, and J. M. W. Turner

The Eighth House: Sex, Money, and Other Important Matters

The eighth house is the second of the three so-called mystical houses, which also are known as houses of endings. (The others are the fourth and the twelfth houses.) This house is about shared resources, including everything from taxes and insurance, and it is about everything from business mergers to inheritances and marrying for money. The eighth house is also known as the house of death and regeneration because it is related to transformation *and* physical death; it deals with transforming physical things back into energy.

Regeneration is about more than death, too. It's also about individual transformation, whether emotional, physical, mental, or spiritual. For this reason, the eighth house includes the life forces, which are concerned with sex, birth, and the afterlife, as well as death. Here is where you'll find your instinctive desire to reproduce, as well as how you cope with and understand the "mysteries" of life. It's also where marriage is consummated, and where all forms of intimacy are found. Part of understanding the mystery of life is considering your intense experiences, whether they be the survival of consciousness after death; merging with another person via sex (orgasm is called *petit mort*—"the little death"—by the French); merging with the God of your understanding (or the Source); or birth. The way you cope with the mysteries of life and death can be found in your eighth house, and all those mysteries or secrets you unearth can be found there, too.

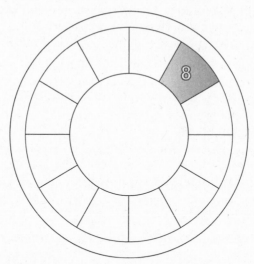

The eighth house: your joint resources, sex, death, and rebirth.

Your eighth house also seems to unveil a bit of the mystery surrounding your death, although when it will occur can never be found in your chart. The eighth house also is the house of psychic powers, occult mysteries, and occult knowledge.

The eighth house is naturally ruled by Scorpio ♏, and its associated planets are Mars ♂ and Pluto ♀, so it's also associated with all forms of subtle energies. For this reason, it's related to higher mathematics, atomic energy, and sciences that deal with complex energies, such as physics. In addition, the eighth house is the area of corporate or political resources, and some people with strong eighth houses might be active in one of these areas.

Ready ... Set ... Transform!

Your eighth house sign describes how you make your life changes and what attitudes or areas you need to transform. Your eighth house ruler describes where and how you encounter areas of your life that need to be transformed. The house where Scorpio ♏, the corresponding natural sign, lies reveals what areas of your life need to be regenerated and where you need to merge your energies with others.

The Sun ☉ in the Eighth House

People with an eighth house Sun constantly seek self-improvement or regeneration, and they do so by applying their willpower. Because these people are both intensely interested in deep mysteries and magnetic, they can often attract the support of others to their causes. This placement also can indicate an inheritance or the managing of other people's money, and while there might be early life difficulties, there might be fame or fortune later in life as well—possibly even recognition after the person's death. People with the Sun in the eighth house are primarily concerned with a need to transform and regenerate, with understanding the deep mysteries of life, and with mysteries in general. Vocationally, they might deal with matters of the dead, such as insurance or funerals, or they might be psychologists or sex therapists.

Eighth house Sun ☉ Notables: Carrie-Anne Moss, Prince, Humphrey Bogart, Nelson Mandela, and Charles Baudelaire

The Moon ☽ in the Eighth House

An eighth house Moon has a deep-seated need for emotional security and is very interested in questions about death and the afterlife. There might be a psychic ability here and an inheritance, especially through the mother. This placement also indicates an instinctive understanding of others' needs and wants, and these people often have changeable circumstances involving intimate relationships and shared resources.

Eighth house Moon ☽ Notables: Nicki Minaj, Zac Efron, Bill Clinton, James Taylor, and Graham Greene

Mercury ☿ in the Eighth House

With its penetrating mind, eighth house Mercury has a talent for research and analysis. There's an attraction to the occult with this placement, too, and people with eighth house Mercury might be intuitive, secretive, and psychic. This placement also might indicate the death of someone very close who greatly influences the person's life, or this person might get money from someone else (or both!). In addition, people with this placement have penetrating insight into sciences that deal with energy, occult mysteries, and life in general. They are likely to understand the true motivations of others and can ferret out secrets. They might work in corporate finance, taxes, insurance, or research, or they might write about mysteries or occult topics.

Eighth house Mercury ☿ Notables: Emma Watson, Carrie Underwood, Buzz Aldrin, Carrie Fisher, and Galileo Galilei

Venus ♀ in the Eighth House

Venus in the eighth house wants security through other people's resources, such as partners. This placement looks for and finds sexual fulfillment, often inherits money from a loved one, and is generally promised a peaceful death. (We'd probably all like to move our Venus here!) The sexual and creative potential of this placement can be helpful to other people as well. Venus in the eighth house might show either an overemphasis on sex or the possibility of marrying for money. It might also indicate intense emotions, jealousy, or possessiveness.

Eighth house Venus ♀ Notables: Chris Evans, Carrie Fisher, Debbie Reynolds, Nancy Reagan, and Jackson Pollock

Mars ♂ in the Eighth House

Because of its natural placement, eighth house Mars is passionate about life and sex, and it is attracted to medicine and the healing arts, as well as to research in a variety of areas. There's a possibility of family conflict over inheritances or shared resources here, and it's also possible that an eighth house Mars might experience sudden death or come into contact with death through war or violence. This placement shows intense energy, persistence, and strong desires, especially when it comes to meeting goals and desires through the use of corporate or shared resources. These people also can be very interested in psychic or occult forces.

Eighth house Mars ♂ Notables: Colin Firth, Steve Jobs, Princess Diana, Joseph Stalin, and Abraham Lincoln

Jupiter ♃ in the Eighth House

Jupiter in the eighth house indicates an optimistic and healthy attitude toward life, death, and sex, and this placement can inspire others as well. Eighth house Jupiter indicates financial gain through inheritance or marriage and an ability to manage money and resources well. People who have this placement also are talented in manifesting their deepest realities. The conditions at death will likely be easy and peaceful, and death will usually come only after a long and healthy life. This placement also can show a strong sex drive or even an overemphasis on sex, and these people might overspend their shared resources.

Eighth house Jupiter ♃ Notables: Mandy Moore, Zooey Deschanel, Pink, Richard Branson, and Carrie Fisher

Saturn ♄ in the Eighth House

Eighth house Saturn often takes responsibility for the affairs of others and is prudent about putting money away for loved ones. People with this placement either have or need to develop appropriate stewardship for material resources because they are often asked to be accountable for other people's money or taxes. This placement can indicate sexual inhibition of some kind or difficulty in expressing oneself emotionally. Eighth house Saturn usually means living to a ripe old age, caring for old antiques or vintage items, maintaining correspondence (such as collecting letters), or maintaining long ties of family or friendship.

Eighth house Saturn ♄ Notables: Robert Downey Jr., Elton John, Placido Domingo, George Harrison, and Salvador Dali

Uranus ♅ in the Eighth House

Uranus in the eighth house is interested in unusual ideas about life, sex, and death, and it is unconventional in its approach to any or all of them. They might have sudden financial gain from unexpected sources, unreciprocated love, and/or prescient dreams. Eighth house Uranus is often highly psychic and intuitive. These people also are very interested in occult topics, telepathy, or the survival of consciousness after death. People with Uranus in the eighth house might attract conditions in which there is sudden danger and must use their intuition to avoid a negative outcome. People who have this placement might put themselves at risk to save others (like rushing into a burning building) without conscious thought for the danger to self.

Eighth house Uranus ♅ Notables: Miley Cyrus, Hillary Clinton, Robin Williams, Frank Capra Jr., and Catherine the Great

Neptune ♆ in the Eighth House

Neptune in the eighth house can be visionary and charismatic, with strongly developed ESP and psychic abilities, as well as an idealistic desire to help others. There might be a partner whose extravagance leads to financial difficulties. This placement can indicate confusion, difficulties, or deception concerning the partner's money, taxes, or insurance. Strong interests in spiritualism also might lead to clairvoyance and an ability to contact the dead. Eighth house Neptune might indicate a death while asleep.

Eighth house Neptune ♆ Notables: George Clooney, Francis Ford Coppola, Diane Arbus, Michael Jackson, and Jim Morrison

Pluto ♀ in the Eighth House

With Pluto in the eighth house, you come face-to-face with the limits and parameters of who you are, as opposed to whom or what you are not. You have a strong need to not only eliminate but also transform all your limitations. To do so, you might be intensely drawn to "taboo" experiences, sex, money, relationships, rituals, shamanism, magic, meditation, or in-depth knowledge as ways of overcoming your limitations. By merging with your chosen symbol, you become whatever you were seeking, and you might gain power by doing so. But the evolutionary intent of your soul is to learn self-reliance and how to identify internal values and resources to sustain yourself. What you are *really* searching for is *within yourself.*

Eighth house Pluto ♀ Notables: Bob Dylan, Bono, Patti Smith, Bob Geldof, and Leonard Bernstein

North Node ☊ in the Eighth House/South Node ☋ in the Second House

With an eighth house North Node/second house South Node, you're learning to overcome possessiveness and learn about self-control in terms of money and possessions. It's time to move beyond self-values and what you have to a point where you integrate with the values of others. You might have a symbolic rebirth after pushing yourself beyond your limits from excessive behaviors. This is a particularly difficult lesson because you might seem to be starting over again, but the main lesson here is about faith and not looking back at your old ways.

Eighth house North Node ☊ Notables: Paris Hilton, Diane Keaton, Albert Einstein, Thomas Hardy, and George Washington

The Ninth House: Don't Know Much About History

Your ninth house is where everything from higher education, philosophy, religion, law, travel, and foreign concerns resides. It also includes the medical system and politics, as well as all areas of collective thought structures. In addition, it's the area involved in the development of a social conscience. In other words, it's the house of your social areas of beliefs.

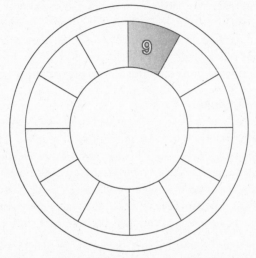

The ninth house: higher education, philosophy, religion, law, and travel.

This is the house of mental exploration and long-distance travel, and it is traditionally the house of long journeys over water. We love the sound of that, and seeing new cultures and more of the world is one way to gain a new perspective of the world in general.

Your ninth house also is the place where you'll find your patterns of behavior—and how you break them. This is where you'll confront the tendency of your life to become routine. This is where you'll encounter unpredictable awareness—the "aha!" experience—to shake you out of routine. This is primarily because it's our beliefs, religion, and philosophical systems that are behind everything we do. In the ninth house, you learn about your inner self and your perception of your life.

You could think of your ninth house as your mental "model of the universe," but remember, *your* model is but one of many. Unsuccessfully navigated, your ninth house can become a place where you mistake that model for the real world. Successfully navigated, it's the place where you'll make room in your life for miracles.

In addition to being where your cultural customs and beliefs exist, this house is where you'll find how you publicly convey your ideas and beliefs. And the ninth house also is considered the house of publishing and teaching.

Naturally associated with Sagittarius ♐ on its cusp, the ninth house is the house of the higher mind and exploration, especially of philosophical subjects. The planet that naturally rules the ninth house is Jupiter ♃, the planet of abundance, or, when overdone, misfortune.

What's Behind Your Beliefs?

Your ninth house sign describes your beliefs, your philosophies, and how you seek opportunities for expansion. Your ninth house ruler describes where and how you expand your mind and experiences and develop your understanding of life. This is the house where Sagittarius ♐—the corresponding natural sign—lies, and it shows what areas of your life can provide you with growth experiences that will lead to a greater understanding of life.

The Sun ☉ in the Ninth House

A ninth house Sun pursues philosophical or religious ideas through one of the areas described by this house: higher education, publishing, or foreign affairs, for example. There's a need for truth here; so, of course, there's a tendency to stick to one's word. These people are both philosophical and full of optimism, which is mainly due to their great faith and strong moral convictions. This placement could indicate a great deal of foreign travel, as well as the pursuit of higher education. Ninth-house Suns are often successful in law, travel, medicine, publishing, or religion. However, there also can be dogmatic tendencies and an inclination to force their ideas and beliefs on others.

Ninth house Sun ☉ Notables: Robert Downey Jr., Michael Jordan, Mark Hamill, Carrie Fisher, and Virginia Woolf

The Moon ☽ in the Ninth House

The primary factor for ninth house Moon is that the person's religious and philosophical beliefs and views of reality are emotionally tied to the past and early home or parental conditioning. Great happiness can come from traveling, and journeys or broadening experiences can create further development of their beliefs and views of reality. This placement has an imaginative and receptive mind, and there's a high consciousness of the supernatural. These people can be natural teachers, putting their imaginative tendencies to practical use. They also tend to learn in a holistic way, and they may be interested in learning about Wicca.

Ninth house Moon ☽ Notables: Kanye West, Whoopi Goldberg, Margaret Thatcher, Gustave Flaubert, and Gustave Courbet

Mercury ☿ in the Ninth House

Mercury in the ninth house is adaptable and exploratory, eager to gain further knowledge and meet new people. There can be a great deal of travel with this placement, as well as interest in everything from higher education to foreign cultures. This placement often wants to understand the development of social ideas, law, justice, government, societal consciousness, and attitudes over time because attitudes determine how and what facts people will integrate. Ninth house Mercury can be intuitive and philosophical, and there might be intellectual snobbery or dogmatic beliefs. This placement involves good oratory skills.

Ninth house Mercury ☿ Notables: Mila Kunis, Al Pacino, Jacqueline Kennedy Onassis, Michel Legrand, and Niels Bohr

Venus ♀ in the Ninth House

Venus in the ninth house has high ideals, an appreciation for fine arts and higher education, and respect for cultural institutions. There will be a great understanding of foreign people and places. This placement indicates you might marry a foreigner, or you might spend much of your life abroad. People with Venus here also might marry someone they meet at an educational institution or church or through their travels abroad. Venus in the ninth house desires education and study about other cultures. People who have this placement might be very well educated in artistic or cultural subjects or religious music and art.

Ninth house Venus ♀ Notables: Venus Williams, The Rock (Dwayne Johnson), Toni Collette, John Updike, and Samuel Taylor Coleridge

Mars ♂ in the Ninth House

Ninth house Mars indicates beliefs translated into action and an active enjoyment of travel and adventure. This placement seeks out new experiences and often finds gain through higher education. There also can be fervent religiosity in this placement. (This is the placement of a crusader for religious, philosophical, social, legal, or educational causes.) Ninth house Mars might also indicate a great restlessness that requires constant travel or interest in sports or outdoor activities. When challenged by aspects, this placement can lead to impatience and intolerance concerning the views of others.

Ninth house Mars ♂ Notables: Rihanna, Kate Winslet, Tiger Woods, Neil Young, and Louisa May Alcott

Jupiter ♃ in the Ninth House

In its natural home here, Jupiter is adventurous and optimistic, and travel and education promise great rewards. The primary distinguishing trait of this placement is the meaningful pursuit of philosophy, religion, or higher education, and many of these people pursue careers as teachers or find their calling in religious occupations. They might have a flair for foreign languages and linguistics, and foreigners might contribute to a ninth house Jupiter's success. This placement can indicate success in writing or publishing as well; in business, it can point to people who lecture, educate, or travel.

Ninth house Jupiter ♃ **Notables:** LeAnn Rimes, Matt Damon, Shaquille O'Neal, George Harrison, and Tennessee Williams

Saturn ♄ in the Ninth House

With Saturn in the ninth house, a person has a great desire to learn and carefully explore philosophy or religion. There's an inherent evaluation of new ideas because ninth house Saturn is interested in social stability, but there's also a desire to know about everything. There can be a tendency toward fanaticism here, but these people often mellow with age as their wisdom develops. Ninth house Saturn often seeks positions of authority or status in education, religious institutions, or businesses that deal with publishing, law, politics, or international affairs. They also might be university professors or public officials.

Ninth house Saturn ♄ **Notables:** Rihanna, Harry, Duke of Sussex, Queen Elizabeth II, Winston Churchill, and Marcel Proust

Uranus ♅ in the Ninth House

Ninth house Uranus always seeks to expand its intellectual horizons and can often be found traveling at the drop of a hat. Someone with this placement might have unusual experiences during global travels and also might have a unique approach to religion, philosophy, or belief systems. People with Uranus here can be unusually gifted in their understanding of religious or metaphysical concepts, with futuristic ideas in philosophy, religion, or education. If they teach, they use technological tools, such as computers or audiovisual equipment, to create stimulating classes. They often study unusual systems of thought, such as astrology, reincarnation, or occult subjects. When challenged by aspect, this placement might become fanatical about religious cults, politics, or social issues.

Ninth house Uranus ♅ **Notables:** Jodie Foster, Julia Child, Charles Addams, Mahatma Gandhi, and William Blake

Neptune ♆ in the Ninth House

Neptune in the ninth house is both imaginative and insightful (and might be prophetically visionary), and it is often drawn to philosophical questions that are not easily answered. This placement is often associated with mystical forms of religion, meditation, and other metaphysical modalities. With their capacity for tolerance and love of travel, people with Neptune here relate well to foreign cultures. They're also interested in social reform. They have strongly intuitive minds, but there can be problems from following misguided spiritual leaders or neglecting to pursue higher education.

Ninth house Neptune ♆ **Notables:** Barack Obama, Bob Dylan, Noam Chomsky, Carrie Fisher, and Claudette Colbert

Pluto ♀ in the Ninth House

With Pluto in the ninth house, you want to understand life in its broadest possible sense and to explain its connection to the Universe as well. Because your emotional security is based on your beliefs, you want to get in touch with larger forces and even tell others about your beliefs. You might try to convert others to your ideas because this reinforces your sense of security and the feeling that you're right. However, the evolutionary intent of your soul is to learn that truth is relative and that the path to truth is ultimately an individual one. This placement is excellent in dealing with karmic, spiritual, and societal laws and systems. Ninth house Plutos are intuitive, conceptual thinkers and are, above all, concerned with truth. Many judges and religious leaders have Pluto in the ninth house.

Ninth house Pluto ♀ Notables: Björk, Robin Williams, John F. Kennedy, Kahlil Gilbran, and Michelangelo

North Node ☊ in the Ninth House/South Node ☋ in the Third House

With a ninth house North Node/third house South Node, you are constantly getting entangled with others on the road to freedom from past conditioning. You like to listen to other people's problems and to give them advice, but you need to learn that truth is much larger than these day-to-day issues and the stored knowledge in your head. Your greatest growth will occur when you make the transition from lower to higher mind and open your eyes to the broader horizons before you. You're here to develop faith and intuition and live a life of spiritual growth.

Ninth house North Node ☊ Notables: Rob Reiner, Margaret Thatcher, Michel Foucault, Orson Welles, and Vladimir Nabokov

Chapter 16

HOPES AND DREAMS: TENTH, ELEVENTH, AND TWELFTH HOUSES

The last three houses are the stuff of dreams—and of ambitions, reputations, interests, and goals. There are secrets here, too, but if you unlock the doors they're behind, you might find greater fulfillment. The tenth house is the area of your reputation and career; the eleventh house represents your long-term dreams and goals; and the twelfth house is where you'll find your secrets, including those you're keeping from yourself. You can look back to Chapter 3 to review the natural associations of signs and houses, and Chapter 2 for a refresher on astrological qualities.

Tenth, Eleventh, and Twelfth Houses

House	Natural Ruler	Natural Planet	Quality
Tenth	Capricorn ♑	Saturn ♄	Cardinal, Angular
Eleventh	Aquarius ♒	Uranus ♅ Saturn ♄	Succedent
Twelfth midheaven	Pisces ♓	Neptune ♆ Jupiter ♃	Cadent

The Tenth House: The Neon Lights Are Bright

Your tenth house is the house of your reputation and your career; in other words, it's your personal Broadway. Just as the fourth house is where you'll find your home, the tenth house, its opposite, is where you'll find everything outside your home: your profession, your community standing, your social role, and what others think of you.

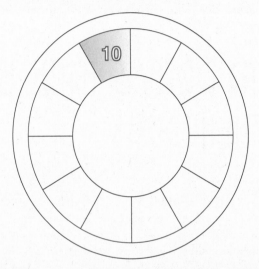

The tenth house: your reputation, career, and social responsibilities.

Some call this the house of ambition, aspiration, and attainment, so it's interesting to note that it's also the house where you'll find your dominant parent. Still, this house is where you'll achieve success through your efforts. It's a reflection of your image and achievements, as shown by the rewards that you receive for your position in life.

Your tenth house is naturally associated with goal-oriented Capricorn ♑ on its cusp, and its planetary ruler is serious, responsible Saturn ♄; naturally, the tenth house also represents positions of power and authority—especially high-government posts. Just as your fourth house cusp is your lower heaven, or I.C., your tenth house cusp is your midheaven, or M.C. This means that this house contains things so obvious about you that they can be seen from a distance. Successfully navigated, your tenth house will give you a sense of fulfilling your destiny and an enormous sense of personal satisfaction as well.

Your tenth house represents your public identity, and at its best, it will match your needs and desires and reflect who you are as a person. After all, developing your social identity should be based on who you are, but accepting a role someone else gives you can happen when you don't get the tenth house right.

Your Supporting Cast

Your tenth house sign describes your ambitions and how you express yourself socially through your profession and community standing. Your tenth house ruler describes where and how you build your social reputation and position. The location of Capricorn ♑, the corresponding natural sign in your chart, shows what areas of your life provide your greatest responsibilities and a need for respect from others.

The Sun ☉ in the Tenth House

A tenth house Sun indicates a strong sense of self, a will to succeed, and a desire to make a difference in the world. Tenth house Sun combines ambition with power. This is a good placement for someone interested in politics or administrative work, or it's a good placement for someone who wants to take on a position of authority and leadership. There's both drive and ambition here, as well as the desire for social status. Although this placement needs power, there might not be the ability to handle it appropriately. Someone with a Sun in the tenth house might use unethical methods to gain power or position. (This might sound familiar when you think of some politicians.) In general, however, this placement is careful not to taint its respectability or dignity.

Tenth house Sun ☉ Notables: James Clavell, Bryan Cranston, Joe DiMaggio, Harold Wilson, and Honore de Balzac

The Moon ☽ in the Tenth House

A tenth house Moon indicates an emotional connectedness to one's work and service to the public. This is a good placement for "lunar" occupations, such as marketing, commodities, or shipping by water. Reputation matters to tenth house Moons, and there can be a tendency to sacrifice one's private life for the attainment of success. People with the Moon in the tenth house are charismatic and are often successful in politics or other careers that deal with the public and community service. Usually, the mother of a person with the Moon in the tenth house works very hard and has a strong influence that sets the stage for a drive toward achievement. The emotional need is strongly linked to the desire for success, and until success becomes linked to the welfare of the public, that person's career might go through changes.

Tenth house ☽ Notables: Adele, Meryl Streep, Nancy Reagan, Robert F. Kennedy, and Rudyard Kipling

Mercury ☿ in the Tenth House

Mercury in the tenth house has no trouble communicating ideas to others and can often do so in a variety of ways. People who have this placement have intellectually stimulating careers and might be found in writing, communications, or public speaking. They're influencers on social media, and they might moderate panel discussions or host a podcast. They acquire added education, so they can achieve significant social positions. Mercury in the tenth house also can be associated with high-level political leaders, and people who have this placement might become speech writers or political strategists. Politicians with this placement become known for their intelligent ideas. There might be travel involved in their careers, or there might be more than one job. Mercury in the tenth house often brings many opportunities to travel or change residence because of career aspirations.

Tenth house Mercury ☿ Notables: Forest Whitaker, Tom Hanks, Heidi Klum, Friedrich Nietzsche, and Marie Curie

Venus ♀ in the Tenth House

Tenth house Venus might have a career involved in the arts or in cultural work and is likely to enjoy social success and prosperity from that career. There's a natural diplomacy at work here, as well as an ability to use one's social charisma and magnetism to achieve public success. Venus in the tenth house desires to counsel, negotiate, facilitate, and arbitrate to create win-win situations and outcomes. People with this placement often partner with others who have the same ideas, values, social status, and development of wealth or prosperity.

Tenth house Venus ♀ Notables: Kanye West, Michael Moore, Al Gore, Robin Williams, and Johann Wolfgang von Goethe

Mars ♂ in the Tenth House

Mars in the tenth house has intense energy, initiative, and drive in its career, and it will want to be the one in charge. This is a very competitive placement, but there's self-reliance, too, which means these people do very well in any executive position. They also can do well in the military or in engineering, and they make effective political leaders and entrepreneurs. This placement also can indicate problems with authority figures—Mars in the tenth house does *not* like to be told what to do!

Tenth house Mars ♂ Notables: Beyoncé, Andy Warhol, Janis Joplin, Muhammad Ali, and Mao Zedong

Jupiter ♃ in the Tenth House

Tenth house Jupiter works very well with others and has a natural ability to lead, inspire, and bring hope and enthusiasm. There's a strong sense of justice here, and this placement can do well in law, politics, or business. Tenth house Jupiter has high moral standards and broad vision, and with its ambition and pride, it will achieve a good reputation and create a good reputation for the group. In the latter part of a tenth house Jupiter's life, there's likely to be renown or high standing in the profession. This also is an excellent position for a career in medicine, healing, religion, philanthropy, or social reform.

Tenth house Jupiter ♃ Notables: Emma Watson, John Malkovich, Chevy Chase, Truman Capote, and Harry S. Truman

Saturn ♄ in the Tenth House

Saturn in its home, the tenth house, indicates someone who is determined, disciplined, and self-reliant, and this person is very likely to achieve success because these people have extremely strong career ambitions and drive, above all else. This placement likes and needs responsibility and so is excellent in business and politics. When well-aspected, this position leads to authority, high position, and high pay. But when this placement is challenged by aspect, there can be a fall from position after compromising values to achieve goals. Tenth house Saturn may fall victim to cancel culture, finding pathways to social media platforms and career advancement (justly or unjustly) blocked. It's important for these people to focus their ambitions on serving others instead of just seeking personal gain or misusing their power. People who have Saturn in the tenth house usually had to learn responsibility early in life because of the absence of authority figures. However, this can translate into a strong sense of responsibility toward one's own family.

Tenth house Saturn ♄ Notables: Will Smith, Chelsea Clinton, Angela Merkel, Kurt Vonnegut, and Arthur Schopenhauer

Uranus ♅ in the Tenth House

Tenth house Uranus needs its freedom and will find its career success in unusual and often autonomous ways. Talk about doing it *my* way! This is the placement of going where no one has gone before. Many engineers, scientists, social reformers, astrologers, broadcasters, people in electronics or mathematics, and those who work in humanitarian fields have Uranus in the tenth house. But it's also an excellent placement for changing the old ways; the originality, insight, and altruism here can make tenth house Uranus a visionary leader. There might also be difficulty getting along with authority figures, so these people might prefer to work for themselves. When this placement is challenged, there can be sudden changes in career or career disappointments.

Tenth house Uranus ♅ Notables: Adele, Jim Carrey, Julie Christie, Dolly Parton, and Thomas Jefferson

Neptune ♆ in the Tenth House

Tenth house Neptune translates into a career that involves creativity, intuition, and imagination. People who have this placement also might serve humanity in some way while having an unusual career at the same time. This placement is often found in actors, artists, musicians, and television personalities, and the world sees these people as glamorous and exciting. Tenth house Neptune thrives in the gig economy. They achieve their success through their own talents and abilities, without much help from at least one of their parents. (The other parent might compensate for this.) This placement also is good for ministers, astrologers, psychics, psychologists, or psychiatrists; people who work in institutions, medical missions, or humanitarian efforts; or people who serve the God of their understanding. This placement also can indicate confusion, changing career goals, or uncertainty about one's calling.

Tenth house Neptune ♆ Notables: Ivana Trump, Jamie Lee Curtis, Agatha Christie, Arthur Miller, and Albert Einstein

Pluto ♀ in the Tenth House

With a tenth house Pluto, your soul is learning the lesson of how to establish your individuality and authority within your culture. This placement is all about laws, customs, and a need to learn how to integrate your own identity into the larger framework of the social order. There is a primary need for discipline and sustained effort to achieve a major commitment or goal. Your soul's evolutionary intent here, though, is to develop internal security and personal fulfillment and to see one's self *without* the trappings of the social role. You might be forced into a deep self-examination of your inner emotions to make this transformation, but this process will ultimately provide a real sense of internal security.

Tenth house Pluto ♀ Notables: Ariana Grande, Will.i.am, Debbie Reynolds, Federico Fellini, and Albert Camus

North Node ☊ in the Tenth House/South Node ☋ in the Fourth House

With a tenth house North Node/fourth house South Node, you're learning about the demands of family and the conflict between doing what you want to do for yourself and your career versus what you must do for your loved ones. The lesson here is to learn how to mature and rise above family issues to arrive at your own sense of contribution to the world. After you learn this lesson, you will move away from self-interest to joyously sharing with others. This placement is all about leaving behind emotional immaturity and then developing responsibility and in the process, reaping the benefits of sharing.

Tenth house North Node ☊ Notables: Julia Roberts, Keanu Reeves, Prince Charles, Carrie Fisher, and Freddie Mercury

The Eleventh House: When You Wish upon a Star

Living in your eleventh house are the groups who will help you achieve your goals and your group involvements. Traditionally, this is the house of friends, hopes, and wishes, and it is concerned with long-term dreams and goals, as well as with the people who share your interests and objectives. It's where you'll find your sense of future direction and purpose, your plans and goals, your hopes and dreams, and the people who can help you get there.

Your eleventh house also is the house of your idealism and vision because it's where your ideas and intellectual growth for collective good reside. This house is naturally ruled by Aquarius ♒ on its cusp, and its associated planet is Uranus ♅, with Saturn ♄ as its co-ruler.

Your eleventh house identifies you with other people and with the goals of those people who parallel and assist your own. Unlike your seventh house primary relationships, these are the friends whose goals and desires parallel your desires, so it's a place where you give and take in your journey toward your future.

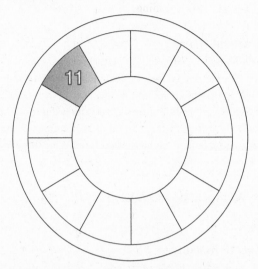

The eleventh house: your goals, groups, and friends.

Social goals or reform and the need to contribute to larger goals take a front seat here. After all, this house is associated with social contributions and accomplishments. Successfully navigated, your eleventh house can provide you with strategy and direction. Unsuccessfully navigated, you'll seem to drift through your life with no purpose, unable to make commitments or decisions, and perhaps lonely as well.

Reaching for the Stars

Your eleventh house sign describes your group involvements and goals and how you express your sense of direction for the future. Your eleventh house ruler describes where and how your hopes and dreams are developed, along with your group contributions. This house, where Aquarius ♒ is its corresponding natural sign, shows what your group involvements are tied to and where you share your unique ideas for the benefit of groups or social goals.

The Sun ☉ in the Eleventh House

Often socially popular and active, an eleventh house Sun indicates someone who needs to integrate personal goals, creativity, and willpower into the larger collective or social order. For this reason, there is a strong desire to accomplish something important that will benefit others. These people are often helped by friends and associates in positions of power or influence. They often have humanitarian goals, and/or they seek to achieve distinction by accomplishing unique or innovative goals. The Sun in the eleventh house might be a leader or might inspire others in some new field, especially one that encompasses both idealism and innovation.

Eleventh house Sun ☉ Notables: Rihanna, Robert Pattinson, Goldie Hawn, Ron Howard, and Vladimir Putin

The Moon ☽ in the Eleventh House

The Moon in the eleventh house is emotionally intuitive when it comes to people, and its charm can attract many admirers. These people might use their homes for group meetings or activities, and they often join up with a variety of causes. These are primarily people who need to develop their goals and future through a constantly growing and changing social sphere. There is also a deep emotional need to bond through friendships and associations with others. Moon in the eleventh house might have many female friends and associates, or they might meet other people primarily through their family members. They often attract a wide extended family and support network.

Eleventh house Moon ☽ Notables: Mark Zuckerberg, Venus Williams, Keanu Reeves, John McCain, and Bruce Lee

Mercury ☿ in the Eleventh House

Eleventh house Mercury has a wide variety of friends, often based on intellectual connections, and is socially minded as well. This placement is very good at thinking of the best ways to achieve goals and is idealistic and original. Mercury in the eleventh house brings a lively mind to group enterprises. People with Mercury in the eleventh house are interested in communications or open exchanges of information with others. They're often dedicated to or interested in sciences, humanitarian causes, astrology, or occult subjects. They also might need to develop persistence in attaining their goals.

Eleventh house Mercury ☿ Notables: Lorde, Margaret Thatcher, Henry Ford, Anne Frank, and Henry Wadsworth Longfellow

Venus ♀ in the Eleventh House

Venus in the eleventh house has lots of friends and benefits from its associations with people, both socially and financially. This placement indicates an idealism and interest in social values, which can lead to involvement with philanthropy or other charitable causes. People with Venus in the eleventh house might have musicians or artists as friends, or they might be involved in artistic associations. Their cooperative spirit makes them excellent team players.

Eleventh house Venus ♀ Notables: Jimmy Carter, George H. W. Bush, Lyndon B. Johnson, Calvin Coolidge, and George Washington

Mars ♂ in the Eleventh House

An eleventh house Mars is often the leader in its circle of friends and actively pursues its well-defined goals. There's energy to spare with this placement, and eleventh house Mars makes friends quickly—although he or she might also lose them quickly by pushing them to keep up. People with an eleventh house Mars have friends or are aligned with groups that might be aggressive or masculine, and they often achieve their personal goals through such people. Someone with Mars in the eleventh house can become dissatisfied with the present social order and might have revolutionary tendencies.

Eleventh house Mars ♂ Notables: Harry, Duke of Sussex, Reese Witherspoon, Nelson Mandela, Eleanor Roosevelt, and Sigmund Freud

Jupiter ♃ in the Eleventh House

Jupiter in the eleventh house is popular and successful through groups and friends, and often benefits and grows from its associations with others. This placement does particularly well in large organizations, and if well-aspected, has good judgment and intuition. People with Jupiter in the eleventh house are usually successful in very large projects, which might be associated with humanitarian, religious, educational, or charitable efforts. In business pursuits, group activities are often related to the sciences, engineering, new inventions, or organizational pursuits. Eleventh house Jupiters also might benefit through travel and foreign associations.

Eleventh house Jupiter ♃ Notables: Ellen DeGeneres, Prince, Diane Arbus, Frida Kahlo, and Karl Marx

Saturn ♄ in the Eleventh House

An eleventh house Saturn has a few strong and meaningful friendships and avoids any superficial relationships. This placement will not be doing much swiping right (or left); tenth house Saturn is faithful. There are high hopes here, but there can be delays and obstacles before one achieves them. Although there might be inner insecurities, there is also strong loyalty to friends and family. Older people are often very helpful to these people. This placement can add structure to ideas and ideals, turning them into practical inventions, uses, or applications. There also can be strong organizational ability because this is one of Saturn's "home" houses.

Eleventh house Saturn ♄ Notables: Mark Zuckerberg, Sarah Jessica Parker, Dolly Parton, Nancy Reagan, and Queen Victoria

Uranus ♅ in the Eleventh House

Eleventh house Uranus people are often associated with humanitarian, astrological, scientific, broadcast, electronics, or technical groups. Remember, this is Uranus's home house, so it's very happy here. These people will have unusual goals and generally aren't concerned with approval or traditions; they can be game changers. This placement often gives strong intuition and the ability to perceive universal laws or principles. For this reason, people with this placement often develop strong interests in humanitarian concerns, the occult, or astrology, as well as new inventions or the natural sciences. Eleventh house Uranus also might change their goals unexpectedly, sometimes more than once during their lives before finding their paths. They also might have more than one set of friends—one set of eccentrics and another set of "normals"—because both Uranus and Saturn are associated with this house.

Eleventh house Uranus ♅ Notables: Princess Charlotte; Harry, Duke of Windsor; Prince William; Prince Charles; and Camilla, Duchess of Cornwall

Neptune ♆ in the Eleventh House

Neptune in the eleventh house is drawn to artistic, spiritual, or humanitarian people and often shares common goals with them. This placement indicates people who join organizations with idealistic, mystical, secret, spiritual, religious, or visionary aims because they're so sensitive to the needs of humankind. People who have this placement might receive beneficial intuitive or spiritual advice from others, though they might be misled by friends or unreliable associates. It's important for people with eleventh house Neptune to exercise care in choosing friends and to avoid unrealistic expectations about them.

Eleventh house Neptune ♆ Notables: Brad Pitt, Debbie Reynolds, Yoko Ono, William Shakespeare, and Michelangelo Buonarroti

Pluto ♀ in the Eleventh House

If you have an eleventh house Pluto, your evolutionary purpose is to move away from old ideas about self-definition into new, uncharted areas. You don't like to be defined by situations, others, or anything external; you want to define yourself outside the mainstream and outside any cultural identity. The evolutionary intent of your soul is to use your ideas about yourself to visualize and plan your future. Most importantly, you must act on them. It's vital that you learn not to wait for approval or support from others before pursuing your life's directions and goals. You are here to be an innovative and creative change agent in whatever area of life is most appropriate for you. Your power here lies in understanding that it's okay to be different.

Eleventh house Pluto ♀ Notables: James Franco, Scarlett Johansson, Sinclair Lewis, Vincent Van Gogh, and Leo Tolstoy

North Node ☊ in the Eleventh House/South Node ☋ in the Fifth House

With an eleventh house North Node/fifth house South Node, you're learning to move beyond being a solitary creator to create for a global community. You need to trust your dreams and learn the value of friendship and the greater good. In the process, you need to let go of pride and self-consciousness and become a part of the collective consciousness. Past creativity and love are needed for larger purposes in this lifetime, and once you develop objectivity, you'll be able to achieve them.

Eleventh house North Node ☊ Notables: Robert Downey Jr., Arnold Schwarzenegger, Julia Child, Boris Leonidovich Pasternak, and Charles Darwin

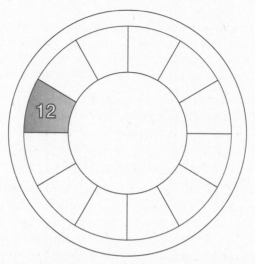

The twelfth house: your subconscious, privacy, and past karma.

The Twelfth House: Secret Agent

The twelfth house gets a bad rep in many astrology books, particularly the older ones. Sometimes, it's called the house of secrets; others call it the house of self-undoing or the house of sorrows. But let's take a moment to look at where this tarnished reputation came from. The twelfth house is certainly the most mystical of the houses. After all, it's where you'll find your subconscious and the unknown. However, like most fields, astrology had a patriarchal philosophy. Until recently, this meant "feminine" signs like Cancer ♋ and Pisces ♓ were called "emotional" and "weepy," and the mystical houses like the fourth, eighth, and twelfth were called "disappointing" or "irrational."

Well, it can be scary for some behind-the-times guys to get in touch with things like intuition and secrets and dreams; they operate in what some men want to be a rational, ordered, and "masculine" world. However, we all know the world isn't always as rational or ordered as we'd like. Many men (and women, too) still deal with issues of *intersectionality*. The textbook definition of intersectionality is: *Cultural patterns of oppression that are not only interrelated but are bound together and influenced by the interconnected systems of society, including race, gender, class, ability, and ethnicity.* Searching for a harmonic balance of consciousness—both in our inner lives and in our outer experiences of the world—is a goal of the twelfth house.

Astrologer Steven Forrest calls the twelfth house "the house of troubles," but he also makes clear that consciousness itself resides here. This is the point at which self meets soul and where ego can merge into spirit.

Successfully navigate your twelfth house, and you'll transcend your everyday worries. Planets in this house also can help you learn lessons that free you from past destructive patterns. Unsuccessfully navigate it, and your self-image will be blurry. You might self-destruct through alcohol, drugs, or the wrong people, or you might seem to have chronic "bad luck."

Among the many things lurking in the closet of your twelfth house are your secret enemies. These are the people who smile to your face and then stab you in the back on social media. Look more closely, though, and you may discover that these are your own energies projected onto someone else. Be aware of what you're hiding from yourself in your twelfth house, and you'll get your enemies out in the open where you can address issues head-on.

Your twelfth house can lead to self-transcendence, moving beyond the ego to what's beyond the self. It's here you'll find your higher consciousness, your unconscious, and what you don't yet know. Poorly aspected, though, it can be your undoing. How you navigate your twelfth house is up to you. Its ruler is Pisces ♓, and its associated planets are Neptune ♆ and Jupiter ♃: Neptune, the mystical, and Jupiter, the fortunate (or when overdone, the unfortunate).

Skeletons in Your Closet

Your twelfth house sign describes your past, the types of social services you might perform, and how you express (or don't express) your unconscious. Your twelfth house ruler describes where and how you can develop beyond yourself and serve the larger collective. Pisces ♓ is the corresponding natural sign, and this house shows where you need to be of service to others and the areas of your life in which you have great potential to develop your unconscious.

The Sun ☉ in the Twelfth House

A twelfth house Sun has a strong desire for solitude, peace, and quiet, and might be close to only a few carefully chosen people. There may be success later in life, along with deep spiritual understanding. This placement also can be both resourceful and self-expressive. The essence of this placement is a person who works behind the scenes instead of in the public eye. These people are here to serve others instead of themselves, and they often have profound inner lives. Many can be found working for large companies or institutions, such as hospitals, prisons, or places of spiritual retreat. This is a good position for medical researchers, doctors, or people who work with the disabled or disadvantaged.

Twelfth house Sun ☉ Notables: Keanu Reeves, Hillary Clinton, Andy Warhol, Judy Garland, and Mahatma Gandhi

The Moon ☽ in the Twelfth House

The Moon in the twelfth house is sensitive, receptive, and intuitive—almost as if it has radar—but can also be easily hurt and might hide its true feelings. There will be a need for alone time or seclusion to process these feelings, meditate, or pursue spiritual teachings. If they don't get time alone, these people might feel pressured and will need to escape, either by "zoning out" or through fantasy. Twelfth house Moons also have a creative imagination, so this placement is commonly found in writers. These people also make good counselors because they're so sensitive to the feelings of others. They may be chefs or bakers, who know instinctively how to nourish others. This placement primarily indicates people whose feelings and emotional responses are heavily tied to their subconscious or past lives. For this reason, they might not understand why they feel the way they do.

Twelfth house Moon ☽ Notables: Allen Ginsberg, James Agee, Virginia Woolf, Percy Bysshe Shelley, and William Blake

Mercury ☿ in the Twelfth House

Twelfth house Mercury is contemplative, and these people work things out for themselves. Also, they might be very reluctant to share what they think. Mercury here is subtle but good at analyzing other people's problems, and might base its decisions on reason and logic. This is because twelfth house Mercury's thinking is heavily influenced by past experiences, unconscious memories, or the subconscious. Close to the ascendant, this Mercury might behave more like a first-house Mercury and be more communicative. (See Chapter 13 for a discussion of Mercury in the first house.) If Mercury is aspected astrologically to any of the outer three planets, these people might gain important knowledge through their intuitive or psychic abilities. (See Chapter 17 to learn more about aspects.)

Twelfth house Mercury ☿ Notables: Beyoncé, Kristen Stewart, Heath Ledger, Stephen Hawking, and Robert Oppenheimer

Venus ♀ in the Twelfth House

Venus in the twelfth house is both artistic and creative and prefers a private, secluded life. This is a compassionate and sympathetic placement because Venus is extremely happy here and has a great desire to serve others in some way. People with Venus in the twelfth house also like to look at life's deeper meanings and might find a good outlet through their devotion to the God of their understanding or an ideal. Worldly success and contributions to help others are both important with Venus in the tenth house. For this reason, this placement might pursue a spiritual life. Often noted for secretive love affairs or personal contacts, this position is primarily distinguished by its artistic and strong emotional ties to the subconscious, which can result in deeply inspired art.

Twelfth house Venus ♀ Notables: Gianni Versace, Steve Martin, Gertrude Stein, Pierre Teilhard De Chardin, and Gustave Courbet.

Mars ♂ in the Twelfth House

Twelfth house Mars people have strong feelings but prefer to keep them secret from everyone else because their desires, anger, or feelings are connected to past experiences or their subconscious, so they might not understand them. People with Mars in the twelfth house have an active imagination and might fight for those less fortunate. These people can be good strategists, planning things behind the scenes. This placement is also very self-motivated and able to work independently without supervision. Primarily, they need *not* to be discouraged by others, which is why they might unconsciously decide to work behind the scenes to accomplish their purposes. They might appear to be mild mannered, but when pushed to their limits and forced to release their suppressed anger, they will fight back like a caged tiger and make formidable foes. These people also might have a partially hidden identity that is not shared with others.

Twelfth house Mars ♂ Notables: Mick Jagger, Arnold Schwarzenegger, Albert Brooks, Yoko Ono, and Edgar Allan Poe

Jupiter ♃ in the Twelfth House

Jupiter in the twelfth house is kind, compassionate, and charitable, and is often found helping others in some way. These people have a strong religious or philosophical faith or are likely to pursue an inner spiritual path. Some have called a twelfth house Jupiter "an angel on your shoulder." This is because people with this placement are often benefited by others anonymously, just as they often help people in need the same way. It's a reward for "good behavior." This is one of Jupiter's home houses because it co-rules Pisces, so it's very happy here; these people are often very intuitive. If challenged by aspect, however, they might fall into impractical idealism, overindulgence, or neglect to develop their creative abilities to help others.

Twelfth house Jupiter ♃ Notables: Barack Obama, Michael J. Fox, Sarah Jessica Parker, Yoko Ono, and Paul Newman

Saturn ♄ in the Twelfth House

Twelfth house Saturn is reserved and cautious, preferring to work alone. This placement can be lonely or afraid, especially because these people won't share their feelings with others for fear they'll be used against them. But this also can be a very good placement for those who require seclusion for their work. This placement might have unconscious—or what seem to be unfounded—fears about their own worth or about the structures of their world dissolving before them. Normally, these fears are either imaginary or linked to past-life memories. It's often wise for these people to develop practical ways to help others, which they are talented at doing; also, doing so helps them get past focusing on their fears and insecurities. This placement is often found in people who work in large companies, large institutions, or for the government. They also might work for charitable foundations or in psychology.

Twelfth house Saturn ♄ Notables: Barack Obama, Angelina Jolie, Robert Redford, Julia Child, and Dante Alighieri

Uranus ♅ in the Twelfth House

A twelfth house Uranus indicates compassion and intuition, and although people with this placement want to free themselves from society's constraints, they are the ones who hold themselves back due to their fears. They have a particular enchantment with the mysterious and romantic, but this also is an intellectual placement. These people not only want to work in unusual ways, they *do* work in unusual ways. This placement is good for researchers or those who work behind the scenes alone. People with Uranus here might also be loners, feeling too different to make strong connections with others. Although they're very intuitive, they might not listen to their higher selves, and so might ignore information.

Twelfth house Uranus ♅ Notables: Chris Evans, Ariana Grande, Jennifer Aniston, Tony Shalhoub, and Steven Spielberg

Neptune ♆ in the Twelfth House

Those who have Neptune in the twelfth house prefer to work in a quiet place that allows their creativity to flow. This placement can indicate an almost otherworldly type of person who is also very helpful to others and who is finely tuned to his or her own subconscious. Because this is Neptune's home house and it's very happy here, this placement can be a strong source of wisdom. These people are highly intuitive and might be in touch with the collective mind, which could be thought of as a pool of ideas we're all plugged into. If Neptune is well-aspected, those with this placement also might be artistic, musical, or poetic, and could have a strong talent for psychology, psychic abilities, or healing. Their search for an inner spiritual path is important, and until they find it, their lives can be "in a fog" or isolated. Their strong ability to absorb other people's feelings and energies makes it difficult for them to be around negative people.

Twelfth house Neptune ♆ Notables: Ariana Grande, Eric Clapton, Julie Andrews, Prince, and Robert Browning

Pluto ♀ in the Twelfth House

If you have Pluto in the twelfth house, you have the potential to spiritualize all aspects of your life, and your unconscious intention is to merge or identify with the Source, the God of your understanding, or a higher power. To do this, you are trying to dissolve any emotional, mental, physical, or spiritual blockages . Naturally, this is a frightening prospect given that we all, as human beings, have a strong concept of "self." This fear can lead to avoidance behaviors, such as living out dreams and illusions or taking compulsive actions, manifesting destructive self-behaviors. The lesson here is faith—and what you're willing to take on faith—to find the ultimate meaning of life. The evolutionary intent of your soul is to develop specific, useful methods for learning to analyze yourself and hone transcendental meditation techniques that enable you to experience the Source, so that you find your blockages and eliminate them. Also, you need to perform some type of "right work," which is work that helps or serves others. You need to learn to believe in your own intuitive abilities, develop faith, and, in the process, let go of the idea of self. This is particularly hard for people from Western civilizations to do.

Twelfth house Pluto ♀ Notables: Keanu Reeves, Tom Hanks, Freddie Mercury, Kurt Cobain, and Virginia Woolf

North Node ☊ in the Twelfth House/South Node ☋ in the Sixth House

With a twelfth house North Node/sixth house South Node, you're learning to move beyond yourself, but it's a tough lesson and you might spend far too much time either wallowing in self-pity or criticizing everyone else. You need to learn to see yourself as part of a larger whole while also seeing that the whole universe is also contained in you. When you learn this, you'll see the greater harmony and synchronicity of all things. This is an opportunity to find all the answers you need within yourself, serve others, and become part of a higher cause or purpose.

Twelfth house North Node ☊ Notables: Cher, John F. Kennedy Jr., Neil Armstrong, Pierre Curie, and Vincent Van Gogh

USING ASTROLOGY: ASTRO-NERDS ASSEMBLE!

Well, here you are! Through astrology, you hold the key pieces to understanding yourself and your journey through your life. All you have to do is put them together! Relax … that's exactly what these final chapters will help you do. From aspects to planetary cycles and from Moon phases to retrogrades, astrology gives precise meaning to your life under the heavens.

Your birth chart is astrology's own data-driven metaphor of the heavens—more specifically, your heavens. Enjoy interpreting charts with confidence for yourself, and for friends. Remember, interpretations made from birth charts by human beings for human beings (even if the chart is computer-generated) contain within them the humanity of personal understanding and relationship.

Part

5

Chapter 17

CONSIDERING ASPECTS IN YOUR BIRTH CHART

It's time to start putting together everything you've learned so far to interpret your birth chart. But first, we need to cover one more aspect of your birth chart: astrological aspects! In this chapter, we now can look at how these planetary relationships flavor your birth chart and unlock more secrets about why you behave the way you do.

Chart Basics: A Language of Symbols

The powerful symbolic language of astrology pictorially illuminates the signs, planets, and houses, and it shows the various relationships among them. If your child were to draw a picture of your family standing in front of your house, the stick person with the longer hair would be Mom; the one with the glasses would be Dad; and the short one would be Junior (or maybe a Balloon Dog, if your kid has some Jeff Koons talent).

Just as Mom, Dad, Junior, and Balloon Dog are much more than "Mom," "Dad," "Junior," and "Balloon Dog," astrological symbols represent much more than "Aries," "Mercury," or "the first house." For example, Aries ♈, the first sign of the zodiac, is ruled by Mars ♂, a cardinal Fire sign, and has yang energy. All that should come immediately to mind when you see the symbol ♈.

In turn, each of these symbols when they appear in a birth chart represents a larger meaning as well. For example, cardinal signs like to lead and to get things started, though they aren't always around to see things through to completion. When the symbol for Aries ♈ appears in a birth chart, these concepts are part of what's represented, plus a whole lot more. The aspects between planets, too, have symbols, and in this chapter, we illuminate the power and resonance of each and how to interpret the aspects in your birth chart.

Before we get started, though, let's review all the basic astrological symbols here for easy reference. When you begin working with your birth chart and considering aspect relationships, these symbols will become second nature to you, bringing to mind instantly all the richness of nuance, meaning, and potential they convey.

Astrological Symbols

Sign	Symbol
Aries	♈
Taurus	♉
Gemini	♊
Cancer	♋
Leo	♌
Virgo	♍
Libra	♎
Scorpio	♏
Sagittarius	♐
Capricorn	♑
Aquarius	♒
Pisces	♓

Planet	Symbol
Sun	☉
Moon	☽
Mercury	☿
Venus	♀
Mars	♂
Jupiter	♃
Saturn	♄
Uranus	♅

Planet	Symbol
Neptune	Ψ
Pluto	♀
North Node	☊
South Node	☋

Aspect	Symbol
Conjunction	☌
Sextile	✶
Square	□
Trine	△
Opposition	☍
Quincunx	⚻

Other	Symbol
Retrograde	℞

Aspects: Specifics on Experience

You probably remember *aspects* from walking through the houses in Part 4. There we mentioned that a planet's aspects can determine how its energies manifest in a certain house. In astrology, *aspect* has a technical meaning. When two planets are in aspect to each other, they are related by one of a set of geometric angles between them; some of these angles are beneficial, and others are challenging.

Looking at aspects means answering the question "How do these planets get along?" There are five major aspects and many more minor aspects. Most planets can form any aspect to another, except for Mercury ☿, which is never more than 28 degrees from the Sun ☉, and Venus ♀, which is never farther than 48 degrees from the Sun ☉. Their orbits are such that they cannot create all of the aspect relationships.

The following are the major aspects:

* **Conjunctions** ☌, which are the strongest aspects.

* **Squares** □, which are considered to be challenging. Their tension provides dynamic action in your life.

* **Oppositions** ☍, which show a need for balance between two competing or different energies or needs.

* **Trines** △, which are considered the most favorable aspects, as their signs usually share the same Element.

* **Sextiles** ⚹, which are harmonious, bringing opportunity and attraction.

Before we walk through the aspects, it's important to understand precisely what aspects are and how they're determined. Remember those numbers before and after each sign next to the planets of your birth chart? Those are the *degrees* of each planet at your birth, and they take on prime importance when we begin aspecting. Planetary degrees show the position of the planets in the signs. The number of degrees one planet is from another planet determines its aspect to that planet.

Most astrologers agree that aspects occur within *orbs* rather than just those that create exact angles. Orbs are the variances in degree allowed in determining aspects. For example, while an exact square is 90 degrees, angles from 83 to 97 degrees are commonly considered to be squares—but even these orbs of 7 degrees depend on the planets involved. Exact aspects, of course, create the strongest connections, but wider orbs cannot be ignored. Some astrologers don't consider orbs beyond 6 degrees, while others will go as high as 10 degrees.

In general, different orbs are allowed for different types of aspects. This is based on the planets involved—the Sun ☉ and Moon ☽ often get 10-degree orbs—and the type of aspect. For example, conjunctions ☌ get more of an orb than sextiles ⚹ because a conjunction is a stronger aspect. We explain the meaning of conjunctions and sextiles—and all the other major aspects—in the next section of this chapter.

To explain this concept a little more, a conjunction is two planets within, say, 7 to 10 degrees of each other (out of 360 degrees); this means the percentage of variance is small. Ten degrees out of 360 is $\frac{1}{36}$ or 2.7 percent, only.

On the other hand, if a sextile ⚹, which is only 60 degrees to begin with, had a 10-degree orb, that would be a nearly 17 percent variance. So, orbs for an aspect such as a sextile ⚹ are smaller than orbs for something like a conjunction ☌ or an opposition ☍.

One helpful way to determine aspects is to recognize what part of a circle a particular angle represents. (And you thought your geometry days were over!) We've provided a list for you.

Aspects Are Angles of the Circle

Portion of Circle	Angle	Aspect Name (* Major Aspect)
½	180°	Opposition*
⅓	120°	Trine*
¼	90°	Square*
⅕	72°	Quintile
⅙	60°	Sextile*
⅐	51½°	Septile
⅛	45°	Semi-square
⅑	40°	Novile
¹⁄₁₀	36°	Semi-quintile
¹⁄₁₂	30°	Semi-sextile

Note that the major aspects are the opposition ☍, trine △, square □, and sextile ✳. There's also the *conjunction,* which isn't listed because it's not an angle; planets in conjunction are in the same area. ("Planet A" conjunction "Planet B" occurs when two planets are in the same area of the birth chart.) All the other aspects are considered minor, though some might not be *quite* as minor as once thought.

In addition, all the major aspects are essentially same-degree aspects, so planets in different signs share the same degree. Most minor aspects involve aspects that are not the same degree.

Another way to determine aspects is to remember which signs are which quality, Element, and/or energy. As a rule (there are exceptions), sextiles ✳ and trines △ are formed by signs with the same Element or energy, and squares □ and oppositions ☍ are formed by signs of the same quality.

The New Math: From Conjunctions ☌ to Sextiles ✳

We concentrate on the major aspects here, with one exception. Astrologers have recently found that *quincunxes* ⚻, or angles of 150°, have far more importance than had been previously thought. Astrologers have come to recognize the quincunx as a "crisis" aspect. This aspect signals an internal need to change an old pattern or accommodate a new routine that wasn't planned for.

It can also signal a lack of shared energy or intention, meaning that solutions will come from unexpected collaboration and yield unexpected—and often brilliant—results.

Like so many things in astrology, aspects used to be characterized as good or bad. These days, astrologers (and psychologists) recognize that we need our challenges to make the most of our lives, so aspects that were once called "bad" are now viewed in a new light. And aspects that once were "good" in the past can sometimes make you too complacent. Let's start at the very beginning, though.

Aspect: Conjunction ☌ 0°

Conjunctions ☌ are the strongest aspects in astrology. The two (or more) planets involved are a focal point of the chart, and their meaning is emphasized. They can be either easy or challenging, depending on which planets are involved and other aspects in the chart.

Aspect: Sextile ⚹ 60°

Sextiles ⚹ are considered quite favorable because their signs usually share the same energy. They do require some effort on your part, though, unlike easy trines. Sextiles are like development opportunities, so if you don't take action to develop them, you can miss out.

Aspect: Square □ 90°

Squares □ are considered to be challenging, and their tension can provide dynamic action in your life and development. Most of us would never do anything if we weren't being motivated by squares (or oppositions)!

Aspect: Trine △ 120°

A trine △ is considered the most favorable aspect because its signs usually share the same Element and energy. These are well-developed skills and strengths, which many people fail to recognize within themselves because their energy is manifested so well. Too many trines can make you weak or lazy because there's no resistance in the energy here at all; instead, there's just an easy flow of energy between the two planets involved.

Aspect: Opposition ☍ 180°

Oppositions ☍ are considered challenging, especially in areas of growth and achievement. They also can show a need for balancing opposite needs and/or energies, such as career versus home or self versus others.

Aspect: Quincunx ⚻ 150°

In a quincunx ⚻ or inconjunct relationship, there's no connection between the signs involved—neither quality, nor Element, nor energy. This aspect indicates a need to adjust in some way, whether it be a change in attitude, habit, or behavior. A quincunx ⚻ is sometimes called the "genius" aspect, as it calls on an individual to act when there is nothing held in common. Some find their best selves under this aspect, though it is not an easy process. Quincunxes lead to unexpected results, as there is no shared energy for a solution; you can't see ahead.

Some planets or energies get along well together, whereas others are uncomfortable with one another. When two planets are in aspect to each other, they're essentially talking and communicating, and the slower planet is telling the faster planet how to behave, think, and act. This is because the slower planet takes longer to move, so it has a greater impact. In other words, Pluto's ♀ aspects have more far-reaching effects than the Moon's ☽, which we feel in a more fast-paced way.

Planets, Fast to Slow

These are the planets, from shortest (fastest) to longest (slowest) orbit:

Moon	☽
Mercury	☿
Venus	♀
Sun	☉
Mars	♂
Jupiter	♃
Saturn	♄
Uranus	♅
Neptune	♆
Pluto	♀

Getting Along: Venus ♀/Jupiter ♃ Aspects

Although we don't have enough pages to take you through all the aspects, we thought we should illustrate how aspects work by showing you two planetary relationships through each of the major aspects. First, we have charismatic Venus ♀ and expansive Jupiter ♃. These two planets get along quite well because Jupiter, the slower planet, expands Venus's function, so there'll be more money, more love, and more relationships.

Venus Conjunct Jupiter ♀☌♃

People with this conjunction love a good time and are charming, generous, and popular. Honest and helpful, they're inclined to help those less fortunate. Also, they have artistic ability and might be talented as peacemakers.

Venus Sextile Jupiter ♀⚹♃

Jupiter's expansiveness enhances Venus's charisma with this aspect, making these people graceful, charitable, outgoing, and affectionate. This is a highly favorable aspect, and it is often considered good luck.

Venus Square Jupiter ♀□♃

This more challenging aspect can make people vain, lazy, extravagant, or ostentatious. This is the aspect of someone who might blow all his or her money on luxury items. Used constructively, this aspect can lead to success in public relations, counseling, or the media.

Venus Trine Jupiter ♀△♃

There's a great deal of grace and elegance with this aspect, plus there's a knack for making big money, having successful partnerships—and enjoying lots of love affairs! This aspect indicates success in music and the arts, and it indicates harmony in marital and domestic affairs.

Venus Opposition Jupiter ♀☍♃

This aspect is extravagant like Venus square Jupiter ♀□♃, and is often found in social climbers who acquire and discard friends in a never-ending pursuit of finding the "in crowd." Navigated well, this aspect can learn to relate well to others—but it's a major challenge.

Venus Quincunx Jupiter ♀⚻♃

This aspect needs to learn self-respect rather than rely so much on what others think. These people lack faith in themselves, which can make them defensive or lead others to walking all over them. Growth with this quincunx comes when these people truly understand that the greatest approval comes from within.

A Harder Row to Hoe: Sun ☉/Saturn ♄ Aspects

In the second pairing we look at, strict Saturn ♄ gives just about everybody a hard time. The Sun ☉ is about creativity, a person's vitality, and his or her sense of self; Saturn is about structure, limitations, losses, or responsibilities, and there's no exception here.

Saturn is the slower planet, so it's the one in charge here. People with this combination might find it hard to enjoy life or might end up censoring themselves, even when Saturn and the Sun are in good aspect to each other (conjunctions, trines, sextiles). There might be problems with authority figures or the father, especially when the two planets are in challenging aspects to each other (squares, oppositions, quincunxes). Even in its more favorable aspects, Sun/Saturn aspects make for a no-nonsense, hardworking relationship.

Sun Conjunct Saturn ☉ ♂ ♄

People with this aspect will have material success because they are hardworking and single-minded. A Sun/Saturn conjunction means these people take their lives very seriously and learn from their experiences, but they should also learn to find some easygoing friends to offset the demands they make on themselves.

Sun Sextile Saturn ☉ ✳ ♄

This aspect means a long, well-ordered, successful life, and these people will joyfully accept all duties and responsibilities that come their way. Working together, the Sun and Saturn lead to good common sense and solid self-confidence.

Sun Square Saturn ☉ □ ♄

There's a major challenge at work here, and these people must work very hard to achieve what they desire. There can be a feeling of underachievement or internal insecurity, and these people want to make certain that they hang on to any position they have.

Sun Trine Saturn ☉ △ ♄

Success with this aspect comes through one's own efforts and powers of concentration, and these people not only grow easily, but they prosper as well. Accepting responsibility comes naturally to people with this aspect, so they might be gatekeepers or supervisors.

Sun Opposition Saturn ☉ ☍ ♄

This challenging aspect can actually cause people to fight against themselves or refuse to accept the obstacles in front of them. The lesson with this aspect is to learn to work with limits and conform to structures and limitations, a hard thing for a strong Sun to do.

Sun Quincunx Saturn ☉ ⚻ ♄

People with this quincunx often have authority issues and can become self-righteous if challenged. They might let others take advantage of them or simply ignore others' wishes. The lesson for people with this aspect is to learn to relax and live and work constructively with other people.

Aspect Grid

When your birth chart is created, an *aspect grid* is created at the same time. This is a chart of boxes with the planets listed across the top and down the side; this chart shows the various aspects those planets make. To illustrate, we show you the Dalai Lama's aspect grid.

Dalai Lama
Natal Chart, Aspects Grid
Jul 6 1935
4:38 am -6:44:48
Takster Tibet
36°N38' 101°E55'
Geocentric
Tropical
Placidus
True Node

Your birth chart also might show aspects at its center, represented as lines, with the type of aspect shown on each line. Lots of astrologers use either a color printer or colored highlighter to differentiate between the aspects on a hard-copy birth chart.

Easy Chart Interpretations

One easy way to start making chart interpretations that include the aspects is to think of aspects as planetary relationships. Ask the question, "How do these planets get along?"

For example, we noted earlier that charismatic Venus ♀ and expansive Jupiter ♃ get along quite well and that Jupiter, the slower planet, expands Venus's function. This means there'll be more money, more love, and more relationships.

We also said that the Sun ☉ is about creativity, a person's vitality, and his or her sense of self, but Saturn ♄ is about structure, limitations, losses, or responsibilities. Knowing this, we can see why this is going to be a more challenging relationship.

In matters of love, it takes more than a good Sun ☉ sign aspect to make a good relationship. Matches "made in heaven" have several good aspects between other planets in their charts. For example, a good aspect between two people's Moons ☽ is very helpful because the couple will be comfortable together on a daily basis and emotionally compatible at the same time. But the best love matches have some challenging aspects between them as well because without a little challenge, the couple might never get together because they'd have nothing to learn from each other! The comparison of relationship charts is called *synastry*. You can learn more about synastry in Appendix C in the charts of Carrie Fisher and her mother, Debbie Reynolds.

It might help you now to go back and look at the keyword concepts for each planet. Better yet, we've provided a quick reference for you in the following table. So now you can use those keywords to begin answering the question about how these planets get along.

Planetary Keywords

Planet	Keywords
Sun ☉	Purpose and self, the person's center
Moon ☽	Emotions, habits, and unconscious patterns
Mercury ☿	Thinking and communication
Venus ♀	Relationships, possessions, money, and harmony
Mars ♂	Action and independence
Jupiter ♃	Growth, optimism, success, and generosity
Saturn ♄	Responsibilities, rules, and limitations
Uranus ♅	Invention, originality, and sudden change
Neptune ♆	Spirituality, dreams, and the mystical
Pluto ♇	Renewal and transformation

Don't forget that the slower planet will always act on the faster planet; in other words, it's the one that will be dominating the relationship.

Your Astrological Signature

Your astrological signature is determined by counting up all the planets you have in each Element. How many planets are in Earth signs, for example? Air signs? Fire signs? Water signs?

You'll be using only planets, not Nodes ☊☋ or angles, in the chart—at least to start. In the same way, you then count up how many planets are in each quality. How many are in cardinal signs? Fixed signs? Mutable signs?

Next, check to see which Element and quality have the largest number of planets. Only one sign represents each pair. That sign is your astrological signature.

For example, the Dalai Lama has four Water planets and four mutable planets. The mutable Water sign is Pisces ♓, so the Dalai Lama's astrological signature is Pisces ♓. This spiritual sign is a perfect expression of the Dalai Lama's life and his presence in the world.

The astrological signature is valuable because it gives the overall tenor or flavor of the chart. If a person has an Aries ♈ signature (that is, the majority of the planets were in cardinal and Fire signs), for example, but only one of the planets is in Aries, this emphasis won't be obvious at first glance. Yet that person will want to lead and start or pioneer new things; in other words, this person will act somewhat like an Aries.

In the Dalai Lama's chart, he has only one planet in Pisces, so the fact that it's his astrological signature reveals a great deal.

What if there's a tie? Well, first look to see if the Sun ☉ or the Moon ☽ is in the groups that tie. If only one or both are in the same group and neither is in the other, that breaks the tie. But if the Sun is in one and the Moon is in the other, you still have a tie.

That's when you add first the ascendant, and then, if there's still a tie, the midheaven. Usually the tie is broken by then, but not always. If it's not, it really *is* a tie.

Sowing or Reaping: Which Lifetime Are You In?

Whether you're sowing or reaping in this lifetime can be determined by counting the number of planets on the eastern half (the left half, houses 10 through 3) of your chart and then counting the number of planets on the western side (the right side, houses 4 through 9).

If there are more planets in the east than the west, then this lifetime is a *sowing lifetime*, and you'll have a great deal of freedom and choices about what you do. (Remember in Chapter 3 that Scarlett Johansson's planets were clustered in her chart's eastern hemisphere, so now we know that she is in a sowing lifetime.) In a sowing lifetime, things won't usually fall in your lap from others, but anything you work toward consistently can work out. You'll have to put in a lot of energy to make things work, but you *will* have lots of choices as to what you work on. This time around, you're sowing your seeds and creating your own opportunities.

On the other hand, if there are more planets in the west than the east, you're in a *reaping lifetime* and will have less freedom. However, you could say your life is set up for you to walk through, and you'll usually find that it opens up to new opportunities from others just when you need it to do so. (Take a look at film director Steven Spielberg's birth chart in Appendix A for an example of a reaping lifetime.)

In essence, in a reaping lifetime, you're harvesting the seeds you planted in previous lives, so your life is already "in place," so to speak. You might have fewer choices, but you don't have to work so hard to get where you're going: you just reap your harvest from previous lives. If you believe this is your only lifetime, then this will still reveal whether you create your own opportunities or receive them through others.

Chart Interpretation: Considering the Aspects

Following is the Dalai Lama's chart once more, but you might notice a difference this time. If so, good for you. The difference is that we've put in the aspects at the center of the chart wheel.

First, note that by using the preceding formula, the Dalai Lama is in a *sowing lifetime*. He's a great example of that type of life as he has the freedom to set his pace as a world spiritual leader. He is in the driver's seat, so to speak, when it comes to sowing seeds of peace and spiritual focus in the world. The Dalai Lama has suggested that his present incarnation may be the last, making this life the ultimate sowing lifetime for the Tibetan spiritual leader. Next, let's look at some of the aspects in the Dalai Lama's chart and apply them to what we've just learned so that we can see what else we can discover about him.

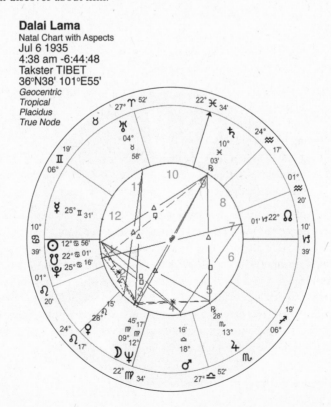

Dalai Lama
Natal Chart with Aspects
Jul 6 1935
4:38 am -6:44:48
Takster TIBET
36°N38' 101°E55'
Geocentric
Tropical
Placidus
True Node

The Dalai Lama's chart has lots of trines △. Seven trines △ appear, to be exact, and only two squares □ to challenge him. Dalai Lama's trines are special, however, as three of them form a perfect triangle called a *grand trine*. This formation lowers resistance for the flow of energy by creating a kind of "zone of ease", giving the Dalai Lama optimal energetic flow in accomplishing tasks and achieving goals within the grand trine's areas of influence. The Dalai Lama's Sun ☉, Saturn ♄, and Jupiter ♃ are all trine △ to each other and form the grand trine. With the Dalai Lama's first house Sun, this configuration is a perfect expression of a very spiritual leader. The Dalai Lama's ninth house Saturn further tells us the Dalai Lama is able to serve as an anchor or foundation for his people's spirituality.

But the trines don't end there. The Dalai Lama has three additional trines from Venus ♀, the Moon ☽, and Neptune ♆ to his eleventh house Uranus ♅. The eleventh house is the house of the masses, and with Uranus there, this configuration is a statement about bringing change by thinking outside the box. These three trines signify ease in bringing love and peace to the forefront of the world's attention in ways that create change in worldviews (the influence of Uranus).

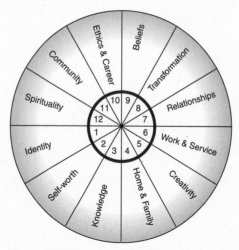

The astrological houses and their areas of influence.

No planets form more aspects on the Dalai Lama's chart than the Moon ☽ and Neptune ♆, which appear in Virgo ♍ in his third house. First of all, the Moon and Neptune are conjunct ☌, creating a laser of strength in his ability to be spiritually attuned to the emotions (Neptune) of the people (Moon). These two planets are then opposed by Saturn ♄ in Pisces ♓ in the ninth house; they are trined △ by Uranus ♅ in the eleventh house; they are sextiled ✳ by Jupiter ♃ in Scorpio ♏ in the fifth house and his Cancer ♋ Sun ☉ in the first house.

All these aspects to the Moon ☽ and Neptune ♆ show how capable he is of being a spiritual leader with the ability to tune into the pulse of people's emotions. Neptune is the planet of unconditional love; therefore, it gives the Dalai Lama the ability to model that love in this world.

As we continue to take a peek into the Dalai Lama's chart, let's review the houses and their areas of influence.

Here Comes the Sun ☉

Before we get into more specific aspects of the Dalai Lama's chart, we need to get a general feel for him. We notice his Sun ☉ is in Cancer ♋ in the first house. Remember that this Sun sign seeks to nurture and create a sense of family. This is a sign that is very sensitive and operates primarily on feelings.

The Dalai Lama's Sun ☉ is square □ to Mars ♂ in Libra ♎ in the fourth house, which is again a statement of the Dalai Lama's desire to use his energies (the influence of Mars) to create a spiritual home for his people. Mars in Libra blends the warrior and the peacemaker, one who is able to see both sides. But with his Pisces ♓ midheaven, the Dalai Lama is a peaceful warrior. The Dalai Lama's Sun ☉ is also sextile ⚹ to his very strong Moon/Neptune conjunction ☽☌♆ in the third house of communication, so he is an excellent spokesman for his beliefs. We've already talked about the Dalai Lama's grand trine involving his Sun ☉, which adds ease for accomplishing all these things.

Now notice that the Dalai Lama's Sun ☉ is square □ to the midheaven, the symbol for his career. This aspect indicates that he will put much energy into his career or life mission. With his first house Sun ☉, this square □ causes him to thrust himself into the public spotlight.

When we look at the sign on his midheaven, we see that it's Pisces ♓, the sign associated with pursuing spiritual matters, being of service, having a vision of unconditional love for the world, and inspiring others. In his gentle way, the Dalai Lama brings his vision and truth to the world.

Interestingly, Jupiter ♃ in Scorpio ♏ trines △ his Sun ☉ along with Saturn ♄ in Pisces ♓, allowing the Dalai Lama to bring a deep flavor of transformation, as well as to create a very stable, compassionate foundation for these transformational changes to happen.

Moonshadow (a.k.a. Moon ☽ in Virgo ♍)

Now that we've looked briefly at his Sun ☉, we move on to the Dalai Lama's Moon ☽, the second part of the important triad. Notice that his Moon is in Virgo ♍ in the third house; it tells us that this is someone who is devoted to sacred service. Because the Moon ☽ is in the third house, his service could be in speaking, writing, and communication. The Moon conjunct Neptune ☽☌♆ further tells us his communications are of a spiritual or religious nature. Additionally, because Virgo is a mutable sign, he is able to constantly shift and change to be in step with current world events.

And He's Got Personality!

Looking beyond, we remember from Chapter 3 that the Dalai Lama's ascendant is Cancer ♋. Now this is a perfect fit and one we might expect for a person whose mission in life is to nurture a belief system. Because his Sun ☉ is also in Cancer ♋, the Dalai Lama is well equipped to be sensitive and to express this sensitivity in the world. However, because the Moon ☽, which is the ruler or landlord of his ascendant, is in Virgo ♍, it brings a certain humbleness and mental practicality to his personality. This gives calmness to his presentation of himself. Because the Moon is conjunct Neptune ☽☌♆, it also lends an air of charisma and gives the ability to be popular.

However, a powerful planetary placement in the Dalai Lama's chart is Pluto ♇ in the first house. Pluto also is placed in the sign of Cancer ♋. This placement gives a very strong person who is able to serve as a catalyst for the transformation of the masses. It adds mystery and additional charisma to his personality. This Pluto placement gives the ability to face cold, hard realities and not flinch. The overall gentle tenor of his chart combined with his Pluto placement gives a very, very strong person who is indeed a gentle giant.

Add to this the South Node ☋ conjunct ☌ Pluto ♇, and you have a powerful statement that the Dalai Lama's life mission is to use his spiritual evolvement from the past to transform the masses. The Buddhist faith has a strong belief in reincarnation, and the Dalai Lama's followers consider him to be the reincarnation of Chenrezig Buddha. This South Node conjunct Pluto powerfully supports a person who indeed would have those strong traits that his followers believe him to have. This is further supported by the fact that this is a sowing rather than a reaping life for the Dalai Lama. He brings much spiritual wisdom forward to sow a new belief system onto the planet. His North Node square Mars ☊□♂ gives credence to his assertion that he may be the final incarnation of the Dalai Lama and that he may choose not to reincarnate. Mars supports aggression and controversy, which certainly surround the current Dalai Lama as he works to bring a peaceful message to an often violent world.

An *interception* occurs when a sign doesn't appear on a house cusp. Instead, it appears totally within a particular house, with the sign before it beginning the house and the sign after it ending the house. Intercepted signs represent areas that people need to develop on their own because others won't be aware of those needs. The Dalai Lama does not have any interceptions, which gives him an easy connection to the energies of each house and allows him to easily express those energies in the world. Interceptions are fairly common, however. Does *your* birth chart have any intercepted signs?

Happy Trails to You!

Finally, we note that the Dalai Lama's Venus ♀ is in Leo ♌ in the third house, trine △ to Uranus ♅ in the eleventh house of life goals. Venus ♀, the planet of love, in Leo ♌, the sign of love, trining △ Uranus ♅ in Taurus ♉, the sign of values, really summarizes the Dalai Lama's life. His theme of love and peace is the foundation of the new values he is striving to bring to the world through unique and unusual ways of being.

We need to keep in mind that we have a trailblazer here, seeking to be a catalyst for change in the world, and that all these parts of his chart are like different internal parts of himself. We don't have enough space to tell you everything about the Dalai Lama's birth chart or life, but you can see from this short demonstration that there's a *lot* to the aspects of anyone's chart—including, of course, your own.

When You Need to Know More: Professional Readings

You can easily get your chart online, along with a basic interpretation. Today, entrepreneurs are building algorithmic databases to give app users complex birth chart interpretations, usually for a fee. The database is built from the input of human beings, and the composite chart is then created algorithmically. Whether algorithmic computer-generated chart readings are as good as readings from *actual* human beings will be up for debate for some time. We believe nothing can replace the intuitive authority of a chart reading human to human.

Just as with everything in astrology, reading and interpreting a birth chart takes years and years of training, as well as a psychically intuitive sense of what it all means. This is just one reason you might choose to get a professional reading. But there are other reasons as well. Let's say, for example, you have specific questions. When should I start my business? Is there a good time soon for me to become pregnant? How can I understand my relationship to my parent(s)? Where is the best place for me to live? A professional reading, with a living, breathing astrologer, can help you answer those specific questions, which involves even more complicated analyses comparing multiple charts. Astrologers perform these analyses to look at *progressions, transits,* and *synastry.* Read on to learn more about how astrology reveals how we relate to each other and how we relate with dimensions of time, space, and place.

Chapter 18

PROGRESSIONS AND TRANSITS ARE WINDOWS OF OPPORTUNITY

With astrology's progressions and transits, we begin to explore how the movement of the planets through the heavens interconnects with what's happening in your life and your relationships *now—right now*. Understanding progressions and transits can give you the foresight to take advantage of your life's favorable times and not allow the less-favorable ones to get you down.

What Progressions and Transits Have to Do with You

Progressions contain the primary timing for your development and growth and show how you evolve and grow. Progressions show how you and your chart progress throughout your life and contain the timing for your development and growth. They are generally felt internally. You might make external changes based on them, but they are like the unfolding of your astrological DNA. The timing for all these changes is very personal and is based solely on your particular chart. Because evolution is slow, these are slow changes.

Transits, on the other hand, are based on the movement of the planets overhead in comparison to the position of the planets in your chart. They occur when the present positions of the planets overhead aspect their various positions in your birth chart. They're much faster than *progressions* and often act as triggers or release points for whatever themes of development your progressions are suggesting.

Transits can also appear to us as events, external matters, or issues with our environments and the people around us. Until we learn to recognize our external circumstances as metaphors for our internal self, transits that are challenging can feel like we are being hit with obstacles and problems.

Progressions, or I Can't Stand Still

You might have been born with your Sun ☉ in Libra ♎ and your Venus ♀ in Scorpio ♏, but as you progress through your life, so do your planets. How your planets progress as you age is what progressions are all about. Progressions show how you evolve and develop over time.

A *progressed chart* is different from your birth chart, in that it moves each planet by however far it moves in 1 day for each year of life. The Sun ☉, for example, moves about 1 degree per day, so in a progressed chart, the Sun would move about 1 degree per *year*. The slowness of this process means that only the inner planets (Sun ☉, Moon ☽, Mercury ☿, Venus ♀, and Mars ♂) are going to move significantly within a lifetime. The outer planets might progress into an exact aspect or placement and then get your attention, but it's generally the inner planets and the angles (ascendant and midheaven) of the chart that evolve over time.

To look at your progressions, you must use a double astrological wheel, called a *bi-wheel*, with your birth chart on the inside and your progressed chart on the outside. When you look at these two charts, you see how your birth planets are evolving over time.

Basically, your progressions move all your planets by 1 day for each year of life after birth. So, you can look up your birth date in an ephemeris and find (roughly) that the planetary positions each day after your birth are going to represent the way your chart unfolds year by year. (An *ephemeris* is a book showing where the planets are at noon or midnight Greenwich Mean Time; find out more about an ephemeris and how it is used to calculate birth charts in Appendix A.)

There are some more technicalities to finding your progressions than what we cover, but the "formula"—1 day for each year—gives you the general idea. You can see then that individual progressions and the unfolding of your development are determined over time by your chart alone.

The Moon ☽, for example, moves about 13 degrees a day, which translates in a progressed chart to about 13 degrees a year. Because each sign covers 30 degrees, this means that about every 2½ years, your progressed Moon moves into a new sign. It also means that approximately every 28 years, you will have a progressed lunar return, where the Moon returns by progression to its original position in your chart.

Themes for Personal Change

Progressions signal the themes and changes in your chart that are waiting to unfold over time. They are often felt internally before they manifest as external changes. As an example, someone might become an author when her Sun ☉ and Mercury ☿ both move into her third house, the house of communications. Before this change occurred on an external level, though, it would be first experienced as an internal need or desire to start writing about important experiences and ideas.

The changes in you represented by progressions can appear as a planet that …

* Changes signs or houses
* "Changes direction" (goes retrograde or goes direct)
* Makes an aspect to a natal planet
* Makes an aspect to another progressed planet

Each of these can unlock a different type of change in you as you progress through your life.

When progressed planets make aspects to your natal planets, they're allowed only very tight orbs because they take such a long time to move. A 1-degree orb is allowed for both before and after the aspect is exact. Even so, except for the Moon ☽, it normally takes a few years for a progressed planet to move out of aspect with a birth planet.

Knowing what your progressions are and when they'll occur can help you unlock the potentials of these cycles. But even if you don't know what's happening and when, you'll evolve anyway, according to the timing of your astrological schedule.

Who, Me? Evolve?

Yes, you. It takes the Sun ☉ about 30 years to move through a sign, so depending on the degree at which your Sun began, either you have already moved into a new Sun sign, or you will someday. A 39-year-old with a 16♊03 Sun, for example, progressed into a Cancer ♋ Sun at about age 14, and at age 44, this person will move into a Leo ♌ Sun.

Notice how slowly this change takes place—every *30 years* after the first progression. Sun ☉ sign changes are *major* changes in how you behave, and this includes your interests, attitudes, and outlook, too. Of course, a progressed Sun never gets around the entire zodiac because it moves only about 1 degree per year.

Some of the progressed Sun aspects you can expect include a helpful sextile ✶ to your natal, or birth, Sun from your progressed Sun ☉ when you're about 60. At 45, there will be a less-helpful semi square, and, when you're 90, you'll get a square □. Unless you're as old as Methuselah, though, your progressed Sun never gets much more than a quarter of the way around your chart. Still, your progressed Sun can be busy aspecting any of your other planets while it's progressing through your chart.

Your Moon ☽ evolves as well, in a very different way. It takes the Moon about 2½ years to move into a new sign and about 28 years to return to its original sign. When this progression happens, the area of life with Cancer ♋ on the cusp (that is, the house ruled by the Moon ☽) might have significant changes. Also, this progression occurs near another important transit at age 29, so there can be major issues coming up at this time.

Rosa Parks's Chart: Progressed to Montgomery, Alabama, December 1, 1955

Let's introduce Rosa Parks's chart, progressed to the day she refused to move to the back of that bus in Montgomery, Alabama, on December 1, 1955. We don't know the exact time of Parks's birth on February 4, 1913, so we've generated a natal chart for her with a noon birth time. A noon chart places the Sun ☉ on the midheaven. Although casting any birth chart without a precise birth time introduces some imprecision (for example, the ascendant sign changes every 2 hours), a noon chart allows a method for casting a chart that anyone can use when the birth time is unknown. It is altogether possible that Rosa herself, along with many people born nearly a century ago, did not know her precise birth time. A professional astrologer has more sophisticated methods to rectify a birth chart when the precise birth time is not known.

Parks's natal chart, shown in the inner wheel, represents the foundation or the blueprint of her life. Here, we see the basics of who she is already appearing on her natal chart. She was a humanitarian through her Aquarius ♒ Sun ☉. She was hardworking, persevering, and serious about life through her Capricorn ♑ Moon ☽. She was a steadfast study of human nature, and she was articulate, aware, and constantly asking the question "Why?" through her ascendant Gemini ♊. And, her strong natal *stellium* in Aquarius ♒ was certain to evolve into a rebel with a cause, a humanitarian seeker of truth, and someone who will cut away the dead wood along her path in life. (A stellium of planets in a birth chart represents a star-like focal point because of the many planets and the aspects these planets form.)

In progressions, the Moon ☽ is often the "timer" because it moves faster than any other planet. In this case, it's pointing to an important social achievement for Parks. Her progressed Moon is in the fixed Fire sign of Leo ♌. Because Aquarius ♒ is in opposition ☍ to the progressed Moon ☽, Parks evolved into someone who needed to express an emotional concern. To put it another way, she became the opposition herself. Plus, this suggests that exactly two months before her famous bus ride, she was thinking and planning something to make a point.

Parks's desire to create awareness was also evident in this progression. Her inner self would have been struggling with her outer image. Chances are, she had been mulling some kind of statement for a while, and no one who has this type of opposition ☍ from her progressed chart to her birth chart could keep quiet for too long. Because Parks has this opposition from the fourth house of her roots, beliefs, and home, she would want to extend that to the opposite house and her natal Sun ☉ in the tenth house of public recognition, career, and contributions to society.

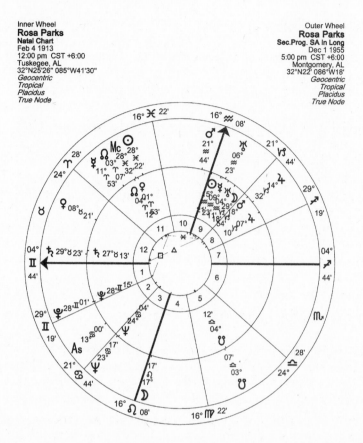

Inner Wheel
Rosa Parks
Natal Chart
Feb 4 1913
12:00 pm CST +6:00
Tuskegee, AL
32°N25'26" 085°W41'30"
Geocentric
Tropical
Placidus
True Node

Outer Wheel
Rosa Parks
Sec.Prog. SA In Long
Dec 1 1955
5:00 pm CST +6:00
Montgomery, AL
32°N22' 086°W18'
Geocentric
Tropical
Placidus
True Node

As amazing as it must have been to watch this woman do what most would fear, the fixed Aquarius ♒/Leo ♌ opposition, as with all fixed signs interacting through their aspects, would result in an event that would be lasting.

Parks's progressed Saturn ♄ is at 29 degrees of Taurus ♉, signaling the ending of a crisis. In her twelfth house of karmic duty and destiny, we find her progressed Saturn ♄ trine △, her natal Moon ☽, at 29 degrees of Capricorn ♑. This indicates that she was determined to enlighten the public on injustices done to the group consciousness. It was about her, yes, but it was also about changing an existing attitude. At this point in time, Parks didn't care about the cost to her or her future. She was "pushed" by a strong obligation to "do something," almost as if she was being compelled by a debt to society. In other words, she did what she felt was obligatory to her world. Parks's chart indicates that she had a debt to pay to her culture and country, that she was here to enlighten *all* of society, and that she would choose an unusual and even unpredictable way to effect this change.

Throughout the next year, Parks continued to have the Moon ☽ in Leo ♌. By the time November 1956 came, her progressed Moon in Leo had made an exact square □ to her natal Saturn ♄ at 27 degrees of Taurus ♉ and then *another* exact square □ to progressed Saturn ♄ at 29 degrees of Taurus ♉. Because these are again fixed signs, the squares *forced* Parks to work through a difficult legal process, one that would ultimately generate a wide range of changes in the law. The squares □ these two planets made reflected the public attention and conflict.

Three to four years after this moment, Parks's progressed Sun ☉ in 28 degrees of Pisces ♓ conjuncted ☌ her natal Venus ♀ at 1 degree of Aries ♈. This is when her life would become increasingly public, including public speaking engagements and writing opportunities, as well as invitations to continue what she began.

Rosa Parks's noon birth chart and progressed birth chart show a gentle rebel with a cause. And, aren't we all more fortunate because of it?

Just as with Parks, your birth chart progresses in its own way, with your progressed planets aspecting your natal or birth planets. As your progressed planets move through the signs, they show how and when you develop and evolve.

Transits, or Planetary Triggers

You could think of transiting planets as being part of a cosmic transit system, moving around overhead on a regular schedule (better than most earthly transit systems!). This is one way to keep in mind that these planets are always on the move, changing positions at the rate of their daily travel. It's another kind of transit system, and it's one we can predict and plan by.

Transits are concerned with particular moments in time. Even your birth chart is a transit, one that was frozen in time when you were born. Transits are also concerned with the relationships that occur when the present positions of the planets aspect your natal planets. Like a progressed chart, a transit chart looks like a double wheel: Your birth chart is on the inside, and *the moment's chart,* or transit chart, is on the outside.

Transits are like triggers; they pop the cork right off the bottle. They're quicker—and happen faster—than progressions, and most of them are specific to each person. At the same time, though, there are transits that are aspects between the same natal and transiting planet that occur at the same ages for everyone. We look at those in more detail later in this chapter. But for now, let's look at transits in the birth chart of Nobel Peace Prize winner Malala Yousafzai, to see how a moment in time affects a lifetime.

Malala Day, July 12, 2013

Malala Yousafzai was born in Mingora, Pakistan, on July 12, 1997. As a young woman, determined to receive an education, she defied the Taliban's ban to attend school. In 2012, she was shot by a Taliban fighter and barely survived. She became an advocate for girls' education and achieved global recognition; on July 12, 2013, her sixteenth birthday, she gave a historic address to the United Nations (UN). In October 2014, she became the youngest person to be awarded a Nobel Prize. We're going to look at the transits in Malala's chart on July 12, 2013, which is unusual in that the transits we're looking at also compose her solar return for that year, adding more resonance to the impact they have to her natal chart. Malala's transits resonated globally—so much so that the UN proclaimed July 12 Malala Day in her honor.

Let's look first at Malala's natal birth chart on the inner wheel of the chart's bi-wheel. Born with the Sun rising in Cancer ♋ in the eleventh house, Malala is extremely focused on her desires and hopes for the world, as the eleventh house rules the dreams of a lifetime and socialization with the outer world. (The eleventh house does not rule family, but it rules extended family.) Born with Leo ♌ rising, she is a leader from birth, and because the ruler of her Leo ascendant is the sign Cancer, her natal sign, Malala speaks with no mask, no disguise—what you see is what you get. In astrology, when the ruler of the ascendant (which represents how you are seen in the public domain) is in the eleventh house, this means you put yourself wholeheartedly into your groups—your connectedness to society. Malala is also very connected to her extended family—her home country; her fourth house Pluto ♇ shows a situation that could be volatile—and sometimes violent—into her teen years. Both in the second house of self-esteem and self-worth and the sign of Libra ♎, her Moon ☽ forms a strong conjunction ☌ to Mars ♂, showing she is well-grounded and balanced within herself and her values, while she's also boldly courageous and angry about a just cause.

Malala's natal planets are balanced, with the personal planets on the eastern side of her natal chart and the outer planets on the western. Cancerians don't always maintain their boundaries and want to be connected emotionally to whomever they love and whatever they believe. But Malala's balanced hemispheres show she does have the individuality to maintain her focus and to stand alone to fight her battles when she needs to. She is independent and self-reliant about maintaining her boundaries, while the outer planets on the western side of her chart show she will help society and is strongly connected to cooperating with society at this time in history to achieve her goals.

On July 12, 2013, Malala Yousafzai celebrated her sixteenth birthday by speaking directly to the world at the UN. When you look at the outer wheel of her transits to that day, you can see her natal eleventh house Sun ☉ touching the transiting Sun; her natal twelfth house Venus ♀ touching on transiting Venus; the transiting first house Moon ☽ in Virgo ♍, which is excellent for the public receiving her message; and transiting Saturn ♄ in Scorpio ♏ in her third house of knowledge and communication. Malala's transits also reveal a rare grand trine in Water: Saturn ♄ in Scorpio ♏ in the third house trines △ both Jupiter ♃ in Cancer ♋ and Neptune ♆ in Pisces ♓ in the seventh house. So, the eleventh house of hopes and dreams trines △ the third of communication and then grand trines those two (Jupiter and Neptune) in the seventh house where Neptune is at 5 degrees of Pisces in 2013. A grand trine in Water means Malala will move the masses. From July 12, 2013, all the way through the end of 2014, she would become well-known through her writing, public speaking, and politics, and she accepted the Nobel Peace Prize in October 2014. Malala's grand trine transit in Water reveals her intentions to spread a message of socialization to do with girls and women on a global scale; her karmic and spiritual connections are to the Earth and all of humanity.

Her transiting chart also reveals challenging aspects. Transiting Uranus ♅ in 12 degrees of Aries ♈ is in direct opposition to her natal Mars ♂ and Moon ☽ in Libra ♎. A *T-Square* to the Sun ☉ also appears. In astrology, a T-Square contains two squares □ and one opposition ☍ forming a right-angled triangle. The planet with the two squares □ is the planet holding the tension of the aspect pattern, which can be difficult to overcome. This means that Malala's speech could cause people to become angry and even obsessed with fighting against her ideas. Sometimes the messenger—in this case, a messenger of peace—is going to have oppositions from Uranus ♅ and Aries ♈, both of which are messengers of war. The oppositions to her natal Moon ☽ and Mars ♂ stimulate difficulties regarding her message that could stir a backlash against it … and her. But with so many trines △, sextiles ⚹, and conjunctions ☌ adding positive aspects as well, Malala is extremely courageous to speak her truth, and she will have more people in favor of her message than against it. Uranus ♅ and Mars ♂ in opposition can represent some form of terrorism or disruption in society. Here, in Malala's chart, it stands for changes in traditional cultural values.

Overall, we would say that the transits of July 12, 2013, reflect that Malala has a calling, a karmic duty, and a responsibility, and she must (and will) face it no matter what it takes to do so and no matter the opposition to her on that day. She is an awakener; she stands her ground and speaks her truth to the world. More and more people will rally to her message of education and equality for girls and women. Over time, the group consciousness will change existing laws and traditions into something better. These are Malala's words on July 12, 2013: "Be peaceful and love everyone. Let us pick up our books and our pens; they are our most powerful weapons, more powerful than guns. One child, one teacher, one book, one pen, can change the world. Education is the only solution. Education first!" Remember, transits focus on a moment in time; progressions show how your personal planets move over time. Transits show the actual position of the planets at a given moment; progressions show how you progress personally as you grow older.

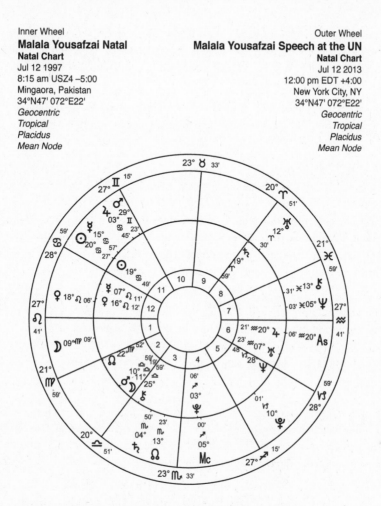

Inner Wheel
Malala Yousafzai Natal
Natal Chart
Jul 12 1997
8:15 am USZ4 –5:00
Mingaora, Pakistan
34°N47' 072°E22'
Geocentric
Tropical
Placidus
Mean Node

Outer Wheel
Malala Yousafzai Speech at the UN
Natal Chart
Jul 12 2013
12:00 pm EDT +4:00
New York City, NY
34°N47' 072°E22'
Geocentric
Tropical
Placidus
Mean Node

Outer and Social Planet Transits

Astrologers look at the transits that the outer planets make more closely than those of the inner planets because they move more slowly, and therefore, they have a much more powerful effect on our lives. We can't stop the planets in their cycles—or our own growth, which they represent—but we can be aware of those cycles and plan our lives accordingly.

Pluto's ♀ motto is "Change or be transformed!" Its transits always pressure you to transform some aspect of your life that isn't authentically you. Generally, with a Pluto transit, you will be forced to change the area ruled by the planet that Pluto contacts. Most people find it *very* painful not to cooperate with Pluto transits.

Neptune ♆ transits encourage us to view old problems from a spiritual or transcending perspective and to let go and move on. Neptune is unpredictable, though, and its transits can either unleash psychic or imaginative powers or lead to confusion, self-doubt, escapism, irresponsibility, or even self-destruction.

Uranus ♅ transits are associated with innovation, rebellion, and unexpected change. A Uranus transit makes you see things in a new way. When you do, you can never go back to the old way of seeing things.

While Saturn ♄ is associated with limitation, its transits also can herald movement to a higher level of responsibility and to rewards for a job well done. If there's still work to be done, though, these transits can make you sit down, reassess, restructure, and seek the right path.

Jupiter ♃ transits often involve broadening your horizons in some way. Your horizons can be broadened through travel or social contacts, or they can be broadened physically, philosophically, or intellectually. Jupiter, remember, is the planet of expansion, and the house it's transiting determines the area of your life in which the expansion is occurring.

The inner planets transit far more quickly, so their effects are not as profound as those of the outer and social planets. Often when an astrologer looks at the transiting cycles for a client's chart, he or she checks only the major ones shown by the outer and social planets.

From the Terrible Twos to the Midlife Crisis and Beyond

These are the cycles, or passages, common to everyone and that occur at about the same age for everyone, too. They're timed by transits of planets that aspect themselves, such as Saturn ♄ to Saturn ♄. Because the planet is aspecting itself, and each planet moves at a certain rate, these transits always occur at about the same age for everyone.

Let's start by looking at the terrible twos. This is the point at which Mars ♂ comes around and conjuncts ♂ itself for the first time. The terrible twos are the equivalent of a person's first taste of independence and assertion. Mars returns occur every two years, so we get more accustomed to them as we get older. But this first time is a lulu, as any parent can tell you!

Next, there's the Jupiter ♃ cycle, which is a 12-year growth cycle. Every 12 years, when transiting Jupiter comes around to conjunct ♂ your natal Jupiter, you start a new growth cycle, learning completely new things and expanding your mind and self in new ways.

Another transit that has a marked effect is when Uranus ♅ is sextile ✳ to itself for the first time during the teen years. This is when people get their first need for independence, to separate from their parents, and to become individuals. We're all familiar with this cycle— from either our own experience or that of our children—and we all know it can be a very chaotic period!

Between ages 28 and 30, people experience their first Saturn ♄ return. This is a major transit: "Grow up," it says, and, if you're not yet on the right path, you'll have a strong feeling of apprehension. All sorts of major changes might occur at a Saturn return if you haven't been on *your* path and have been meeting other people's expectations instead. You might even blow up your life and start over in new surroundings or travel for a time.

However, if you're doing what you're supposed to be doing, then you won't have challenges. You might be rewarded with a promotion for good work or a similar "prize." You could think of a Saturn return as a time to clean up the inappropriate parts of your life and to ensure that you're on the right path for you (or reassess your path) instead of worrying about what others think.

The second Saturn return, which occurs between the ages of 58 and 60, is also a major transit. People achieve recognition for a fulfilling career at this point, or they reach an important goal. A human life is roughly two-thirds over at this point, and interestingly, statistics indicate that people who feel unhappy with their lives, are depressed, or feel like a failure in some way might end up using this as their exit point from the planet. Really, the second Saturn return represents an opportunity to renew old passions or begin to explore new ones now that the path you've been on so long has matured and may not hold anything new.

The Midlife Crisis

The midlife crisis used to occur at age 42. This cycle coincides with when transiting Uranus comes opposite natal Uranus ♅☍♅, transiting Neptune squares itself ♆□♆, and shortly afterward, when transiting Saturn opposes itself ♄☍♄. However, because some of the outer planets are in the faster portions of their orbits right now, this has been happening during millennials' late 30s. In addition, another planet has gotten into the fray.

Because of its erratic orbit, Pluto ♇ is moving through the signs faster than its average. For this reason, transiting Pluto is currently squaring personal Pluto ♇□♇at age 36 or 37, well before the midlife crisis. (We're speaking here about people who have Pluto ♇ in Virgo ♍; those with Pluto ♇ in Leo ♌ experienced this right *during* their midlife crisis, at around 39 to 40 years old.) Transiting Pluto square natal Pluto signals a general transformation. This square used to appear late in people's lives. (In 1900, the average life span in the United States wasn't much over 40!) There is a major evolution in the meaning of this aspect for us—and future generations.

Preparing for the latter part of your life (and eventually death) is a big step, but it isn't one that's necessary when this aspect occurs in midlife. Instead, this transit's intensity should be focused on changing one's life for the better and giving up whatever is being brought up from the past that isn't appropriate or authentic.

People who successfully make it through this series of "midlife" transits develop a new maturity to become their true selves. The purpose of the midlife crisis is to reorient themselves away from just meeting external demands toward more internal needs that give real meaning to their lives.

Before we discuss the specifics of the midlife transits, let's look at the transiting Pluto square natal Pluto ♇□♇ in more detail.

Oh, What Fun It Is to Transform Ourselves!

General transformation is a period when past issues that are no longer relevant are dug up and eliminated. This can include aspects of yourself that have been forgotten or repressed for so long that you no longer remember them.

The Pluto square natal Pluto ♇□♇ transit lasts almost two years, and by the time it ends, a person's life and consciousness are quite changed. Sometimes, a person's life is completely rebuilt after this occurs. It's better to cooperate with the changes that need to happen to you during this period than resist them because the consequences of resistance can be quite destructive.

Transiting Pluto square natal Pluto ♇□♇is happening to many people who are still young—people who have half their lives to live at this higher level of consciousness. This unusual situation is one indicator of the High Renaissance period the Earth is experiencing now, which is a time of rapid and profound change, growth, and transformation.

This early Pluto ♇ transit is going to happen, at least during this period in time, *before or during* the midlife crisis. So, by the time the midlife crisis is over, the men are separated from the boys, and the women are separated from the girls! Pluto transits are just too demanding to ignore. People find they can't hang on to their old behavior patterns during these periods in their lives, so they give up and make the change!

Uranus ♅ and Neptune ♆ and Saturn ♄—Oh, My!

Yes, indeed! The midlife crisis can be a lot like encountering lions and tigers and bears! And with Neptune ♆ in the act, even if these aren't real dangers, you might *believe* they exist. Here's an up-close and personal look at these midlife transits.

When transiting Uranus opposes natal Uranus ♅☍♅, its purpose is to reorient you to doing things with personal meaning. At this point in your life, you've spent most of it trying to have an impact on the external world and meeting the expectations of others. Now it's time to shift toward doing the things that have *internal* meaning for you.

For people who've been doing what they were "supposed" to be doing, this period is often an epiphany. For those who've gotten into premature ruts or who've stopped growing along the way, though, there's a sudden "last chance" feeling about it that sends some people off on radical changes quite unlike their normal selves. This could mean a career change. More negatively, it could mean leaving one's spouse for someone younger, buying a snazzy sports car, or seeking new adventures.

The most appropriate response to this transit is to withdraw internally and figure out *what you really want to do with the rest of your life*. If you don't take the time to examine what you want and then make the needed changes, you might find yourself living a hollow life later and never understanding why.

When transiting Neptune squares natal Neptune ♆□♆, you can expect another period of intense questioning of yourself, your ideals, and how well you've lived up to them. But because it's Neptune, it's difficult to see where you're really going during this period—and whether it's even worth going there.

This is a lot like driving a twisty road in heavy fog. While you might decide you should make some changes in your life, you might *not* understand which ones to make. Instead of actually making these changes during this time, it's best to consider which course to take until the fog clears. This period or transit takes almost three years.

When transiting Saturn is opposite natal Saturn ♄☍♄, this can mean a successful culmination of your effort and work, or it could mean a time when old patterns that weren't cleared out earlier challenge your career and relationships. Once again, it's a time for reassessment and refocusing. This transit occurs a little later than the Uranus ♅ and Neptune ♆ transits, but in past times, all three used to happen together.

This entire process is geared toward questioning your present life and yourself. If you ever thought you knew yourself, this period may prove otherwise. But instead of responding with an intense desire to recapture your youth, it's best to find out what in life really has meaning for you and then find a way to refocus your life on that.

Unlocking Personal Transits

Personal transits are cycles with timing based on the placement of your own planets. Unlike the cycles that occur at specific ages when a planet aspects itself, these transits can occur at any age. For example, transiting Saturn will conjunct each person's Sun at a different age ♄☌☉, and the timing of that depends on what sign your Sun is in and where Saturn was when you were born.

For example, if your Sun ☉ is in Cancer ♋ and Saturn ♄ was in Gemini ♊ when you were born, this transit would have happened for the first time when you were a young child. But if Saturn ♄ was in Leo ♌ when you were born (and you have a Cancer Sun ♋☉), you would have been in your mid-20s before this occurred for the first time.

In general, you can look at your birth chart and the current planetary positions to see what's happening for you at any given moment in time.

Astrology Is Your Compass

Now that you understand how your chart unfolds with progressions and transits, you can see how astrology can be used to look ahead into your life.

It's always a good idea to check out your progressions and transits regularly, and it's also good to know three to five years in advance what's coming down the pike in the way of major changes. You can anticipate and plan for everything, from job or career changes, financial difficulties, having children, to even relocating. Looking ahead gives you the room to plan what responses you might choose and to accept responsibility for what the changes end up being. For example, if you're trying to make a career change, it's best to look for trines △ or sextiles ✳ with planets to the midheaven, tenth-house ruler, or look for the planets in the tenth house to initiate that change. Why make things harder for you than they need to be? Make the most of your windows of opportunity, and your career will be rewarded accordingly.

Relationship issues might come up, too. If you know a troubling time in a relationship is approaching, you can understand what the likely issues of timing are and learn appropriate ways to handle and deal with them. Then when that troubling time actually arrives, it's not a cataclysmic period; instead, it becomes one of growth and understanding of how you and your relationships are changing. (To find out about the dynamics of compatibility in relationships between people, you'll want to explore astrological synastry. See Appendix C.)

Astrology can be used as a compass because you can see the kinds of events or changes that are going to unfold and how you're evolving and growing during your life. This kind of knowing gives you a road map for your life and a more conscious approach for dealing with changes. After all, wouldn't you rather know where you're headed on your life's journey than move ahead blindly?

Windows of Opportunity

Windows of opportunity are periods when your progressions and transits are beneficial. These are good times to make changes, make progress, and develop things easily. These progressions and transits are usually trines △ and sextiles ✳ (sometimes conjunctions ☌), and they're just waiting for you to take advantage of them.

Often, though, when these periods hit, there's a tendency to sit back and take it easy, so it's important to use them to your advantage and not squander them.

But you won't know there's an opportune period unless you're looking at your progressions and transits to determine when they are. So, do it yourself or visit an astrologer at least once a year. It's a good investment!

Jump or Be Pushed, Your Choice

Unlike a trine △ or sextile ✳, when squares □ or oppositions ☍ come up by progression or transit, you'll be *forced* to do something. Either you'll take matters into your own hands and act, or an external action will *force* you to do something. Some of these squares □ from outer planets, like Neptune ♆ or Pluto ♀, can take a couple years to get through. If you don't consciously understand what's happening and, as a consequence, respond inappropriately, you can end up projecting the energy outward. That energy will come back to you as difficult external events.

Anything that's blocking positive growth—be it a job, a relationship, or personal property—will be removed to ensure that the needed growth occurs. Some of these external events can be cataclysmic—a serious accident, a severe illness, or even a death in the family—and they can *force* you to make the change. But challenging progressions and transits can trigger internal desire for change, too. The important thing is to notice them. Obviously, it's best to take the appropriate action before a catastrophe occurs. Serious accidents, something terrible happening in one's career, or a major blow-up in a relationship are all manifestations of a "jump-or-be-pushed" aspect. Something's gotta blow to send you in the direction that you must go. If you get to that point without doing anything constructive, you'll be pushed.

Chapter 19

MOON ☽ SHADOWS: MOON PHASES, MOON CYCLES, AND VOID OF COURSE MOONS

Most people know the four major phases of the Moon ☽: Full Moon ○, New Moon ●, First-Quarter Moon ◑, and Third-Quarter Moon ◐. Astrologers use four additional *Moon phases*—Crescent Moon, Gibbous Moon, Disseminating Moon, and Balsamic Moon. The eight Moon phases of the Moon's 29½-day cycle are, in order: New Moon, Crescent Moon, First-Quarter Moon, Gibbous Moon, Full Moon, Disseminating Moon, Last-Quarter Moon, and Balsamic Moon. In its 29½-day cycle through the zodiac, the Moon spends about 2½ days in each sign.

Moon ☽ Phases: Dancing with the Sun ☉

As the Moon ☽ moves through the heavens on its monthly dance with the Sun ☉, its angle to the Sun changes. This angle determines how much of the Moon the Sun illuminates and how much of the Moon we see. We say the Moon ☽ is waxing (growing in intensity and the amount of light it reflects) as it journeys away from the Sun ☉; it is waning (diminishing in intensity and the amount of light it reflects) as it travels toward the Sun ☉. We see these changes in the Moon's appearance.

A New Moon ● begins in darkness and emerges as a crescent that looks like the curve of the letter *D*. This is the Moon that is full of possibilities and the Moon of beginnings. It's also a period when people have a natural urge to start something.

The First-Quarter ☾ or Waxing Moon ☾ is also known as the Half-Moon and appears to us as a filled-in *D*. This is the Moon that will see projects through and is the Moon of action and independence. It also can bring external challenges to light; the astrological definition of a First-Quarter Moon ☾ is "crisis in action" because there's often a crisis or challenge associated with things started at the time of the New Moon.

The Moon is always exactly opposite the Sun ☉ when it is Full ○ and activities are brought to fruition. Whatever was being developed comes to light at this time. All is visible during a Full Moon, truly a "full circle." The Third-Quarter or Waning Moon ☾ looks like a filled-in *C* and is the midpoint of the Moon's waning phase. It's a time to assess, to look over what has been accomplished, to learn from one's mistakes, to wind down, and prepare for the next cycle. During the Moon's dark night, called a Balsamic Moon, psychic energy peaks. It's time to retreat, reflect, and get ready to begin again.

How Moon ☽ Phases Affect the Way We Do Things

The phase of the Moon at the time of your birth provides another overlay of meaning for interpreting and understanding your birth chart. However, your natal Moon phase is not always obvious when you look at your birth chart because the only way to identify it is to know the number of degrees between the placements of the Sun and the Moon. Back in the day of paper and pencil, an astrologer usually had to figure out this information for you. Today, astrology sites and online apps can likely figure your natal Moon phase instantly. It is very useful for you to know because your natal Moon phase influences the energies of the signs and planets in your birth chart.

Understanding the Moon's phases and how they affect our daily lives can help us work with these energies rather than against them. Let's take a walk through each Moon phase to see what this means.

New Moon ●: New Beginnings

The New Moon ● is the time of new beginnings. This is life at its most basic, with only instinct to guide it, and it is the starting point for all ventures. Like the seed first germinating, all experiences are new. The New Moon is 0° to 45° in front of the Sun and is the most active, primitive, and impulsive Moon phase. Aries ♈ is the sign associated with this Moon. This is a good time to begin new projects, to set the plans you've made in motion, and to plant what you hope to see succeed.

When the Sun ☉ and the Moon ☽ are very close to each other in your birth chart, it can be difficult to tell whether the Moon ☽ is New or Balsamic. But their energies are nearly opposite.

Most astrology sites and online apps provide the information, taking the guesswork out of this determination.

Crescent Moon: Pulling Away from the Past

The Crescent Moon is the emerging seedling putting out roots and a stem. At this Moon phase, the Moon is 45° to 90° in front of the Sun. Astrologers view this Moon as pulling away from the past to establish a new foundation. When the Crescent Moon is in your birth chart, you are preparing your life for the new direction you want to follow.

First-Quarter Moon ◐: External Challenges

The First-Quarter Moon is 90° to 135° in front of the Sun. This is the Moon of revolutionary change, and people born under the First-Quarter Moon are very action-oriented about changing what does not work. They experience much personal change and are the movers and shakers in their communities and in the world. This Moon is the stem and leaves—the structures of growth.

The First-Quarter Moon is square to the Sun, which is a position of challenge. During the First-Quarter Moon, a new project just gaining its own momentum may suddenly encounter a bureaucratic snafu. Often such challenges come in the form of crises that require rapid responses to save the projects. People born under a First-Quarter Moon often have an instinctive understanding of how to resolve issues and get projects back on track.

The First-Quarter Moon is a time to anticipate challenges, so you can prepare for and address them before they reach crisis states. This is a time to take the extra effort to make sure that everything continues to go smoothly. This Moon is associated with nurturing Cancer ♋.

Gibbous Moon: Refining and Expanding

The Gibbous Moon, 135° to 180° in front of the Sun, is the bud preparing to bloom. The structure is in place and the Gibbous Moon provides the energy to finesse the details. For projects under way, this may mean correcting flaws or working out the bugs. People born under a Gibbous Moon are often writers and researchers. They've gathered information and knowledge, and now they have the ability to expand and grow because of it.

Full Moon ○: Full Bloom

The Full Moon ○ glows bright with the Sun's illumination. This Moon has traveled as far as it can from the Sun and now rests directly opposite the Sun. Its placement is 180° to 135° *behind* the Sun. This is the Moon of high energy, the Moon's highest peak before it begins its waning phase, and the Moon most closely associated with Libra ♎.

The Full Moon's shine lights up the harvest, a time to reap the rewards of all your hard work. A Full Moon can be a time of grand achievement, putting you in the spotlight. People born under a Full Moon love being the center of attention. Because the Full Moon shows what you—or others—are doing, its glare may also reveal disappointments and disillusions. Crazy things also happen during Full Moons, often because all that lunar energy hasn't been channeled during earlier Moon phases.

Many report that Full Moons keep hospital staff busy. Emotions are higher, and the release of excess energy that comes with the Full Moon may result in moodiness and even accidents. Many pregnant women start labor with the Full Moon.

Disseminating Moon: Sharing Life's Experiences

At 135° to 90° behind the Sun, the Disseminating Moon is the bloom turned to fruit and it is time to share the fruit with others. People born under a Disseminating Moon have had intense life experiences, and they want to share what they've learned from them with others. Sometimes, there is a sense of urgency to this sharing that may make the person seem zealous. But this is only because knowledge is often timely and must be passed on while it's still fresh.

Third-Quarter Moon ◑: Inner Evaluation

By the Third-Quarter Moon ◑, the fruit has fallen, the leaves are dropping, and the plant is returning to the Earth. This is a Moon of inner evaluation and a time to look back at what we've done and see where we can make improvements. The Third-Quarter Moon ◑ stimulates inner assessment that may lead to questioning whether we've made the right choices or done the right things.

People born under a Third-Quarter Moon ◑ often make total shifts in their lives that appear sudden to others but really have been brewing within the person for a long time. The Third-Quarter Moon ◑ is the Wise Woman, whose knowledge of the mystical and unknown can help us find greater understanding. This is the Moon associated with Capricorn ♑.

Balsamic Moon: Retreat and Release

The final Moon phase is the Balsamic Moon, 45° to 0° behind the Sun. During this dark Moon that is not visible in the night sky, the seed lies waiting beneath the soil. Though it often seems nothing is happening, this is a very busy time of preparation.

The Balsamic Moon is a time of retreat into your deepest self. During the Balsamic Moon, you may find yourself lost in contemplation. Though on the surface, there doesn't seem to be much going on with you, below the surface, you are working through and resolving significant life issues.

People born under a Balsamic Moon are often prophets and visionaries. They are connected to the past but see the future, putting them out of step with their time. Their life situations tend to change quickly because they're finishing up with people, places, and events to create a legacy for the next cycle.

Using Moon ☽ Energies

As it waltzes through its phases, the Moon is moving through the signs as well, spending about 2½ days in each sign. The Moon travels about 1° every 2 hours (sometimes faster or slower), which translates into crossing a sign about every 60 hours. Your Moon ☽ sign reveals your emotional, feeling self. Along with your Sun ☉ sign and ascendant, your Moon sign is one of the power points that reveal the essence of your nature in your astrological birth chart, as we explored in the birth charts of Carrie Fisher and Debbie Reynolds in Appendix C. And as you might recall from Chapter 9, the Moon's energies manifest differently in each of the zodiac signs.

Moonwalking Through the Zodiac

Ever notice how some days you feel like starting new projects or adventures, and other days you feel like staying in bed with the covers pulled over your head? Sometimes, it feels as though each day has a distinct flavor. A day in an Aries Moon ♈☽ feels like a good day to start things, for example, and a day in a Pisces Moon ♓☽ feels like a good day to imagine them. Here's a key to the Energy of the Day by the Moon ☽ signs.

Moon ☽ In	Moon ☽ Energy
Aries ♈	Beginnings/pushiness
Taurus ♉	Steady course/getting bogged down
Gemini ♊	Communication/lack of listening
Cancer ♋	Sensitivity/moodiness
Leo ♌	Exuberance/boisterousness
Virgo ♍	Organization/nitpicking
Libra ♎	Equilibrium/indecision
Scorpio ♏	Power/possessiveness
Sagittarius ♐	Enjoyment/restlessness
Capricorn ♑	Control/challenges
Aquarius ♒	Independence/detachment
Pisces ♓	Dreaminess/overimagination

When we learn to associate the Moon's natural cycles—both through its phases and through the signs—with our own, we can plan our lives to move *with* these Moon ☽ rhythms rather than *against* them. And don't forget—the Moon has been a woman for as long as anyone can remember. With the recent resurgence of interest in goddesses and goddess cycles, the phases of the Moon have reclaimed their ancient stories as well.

Drawing Down the Moon ☽

In Nature-based Wicca, the Goddess is a powerful energy of the Source and is represented by the Moon. Wiccans practice the ceremony of Drawing Down the Moon to give thanks and to gather Goddess energy when there is a Full Moon ○. Whether you are a believer in Wicca or just curious about it, we all can agree that standing in full moonlight has its power and can be a mystical, emotional experience.

To tap into this ancient practice of calling upon Moon energy, stand outdoors in the path of the moonlight. Take a deep breath and straighten through your body, feeling your feet take root in the Earth while your eyes rise to the Moon herself. Take another deep breath and on the exhale, feel your fingertips extend downward as Moon energy moves through your body from the crown of your head to your feet. Continue breathing deeply and fully, and with your eyes open and focused on the Moon, begin to meditate on your blessings from the Moon cycle just reaching fruition and on your prayers for the cycle about to begin.

As you feel your intent settle within you, raise your arms straight out to your sides and then upward to the heavens, joining your palms. Now, breathe in fully and as you begin to exhale, lower your palms before your forehead, chin, voice box, collarbone, and down to your heart in a Namaste pose. Bow your head and give thanks to the Goddess. Open your arms by reaching your palms to the Moon and opening outward to trace your own Full Moon in the air. Take one more deep breath and return to your surroundings.

Gardening by the Moon ☽

The Moon's energies also influence gardening and farming. It's best to plant when the Moon is waxing, from the New Moon to the Full Moon. The earlier in the Waxing Moon ◑ you can do your planting, the better. During this part of the Moon's cycle, the Moon's energy grows and nurtures. It's best to harvest during the Balsamic Moon, which is at the end of the Moon's waning energy.

If you are planting bulbs or root crops, such as radishes or potatoes, you'll want to use the Moon's energy in a different way by planting from the Full Moon ○ to the Third-Quarter Moon ◐. This waning energy supports things that grow underground and store their energy in their roots. Are you pruning rather than planting? Prune for growth during the Waxing Moon ◑ and prune to slow growth during the Waning Moon ◐.

Gardening by the Moon Phases and Moon ☽ Signs

Activity	Moon ☽ Phases and Moon ☽ Signs for Best Results
Plant, fertilize, water	Waxing Moon (New Moon, Crescent Moon, First-Quarter Moon) Fruitful signs: Cancer ♋, Scorpio ♏, Pisces ♓, Taurus ♉; Semi-fruitful signs: Libra ♎ and Capricorn ♑ for certain circumstances
Weed and do pest control	Waning Moon (Third-Quarter Moon) Barren signs: Aries ♈, Gemini ♊, Leo ♌, Virgo ♍, Sagittarius ♐, Aquarius ♒
Harvest	Waning Moon (Balsamic Moon) Dry signs: Aries ♈, Leo ♌, Sagittarius ♐, Gemini ♊, Aquarius ♒

Void of Course Moon: Time-Out!

Astrologers refer to the void of course Moon as a cosmic time-out. When the Moon ☽ is void of course, its energy is spent, and this is a time for gestation, research, or rest. Either nothing will come of decisions made during this time, or there will be unexpected problems that can prevent a successful completion. When the Moon ☽ is void of course, it's best not to take any action. Void of course Moons, or cosmic time-outs, are periods when the Moon ☽ is no longer making major aspects—conjunction ☌, sextile ⚹, square □, trine △, or opposition ☍—to the other planets. Void of course Moons last until the Moon enters the next zodiac sign.

In addition, the last aspect made by the Moon ☽ before it goes void determines the final outcome of an event. This means, for example, that if you begin a new venture while the Moon is in Leo ♌, the last aspect that the Moon makes while it's in Leo is what the final outcome of your venture will be—even if the final aspect is a day or two away. So, it makes good astrological sense to know what the Moon is doing and to adjust your schedule to be in tune with it.

Swimming Against the Tide

When decisions are made or actions are taken during these cosmic time-out periods, either nothing comes of them or there are unexpected difficulties. Meetings convened often fail to come to any decisions because the key information required is usually missing, or the person with the best understanding of the issue or the power needed to implement a solution isn't present. When decisions are made anyway, they're plagued by false starts, mistakes, and difficulties. Frequently, remaking the decision becomes necessary later. This often means changing course after spending valuable resources on an erroneous path.

Cosmic time-outs, or void of course Moons ☽, are gestation periods that are better used for rest and regrouping. These times are good for conducting research, gathering information, brainstorming, catching up, cleaning, reading, writing proposals or grants (but not sending them … not yet!), reviewing ideas, meditating, engaging in introspection, and getting centered. These times are also perfect for just enjoying yourself!

Other typical examples observed under this cycle include flight delays or car problems. Misunderstandings about meeting times or places abound. New products might be approved but don't make it to market. Items purchased often have quality or delivery problems or parts missing. Public speaking falters and performances fizzle. People waffle on decisions. Investments go nowhere, and contracts and other legal matters signed during this period go astray. Sounds like fun, right?

A Message from the Universe: Relax!

In essence, during void of course Moons ☽ the Universe is asking us to use this time to slow down. It wants us to recognize that the creative process of life includes time for regrouping, gestating our ideas, and collecting our thoughts or data. Nothing in nature demands constant progress and action, except human beings! There's often a clear reason not to push forward during these times, and when we do so anyway, we're disregarding our better senses and the Universe's plan. A better scenario is to make and implement important decisions only during action cycles, when the Moon ☽ is still making aspects.

But there are many positives about void of course Moons. They present ideal times to go inward in meditation or prayer. A void of course Moon is a great time to study or simply to rest and relax. Take a mini-vacation or a short getaway. If you must *do* something, clean closets or start an exercise plan or cook a meal from scratch for your family or friends. A void of course Moon can be a time of creativity or a time for getting your thoughts and ideas down on paper or in your sketchbook. Void of course Moons are the perfect time for exploring all the many "Ors" of your life!

Walking on the Moon, July 20, 1969

Perhaps the greatest collective achievement of humankind, after discovering fire, of course, is the Moon landing, which took place on July 20, 1969. Three American astronauts—Neil Armstrong, Buzz Aldrin, and Michael Collins—flew the Apollo 11 mission to the Moon. Collins piloted the command module *Columbia* in its orbit around the Moon, while Armstrong and Aldrin landed the Apollo lunar module *Eagle* in the Sea of Tranquility. At 10:56 P.M. EDT, half a billion people on Earth united by the technology of television and watched as Armstrong placed humankind's first foot forward onto the Moon's surface. "That's one small step for (hu)man (beings), one giant leap for (hu)mankind." (Parentheses *ours*.)

Only a short fifty years more or less (in the Universe's understanding of time) has passed since that momentous moment, linking Earth, Moon, and Humankind in space and time. But using astrology by preparing an *event* chart puts us right back there, under the same heavens with Armstrong, Aldrin, and Collins. Astrologers prepare event charts to study the energies surrounding a given time and place; specific people can be added, too, if that's desired. Our Moon Landing event chart considers all humankind. Let's look at the chart's three defining points: the Sun ☉, the Moon ☽, and the ascendant.

First, we consider the ascendant, which gives us the public image of a situation or an event; here, the Sun ☉ at 22 degrees of Pisces ♓ is rising with the North Node ☊ at 23 degrees of Pisces ♓, just as Armstrong puts his first foot down. This placement of the ascendant means we are shooting for the heavens and going toward a futuristic situation that we have no idea where it will lead us. The North Node ☊ is always a positive point in any chart because it has to do with accessing the future, where we need to go. Here, in the first house, it means that the first step on the Moon on July 20, 1969, is the first step to understanding a new dimension of life and a passionate connection to seeking information to help the good of all humankind. This is the Piscean influence. With Pisces rising at that later degree, it meant we, as a species, were ready to try something new, even it if included walking "into the void" and not knowing the outcome. Certainly, we were passionate about making the trip.

Now, we look at the Libra Moon ♎☽ at 11 degrees of Pisces ♓, next to Jupiter ♃ in the sky in the seventh house. (Libra Moon is wonderful next to expansive Jupiter). So, this means that the astronauts and the assembled NASA team had a passionate, enthusiastic, and emotionally connected commitment to the goal of putting humankind on the Moon. Libra means everyone worked well together in the research and planning stages and during the voyage and landing. Everyone intuited the value this mission could hold for humankind and agreed to work together to make it happen.

Lastly, the Sun ☉ is in Cancer ♋ in the fifth house of creativity, at 28 degrees of Cancer formed a grand trine △ to the North Node in Pisces ☊♓ in the first house and to Neptune ♆ in Scorpio ♏ in the eighth house. There were actually *two* grand trines △ including the ascendant, so the Sun ☉ was trining, and the Sun was being trined by Neptune ♆ (a planet further out there in the Universe). Neptune is mystery, and in the eighth house of soulful transformation, it shows that we were looking for the answer to a mystery—and that we needed to do so by our own travel. We needed to travel into the void in order to emerge in the light of the Sun ☉. There was actually a grand trine for about two days before July 20 and for 5 days after. So, a long-lasting grand trine from the Sun to Neptune to the North Node and ascendant would reveal that there is protection—spiritual protection, emotional protection, financial protection—the spiritual world and the material world were in harmony and union with each other.

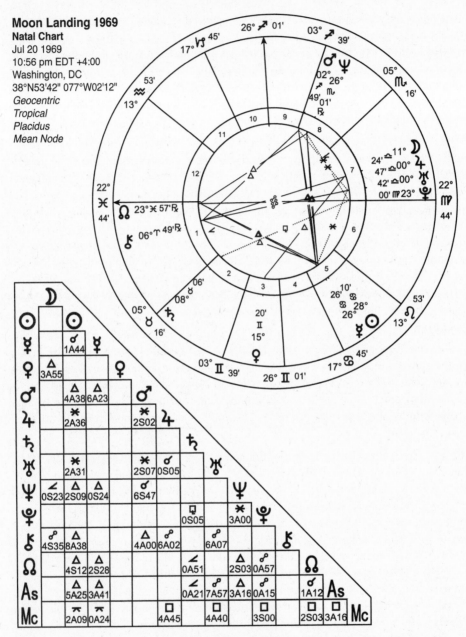

The event chart for the Moon Landing, 10:56 P.M., July 20, 1969. Study the relationship of the Sun, Moon, and ascendant to get to the heart of the matter.

Remember, the Sun in Cancer ☉ ♋ is ruled by the Moon ☽. Add to that the Pisces ♓, Cancer ♋, and Scorpio ♏ combination of Water signs in grand trine in late degrees shows humankind setting off in a new direction, ready to explore the next uncharted territory, and crossing the ocean of space. All the research and work has been done; all that is left is to go! The Ancients used to say that if you have a grand trine connected to the Sun or the Moon and connected to the ascendant at either point, you are protected by heaven, everyone is cheering for you, and everyone has the same positive energy directed toward your goal. The ancients also believed that a grand trine related to the Sun ascendant on the Moon would show that heaven and earth were, on that day, in communion with each other. On July 20, 1969, humankind was heir to a kind of manifest destiny of space exploration.

When you think about the seventh house of human partnerships, and think about how it took many, many people to get humankind on the space journey that put human beings on the Moon—and when you also consider the fact that the Moon ☽ and Jupiter ♃ were conjunct ☌ in the seventh house with the outer planets of Uranus ♅ and Pluto ♀—you realize that everyone was emotionally connected to this event before it ever happened. All humankind was dedicated to the goal of reaching the Moon, and that is why of course the outcome would have manifested as a grand trine. In the words of U.S. president John F. Kennedy speaking to Congress in May 1961: "But in a very real sense, it will not be one man going to the Moon—if we make this judgment affirmatively, it will be an entire nation. For all of us must work to put him there."

In casting event charts, astrology reveals the heart of the matter. Whether a wedding, a trip abroad, a move to a new city, or a new job, everything you'll need to know about the nature of that event—its people, time, and place—will be revealed, even on a trip to the Moon! Oh, yes, and those of us who stood together on Earth on July 20, 1969, looked up in the night sky to see a Waxing Crescent Moon ◐.

HOW A COMPUTER CALCULATES A BIRTH CHART

To cast a birth chart by hand takes years of study into the science and mathematics behind the theory of astrology. Despite the meme "astrology is fake but …," the underpinnings of a birth chart are technical, precise, and intricate. You need to be an expert to hand-cast a birth chart. To become an astrologer certified by the International Society of Astrological Proficiency (ISAR CAP), you need to take a vigorous exam complete with calculating a birth chart by hand and going on to interpret it accurately.

Once you learn all that goes into calculating a birth chart by hand, you'll appreciate exactly how much astrology balances our time's techno-rationalist, data-driven lifestyle. Your birth chart is astrology's own data-driven metaphor of the heavens—more specifically, *your* heavens. Astrology embraces the big question our physicists, geneticists, and natural scientists grapple with: *what is our place in the Universe?*

So, what *are* the calculations behind a computer's creation of a birth chart? Okay, astro-nerds, put on your Copernicus Renaissance astrologer's thinking cap and follow along as Madeline takes you through the calculation of brilliant American film director Steven Spielberg's birth chart. Make your pour-over coffee, settle in, and get ready to concentrate as we journey through space and time to the precise technical expression of Steven Spielberg's essential nature—his astrological birth chart.

Resources Your Computer Has Replaced

To do the calculating, you may be surprised by just how many books and equations your computer is replacing to cast a birth chart. For starters, these include an ephemeris, a *table of houses,* an atlas, and a book of time zone changes; there are a lot of other books we don't mention here, but these four are essential resources. Let's look at what they include to help you understand how your birth chart is calculated.

Ephemeris

An ephemeris (the plural is *ephemerides*—it's Greek) is a book that shows where the planets are at noon or midnight Greenwich Mean Time every day of every year. Your computer looks up the planetary positions that are contained in an ephemeris for you. Later in this appendix, we show how to look up the planetary positions yourself.

Table of Houses

You find your ascendant, midheaven, and house cusps with a table of houses. These charts are arranged in 1-degree increments of longitude, but amazingly enough, most people were born in between two of these. The latitudes along the side of the column are also in 1-degree increments, so most people also live between those.

Based on the birth information you provide, the computer program calculates the actual house positions; it has a built-in table of houses to save you all the trouble.

Atlas

When was the last time you texted a friend for their coordinates? GPS uses latitude and longitude to track the precise location you desire, such as the walking route to the coffee house where you'll meet. Renaissance astrologers had atlases that showed both latitude and longitude. The atlas is used to find the specific latitude and longitude, the coordinates for your exact place of birth. Almost all atlases show latitude and longitude to the minute. (For example, the Four Corners of Arizona, Colorado, New Mexico, and Utah are 37N00 and 109W00.) Many atlases show the seconds as well. In addition, *The American Atlas* shows both locations *and* the time zone changes, as well as seconds.

Chart-creation programs have built-in atlases; you or the astrologer enters the name of the place, and the computer does the rest. A few still use a separate atlas program to do this. By hand, of course, you look up coordinates the old-fashioned way to locate the latitude and longitude for your birthplace. The more accurate the coordinates entered, the more precise the birth chart will be. To be *really* precise, let's say your mom had a natural childbirth and you were born at home; you can compare GPS coordinates for your birth house with the coordinates you'd find for your birth town, which is the difference between saying "82 Main Street" and "Seattle." No matter how it's obtained, the important thing is to enter accurate coordinates from the best information you know about birthplace.

Book of Time Zone Changes

Now, don't forget, we also have that pesky daylight-saving time to contend with. You know, that "fall back, spring ahead" deal, which we never seem to get straight, no matter how many years we've been setting those clocks back and forth. In the United States, only Arizona (except the Navajo Nation) and Hawaii don't use daylight-saving time (DST). About 70 countries around the world observe some form of DST, though the dates and amount of time change vary.

A book of time zone changes makes all this simple. It tells you when and whether the place you were born switches to daylight-saving time, and when it switches back. In the past, something called war time was also used. All places have undergone time changes at some time. These books include all time changes for the past, present, and future. Maybe we should all have one of these—whether we're doing our birth charts or not! Of course, this is one more thing your computer program will have in its database and do automatically.

Basic Information

For all the math and science that go into your birth chart's creation—whether cast by hand or by computer—you need three simple, though essential, pieces of information to perform accurate birth chart calculations:

* Your date of birth
* Your precise time of birth
* Your place of birth, as exactly as is known

It's About Time, It's About Space

One of the most important things to understand about chart calculation is that it's all about time—three kinds of time, to be exact: *Greenwich Mean Time (GMT)*, sidereal time (or star time—there's an explanation coming up later), and local time. Greenwich Mean Time (GMT) is the time standard used in astronomy for locations at 0 degrees longitude or meridian. It's 4 hours later than Eastern Daylight Time and 5 hours later than Eastern Standard Time.

We talk about each time at a particular point in the birth chart calculation process, and we tell you some of the astronomy behind time as well.

Working in Base 60

Sixty seconds make up a minute, and 60 minutes make up an hour. This is called base 60—quite simply, a system that uses 60 instead of 10 as its basis. Base 60 is used to calculate clock time or distance: 60 seconds make up a minute, and 60 minutes make up an hour or a degree.

Geographical distances also are calculated using the base 60 system and are measured in degrees, minutes, and seconds. All calculations for your birth chart are done in hours or degrees, minutes, and seconds, and it's important that you keep these three things separate—for example, 7 hours, 29 minutes, 13 seconds. This also can be written as 07:29:13.

Sixty seconds converts to 1 minute, and 60 minutes is either 1 hour or 1 degree, depending on whether we're measuring time or distance. Also remember that if you subtract and need to borrow a minute, you're borrowing 60 seconds. Or if you borrow an hour, you're borrowing 60 minutes. We're starting with this so you understand the measurement system that's behind the calculation a computer performs so easily.

Converting to GMT

The first thing calculated is your Greenwich Mean Time (GMT), based on the time zone in which you were born. The person doing your birth chart will have checked a time changes book first to make sure the time zone entered into the computer is correct. Nowadays, though, time zone changes are already programmed into computer apps and software. GMT is the time for which the ephemeris is set up, with the position of the planets calculated for midnight or noon. If a person was born anywhere other than in England or the other locations that lie within GMT, the computer must convert the birth time to GMT, which, in turn, is used to calculate the actual position of the planets.

The conversion to GMT (for the Western Hemisphere, anyway) is made by adding to your birth time the difference in hours between the time zone where you were born and GMT. GMT is later than time in the United States, and the computer calculates this using a look-up table similar to the following table. However, this is such an easy calculation, anyone could do it!

If a person was born during daylight-saving or war time, the computer adds 1 less hour than when converting to GMT from a standard time zone. It's easy to determine whether a person was born during daylight-saving or war time by using a time changes book or a computer with such changes programmed into it.

Converting to Greenwich Mean Time (United States)

Time Zone	Add
Eastern Standard	5 hours
Central Standard	6 hours
Mountain Standard	7 hours
Pacific Standard	8 hours
Daylight-Saving or War Time Zone	**Add**
Eastern Daylight	4 hours
Central Daylight	5 hours
Mountain Daylight	6 hours
Pacific Daylight	7 hours

The possibility exists that one's Greenwich Mean Time of birth is on a different day than the actual date of birth at the birth location. If you were using a midnight ephemeris, for example, and you were born on August 1 at 8 P.M. Central Daylight Time, you'd add 5 hours, which would equal 1 A.M. GMT. That, of course, is the next day! So, you'd be looking for your planets on August 2 instead of August 1.

Let's Calculate Steven Spielberg's Birth Chart

First, we look at Steven Spielberg's birth information. Spielberg was born on December 18, 1946, at 6:16 P.M. in Cincinnati, Ohio. We note that he was born at 6:16 P.M. Eastern Standard Time. To change this to GMT, the computer first converts this to the 24-hour system (by adding 12 hours because Spielberg has a P.M. birth) to come up with 18:16. Then it adds 5 hours (to convert from EST) to get a GMT time of 23:16.

To Boldly Seek Those Planetary Positions

Let's begin our mission by looking at an ephemeris page for December 1946, the month of Steven Spielberg's birth. We use a midnight ephemeris throughout the rest of this chapter, so all our references and examples are for a midnight ephemeris instead of a noon ephemeris.

Looking at the sample page in the following figure, let's find the date, December 18, for Spielberg's planets. The first thing you see is that a sidereal time (abbreviated SID time) is shown next to the date. We don't use that here, but we come back to it when we calculate the houses. For now, just note where it is.

DECEMBER 1946 **LONGITUDE**

Day	Sid.Time	☉	0 hr ☽	Noon ☽	True ☊	☿	♀	♂	♃	♄	♅	♆	♇
1 Su	4 36 59	8♐11 39	27♒39 39	3♓56 1	11♊45.0	21♏ 9.4	18♏14.6	17♐41.3	14♏18.0	8♌47.4	20♊14.8	10♎18.0	13♌18.6
2 M	4 40 56	9 12 29	10♓17 28	16 44 32	11R45.0	21D 13.5	17R57.6	18 25.8	14 30.5	8R46.1	20R 12.3	10 19.4	13R18.2
3 Tu	4 44 52	10 13 20	23 17 37	29 57 7	11 45.0	21 27.6	17 43.0	19 10.4	14 43.0	8 44.8	20 9.8	10 20.7	13 17.7
4 W	4 48 49	11 14 11	6♈43 19	13♈36 23	11D44.9	21 50.9	17 30.9	19 55.0	14 55.5	8 43.4	20 7.3	10 22.0	13 17.2
5 Th	4 52 45	12 15 3	20 36 23	27 43 12	11 44.9	22 22.4	17 21.2	20 39.6	15 8.0	8 41.8	20 4.8	10 23.3	13 16.6
6 F	4 56 42	13 15 57	4♉56 35	12♉16 3	11 45.0	23 1.3	17 14.0	21 24.3	15 20.3	8 40.2	20 2.3	10 24.6	13 16.1
7 Sa	5 0 39	14 16 51	19 40 59	27 10 35	11 45.2	23 46.9	17 9.3	22 9.1	15 32.7	8 38.4	19 59.7	10 25.8	13 15.5
8 Su	5 4 35	15 17 45	4♊43 51	12♊19 42	11R45.3	24 38.2	17D 7.1	22 53.9	15 45.0	8 36.6	19 57.2	10 27.0	13 14.9
9 M	5 8 32	16 18 41	19 56 56	27 34 18	11 45.3	25 34.7	17 7.4	23 38.7	15 57.2	8 34.6	19 54.6	10 28.1	13 14.3
10 Tu	5 12 28	17 19 38	5♋10 31	12♋44 25	11 45.1	26 35.6	17 10.1	24 23.6	16 9.4	8 32.5	19 52.1	10 29.3	13 13.6
11 W	5 16 25	18 20 36	20 14 51	27 40 51	11 44.5	27 40.5	17 15.1	25 8.6	16 21.6	8 30.4	19 49.5	10 30.4	13 12.9
12 Th	5 20 21	19 21 35	5♌ 1 35	12♌16 25	11 43.6	28 48.7	17 22.6	25 53.6	16 33.6	8 28.1	19 47.0	10 31.5	13 12.2
13 F	5 24 18	20 22 35	19 24 51	26 26 37	11 42.7	29 59.9	17 32.3	26 38.6	16 45.7	8 25.7	19 44.4	10 32.5	13 11.5
14 Sa	5 28 14	21 23 36	3♍21 35	10♍ 9 49	11 41.9	1♐13.6	17 44.3	27 23.8	16 57.6	8 23.2	19 41.9	10 33.5	13 10.7
15 Su	5 32 11	22 24 37	16 51 27	23 26 46	11D41.4	2 29.6	17 58.4	28 8.9	17 9.6	8 20.7	19 39.3	10 34.5	13 10.0
16 M	5 36 8	23 25 40	29 56 8	6♎19 58	11 41.4	3 47.5	18 14.7	28 54.1	17 21.4	8 18.0	19 36.7	10 35.4	13 9.2
17 Tu	5 40 4	24 26 44	12♎38 43	18 52 54	11 42.0	5 7.1	18 33.0	29 39.4	17 33.2	8 15.2	19 34.2	10 36.3	13 8.3
18 W	5 44 1	25 27 49	25 2 59	1♏ 9 30	11 43.1	6 28.2	18 53.3	0♑24.7	17 44.9	8 12.4	19 31.6	10 37.2	13 7.5
19 Th	5 47 57	26 28 54	7♏12 56	13 13 45	11 44.5	7 50.6	19 15.6	1 10.0	17 56.6	8 9.4	19 29.1	10 38.1	13 6.6
20 F	5 51 54	27 30 1	19 12 24	25 9 19	11 45.8	9 14.1	19 39.7	1 55.5	18 8.2	8 6.3	19 26.6	10 38.9	13 5.7
21 Sa	5 55 50	28 31 8	1♐ 4 53	6♐59 27	11R46.9	10 38.6	20 5.5	2 40.9	18 19.7	8 3.2	19 24.0	10 39.7	13 4.8
22 Su	5 59 47	29 32 16	12 53 23	18 46 59	11 47.2	12 4.0	20 33.1	3 26.4	18 31.2	7 60.0	19 21.5	10 40.4	13 3.9
23 M	6 3 43	0♑33 24	24 40 33	0♑34 19	11 46.6	13 30.2	21 2.4	4 12.0	18 42.6	7 56.7	19 19.0	10 41.2	13 2.9
24 Tu	6 7 40	1 34 33	6♑28 34	12 23 33	11 45.0	14 57.0	21 33.2	4 57.6	18 53.9	7 53.3	19 16.5	10 41.8	13 2.0
25 W	6 11 37	2 35 42	18 19 30	24 16 38	11 42.3	16 24.5	22 5.6	5 43.2	19 5.2	7 49.8	19 14.1	10 42.5	13 1.0
26 Th	6 15 33	3 36 52	0♒15 14	6♒15 32	11 38.7	17 52.6	22 39.5	6 28.9	19 16.3	7 46.2	19 11.6	10 43.1	12 60.0
27 F	6 19 30	4 38 1	12 17 49	18 22 22	11 34.7	19 21.1	23 14.7	7 14.6	19 27.4	7 42.5	19 9.2	10 43.7	12 58.9
28 Sa	6 23 26	5 39 11	24 29 30	0♓39 33	11 30.7	20 50.2	23 51.4	8 0.4	19 38.4	7 38.8	19 6.7	10 44.3	12 57.9
29 Su	6 27 23	6 40 21	6♓52 52	13 9 49	11 27.1	22 19.7	24 29.3	8 46.2	19 49.3	7 35.0	19 4.3	10 44.8	12 56.8
30 M	6 31 19	7 41 30	19 30 47	25 56 10	11 24.6	23 49.6	25 8.5	9 32.0	20 0.2	7 31.1	19 1.9	10 45.2	12 55.7
31 Tu	6 35 16	8 42 40	2♈26 21	9♈ 1 42	11D 23.3	25 19.9	25 48.9	10 17.9	20 10.9	7 27.2	18 59.5	10 45.7	12 54.6

A page from the ephemeris for December 1946.

(Illustration from *The American Ephemeris for the 20th Century,* used by permission. Copyright© ACS Publications, 5521 Ruffin Road, San Diego, CA 92123-1314. Call 1-800-888-9983 to place orders.)

What you need to notice now is that the positions that are given for each planet for each day are accurate only for midnight. So, the computer needs to calculate the distance traveled from the *start time* (midnight, in our case) in the ephemeris to the time Spielberg was born. The start time, or reference time, is either midnight or noon for a given date, depending on the ephemeris. The computer uses this to determine the daily travel of the planets.

Find the sign a planet is in by looking *up* to the nearest sign shown in the column; or, if there is a new sign change on that day, you might use that one. This depends on whether the planet changed signs after or before the person was born. If a planet hasn't changed signs during that month, though, the planet will be the sign shown at the top of the column.

Daily Travel

To calculate the distance from the start time, the computer must find out how far each planet traveled between the start time and the next day's position. Then it calculates how much of that distance was traveled by the planet at the time Spielberg was born. Remember that we must use the GMT here, not the birth time.

Let's use Spielberg's birth data—December 18, 1946, at 23:16 GMT—as an example. The computer subtracts the position shown for the planets on December 18 at midnight from the position of the planets shown for midnight on December 19. This shows you that planet's *daily travel*. Daily travel is the distance a planet moves in a 24-hour period.

Next, the computer calculates how much time elapsed between midnight and when Spielberg was born. Using his GMT of 23:16, this is calculated as follows: 23:00 is 23 hours past midnight, and 16 minutes divided by 60 minutes = .26 hours. So, 23.26 hours divided by 24 hours = .9691666. In this case, each planet traveled 23.26 hours, or .9691666 of a day from the position shown at midnight.

Now the computer multiplies this number (.9691666) by the amount of daily travel for each of the planets that day. The Sun ☉, for example, travels about one degree per day. And on the day that Spielberg was born, it traveled a total distance of 1 degree, 1 minute, 5 seconds. So, its travel until Spielberg was born was .9691666 times the Sun's total travel for that day of 1 degree, 1 minute, and 5 seconds. (Aren't you lucky that unless you're a devoted astro-nerd, the computer, not you, gets to figure this stuff?)

The Sun's travel also can be expressed as 61 minutes and 5 seconds (or a total of 3,665 seconds). So, .9691666 times 3,665 seconds equals 59 minutes and 2 seconds. The computer then adds this amount to the December 18 position shown in the ephemeris (25 degrees, 27 minutes, 49 seconds) to arrive at the position for Spielberg's Sun. Adding 59 minutes, 2 seconds gives a final position of 26 degrees, 26 minutes, and 51 seconds. The computer rounds this to 26 degrees, 27 minutes of Sagittarius ♐, which is what is shown on the chart. Then the computer does the same thing to find all Spielberg's other planets' positions, plus his North Node.

What About Retrogrades?

Now, if a planet is retrograde, or appears to be moving backward (see Chapter 12), the computer works in the opposite direction. You can see for yourself when you look at the ephemeris that some of Spielberg's planets are losing ground; this tells you right away that they're retrograde. The computer knows this, too. There's also an "R" in the column above on the date when the planet went retrograde. If it started the month in retrograde motion, this is shown on the second day for the month, as the sample ephemeris page shows for Venus ♀, Saturn ♄, Uranus ♅, and Pluto ♇.

In this case, the computer does exactly the reverse of what we've just shown you. Because the second entry is smaller than the first entry, the computer *subtracts* it from the first position.

In our example, this means that the computer subtracts the December 19 position for Saturn from its position on December 18. Then it calculates how far it traveled until Spielberg was born and *subtracts* it from the December 18 position because Saturn ♄ is retrograding.

A Wrinkle in Sidereal, or Star Time

Sidereal time, or star time, is based on the actual amount of time it takes Earth to rotate once on its axis in relation to the fixed stars. Whereas clock time measures a day as 24 hours based on the apparent movement of the Sun, sidereal time measures it at its astronomical (or star) speed, which is about 4 minutes less.

Sidereal time is time as measured by the heavens, and a sidereal day is the length of time it takes Earth to rotate on its axis once, relative to the fixed stars. On the other hand, our calendar day (or mean [average] solar day) is the length of time it takes Earth to rotate on its axis relative to the Sun. (This also is sometimes referred to as the apparent movement of the Sun because, to us, the Sun appears to move around Earth.) The mean solar day is slightly longer than the sidereal day because while Earth is rotating on its axis, it's also moving in orbit around the Sun.

Earth gets back to the same place it started, in relation to the fixed stars, about 4 minutes earlier than it does in relation to the Sun. So, by our clock time, the sidereal time is about 4 minutes later at the beginning of each new day. You can see this in the ephemeris under the column for sidereal time.

The local sidereal time tells you which degree of the zodiac is on the midheaven. This is the starting point for calculating the houses, which we explain later in this appendix.

But let's make this a little simpler by giving you an example. Imagine a line extending directly over your head into the heavens. That's your local zenith. If you went outside at the same sidereal time every night, you would find the same fixed stars crossing your local zenith at that moment. You could also call this *star time,* because it takes a little less time for Earth to get back to its initial position, relative to the stars—by about 4 minutes. Our clock day is actually a little bit longer than the real star time (or sidereal time).

We need to convert everything into sidereal time to calculate an astrological birth chart, so that we can determine the ascendant, midheaven, and houses by star time.

Calculating Sidereal Time

Let's go to our example to see how this works. On the sample ephemeris page, look up the sidereal time for Spielberg's birth date, December 18, 1946. Keep in mind that the start time of our sample ephemeris page is midnight.

You'll find the sidereal time next to the date. Did you find it? It's 5 44 1. The computer must update it to the time Spielberg was born. To do this, the computer looks up the sidereal reference time for the date and year of birth. Then it adds (at least, in North America) the true local time (also known as local mean time) of birth; this is added as hours, minutes, and seconds to the reference time of the ephemeris. Then it adds an acceleration factor based on the *time* of birth to correct for the 4-minute difference between our clock time and sidereal time. Finally, it adds another acceleration correction factor for the 4-minute difference, based on the *location* of the birth.

The sum of these factors give the computer the sidereal time of the birth. For you hardcore math whizzes, we're going to show you how Spielberg's sidereal time was calculated by the computer. If you're not interested in these details, of course, you can go ahead and move along to "Desperately Seeking House Cusps" later in this appendix.

First, the computer looks up Spielberg's date and year of birth in the ephemeris to get the sidereal time. In this case, it's 5 hours, 44 minutes, and 1 second at midnight on December 18, 1946. Then the computer calculates the true local time or the amount of time that passed between the reference or start time in the ephemeris and the exact time of birth.

Remember that the reference time for our ephemeris is midnight Greenwich Mean Time. So, we have to make a few corrections to find out how many hours and minutes it was past that time when Spielberg was born in Cincinnati, Ohio. And this leads us to another discussion of time—in this case, true local time.

Will the True Local Time Please Stand Up?

Now, really, there isn't a false local time. But there *is* a true local time, which is based on where the Sun actually is, instead of our clock time conventions. The Sun appears to move 60 miles every 4 minutes, which is the same as moving 1 degree in longitude every 4 minutes. This is why the time zones around the world change by 1 hour for every 15 degrees of longitude around the world.

Only at the primary meridians (every 15 degrees from Greenwich) does the clock time equal the Sun time. Everywhere else, it's either earlier or later by actual local or solar time. So, unless a person was born directly on one of the primary meridians—in the case of North America, at 60W00, 75W00, 90W00, 105W00, or 120W00—the computer makes a correction of 4 minutes of time for each degree of difference in longitude for the birth location.

Greenwich, England, was selected to be 0 degrees in longitude. When we travel west of Greenwich—as we do to get to the United States from England—for every 15 degrees of longitude we travel, there is 1 hour of difference in time. In this case, time is 1 hour earlier for every 15 degrees of longitude that we travel west of Greenwich.

Imagine, for example, that the birth location is 3 degrees to the east of the prime meridian 75W00, at 72W00. The Sun already reached this area and passed over it before it reached the 75W00 meridian. Basically, it's later in this location by Sun time than at the primary meridian by 3 degrees times 4 minutes, which equals 12 minutes. And because it's later in time at 72W00 than at 75W00, the 12 minutes are *added* to get the correct local time.

At 78W00, this is 3 degrees past the primary meridian of 75W00, so the computer corrects for those 3 extra degrees and *subtracts* 12 minutes from the time for the primary meridian to get the local time. In essence, it's earlier at 78W00 than it is at 75W00 because the Sun reaches it later.

Calculating True Local Time

Now that you understand what local time is, we will walk you through what the computer calculates for Spielberg's local time. First, it must determine whether he was born during Daylight Saving, War Time, or Standard Time. If he had been born during either Daylight Saving or War Time, the computer would have subtracted 1 hour from his birth time. But because it was an Eastern Standard Time birth, no changes were made at this step.

Next, his birth location is Cincinnati, Ohio, which has a longitude of 84W31. This is 9 degrees, 31 minutes west of the 75W00 primary meridian. The clock time when he was born was 6:16 P.M. EST, but that was accurate only at 75W00. In Cincinnati, the solar time was a little bit earlier. So, the computer multiplies the difference in longitude by 4 minutes and gets 36 minutes and 124 seconds, which converts to 38 minutes and 4 seconds.

Because Cincinnati is west of the 75W00 meridian and it's earlier there, the computer subtracts this amount from the time of 6:16 P.M. to get 5 hours, 37 minutes, and 56 seconds as his true local time. But to keep this in a 24-hour clock system so we don't confuse A.M. and P.M., 12 hours are added, and his true local time is shown as 17 hours, 37 minutes, and 56 seconds (17:37:56). This is what the computer adds to the sidereal time shown in the midnight ephemeris because this is the real difference in time between the start, or reference, time shown there.

If Spielberg had been born somewhere east of England, such as Russia or China, of course, calculating the true local time would be a slightly different process from what we've used because the time there is later than in Greenwich.

So far, we have the sidereal time and the true local time, which are added together as follows (in a 24-hour system):

Sidereal time shown in ephemeris:	5 hours	44 minutes	1 sec
+ True local time (past midnight):	17 hours	37 minutes	56 sec

But there are still a few minor corrections to make before the computer has the final calculated sidereal time.

Acceleration

Next, the computer adds something called *acceleration*. Acceleration is a correction factor to compensate for the difference of about 4 minutes between a solar day and sidereal time. Acceleration is calculated for both the time of birth and place of birth. It's added at a rate of 10 seconds for every hour from the start or reference time in the ephemeris—midnight, in our case—to the true local time for North American births.

This equals 10 seconds of time for each hour after midnight that Spielberg was born. The computer uses the true local time, which, for this step, can be rounded to 17 hours and 38 minutes. So the computer multiplies 17 hours and 38 minutes past midnight by 10 seconds per hour, which equals 170 seconds plus about 6 more seconds for the 38 minutes. This adds up to 176 seconds, or 2 minutes and 56 seconds.

So, the computer adds 2 minutes and 56 seconds for the acceleration part of the formula based on his birth time. In our example so far, the computer has the following:

Sidereal time shown in ephemeris:	5 hours	44 minutes	1 sec
+ True local time (past midnight):	17 hours	37 minutes	56 sec
Acceleration (based on time of birth):		2 minutes	56 sec

Correction for Place of Birth

The computer still has *one more* minor correction to make! The computer already corrected for the difference of 4 minutes between sidereal time and a solar day if you were born in Greenwich, England. But because most of us are born elsewhere, the computer corrects for these 4 minutes again, based on our location. In essence, this is a correction for the place of birth, and, if we remember that distance equals time, this makes sense.

To calculate this, the computer adds 10 seconds for every 15 degrees of west longitude. Spielberg was born at 84W31, so for the first 75 degrees of west longitude, it adds 50 seconds. That leaves another 9 degrees and 31 minutes to correct for, which is about 6 seconds, for a total correction of 56 seconds. The computer then adds the 56 seconds to the rest of the corrections, and adds them all up to get the actual sidereal time for Spielberg's birth. So now we have:

Sidereal time shown in ephemeris:	5 hours	44 minutes	1 sec
True local time (past midnight):	17 hours	37 minutes	56 sec
Acceleration (based on time of birth):		2 minutes	56 sec
Acceleration (based on place of birth):			56 sec
Actual calculated sidereal time:	22 hours	83 minutes	169 sec

This converts to *23 hours, 25 minutes, 49 seconds, which is the final sidereal time for Spielberg.* Hooray! We finally have the number we need!

The computer also knows that when the sidereal clock reaches 24 hours, it starts counting over again, beginning at 0. So, it checks to make sure that the final sidereal time is within 24 hours. If it's not, it subtracts 24 hours from the total to get the correct sidereal time. In Spielberg's case, this wasn't necessary.

Let's summarize the corrections the computer makes for North American charts, using a midnight ephemeris to arrive at sidereal time:

1. The computer starts with the reference sidereal time in the ephemeris for the date and year of birth.

2. Then it calculates the true local time for the birthplace. It expresses that birth time in a 24-hour system (adding 12 hours for P.M. birth times) and adds that to the sidereal time it found in the midnight ephemeris.

3. Now it calculates and adds the acceleration factor to compensate for the difference of 4 minutes per day between sidereal time and regular clock time, based on the birth time.

4. The computer calculates the acceleration factor again to compensate for the birth location and adds this, too.

5. Last, the computer adds all these and converts it to within 24 hours to get the final calculated sidereal time.

Houses, Houses, and More Houses!

It's time to talk about house systems, which are very technical. There are a lot of different ways to divide space to come up with houses. One of the most commonly used house systems is Placidus; this might be because for a long time it was the only one available in reference books.

Now that there are computers, though, a wide variety of house systems are available. They have a lot of technical differences between them, which we don't cover here. Different astrologers like different house systems. For example, some astrologers prefer Koch houses for far-northern latitudes.

For the purposes of this book, though, we use the Placidus house system. It's certainly a good system to start with, and many astrologers still prefer to use it today.

Desperately Seeking House Cusps

As you might recall, house cusps are the places where the houses begin. When you look at a birth chart, you'll see lines, with a sign and degrees on each, dividing the houses.

Now that the computer has Spielberg's sidereal time, it "looks up" the houses in a table similar to the one shown here. This is a page from the *AFA Table of Houses, Placidus System.*

N LAT	23h 24m 0s / MC / 351° 0' 0' — ♓ 20° 12' 19"					23h 28m 0s / MC / 352° 0' 0' — ♓ 21° 17' 27"					N LAT
	11	12	Ascendant	2	3	11	12	Ascendant	2	3	
0	♈22 42.3	♉23 23.4	Ⅱ21 43.9	♋19 24.1	♌18 34.0	♈23 46.0	♉24 22.0	Ⅱ22 39.2	♋20 20.3	♌19 35.0	0
5	22 59.0	24 30.5	23 43.1	20 39.5	19 1.5	24 3.5	25 29.8	24 38.5	21 35.3	20 2.0	5
10	23 16.5	25 40.6	25 45.1	21 54.9	19 29.0	24 21.7	26 40.7	26 40.5	22 50.3	20 28.9	10
15	23 34.9	26 55.1	27 51.5	23 11.4	19 56.8	24 40.9	27 55.9	28 46.8	24 6.2	20 56.1	15
16	23 38.8	27 10.7	28 17.5	23 26.9	20 2.4	24 45.0	28 11.6	29 12.8	24 21.6	21 1.6	16
17	23 42.7	27 26.5	28 43.8	23 42.5	20 8.1	24 49.0	28 27.5	29 39.0	24 37.2	21 7.2	17
18	23 46.6	27 42.6	29 10.4	23 58.3	20 13.8	24 53.1	28 43.8	♋0 5.5	24 52.8	21 12.8	18
19	23 50.6	27 59.0	29 37.2	24 14.1	20 19.6	24 57.3	29 0.3	0 32.3	25 8.5	21 18.5	19
20	23 54.7	28 15.7	♋0 4.4	24 30.1	20 25.4	25 1.6	29 17.1	0 59.4	25 24.4	21 24.2	20
21	23 58.9	28 32.7	0 32.0	24 46.3	20 31.2	25 6.0	29 34.3	1 26.9	25 40.4	21 29.9	21
22	24 3.2	28 50.1	0 59.9	25 2.6	20 37.1	25 10.4	29 51.8	1 54.7	25 56.6	21 35.7	22
23	24 7.5	29 7.8	1 28.2	25 19.0	20 43.1	25 14.9	Ⅱ0 9.7	2 22.9	26 12.9	21 41.6	23
24	24 12.0	29 26.0	1 56.9	25 35.7	20 49.2	25 19.6	0 27.9	2 51.5	26 29.4	21 47.5	24
25	24 16.5	29 44.5	2 26.1	25 52.5	20 55.3	25 24.3	0 46.6	3 20.5	26 46.1	21 53.5	25
26	24 21.1	Ⅱ0 3.5	2 55.7	26 9.6	21 1.5	25 29.1	1 5.7	3 50.0	27 3.0	21 59.5	26
27	24 25.9	0 23.0	3 25.7	26 26.9	21 7.8	25 34.0	1 25.3	4 19.9	27 20.2	22 5.7	27
28	24 30.7	0 42.9	3 56.3	26 44.4	21 14.1	25 39.1	1 45.4	4 50.4	27 37.5	22 11.9	28
29	24 35.7	1 3.4	4 27.5	27 2.1	21 20.6	25 44.3	2 6.0	5 21.3	27 55.1	22 18.2	29
30	24 40.8	1 24.5	4 59.1	27 20.2	21 27.1	25 49.6	2 27.2	5 52.9	28 13.0	22 24.7	30
31	24 46.1	1 46.1	5 31.4	27 38.5	21 33.8	25 55.1	2 49.0	6 25.0	28 31.1	22 31.2	31
32	24 51.5	2 8.4	6 4.3	27 57.1	21 40.6	26 0.7	3 11.4	6 57.7	28 49.5	22 37.8	32
33	24 57.0	2 31.4	6 37.9	28 16.0	21 47.5	26 6.5	3 34.5	7 31.0	29 8.3	22 44.6	33
34	25 2.8	2 55.1	7 12.1	28 35.3	21 54.5	26 12.5	3 58.3	8 5.0	29 27.4	22 51.4	34
35	25 8.7	3 19.6	7 47.1	28 54.9	22 1.6	26 18.7	4 22.9	8 39.8	29 46.8	22 58.4	35
36	25 14.8	3 44.9	8 22.9	29 15.0	22 9.0	26 25.1	4 48.4	9 15.3	♋0 6.6	23 5.6	36
37	25 21.1	4 11.2	8 59.4	29 35.4	22 16.4	26 31.6	5 14.7	9 51.5	0 26.8	23 12.9	37
38	25 27.7	4 38.4	9 36.8	29 56.2	22 24.0	26 38.5	5 42.1	10 28.6	0 47.4	23 20.3	38
39	25 34.5	5 6.6	10 15.1	♌0 17.5	22 31.8	26 45.5	6 10.4	11 6.6	1 8.5	23 28.0	39
40	25 41.5	5 36.0	10 54.3	0 39.3	22 39.8	26 52.9	6 39.9	11 45.5	1 30.0	23 35.8	40
41	25 48.9	6 6.6	11 34.5	1 1.6	22 48.0	27 0.5	7 10.5	12 25.4	1 52.1	23 43.7	41
42	25 56.5	6 38.4	12 15.8	1 24.5	22 56.4	27 8.5	7 42.5	13 6.3	2 14.7	23 51.9	42
43	26 4.5	7 11.7	12 58.1	1 47.9	23 5.0	27 16.7	8 15.8	13 48.2	2 37.8	24 0.4	43
44	26 12.8	7 46.5	13 41.6	2 12.0	23 13.8	27 25.4	8 50.7	14 31.3	3 1.6	24 9.0	44

A page from the AFA Table of Houses.

(Excerpts from *the AFA Table of Houses, Placidus System* are reproduced with the permission of Gregg Howe of Astro Numeric Service and the American Federation of Astrologers, Inc. Copyright© 1988 by the American Federation of Astrologers, Inc.)

The computer looks up the sidereal time closest to Spielberg's calculated sidereal time. It's very important to have the right sidereal time before going on to this step, so it's a good thing we have computers to do this for us!

Notice the sidereal times in the top-left corner of each box, and you'll see that the table on the left is for 23 hours, 24 minutes, 0 seconds. The table on the right is for the sidereal time of 23 hours, 28 minutes, 0 seconds.

You can see that Spielberg's sidereal time of 23 hours, 25 minutes, 49 seconds is *between* those two sidereal times. So, the computer knows that it has to *interpolate* between these house tables to get the right houses for Spielberg. Lucky for us, we don't have to know what those steps are! But there are a few things we *can* understand easily.

The Search for Midheaven

Notice the M.C. notations in the middle of the two headers on the page from the *AFA Table of Houses*? An M.C. is the same as the midheaven or tenth house cusp for the chart. Spielberg's calculated chart midheaven is at ♓20°41'.

The two M.C.s shown on the two tables from *Table of Houses* are ♓20°12'19" (20 degrees Pisces, 12 minutes, and 19 seconds) and ♓21°17'27". So, we know the computer has calculated the correct sidereal time because Spielberg's midheaven lies between these two M.C.s. When the computer is done *interpolating* for his correct longitude, it gives Spielberg's midheaven as well, which is 20 degrees Pisces and 41 minutes (written as ♓20°41'). Interpolating the houses means finding the correct positions between two sidereal times for them.

Correcting for latitude can make an enormous difference. In Spielberg's case, most of his house cusps are about 35 to 45 minutes later than shown in *The Table of Houses*. That's not a big difference, but in some charts, this is enough for a planet to move to a different house, or for an ascendant, or M.C., to change signs. And we all know how star-crossed that could be!

Calculating the Other Houses

Now the computer needs to know Spielberg's latitude to find the rest of the houses. Because he was born in North America, he has a northern latitude, and the computer knows to look for it on this chart. It's 39N06, or 39 degrees and 6 minutes north of the equator. That's very close to the house cusps shown for the latitude of 39N00.

Now look at the left table with the sidereal time of 23 hours, 24 minutes, and 0 seconds, and notice the column of northern latitudes next to it. Look at the ones shown for the latitude of 39 degrees, and compare them to the house cusps on Spielberg's chart. They're pretty close, but the computer goes the extra step and interpolates them for latitude corrections, too.

Your midheaven changes degrees at least every 4 minutes, and depending on your birth chart, it could be even more often. Because the interpretation of a chart can't be more accurate than the information used to calculate it, it's worth doing some research to get your birth time right, such as sending away for your birth certificate. Otherwise, you might end up with a birth chart that's not *entirely* accurate. When no birth time is known, noon is the time used generally by astrologers to calculate birth charts.

You will see the house cusps listed for the eleventh house, twelfth house, ascendant, second house, and third house for that latitude. The other house cusps aren't listed because they're exactly opposite the ones shown, in the opposite sign.

In general, house systems operate the same way, so the house opposite will have the same degrees, minutes, and seconds, but they have the opposite sign. Using Spielberg's midheaven as an example, it is ♓20°41', and the I.C. (or the fourth house cusp) will equal ♍20°41' (20 degrees Virgo, 41 minutes), which is the sign opposite Pisces.

A good way to check the computer's work (if you're inclined in that direction!) is the following: If the person was born around sunrise, the Sun should be in the first house, or perhaps just into the twelfth. A noon birth means the Sun will be in the ninth or tenth house. Sunset births occur in the seventh or sixth house—or right on the descendant. And midnight births can be found in the third or fourth house. It's like this for every house. In this table of houses, we know the eleventh (fifth), twelfth (sixth), ascendant (descendant—seventh), second (eighth), and third (ninth). And, of course, we already know the midheaven and I.C.

The Big Reveal: Spielberg's Birth Chart

Finally! The computer puts all these calculations together in a birth chart. It has the planets' positions, and now it has the house cusps. It puts the calculated houses in the appropriate places and then adds the planets in there, too. Thus, we have Steven Spielberg's (or your) birth chart!

Computer software has perfected the method for calculating and preparing astrological birth charts. Unless you are the most gifted of gifted astro-nerds, it will be difficult to calculate a birth chart by hand with the precision and speed with which a computer can access data (even NASA data!). Birth chart interpretations, however, are another matter.

Computer algorithms are being designed to build chart readings, and though they are based on a human being's interpretations, the compiled computer readings may lack a personal human touch. Whether algorithmic birth chart readings will become totally acceptable begs the question of how integral computer algorithms will become in all aspects of a computer society. Some apps champion algorithmic readings, while others use computers to calculate chart data but use human beings to do chart readings for clients.

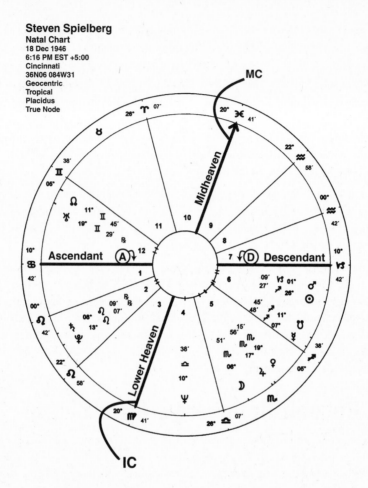

Steven Spielberg
Natal Chart
18 Dec 1946
6:16 PM EST +5:00
Cincinnati
36N06 084W31
Geocentric
Tropical
Placidus
True Node

When doing chart readings, we prefer the human touch. Because a birth chart is a metaphor for the heavens at the time and place of an individual's birth, a truly perceptive interpretation depends on accessing more than data; it's about accessing what it means to be human. Specifically, what it means to be *you*. A reading by a good astrologer, in real time, can probe the nuances and potentialities present in your chart. But who knows? With the coming dawn of artificial intelligence (AI), what it means to be precisely accurate, and what it means to be a human being, may evolve in two different directions.

And so we leave you to interpret Spielberg's chart with the following clues:

* Spielberg is in a reaping lifetime; more of his planets appear in western houses ten through three. (Remember, the Dalai Lama is in a sowing lifetime. See Chapter 17.)

* Pisces ♓ is on Spielberg's midheaven; this is the sign associated with film, movies, photography, spiritual pursuits, and inspiring others.

* Spielberg's Sun ☉ and Uranus ♅ both rule two houses. The Sun is in charge of the second and third houses, while Uranus is in charge of the eighth and ninth houses.

* Spielberg's Moon ☽ is in Scorpio ♏ in the fifth house. Scorpio does not have a house cusp, so Spielberg's Moon is considered intercepted. Interceptions show an area of life that individuals need to develop on their own, outside their usual environment.

* A surprise: Spielberg's ascendant sign is Cancer ♋. He's here to learn responsible nurturing.

What else do you see in the famous director's stars?

ASTEROIDS AND CHIRON

Many astrologers also look for the placements of the asteroids and Chiron ⚷ in your birth chart. The four asteroids—Ceres ⚳, Juno ⚵, Pallas Athene ⚴, and Vesta ⚶—are named after goddesses. The asteroids represent the feminine energy in your birth chart, whether you're male or female, bringing a balance of the masculine and feminine. Until the asteroids were discovered, we only had the Moon and Venus to represent feminine energy.

Specifically, the asteroid Juno represents committed relationships and the wife archetype. Vesta is about commitment and focus and, to some extent, the sister archetype. She is the guardian of the hearth in the home. Ceres represents nurturing, especially in connection to food, and is the mother archetype. Pallas Athene is both healer and warrior energy and somewhat represents the daughter archetype. In mythology, Pallas Athene was born by leaping from Jupiter's forehead, so she is also very mental and represents wisdom.

The planetoid/comet Chiron ⚷ is named after a mythical centaur who was a gifted warrior, teacher, and healer. Astrologers use Chiron to talk about a person's spiritual path, such as how the person may be a maverick or shaman; Chiron also is used to talk about a person's deepest wound. Chiron is also the healer, especially alternative healing methods. The Magi Society has done extensive research on Chiron and believes that it also deals with relationship and money.

Asteroid	Realm	Areas of Responsibility
Ceres ⚳	Motherhood	Fertility, parent/child relationships, crops, natural cycles
Juno ⚵	Marriage	Partnerships, contracts, social obligations
Pallas Athene ⚴	Wisdom	Knowledge, justice, understanding
Vesta ⚶	Power	Devotion, sexuality, health, service to others

Ceres ⚳: Nurturing Growth

Ceres is the goddess of fertility. Her realm—fertility, parent/child relationships, crops, and natural cycles—includes everything that grows. Ceres ⚳ is associated with the sign Cancer ♋ and with the Moon ☽. Ceres in your chart shows your approach to parenting.

Ceres ⚳ Through the Signs

Sign	Your Approach to Parenting
Aries ♈	Enthusiastic
Taurus ♉	Steadfast
Gemini ♊	Communicative
Cancer ♋	Nurturing
Leo ♌	Generous
Virgo ♍	Devoted
Libra ♎	Judicious
Scorpio ♏	Intense
Sagittarius ♐	Adventurous
Capricorn ♑	Cautious
Aquarius ♒	Inventive
Pisces ♓	Unconditional

Juno ⚵: All Things Partnership

Juno is the goddess of marriage and partnership, so her realm covers social responsibilities and the home. Juno is associated with the signs Taurus ♉ (the home) and Libra ♎ (partnerships), as well as the planet Venus ♀. Your Juno placement reveals your approach to partnership.

Juno ⚵ Through the Signs

Sign	Your Approach to Partnership
Aries ♈	Impulsive and fiery
Taurus ♉	Committed and secure
Gemini ♊	Casual and mentally agile
Cancer ♋	Cautious and tenacious
Leo ♌	Dramatic and adored
Virgo ♍	Practical and devoted
Libra ♎	Romantic and balanced
Scorpio ♏	Powerful and magnetic
Sagittarius ♐	Adventurous and exciting
Capricorn ♑	Steady and cautious
Aquarius ♒	Inventive and unusual
Pisces ♓	Idealistic and intuitive

Pallas Athene ⚴: Wise Woman and Warrior

Pallas Athene is the goddess of justice and wisdom, so her realm is diplomacy—knowledge, empathy, and understanding. This asteroid is associated with the humanitarian sign Aquarius ♒ and the quicksilver planets Mercury ☿ and Uranus ♅. Pallas Athene's ⚴ placement in your birth chart shows how you approach decisions and where your potential for diplomatic resolution lies.

Pallas Athene ⚴ Through the Signs

Sign	Your Approach to Decision Making
Aries ♈	Taking the lead
Taurus ♉	Building consensus
Gemini ♊	Forging communication
Cancer ♋	Listening closely
Leo ♌	Creating coalitions

(continues)

Sign	Your Approach to Decision Making
Virgo ♍	Organizing the ideas
Libra ♎	Weighing the issues
Scorpio ♏	Seizing control
Sagittarius ♐	Forging ahead
Capricorn ♑	Managing cautiously
Aquarius ♒	Coming from right field
Pisces ♓	From the heart

Vesta ⚶: Hearth, Home, and Family

The last of the asteroids is Vesta, who is responsible for protecting the hearth and family. The signs associated with Vesta ⚶ are service-oriented Virgo ♍ and powerful Scorpio ♏, and her planet is transformational Pluto ♇. Your Vesta ⚶ placement on your birth chart shows your approach to giving.

Vesta ⚶ Through the Signs

Sign	Your Approach to Giving
Aries ♈	Impulsive
Taurus ♉	Generous
Gemini ♊	Witty
Cancer ♋	Empathetic
Leo ♌	Heart-centered
Virgo ♍	Sensible
Libra ♎	Harmonious
Scorpio ♏	Passionate
Sagittarius ♐	Spontaneous
Capricorn ♑	Careful

Sign	Your Approach to Giving
Aquarius ≈	Unusual
Pisces ⯓	Compassionate

Chiron ⚷: The Wounded Healer

Chiron ⚷ is often called the wounded healer because in mythology, this half man/half beast overcame his own psychic pain to become mythology's greatest healer. In astrology, this planetoid/comet reveals healing patterns. Its placement in your birth chart is an invitation to heal a particular psychic wound.

Chiron ⚷ Through the Signs

Sign	Psychic Wound	Healed By
Aries ♈	Impatience	Patience
Taurus ♉	Doubt	Understanding
Gemini ♊	Self-distrust	Wisdom
Cancer ♋	Indifference	Gentleness
Leo ♌	Overenthusiasm	Tolerance
Virgo ♍	Servility	Strength
Libra ♎	Indecision	Steadfastness
Scorpio ♏	Possessiveness	Selfless love
Sagittarius ♐	Restlessness	Inner peace
Capricorn ♑	Fear	Courage
Aquarius ≈	Aloofness	Sharing
Pisces ⯓	Paranoia	Self-transcendence

Climate Activist Greta Thunberg's Birth Chart

Where better to examine how the asteroids and Chiron manifest in someone's chart than in the birth chart of young climate activist Greta Thunberg. Greta's chart is a perfect example of how the asteroids add nuance and relevance to a chart reading, and it proves there are indeed modern-day goddesses among us. Let's look at Greta's goddess energies.

Greta's Asteroids and Chiron

Greta's Juno ⚵ in Scorpio ♏ is in her sixth house of personal responsibilities, work, and service. The asteroid of marriage in the house of work and service—what a perfect placement for Greta! It indicates that Greta is devoted, with an intense emotional commitment and to all her important relationships and partnerships. She believes in service to others and that one person is never too small to make a difference, she will be devoted to whomever she partners with, and she will hold partners to the same high passion she feels herself for the work they will do together. Pallas Athene ⚴ is in Aquarius ♒ in Greta's eleventh house, indicating that she comes to matters of goals, groups, and friends from a place of thoughtful wisdom. Aquarius ♒ Pallas ⚴ brings the electricity of Air's intellect partnered with a persistence and action-packed desire to bring knowledge and wisdom to the public arena. Greta is a change agent, who brings new ideas that surprise and perhaps confront. When we look at Greta's Vesta ⚶ in Libra ♎ also in her sixth house of work and service, we find someone who has studied and believes her knowledge will bring harmony and a new, restorative balance to humanity's relationship with the Earth. Greta's Vesta reveals just how important she feels her work to be—and the faith she has in the harmony that will come from it.

Greta's Ceres ⚳ is in Aries ♈ in the twelfth house, the house of the subconscious and service to the greater collective consciousness. The asteroid of fertility and motherhood in the house of the past indicates a sense of completion and the fullness of rebirth. Greta's wholehearted enthusiasm for developing her awareness to evolve from the past toward a new consciousness for humanity's soul connection to the Earth reveals an Aries influence and hints at Greta's role as a modern-day Gaia, Earth mother. As a bonus, Greta's chart detail also includes the asteroids Hygeia and Astraea. Hygeia, the goddess of health and medicine, and Astraea, the goddess of justice and innocence, are both located in Taurus ♉ in Greta's twelfth house. Complementing her Ceres ⚳ placement, Hygeia and Astraea reveal Greta's commitment to restoring the health of the Earth and the righteousness of this cause because the Earth is humanity's only home (the Taurus influence). We find Greta's Chiron ⚷, the wounded healer, in Capricorn ♑ in her ninth house of philosophy, travel, and beliefs. This suggests that Greta heals her fears through the courage of her beliefs and is willing to put herself on the world stage, traveling far and wide to spread the global message she believes will bring renewed conviction and healing to the Earth.

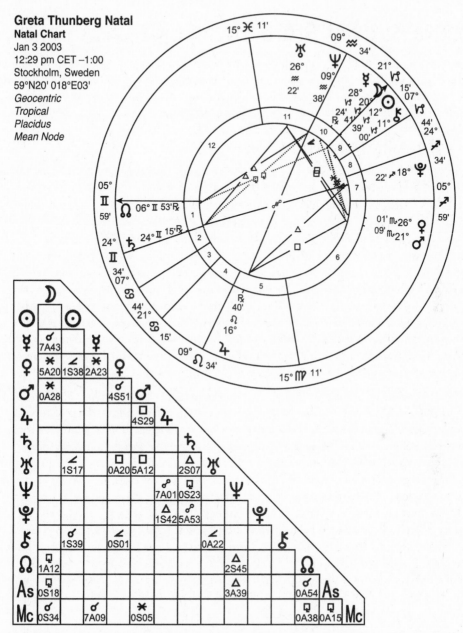

A detail from the birth chart for Greta Thunberg, including the placement of the asteroids Ceres, Juno, Pallas Athene, and Vesta, plus Hygeia and Astraes and the comet Chiron.

Greta's Birth Chart and Chiron

Let's take a look at how Greta's Chiron ⚷ placement in her birth chart unlocks the key to her birth chart reading. Greta has a powerful conjunction ☌ in her natal Sun sign Capricorn ♑. The Sun ☉ and Chiron ⚷ are both in the ninth house of teaching, healing, the philosopher, and the educator. Chiron is at 11 degrees of Capricorn next to her natal Sun at 12 degrees of Capricorn; next to the 20-degree Moon ☽ in Capricorn; next to Mercury ☿ at 28 degrees of Capricorn; and Mercury is retrograde ℞. So, Greta's powerful Sun conjunct Chiron ☉☌⚷ at 11 and 12 degrees of Capricorn ♑ comes from a philosophy of educating people; she's pragmatic, well researched, and well aware of the physical Earth sign environment (Capricorn ♑!) she lives in. Greta has come to this life as a New Moon in Capricorn in the ninth and tenth house. Because her Sun and Chiron are in her ninth house, too, she will travel in her lifetime. Globally, Greta will be out in the world publicly advocating with all her strength, consistently throughout her whole lifetime.

Greta's first house 5 degrees Gemini ♊ rising North Node ☊ reveals that her future depends on her personality; in other words, when Greta gets out in the world, she'll be heard. And all those Capricorn planets in the ninth and tenth houses feed back into Greta's first house, where she also has Saturn ♄, Capricorn's ruler, at 24 degrees of Gemini. Her first house Saturn ♄ makes a positive aspect, a trine △, to Uranus ♅ in her eleventh house of hopes, dreams, and wishes. In astrology, if Saturn is making a good aspect either to an outer planet or a personal planet—which it is in Greta's chart—this indicates an old soul and exhibits wisdom that continues to grow because Greta herself, no matter her age in years, is continually self-challenging to know more and share this knowledge with the public.

So, the Sun conjunct Chiron ☉☌⚷ in Greta's ninth house in Capricorn connects powerfully to the Moon and Mercury, also in Capricorn, and to her first house Saturn (Capricorn's ruler). Greta is a healer who believes everyone needs the best information to work toward achieving goals for the betterment of humanity and the world. But she doesn't want to lead the way; she wants humanity to use the information she brings to light to lead itself in the right direction, to heal the planet, and to live in peace and harmony with the environment.

So, you can see how Chiron and the asteroids deepen an understanding of Greta's birth chart and help reveal her true nature—our Gaia, who will lead humanity to heal the Earth!

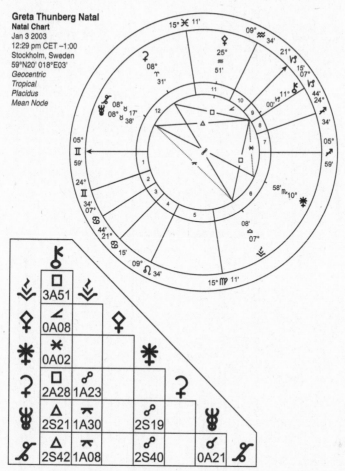

Greta Thunberg Natal
Natal Chart
Jan 3 2003
12:29 pm CET –1:00
Stockholm, Sweden
59°N20' 018°E03'
Geocentric
Tropical
Placidus
Mean Node

Look at what Greta's Chiron ⚷ placement reveals in her birth chart.

COMPATIBLE? TRY SYNASTRY!

Are you ready to explore the synastry of *your* relationships? As you deepen your understanding of astrology's signs, planets, houses, and aspects, you'll possess the confidence to read your own birth chart, for its potential is your own. Each new astrological insight represents a hard-won self-realization. As in your birth chart, so it is in life. While you may get a few online or in-person chart readings with professional astrologers, we believe the work you do on your own to deconstruct your natal birth chart is the most valuable.

Your astrological birth chart is a map of the heavens upon which you chart your life's course. Unlike a road map, birth charts do not reveal a predetermined path. It's up to you to plot or correct course using the data (signs, planets, houses, aspects) within the chart. And as the planets move and time advances, progressed charts and chart transits show you potential for change by evolving house placements degree by degree. Birth charts work because they allow human beings to chart their unique courses through the Universe, a testament to their centuries' old utility and refined design.

But what about *compatibility?* Whether challenging or loving, difficult or easeful, can astrology tell you about the relationships in your life? Well, there *is* a way. *Synastry* is astrology's method for determining compatibility. A natal birth chart is cast for each of the parties of the relationship. Then, a special aspect grid called a *synastry grid* is produced that compares aspect relationships between the charts, looking for issues to nurture or resolve. Synastry can reveal patterns and nuances of the relationship that may be difficult to spot in daily life, and that may even signal karmic connections. Some believe synastry can reveal past-life situations and relationships.

Synastry readings can be complex. We encourage you to obtain birth charts and a synastry grid online for you and for whomever you desire to explore a relationship with. Of course, the more precise the birth date, birth time, and birthplace information you use for all parties, the more accurate your birth charts and synastry grid will be. We know this is the age of oversharing, but please do be aware of and considerate of the privacy of others.

Synastry: Astrology's Relationship App

When looking to do a synastry reading, it's like getting a chance to swipe left or swipe right on the cosmic potential of a relationship in the Universe. Will your relationship grow, or fade? Synastry does chart the potential worth of a relationship; but it does not, surely, chart the worth of a person. Every person is worthy of good relationships with willing partners! Never lose sight of that human truth. To start, make sure you obtain all birth information for your reading in an ethical manner. If the owner is a private citizen (and not a public figure), request permission to cast their charts from each individual owner of birth data. Always offer to share synastry information with its owner and always keep all information private from the public; don't share, publish, or discuss other people's charts in public forums. Should you decide to have charts cast on other private people's data without their knowledge or permission (and we strongly advise against this), be discreet and keep what you find to yourself.

For your first foray into doing synastry readings, we suggest you choose a willing partner and explore your relationship together. The reading's birth charts and synastry grid will be shared between you, and both of you will have the chance to comment and provide insight and interpretation about your relationship. Make the commitment that all charts and interpretations generated for the synastry reading will be kept private and confidential. Collaborative synastry readings can be a creative way to expand the consciousness of your relationship. Remember that the synastry reading is being done for the benefit of the relationship, and make a further commitment to stay positive and work toward enhancing your mutual bond.

We believe that though a synastry grid may be fairly easy to generate online, reading it is not. For a more sophisticated synastry analysis than you can glean on your own or with a collaborative partner, we recommend that you engage a professional astrologer's services. A reading *from* a human being—not a computer—is always superior when assessing the compatibility of human beings. It is more in-depth, more nuanced, more intuitive, and certainly more interactive. (And it's likely done face to face.) When exploring important family or marriage relationships, a professional interpretation from a living, breathing astrologer is well worth the investment, don't you think?

My Mother, Myself: Carrie and Debbie

We're going to walk you through a basic synastry interpretation using the mother/daughter relationship of writer/actress Carrie Fisher and her mom, actress Debbie Reynolds. When looking at a synastry grid, you'll want to note the following.

* Look at the aspects between the Sun ☉ and Moon ☽ in your charts. The aspects here are very important to the type of bond you share.

* Look for trines △ and sextiles ✳ in the synastry grid. These are the supportive aspects, which create a harmonious flow between the two charts.

* Also check for oppositions ☍ and squares □ in the grid. These are the challenging aspects—those that encourage growth—in the relationship.

* Look at Jupiter ♃ and Saturn ♄ connections, which indicate relationship through longevity and strength. These aspects also relate to karma.

Across
Debbie Reynolds
Natal Chart
Apr 1 1932
5:49 pm MST +7:00
El Paso, TX
31°N45'31" 106°W29'11"
Geocentric
Tropical
Placidus
Mean Node

Down
Carrie Fisher
Natal Chart
Oct 21 1956
12:11 pm PST +8:00
Los Angeles, CA
34°N03'08" 118°W14' 34"
Geocentric
Tropical
Placidus
Mean Node

Synastry Grid

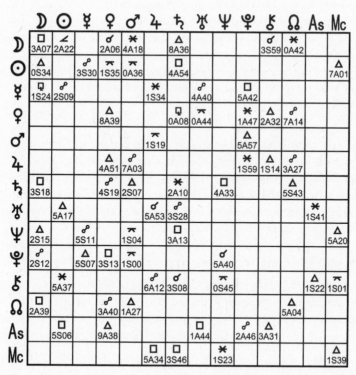

	☽	☉	☿	♀	♂	♃	♄	♅	♆	♇	⚷	☊	As	Mc
☽	□ 3A07	∠ 2A22		☌ 2A06	⚹ 4A18		△ 8A36				☌ 3S59	⚹ 0A42		
☉	△ 0S34		☍ 3S30	⚻ 1S35	⚻ 0A36	□ 4A54								△ 7A01
☿	⚻ 1S24	☍ 2S09		⚹ 1S34		☍ 4A40		□ 5A42						
♀			△ 8A39			⚻ 0A08	⚻ 0A44			⚹ 1A47	△ 2A32	☍ 7A14		
♂				⚻ 1S19						△ 5A57				
♃				△ 4A51	☍ 7A03					⚹ 1S59	△ 1S14	☍ 3A27		
♄	□ 3S18					☌ 4S19	☌ 2S07		⚹ 2A10	□ 4A33	△ 5S43			
♅		△ 5A17				☌ 5A53	☌ 3S28						⚹ 1S41	
♆	△ 2S15		☌ 5S11		⚻ 1S04	□ 3A13								△ 5A20
♇	☌ 2S12		△ 5S07	□ 3S13	⚻ 1S00		☌ 5A40							
⚷		⚹ 5A37				☍ 6A12	☌ 3S08		⚻ 0S45				△ 1S22	⚻ 1S01
☊	□ 2A39					☍ 3A40	△ 1A27				△ 5A04			
As		□ 5S06		△ 9A38			□ 1A44			☍ 2A46	△ 3A31			
Mc						□ 5A34	□ 3S46		⚹ 1S23					△ 1S39

Caption: Counting and comparing aspects between two charts, as revealed in a synastry grid, tells the nature of their connectedness in a relationship.

If there are no major aspects (whether positive or challenging) between the natal personal planets—the Sun ☉, Moon ☽, Mercury ☿, Venus ♀, and Mars ♂, plus the ascendant, then there is no electricity, no spark, and maybe not even a desire to connect in a relationship. In other words, the absence of major aspects between the personal planets means there is no relationship to be kindled. In Carrie and Debbie's synastry compatibility grid, within their personal planets these two have 7 major aspects between them, and that's pretty good. Four of the personal planets are involved—the Moon ☽, Venus ♀, Mars ♂, and the Sun ☉. There is no question that this points to a strong bond between the two of them from the time of Carrie's birth.

In the sense of compatibility, the two most important planets are Jupiter ♃ and Saturn ♄ because they reveal how Carrie and Debbie related to the world they lived in, other family members, the community, and society. There were a lot of aspects between Carrie's Jupiter ♃ and Saturn ♄ and Debbie's. So, in the sense of bonding, there was a strong focus that these two related consistently throughout their lives (because the natal charts represent the journey from birth to death).

With their personal planets strongly aspected, electricity flowed between Carrie and Debbie, and especially between Jupiter ♃ and Saturn ♄ (the outer planets), plus the ascendant also had several good aspects. Carrie and Debbie were strongly connected in a durable and enduring relationship in which they worked through their issues by talking things out. That being said, some of the aspects appear to have been difficult or malefic, squares □ and oppositions ☍. Both within their personal planets and outer planets, the count of challenging aspects (squares □ and oppositions ☍) was balanced with the number of positive aspects (trines △ and sextiles ✶). So, from the time Carrie was born, Debbie was overly worried about her, and she was dedicated to her responsibilities as a mother, regardless of being challenged by her career to find a routine for steady parenting.

On her side, Carrie watched her mom go through a lot of emotional rollercoaster cycles with other family members, with Carrie's father, and in other relationships. Carrie, being a Libra ♎ with some Scorpio ♏ in her, was sensitive and empathic; Carrie's early childhood experiences watching her mom led to a rollercoaster kind of relationship with Debbie. Carrie didn't want to tell her mom everything about her life because she already saw her mom going through so much. Over two or three decades, though, their parent/child bond grew and they became very strongly connected. If Saturn ♄—the planet of the past in this lifetime—is the planet of past lives as well, these two have probably been in each other's previous lives over and over again.

What brought Carrie and Debbie together throughout 30 to 60 years is the connection to the conditions in their charts, the dramatic ups and downs, and their union through crises. These things drew them together year upon year, giving them the foundation to stay together and actually grow through life's crises to strengthen their bond. Their relationship had the same strength, durability, and longevity of a long-married couple, so strong that it was never broken through crisis. Instead, their closeness developed further, and they were never separated for long. On a conscious, subconscious, and soul level these two were always connected in life, and they remain so in death.

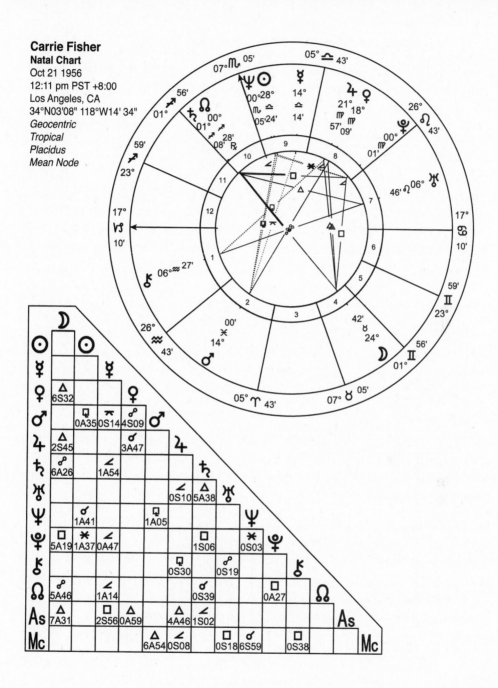

Carrie Fisher
Natal Chart
Oct 21 1956
12:11 pm PST +8:00
Los Angeles, CA
34°N03'08" 118°W14' 34"
Geocentric
Tropical
Placidus
Mean Node

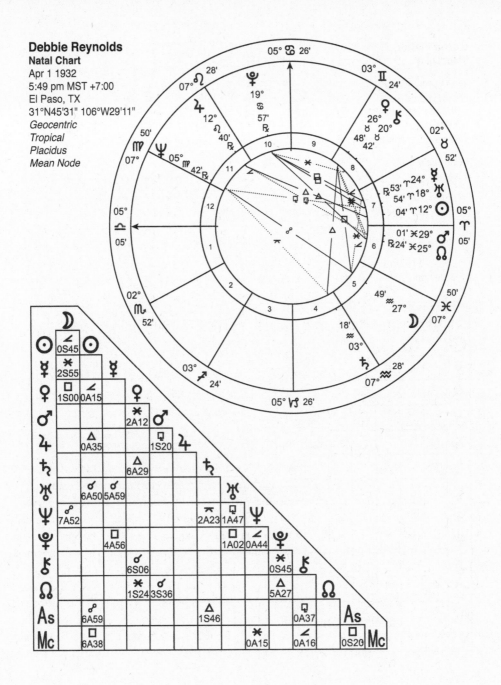

Debbie Reynolds
Natal Chart
Apr 1 1932
5:49 pm MST +7:00
El Paso, TX
31°N45'31" 106°W29'11"
Geocentric
Tropical
Placidus
Mean Node

Synastry Between Birth Charts

To confirm what we've seen in their synastry compatibility grid, let's look at Carrie and Debbie's birth charts as well, specifically the Sun ☉, the Moon ☽, and Rising sign.

* Carrie was born with her Sun in Libra ☉ ♎ in the ninth house of philosophy and beliefs. Her Moon was in Taurus ☽ ♉ in the fourth house of home and family. Her Rising sign was Capricorn ♑.

* Debbie was born with her Sun in Aries ☉ ♈ in the seventh house of important relationships and partnerships. Her Moon was in Aquarius ☽ ♒ in the fifth house of fun, creativity, romance, and children. Her Rising sign was Libra ♎.

Carrie's Libra Sun ♎ ☉ in the ninth house gave her a strong sense of balance and fairness in her beliefs, and her Capricorn ascendant influenced her Sun ☉ to make her believe wholeheartedly in the goals and dreams she had for her life and in their pursuit. To the world, Carrie was an ambitious, intelligent, and focused person. Debbie's ascendant in Libra ♎ meant that she showed herself to be fair and balanced in her public life, and these qualities were important to her. Carrie's Libra Sun ♎ ☉ then embodied within herself the qualities her mother displayed outwardly to the world. Debbie's Sun in Aries ☉ ♈ acted as the foundation for her personality—so her courage and bold action was tempered by her outward desire for balance and fairness (Libra ♎ ascendant). Again, Carrie was watching and internalizing to her very core what she saw outwardly shown in her mother's life through Debbie's ascendant. Their two Moons ☽ mean that Carrie's love and need for home and family was based in Debbie's determination to make that home creative and fun, with an emphasis on stimulating Carrie's intellect.

Carrie and Debbie shared an eighth house Venus (personal planet) and a seventh house Uranus (outer planet). Carrie's Venus was in Virgo ♀ ♍, and Debbie's Venus was in Taurus ♀ ♉. Carrie's Uranus was in Leo ♅ ♌ (alone in her seventh house), and Debbie's Uranus was in Aries ♅ ♈ (Debbie's Sun ☉ and Mercury ☿ were both in Aries ♈, too.) Debbie's Aries Sun, Mercury, and Uranus showed her moving forward through life with a bold set of strong beliefs about family and a bold way of communicating them. Her daughter's Uranus in Leo ♅ ♌, the Sun's ruler, show that she was equally strong-willed and inherently creative when expressing her will in primary relationships. Debbie's Venus in Taurus ♀ ♉ in the eighth house of transformation shows that she grappled with the challenges of an ever-changing home front. Chiron ⚷, the wounded healer, embodied her desire to heal and restore the home. Carrie's Venus in Virgo ♀ ♍ was supported by her eighth house placements of outer planets Jupiter ♃ and Pluto ♇, which were also in Virgo ♍. Carrie held onto sacred patterns that were held within her mother's evolving concept of home. We can see that these two were tightly bound. We've only scratched the surface of an in-depth synastry reading for Carrie and Debbie; yet already so much is revealed in support of their relationship.

Synastry in Your Relationships

Are you ready to discover the partnership dynamics in one of your closest relationships? Has your relationship partner agreed to collaborate on your astrological synastry reading? Do you have accurate birth charts and synastry grid in hand? What you find will be no less than a charting of the evolution of soul with soul. Remember, in analyzing your charts together, you are not just reading a map. You are charting your shared course through life! Press on.

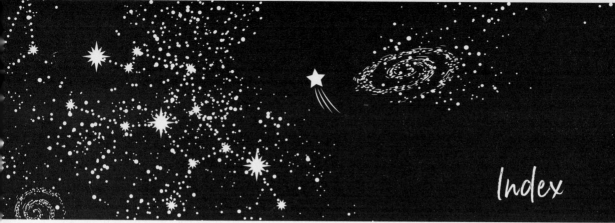

Index

Asimov, Isaac, 208
aspects, 181, 245, 261
   angle of circle, 249
   characterization, 250
   chart interpretations, 254–259
   conjunctions, 247–248, 250
   experience, 247–248
   grid, 253
   interception, 260
   major, 181, 247, 249
   oppositions, 248, 250
   orbs, 248
   planetary keywords, 255
   planets, 251–253
   professional readings, 261
   quincunx, 249–251
   same-degree, 249
   sextiles, 248, 250
   squares, 247, 250
   symbols, 245–246
   trines, 248, 250
Assange, Julian, 137, 196, 200
Astaire, Fred, 145, 186
Astin, Sean, 195
Astraea, 75
astrologers
   Newton, Isaac, 11
   Nostradamus, 10
   Pythagoras, 10
   rectification done by, 31
   Three Wise Men, 11
astrological charts, 6–8
astrological signature, 255–256
astrology
   astrologers, 10–11
   basis of, 5
   celestial rhythms, 6
   defined, 5
   famous people using, 11
   history, 9–11
   houses, 5
   intuitive foundation of, 12
   mathematics of, 41
   natal, 6
   personal agency and, 3–4
   psychological model provided
     by, 5

Rising sign, 6
   use as compass, 276
Atwood, Margaret, 60, 133
Aubier, Catherine, 125
Austen, Jane, 89, 141
authority (Saturn), 143–147
Avengers, 44

B

Baby Boomers, 156
Baldwin, James, 71
Bale, Christian, 124
Balsamic Moon, 280, 282
Balzac, Honore de, 229
Barrymore, Drew, 191
Barth, John, 125
Baryshnikov, Mikhail, 101
Basinger, Kim, 89
Baudelaire, Charles, 218
Beck, 52, 207, 208
Beckett, Samuel, 84, 128, 203
Beckham, David, 56, 132, 195
Beckham, Victoria, 135
Beethoven, Ludwig van, 126
Bell, Alexander Graham, 125
Bell, Vanessa, 60
Belushi, John, 202
Benigni, Roberto, 94
Bergman, Ingmar, 185
Bernal, Gael Garcia, 136
Bernstein, Leonard, 141, 203, 220
Berra, Yogi, 104
Beyoncé, 75, 80
Bezos, Jeff, 137
Billy the Kid, 205
Birkin, Jane, 133, 203
birth charts, 6–8, 29–48
   creation of, 32–44
     ascendant, 32–33
     generational planets, 38
     houses, 41–44
     inner planets, 36
     luminaries, 35
     Nodes, 39–40
     personal planets, 36

planetary rulership, 40
planets, 34–35
   social planets, 37
   transpersonal planets, 38
   visible houses, 41
Dalai Lama, 6–8, 18–20
description of, 4
Internet calculation of, 3
King, Stephen, 115–118
lessons illuminated by, 4
meme-worthy, 13
meridian lines, 182
online access to, 4
reading, 13
as record of potential, 13
Sun signs, 17–20
symbols in, 7
uniqueness of, 6
vital statistics, 29–32
zodiac symbols, 15–17
bi-wheel, 264
Björk, 84, 85, 141, 187
Black Widow, 60
Blair, Tony, 145
Blake, William, 146, 224, 239
Blanchett, Cate, 56, 131, 201
Blige, Mary J., 129
body signs, 8–9
Bogart, Humphrey, 218
Bohr, Niels, 129, 223
Bolt, Usain, 127
Bono, 220
Botticelli, 130
Bowie, David, 94, 142, 213
Bradbury, Ray, 129, 187
Brady, Tom, 71
Brahms, Johannes, 145
Branson, Richard, 219
Brin, Sergey, 124
Broderick, Matthew, 52
Brolin, Josh, 56, 204
Brontë, Anne, 137
Brontë, Charlotte, 56
Brontë, Emily, 87, 190
Brooks, Albert, 145, 240
Brooks, Garth, 201
Brown, James, 215

G